EIGHT MODERN
ESSAYISTS Fifth Edition

EIGHT MODERN ESSAYISTS Fifth Edition

WILLIAM SMART
Sweet Briar College

ST. MARTIN'S PRESS • NEW YORK

Senior editor: Mark Gallaher
Development editor: Bob Weber
Project editor: Emily Berleth
Cover design: Celine Brandes
Cover photo: Phototake

For information, write:
St. Martin's Press, Inc.
175 Fifth Avenue
New York, NY 10010

ISBN: 0-312-01233-0

ACKNOWLEDGMENTS
Acknowledgments and copyrights are continued at the back of the
book on pages 350–352, which constitute an extension of the
copyright page.

"The Death of the Moth" and "Professions for Women" from *The
Death of the Moth* by Virginia Woolf, copyright 1942 by Harcourt
Brace Jovanovich, Inc., and renewed 1970 by Marjorie T. Parsons.
Reprinted by permission of Harcourt Brace Jovanovich, Inc., the
Executors of the Virginia Woolf Estate, and The Hogarth Press.

Excerpt from "Shakespeare's Sister" from *A Room of One's Own* by
Virginia Woolf, copyright 1929 by Harcourt Brace Jovanovich, Inc., and
renewed 1957 by Leonard Woolf. Reprinted by permission of Harcourt
Brace Jovanovich, Inc., the Executors of the Virginia Woolf Estate, and
The Hogarth Press.

To Sarah & Jessie

Preface

THERE HAVE BEEN MANY CHANGES in the twenty-five years since *Eight Modern Essayists* was first published. Some writers in that first edition seem old-fashioned now: Max Beerbohm, James Thurber, Edmund Wilson. Even some of the more "up-to-date" writers who replaced them over the years—D. H. Lawrence and Norman Mailer, for example—no longer seem quite as fresh. In 1965, half the authors in this latest edition had yet to publish their first book. And, should there be other editions in the future, there will certainly be other changes. (Maybe some future edition will include a writer who used this anthology in college!)

The major goal of these collections has always been to present writers whose voices are strong and original and therefore will appeal to intelligent readers—not "easy" writers or "popular" writers, but *good* writers worth studying in depth. Three writers who have remained throughout all five editions best exemplify those elusive qualities: Virginia Woolf, George Orwell, and E. B. White. However different they may be as writers—as thinkers and stylists—they nevertheless appeal nearly equally to all readers.

The idea behind *Eight Modern Essayists* has always been that concentrating on a few good writers helps one learn to write. The point is not to learn rhetorical devices or stylistic stratagems that have been "successful" for other writers but, rather, to learn that good writing is not solely a matter of grammatical correctness.

This Fifth Edition presents two new American writers who meet the standards I have always used in selecting essayists for inclusion: writers whom teachers will like to teach, and students will enjoy reading. Paul Fussell and Carol Bly will, I believe, live up to the expectations of anyone who has used a previous edition. They are intelligent writers with distinctive voices, and they merit our concentrated attention.

Despite the need to keep *Eight Modern Essayists* fresh—for students as well as for teachers—I've always been saddened by the losses that occurred from one edition to the next. No matter how much one liked the *new* essayists, there was no way not to miss E. M. Forster's "My Wood," for instance, or D. H. Lawrence's "Adolf," or James Baldwin's "Notes of a Native Son." With this Fifth Edition I've finally figured out how to eat my cake and have it too—by creating an appendix at the end of the book containing one essay by each of the writers who has been replaced over the years. A breach of principle—indeed!—but one I feel confident will win the approval of anyone who has ever used *Eight Modern Essayists*.

W. S.

Contents

A Note to Students

GOOD WRITING BEGINS with knowing what good writing is, and the only way to do that is by reading the best writers who have preceded you. There is a classic statement on the subject by the seventeenth-century playwright Ben Jonson:

> It is fit for the beginner and learner to study others and the best. For the mind and memory are more sharply exercised in comprehending another man's things than our own; and such as accustom themselves and are familiar with the best authors shall ever and anon find somewhat of them in themselves.

You learn several things when you read a number of pieces by the same author: first, that he or she has a point of view which is fairly consistent; second, that most good writers have a personal style of writing—that is to say, they have distinct "voices." It won't be long before you'll be able to tell George Orwell from Virginia Woolf or E. B. White from Joan Didion just by reading a couple of sentences. By then you will have learned that no single way of writing is better than all others. Different writers write different ways.

This collection of essays should encourage you to be bold, to try to write as well as the writers you are reading. Very likely, you won't be able to do it, but just trying hard will make you a better writer. The key word, of course, is *hard*. Good writing is hard work. It doesn't come easily, even for the best—indeed, *especially* for the best. You must be intelligent and perceptive and honest—and care deeply about things—but that is not enough. I sometimes tell students that if the writers in this collection were students in the course, they would probably be spending the most time on their papers, not the least.

The best writers are often the slowest, most careful writers. Because good writing often reads quickly doesn't mean it was written quickly. Keep in mind that the time you spend writing is never wasted time; you just don't realize when you're making progress. It's so slow sometimes. But good teachers will always give you a chance to write well if you are sincere about wanting to do it.

This is a book of essays for people who would like to learn to write well. Read it carefully, and even after the course is over, *keep* it . . . and read these writers again and again. And write. That is the only way to learn to write well.

EIGHT MODERN
ESSAYISTS Fifth Edition

VIRGINIA WOOLF

HBJ Photo

PERHAPS NO ENGLISH WRITER ever grew up as surrounded by books, writers, and the affluence that makes culture possible as Virginia Woolf. At the time of her birth (in London in 1882) her father, Leslie Stephen, was already distinguished as a philosopher, critic, and editor of the *Cornhill Magazine*. His first wife had been Thackeray's youngest daughter; his second, Virginia's mother, was descended from French nobility. Meredith, Hardy, and Henry James were his close friends, as was James Russell Lowell, who accepted the invitation to be Virginia's godfather by sending along some verses that expressed the wish that "the child would be/ A sample of heredity." Later that same year Leslie Stephen was named editor of the *Dictionary of National Biography,* and it was in the presence of that enormous undertaking that Virginia was educated. Instead of being sent to school, she was simply turned loose in her father's library, and the breadth of the knowledge she gained therein reveals itself in nearly all her essays.

Books, though, were not the whole of her education, and for the rest one must look to St. Ives in Cornwall, where the Stephen family went for its summer holidays. There, close by the sea, Virginia and the other Stephen children, Thoby, Vanessa, and Adrian—along with the children from their mother's first marriage—spent many happy days picnicking, boating, and playing games. In *To the Lighthouse* (1927) Virginia Woolf describes their summers in Cornwall with great fidelity.

When Sir Leslie died in 1904, the four Stephen children gave up the house at Hyde Park Gate and moved to 46 Gordon Square, Bloomsbury. Soon Thoby's friends, Lytton Strachey and Clive Bell, started coming around to carry on the discussions they had begun at Cambridge under the name of the "Midnight Society." And thus began what has since been known as the "Bloomsbury Group," by no means a formal organization, but merely a gathering of friends who believed (as their Cambridge mentor, G. E. Moore, had declared in his *Principia Ethica*) that the appreciation of beauty and the need for personal relationships were man's supreme endeavors.

After Thoby died of typhoid in Greece in 1906 and Vanessa married Clive Bell a year later, Virginia and Adrian moved to Fitzroy Square, a short distance away, and the Thursday night meetings followed them. New friends began coming—among them the art critic Roger Fry, the economist John Maynard Keynes, and E. M. Forster—until, by the late nineteen-twenties, the group was so famous that the word Bloomsbury had become synonymous with highbrow. Nor was it always used as a compliment; D. H. Lawrence called them "Bloomsberries," gilded youth, beetles that stung like scorpions.

In 1912 Virginia Stephen married Leonard Woolf, a socialist and political writer who had been one of Thoby's friends at Cambridge, and three years later she published her first novel, *The Voyage Out*. Then, in 1917, with no other intention than that of printing a few short works by themselves and their friends, purely for the fun of it, the Woolfs bought a hand printing press and set it up in the dining room of their house in Richmond. The first book they produced contained two stories, one by Virginia and the other by Leonard; a little later they published *Prelude* by Katherine Mansfield and *Poems 1919* by T. S. Eliot. What had started out as a lark suddenly became a successful business, and over the years that followed The Hogarth Press became famous as a publisher of new writers. Undoubtedly, the Woolfs made their greatest mistake as editors when they refused to publish Joyce's *Ulysses*.

In 1919 they bought the cottage Monks House in the village of Rodmell, near the River Ouse, in Sussex, and there they spent their weekends and holidays for the next twenty-two years. In March 1941, in a state of depression brought on both by the war and the fear that she might lose her mind and be a burden on her husband, Virginia Woolf committed suicide by drowning herself in the Ouse. Later, her husband revealed that she had suffered several nervous breakdowns earlier in her life, going back as far as her mother's death in 1895.

Along with Joyce and Proust, Virginia Woolf is one of the great innovators of the modern novel, directing the reader's attention away from a sequence of outward actions and toward the complex inner lives of her characters. In her most successful novels—*Jacob's Room* (1922), *Mrs. Dalloway* (1925), *To the Lighthouse* (1927), *The Waves* (1931), and *Between the Acts* (published posthumously in 1941)—almost nothing happens on the surface of her characters' lives. Instead, the action all takes place in their heads, in their responses both to each other and to the objects they are surrounded by. Time, also, changes: the chronological time of outward actions—in which morning is separated from night by a sequence of events or "actions"—is replaced by the *real* time of an alert consciousness; morning to night becomes a sequence of impressions, intuitions, memories, anticipations. In short, the conflicts between the characters all take place within their sensibilities and, because of that, the novels make large demands on the reader's perceptions.

However difficult her novels may sometimes be, as an essayist Virginia Woolf is always perfectly lucid. Seldom does she abandon her father's advice "to write in the fewest possible words, as clearly as possible, exactly what one meant." Moreover, she obviously benefited from the more than two hundred book reviews she wrote for the *Times Literary Supplement* from 1905 until a few years before her death. And yet she was never a formal, systematic critic, but rather a common reader, personal and subjective, who read "for his own pleasure rather than to impart knowledge or correct the opinions of others." And one notices that the books she loved the best and wrote the most engagingly about were not especially the classics, but all those memoirs, letters, biographies, and autobiographies of the obscure, all those "rubbish-heaps," as she put it, of "vanished moments and forgotten lives told in faltering and feeble accents. . . ." For Virginia Woolf was a novelist even when she was writing essays, and it made little difference to her if her characters came from real life or the pages of a book. All she wanted was to illuminate those lives, make them stand before us in all their vitality and confusion. Nothing else really mattered to her. "If one wishes to better the world," she once wrote, "one must, paradoxically enough, withdraw and spend more and more time fashioning one's sentences to perfection in solitude."

THE DEATH OF THE MOTH

Power Behind Life—and death

MOTHS THAT FLY by day are not properly to be called moths; they do not excite that pleasant sense of dark autumn nights and ivy-blossom which the commonest yellow-underwing asleep in the shadow of the curtain never fails to rouse in us. They are hybrid creatures, neither gay like butterflies nor sombre like their own species. Nevertheless the present specimen, with his narrow hay-coloured wings, fringed with a tassel of the same colour, seemed to be content with life. It was a pleasant morning, mid-September, mild, benignant, yet with a keener breath than that of the summer months. The plough was already scoring the field opposite the window, and where the share had been, the earth was pressed flat and gleamed with moisture. Such vigour came rolling in from the fields and the down beyond that it was difficult to keep the eyes strictly turned upon the book. The rooks too were keeping one of their annual festivities; soaring round the tree tops until it looked as if a vast net with thousands of black knots in it had been cast up into the air; which, after a few moments, sank slowly down upon the trees until every twig seemed to have a knot at the end of it. Then, suddenly, the net would be thrown into the air again in a wider circle this time, with the utmost clamour and vociferation, as though to be thrown into the air and settle slowly down upon the tree tops were a tremendously exciting experience.

The same energy which inspired the rooks, the ploughmen, the horses, and even, it seemed, the lean bare-backed downs, sent the moth fluttering from side to side of his square of the window-pane. One could not help watching him. One was, indeed, conscious of a queer feeling of pity for him. The possibilities of pleasure seemed that morning so enormous and so various that to have only a moth's part in life, and a day moth's at that, appeared a hard fate, and his zest in enjoying his meagre opportunities to the full, pathetic. He flew vigorously to one corner of his compartment, and, after waiting there a second, flew across to the other. What remained for him but to fly to a third corner and then to a fourth? That was all he could do, in spite of the size of the downs, the width of the sky, the far-off smoke of houses, and the romantic voice, now and then, of a steamer out at sea. What he could do he did. Watching him, it seemed as if a fibre, very thin but pure, of the enormous energy of the world had been thrust into his frail and diminutive body. As often as he crossed the pane, I could fancy that a thread of vital light became visible. He was little or nothing but life.

Yet, because he was so small, and so simple a form of the energy that was rolling in at the open window and driving its way through so many narrow and intricate corridors in my own brain and in those of other human beings, there was something marvelous as well as pathetic about him. It was as if someone had taken a tiny bead of pure life and decking it as lightly as possible with down and feathers, had set it dancing and zigzagging to show us the true nature of life. Thus displayed one could not get over the strangeness of it. One is apt to forget all about life, seeing it humped and bossed and garnished and cumbered so that it has to move with the greatest circumspection and dignity. Again, the thought of all that life might have been had he been born in any other shape caused one to view his simple activities with a kind of pity.

After a time, tired by his dancing apparently, he settled on the window ledge in the sun, and, the queer spectacle being at an end, I forgot about him. Then, looking up, my eye was caught by him. He was trying to resume his dancing, but seemed either so stiff or so awkward that he could only flutter to the bottom of the window-pane; and when he tried to fly across it he failed. Being intent on other matters I watched these futile attempts for a time without thinking, unconsciously waiting for him to resume his flight, as one waits for a machine, that has stopped momentarily, to start again without considering the reason of its failure. After perhaps a seventh attempt he slipped from the wooden ledge and fell, fluttering his wings, onto his back on the window sill. The helplessness of his attitude roused me. It flashed upon me he was in difficulties; he could no longer raise himself; his legs struggled vainly. But, as I stretched out a pencil, meaning to help him to right himself, it came over me that the failure and awkwardness were the approach of death. I laid the pencil down again.

The legs agitated themselves once more. I looked as if for the enemy against which he struggled. I looked out of doors. What had happened there? Presumably it was midday, and work in the fields had stopped. Stillness and quiet had replaced the previous animation. The birds had taken themselves off to feed in the brooks. The horses stood still. Yet the power was there all the same, massed outside indifferent, impersonal, not attending to anything in particular. Somehow it was opposed to the little hay-coloured moth. It was useless to try to do anything. One could only watch the extraordinary efforts made by those tiny legs against an oncoming doom which could, had it chosen, have submerged an entire city, not merely a city, but masses of human beings; nothing, I knew, had any chance against death. Nevertheless after a pause of exhaustion the legs fluttered again. It was superb this last protest, and so frantic that he succeeded at last in righting himself. One's sympathies, of course, were all on the side of life. Also, when there was nobody to care or to know, this gigantic effort on the part of an insignificant little moth, against a power of such magnitude, to retain what no one else valued or desired to keep, moved one strangely. Again, somehow, one saw life a pure bead. I lifted the pencil again, useless though I knew it to be. But even as I did so, the unmistakable tokens of death showed themselves. The body relaxed, and instantly grew stiff. The struggle was over. The insignificant little creature now knew death. As I looked at the dead moth, this minute wayside triumph of so great a force over so mean an antagonist filled me with wonder. Just as life had been strange a few minutes before, so death was now as strange. The moth having righted himself now lay most decently and uncomplainingly composed. O yes, he seemed to say, death is stronger than I am.

[1942]

SHAKESPEARE'S SISTER

IT WOULD HAVE BEEN impossible, completely and entirely, for any woman to have written the plays of Shakespeare in the age of Shakespeare. Let me imagine, since facts are so hard to come by, what would have happened had Shakespeare had a wonderfully gifted sister, called Judith, let us say. Shakespeare himself went, very probably—his mother was an heiress—to the grammar school, where he may have learnt Latin—Ovid, Virgil and Horace—and the elements of grammar and logic. He was, it is well known, a wild boy who poached rabbits, perhaps shot a deer, and had, rather sooner than he should have done, to marry a woman in the neighbourhood, who bore him a child rather quicker than was right. That escapade sent him to seek his fortune in London. He had, it seemed, a taste for the theatre; he began by holding horses at the stage door. Very soon he got work in the theatre, became a successful actor, and lived at the hub of the universe, meeting everybody, knowing everybody, practising his art on the boards, exercising his wits in the streets, and even getting access to the palace of the queen. Meanwhile his extraordinarily gifted sister, let us suppose, remained at home. She was as adventurous, as imaginative, as agog to see the world as he was. But she was not sent to school. She had no chance of learning grammar and logic, let alone of reading Horace and Virgil. She picked up a book now and then, one of her brother's perhaps, and read a few pages. But then her parents came in and told her to mend the stockings or mind the stew and not moon about with books and papers. They would have spoken sharply but kindly, for they were substantial people who knew the conditions of life for a woman and loved their daughter—indeed, more likely than not she was the apple of her father's eye. Perhaps she scribbled some pages up in an apple loft on the sly, but was careful to hide them or set fire to them. Soon, however, before she was out of her teens, she was to be betrothed to the son of a neighbouring wool-stapler. She cried out that marriage was hateful to her, and for that she was severely beaten by her father. Then he ceased to scold her. He begged her instead not to hurt him, not to shame him in this matter of her marriage. He would give her a chain of beads or a fine petticoat, he said; and there were tears in his eyes. How could she disobey him? How could she break his heart? The force of her own gift alone drove her to it. She made up a small parcel of her belongings, let herself down by a rope one summer's night and took the road to London. She was not seventeen. The birds that sang in the hedge were not more musical than she was. She had the quickest fancy, a gift like her brother's, for the tune of words. Like him, she had a taste for the theatre. She stood at the stage door; she wanted to act, she said. Men laughed in her face. The manager—a fat, loose-lipped man—guffawed. He bellowed something about poodles dancing and women acting—no woman, he said, could possibly be an actress. He hinted—you can imagine what. She could get no training in her craft. Could she even seek her dinner in a tavern or roam the streets at midnight? Yet her genius was for fiction and lusted to feed abundantly upon the lives of men and women and the study of their ways. At last—for she was very young, oddly like Shakespeare the poet in her face, with the same grey eyes and rounded brows—at last Nick Greene the actor-manager took pity on her; she found herself with child by that gentleman and so—who shall measure the heat and violence of the poet's heart when caught and tangled in a woman's body?—killed herself one winter's night and lies buried at some cross-roads where the omnibuses now stop outside the Elephant and Castle.

That, more or less, is how the story would run, I think, if a woman in Shakespeare's day had had Shakespeare's genius.

[1929]

PROFESSIONS FOR WOMEN*

WHEN YOUR SECRETARY invited me to come here, she told me that your Society is concerned with the employment of women and she suggested that I might tell you something about my own professional experiences. It is true I am a woman; it is true I am employed; but what professional experiences have I had? It is difficult to say. My profession is literature; and in that profession there are fewer experiences for women than in any other, with the exception of the stage—fewer, I mean, that are peculiar to women. For the road was cut many years ago—by Fanny Burney, by Aphra Behn, by Harriet Martineau, by Jane Austen, by George Eliot—many famous women, and many more unknown and forgotten, have been before me, making the path

*A paper read to The Women's Service League.

smooth, and regulating my steps. Thus, when I came to write, there
were very few material obstacles in my way. Writing was a reputable
and harmless occupation. The family peace was not broken by the
scratching of a pen. No demand was made upon the family purse. For
ten and sixpence one can buy paper enough to write all the plays of
Shakespeare—if one has a mind that way. Pianos and models, Paris,
Vienna and Berlin, masters and mistresses, are not needed by a writer.
The cheapness of writing paper is, of course, the reason why women
have succeeded as writers before they have succeeded in the other
professions.

But to tell you my story—it is a simple one. You have only got to
figure to yourselves a girl in a bedroom with a pen in her hand. She
had only to move that pen from left to right—from ten o'clock to one.
Then it occurred to her to do what is simple and cheap enough after
all—to slip a few of those pages into an envelope, fix a penny stamp
in the corner, and drop the envelope into the red box at the corner.
It was thus that I became a journalist; and my effort was rewarded
on the first day of the following month—a very glorious day it was
for me—by a letter from an editor containing a cheque for one pound
ten shillings and sixpence. But to show you how little I deserve to be
called a professional woman, how little I know of the struggles and
difficulties of such lives, I have to admit that instead of spending that
sum upon bread and butter, rent, shoes and stockings, or butcher's
bills, I went out and bought a cat—a beautiful cat, a Persian cat,
which very soon involved me in bitter disputes with my neighbours.

What could be easier than to write articles and to buy Persian cats
with the profits? But wait a moment. Articles have to be about some-
thing. Mine, I seem to remember, was about a novel by a famous man.
And while I was writing this review, I discovered that if I were going
to review books I should need to do battle with a certain phantom.
And the phantom was a woman, and when I came to know her better
I called her after the heroine of a famous poem, The Angel in the
House. It was she who used to come between me and my paper when
I was writing reviews. It was she who bothered me and wasted my time
and so tormented me that at last I killed her. You who come of a
younger and happier generation may not have heard of her—you may
not know what I mean by the Angel in the House. I will describe her
as shortly as I can. She was intensely sympathetic. She was immensely

charming. She was utterly unselfish. She excelled in the difficult arts of family life. She sacrificed herself daily. If there was chicken, she took the leg; if there was a draught she sat in it—in short she was so constituted that she never had a mind or a wish of her own, but preferred to sympathize always with the minds and wishes of others. Above all—I need not say it—she was pure. Her purity was supposed to be her chief beauty—her blushes, her great grace. In those days— the last of Queen Victoria—every house had its Angel. And when I came to write I encountered her with the very first words. The shadow of her wings fell on my page; I heard the rustling of her skirts in the room. Directly, that is to say, I took my pen in hand to review that novel by a famous man, she slipped behind me and whispered: "My dear, you are a young woman. You are writing about a book that has been written by a man. Be sympathetic; be tender; flatter; deceive; use all the arts and wiles of our sex. Never let anybody guess that you have a mind of your own. Above all, be pure." And she made as if to guide my pen. I now record the one act for which I take some credit to myself, though the credit rightly belongs to some excellent ancestors of mine who left me a certain sum of money—shall we say five hun- dred pounds a year?—so that it was not necessary for me to depend solely on charm for my living. I turned upon her and caught her by the throat. I did my best to kill her. My excuse, if I were to be had up in a court of law, would be that I acted in self-defence. Had I not killed her she would have killed me. She would have plucked the heart out of my writing. For, as I found, directly I put pen to paper, you cannot review even a novel without having a mind of your own, without expressing what you think to be the truth about human relations, morality, sex. And all these questions, according to the Angel in the House, cannot be dealt with freely and openly by women; they must charm, they must conciliate, they must—to put it bluntly—tell lies if they are to succeed. Thus, whenever I felt the shadow of her wing or the radiance of her halo upon my page, I took up the inkpot and flung it at her. She died hard. Her fictitious nature was of great assistance to her. It is far harder to kill a phantom than a reality. She was always creeping back when I thought I had des- patched her. Though I flatter myself that I killed her in the end, the struggle was severe; it took much time that had better have been spent upon learning Greek grammar; or in roaming the world in search of

adventures. But it was a real experience; it was an experience that was
bound to befall all women writers at that time. Killing the Angel in
the House was part of the occupation of a woman writer.

But to continue my story. The Angel was dead; what then remained? You may say that what remained was a simple and common
object—a young woman in a bedroom with an inkpot. In other words,
now that she had rid herself of falsehood, that young woman had only
to be herself. Ah, but what is "herself"? I mean, what is a woman?
I assure you, I do not know. I do not believe that you know. I do not
believe that anybody can know until she has expressed herself in all
the arts and professions open to human skill. That indeed is one of
the reasons why I have come here—out of respect for you, who are
in process of showing us by your experiments what a woman is, who
are in process of providing us, by your failures and successes, with that
extremely important piece of information.

But to continue the story of my professional experiences. I made
one pound ten and six by my first review; and I bought a Persian cat
with the proceeds. Then I grew ambitious. A Persian cat is all very
well, I said; but a Persian cat is not enough. I must have a motor car.
And it was thus that I became a novelist—for it is a very strange thing
that people will give you a motor car if you will tell them a story. It
is a still stranger thing that there is nothing so delightful in the world
as telling stories. It is far pleasanter than writing reviews of famous
novels. And yet, if I am to obey your secretary and tell you my
professional experiences as a novelist, I must tell you about a very
strange experience that befell me as a novelist. And to understand it
you must try to imagine a novelist's state of mind. I hope I am not
giving away professional secrets if I say that a novelist's chief desire
is to be as unconscious as possible. He has to induce in himself a state
of perpetual lethargy. He wants life to proceed with the utmost quiet
and regularity. He wants to see the same faces, to read the same books,
to do the same things day after day, month after month, while he is
writing, so that nothing may break the illusion in which he is living—
so that nothing may disturb or disquiet the mysterious nosings about,
feelings round, darts, dashes and sudden discoveries of that very shy
and illusive spirit, the imagination. I suspect that this state is the same
both for men and women. Be that as it may, I want you to imagine
me writing a novel in a state of trance. I want you to figure to

yourselves a girl sitting with a pen in her hand, which for minutes, and
indeed for hours, she never dips into the inkpot. The image that comes
to my mind when I think of this girl is the image of a fisherman lying
sunk in dreams on the verge of a deep lake with a rod held out over
the water. She was letting her imagination sweep unchecked round
every rock and cranny of the world that lies submerged in the depths
of our unconscious being. Now came the experience, the experience
that I believe to be far commoner with women writers than with men.
The line raced through the girl's fingers. Her imagination had rushed
away. It had sought the pools, the depths, the dark places where the
largest fish slumber. And then there was a smash. There was an
explosion. There was foam and confusion. The imagination had
dashed itself against something hard. The girl was roused from her
dream. She was indeed in a state of the most acute and difficult
distress. To speak without figure she had thought of something, something about the body, about the passions which it was unfitting for her
as a woman to say. Men, her reason told her, would be shocked. The
consciousness of what men will say of a woman who speaks the truth
about her passions had roused her from her artist's state of uncon-
sciousness. She could write no more. The trance was over. Her imagination could work no longer. This I believe to be a very common
experience with women writers—they are impeded by the extreme
conventionality of the other sex. For though men sensibly allow themselves great freedom in these respects, I doubt that they realize or can
control the extreme severity with which they condemn such freedom
in women.

These then were two very genuine experiences of my own. These
were two of the adventures of my professional life. The first—killing
the Angel in the House—I think I solved. She died. But the second,
telling the truth about my own experiences as a body, I do not think
I solved. I doubt that any woman has solved it yet. The obstacles
against her are still immensely powerful—and yet they are very difficult to define. Outwardly, what is simpler than to write books?
Outwardly, what obstacles are there for a woman rather than for a
man? Inwardly, I think, the case is very different; she has still many
ghosts to fight, many prejudices to overcome. Indeed it will be a long
time still, I think, before a woman can sit down to write a book
without finding a phantom to be slain, a rock to be dashed against.

Imagination

Feminist
sexuality

And if this is so in literature, the freest of all professions for women, how is it in the new professions which you are now for the first time entering?

Those are the questions that I should like, had I time, to ask you. And indeed, if I have laid stress upon these professional experiences of mine, it is because I believe that they are, though in different forms, yours also. Even when the path is nominally open—when there is nothing to prevent a woman from being a doctor, a lawyer, a civil servant—there are many phantoms and obstacles, as I believe, looming in her way. To discuss and define them is I think of great value and importance; for thus only can the labour be shared, the difficulties be solved. But besides this, it is necessary also to discuss the ends and the aims for which we are fighting, for which we are doing battle with these formidable obstacles. Those aims cannot be taken for granted; they must be perpetually questioned and examined. The whole position, as I see it—here in this hall surrounded by women practising for the first time in history I know not how many different professions—is one of extraordinary interest and importance. You have won rooms of your own in the house hitherto exclusively owned by men. You are able, though not without great labour and effort, to pay the rent. You are earning your five hundred pounds a year. But this freedom is only a beginning; the room is your own, but it is still bare. It has to be furnished; it has to be decorated; it has to be shared. How are you going to furnish it, how are you going to decorate it? With whom are you going to share it, and upon what terms? These, I think, are questions of the utmost importance and interest. For the first time in history you are able to ask them; for the first time you are able to decide for yourselves what the answers should be. Willingly would I stay and discuss those questions and answers—but not tonight. My time is up; and I must cease.

[1931]

ELLEN TERRY

WHEN SHE CAME on to the stage as Lady Cicely in *Captain Brassbound's Conversion,* the stage collapsed like a house of cards and all the limelights were extinguished. When she spoke it was as if someone drew a bow over a ripe, richly seasoned 'cello; it grated, it glowed, and it growled. Then she stopped speaking. She put on her glasses. She gazed intently at the back of a settee. She had forgotten her part. But did it matter? Speaking or silent, she was Lady Cicely—or was it Ellen Terry? At any rate, she filled the stage and all the other actors were put out, as electric lights are put out in the sun.

Yet this pause when she forgot what Lady Cicely said next was significant. It was a sign not that she was losing her memory and past her prime, as some said. It was a sign that Lady Cicely was not a part that suited her. Her son, Gordon Craig, insists that she only forgot her part when there was something uncongenial in the words, when some speck of grit had got into the marvellous machine of her genius. When the part was congenial, when she was Shakespeare's Portia, Desdemona, Ophelia, every word, every comma was consumed. Even her eyelashes acted. Her body lost its weight. Her son, a mere boy, could lift her in his arms. "I am not myself," she said. "Something comes upon me. . . . I am always-in-the-air, light and bodiless." We, who can only remember her as Lady Cicely on the little stage at the Court Theatre, only remember what, compared with her Ophelia or her Portia, was as a picture postcard compared with the great Velasquez in the gallery.

It is the fate of actors to leave only picture postcards behind them. Every night when the curtain goes down the beautiful coloured canvas is rubbed out. What remains is at best only a wavering, insubstantial phantom—a verbal life on the lips of the living. Ellen Terry was well aware of it. She tried herself, overcome by the greatness of Irving as Hamlet and indignant at the caricatures of his detractors, to describe what she remembered. It was in vain. She dropped her pen in despair. "Oh God, that I were a writer!" she cried. "Surely a *writer* could not string words together about Henry Irving's Hamlet and say *nothing, nothing.* " It never struck her, humble as she was, and obsessed by her lack of book learning, that she was, among other things, a writer. It never occurred to her when she wrote her autobiography, or scribbled page after page to Bernard Shaw late at night, dead tired after a rehearsal, that she was "writing." The words in her beautiful rapid hand bubbled off her pen. With dashes and notes of exclamation she tried to give them the very tone and stress of the spoken word. It is true, she could not build a house with words, one room opening out of another, and a staircase connecting the whole. But whatever she took up became in her warm, sensitive grasp a tool. If it was a rolling-pin, she made perfect pastry. If it was a carving knife, perfect slices fell from the leg of mutton. If it were a pen, words peeled off, some broken, some suspended in mid-air, but all far more expressive than the tappings of the professional typewriter.

With her pen then at odds and ends of time she has painted a self-portrait. It is not an Academy portrait, glazed, framed, complete. It is rather a bundle of loose leaves upon each of which she has dashed off a sketch for a portrait—here a nose, here an arm, here a foot, and there a mere scribble in the margin. The sketches done in different moods, from different angles, sometimes contradict each other. The nose cannot belong to the eyes; the arm is out of all proportion to the foot. It is difficult to assemble them. And there are blank pages, too. Some very important features are left out. There was a self she did not know, a gap she could not fill. Did she not take Walt Whitman's words for a motto? "Why, even I myself, I often think, know little or nothing of my real life. Only a few hints—a few diffused faint clues and indirections. . . . I seek . . . to trace out here."

Nevertheless, the first sketch is definite enough. It is the sketch of her childhood. She was born to the stage. The stage was her cradle, her nursery. When other little girls were being taught sums and pot-hooks she was being cuffed and buffeted into the practice of her profession. Her ears were boxed, her muscles suppled. All day she was hard at work on the boards. Late at night when other children were safe in bed she was stumbling along the dark streets wrapped in her father's cloak. And the dark street with its curtained windows was nothing but a sham to that little professional actress, and the rough and tumble life on the boards was her home, her reality. "It's all such sham there," she wrote—meaning by "there" what she called "life lived in houses"—"sham—cold—hard—pretending. It's not sham here in our theatre—here all is real, warm and kind—we live a lovely spiritual life here."

That is the first sketch. But turn to the next page. The child born to the stage has become a wife. She is married at sixteen to an elderly famous painter. The theatre has gone; its lights are out and in its place is a quiet studio in a garden. In its place is a world full of pictures and "gentle artistic people with quiet voices and elegant manners." She sits mum in her corner while the famous elderly people talk over her head in quiet voices. She is content to wash her husband's brushes; to sit to him; to play her simple tunes on the piano to him while he paints. In the evening she wanders over the Downs with the great poet, Tennyson. "I was in Heaven," she wrote. "I never had one single pang of regret for the theatre." If only it could have lasted! But somehow—here a blank page intervenes—she was an incongruous element in that quiet studio. She was too young, too vigorous, too vital, perhaps. At any rate, the marriage was a failure.

And so, skipping a page or two, we come to the next sketch. She is a mother now. Two adorable children claim all her devotion. She is living in the depths of the country, in the heart of domesticity. She is up at six. She scrubs, she cooks, she sews. She teaches the children. She harnesses the pony. She fetches the milk. And again she is perfectly happy. To live with children in a cottage, driving her little cart about the lanes, going to church on Sunday in blue and white cotton—that is the ideal life! She asks no more than that it shall go on like that for ever and ever. But one day the wheel comes off the pony cart. Huntsmen in pink leap over the hedge. One of them dismounts and offers help. He looks at the girl in a blue frock and exclaims: "Good God! It's Nelly!" She looks at the huntsman in pink and cries, "Charles Reade!" And so, all in a jiffy, back she goes to the stage, and to forty pounds a week. For—that is the reason she gives—the bailiffs are in the house. She must make money.

At this point a very blank page confronts us. There is a gulf which we can only cross at a venture. Two sketches face each other; Ellen Terry in blue cotton among the hens; Ellen Terry robed and crowned as Lady Macbeth on the stage of the Lyceum. The two sketches are contradictory yet they are both of the same woman. She hates the stage; yet she adores it. She worships her children; yet she forsakes them. She would like to live for ever among pigs and ducks in the open air; yet she spends the rest of her life among actors and actresses in the limelight. Her own attempt to explain the discrepancy is hardly convincing. "I have always been more woman than artist," she says. Irving put the theatre first. "He had none of what I may call my bourgeois qualities—the love of being in love, the love of a home, the dislike of solitude." She tries to persuade us that she was an ordinary woman enough; a better hand at pastry than most; an adept at keeping house; with an eye for colour, a taste for furniture, and a positive passion for washing children's heads. If she went back to the stage it was because—well, what else could she do when the bailiffs were in the house?

This is the little sketch that she offers us to fill in the gap between the two Ellen Terrys—Ellen the mother, and Ellen the actress. But here we remember her warning: "Why, even I myself know little or nothing of my real life." There was something in her that she did not understand; something that came surging up from the depths and swept her away in its clutches. The voice she heard in the lane was not the voice of Charles Reade; nor was it the voice of the bailiffs. It was the voice of her genius; the urgent call of something that she could not define, could not suppress, and must obey. So she left her children and followed the voice back to the stage, back to the Lyceum, back to a long life of incessant toil, anguish, and glory.

But, having gazed at the full-length portrait of Ellen Terry as Sargeant painted her, robed and crowned as Lady Macbeth, turn to the next page. It is done from another angle. Pen in hand, she is seated at her desk. A volume of Shakespeare lies before her. It is open at *Cymbeline,* and she is making careful notes in the margin. The part of Imogen presents great problems. She is, she says, "on the rack" about her interpretation. Perhaps Bernard Shaw can throw light upon the question? A letter from the brilliant young critic of the *Saturday Review* lies beside Shakespeare. She has never met him, but for years they have written to each other, intimately, ardently, disputatiously, some of the best letters in the language. He says the most outrageous things. He compares dear Henry to an ogre, and Ellen to a captive chained in his cage. But Ellen Terry is quite capable of holding her own against Bernard Shaw. She scolds him, laughs at him, fondles him, and contradicts him. She has a curious sympathy for the advanced views that Henry Irving abominated. But what suggestions has the

brilliant critic to make about Imogen? None apparently that she has
not already thought for herself. She is as close and critical a student
of Shakespeare as he is. She has studied every line, weighed the
meaning of every word; experimented with every gesture. Each of
those golden moments when she becomes bodiless, not herself, is the
result of months of minute and careful study. "Art," she quotes,
"needs that which we can give her, I assure you." In fact this mutable
woman, all instinct, sympathy, and sensation, is as painstaking a
student and as careful of the dignity of her art as Flaubert himself.

But once more the expression on that serious face changes. She
works like a slave—none harder. But she is quick to tell Mr. Shaw that
she does not work with her brain only. She is not in the least clever.
Indeed, she is happy she tells him, *"not to be clever."* She stresses the
point with a jab of her pen. "You clever people," as she calls him and
his friends, miss so much, mar so much. As for education, she never
had a day's schooling in her life. As far as she can see, but the problem
baffles her, the main spring of her art is imagination. Visit mad-houses,
if you like; take notes; observe; study endlessly. But first, imagine. And
so she takes her part away from the books out into the woods. Ram-
bling down grassy rides, she lives her part until she is it. If a word jars
or grates, she must re-think it, re-write it. Then when every phrase
is her own, and every gesture spontaneous, out she comes onto the
stage and is Imogen, Ophelia, Desdemona.

But is she, even when the great moments are on her, a great actress?
She doubts it. "I cared more for love and life," she says. Her face, too,
has been no help to her. She cannot sustain emotion. Certainly she
is not a great tragic actress. Now and again, perhaps, she has acted
some comic part to perfection. But even while she analyses herself, as
one artist to another, the sun slants upon an old kitchen chair.
"Thank the Lord for my eyes!" she exclaims. What a world of joy her
eyes have brought her! Gazing at the old "rush-bottomed, sturdy-
legged, and wavy-backed" chair, the stage is gone, the limelights are
out, the famous actress is forgotten.

Which, then, of all these women is the real Ellen Terry? How are
we to put the scattered sketches together? Is she mother, wife, cook,
critic, actress, or should she have been, after all, a painter? Each part
seems the right part until she throws it aside and plays another.
Something of Ellen Terry it seems overflowed every part and re-

mained unacted. Shakespeare could not fit her; not Ibsen; nor Shaw. The stage could not hold her; nor the nursery. But there is, after all, a greater dramatist than Shakespeare, Ibsen, or Shaw. There is Nature. Hers is so vast a stage, and so innumerable a company of actors, that for the most part she fobs them off with a tag or two. They come on and they go off without breaking the ranks. But now and again Nature creates a new part, an original part. The actors who act that part always defy our attempts to name them. They will not act the stock parts—they forget the words, they improvise others of their own. But when they come on the stage falls like a pack of cards and the limelights are extinguished. That was Ellen Terry's fate—to act a new part. And thus while other actors are remembered because they were Hamlet, Phèdre, or Cleopatra, Ellen Terry is remembered because she was Ellen Terry.

[1941]

A SKETCH OF THE PAST

TWO DAYS AGO—Sunday 16th April 1939 to be precise—Nessa said that if I did not start writing my memoirs I should soon be too old. I should be eighty-five, and should have forgotten—witness the unhappy case of Lady Strachey. As it happens that I am sick of writing Roger's life, perhaps I will spend two or three mornings making a sketch.* There are several difficulties. In the first place, the enormous number of things I can remember; in the second, the number of different ways in which memoirs can be written. As a great memoir reader, I know many different ways. But if I begin to go through them and to analyse them and their merits and faults, the mornings—I cannot take more than two or three at most—will be gone. So without stopping to choose my way, in the sure and certain knowledge that it will find itself—or if not it will not matter—I begin: the first memory.

*VW was at work on *Roger Fry: A Biography*.

This was of red and purple flowers on a black ground—my mother's dress; and she was sitting either in a train or in an omnibus, and I was on her lap. I therefore saw the flowers she was wearing very close; and can still see purple and red and blue, I think, against the black; they must have been anemones, I suppose. Perhaps we were going to St Ives; more probably, for from the light it must have been evening, we were coming back to London. But it is more convenient artistically to suppose that we were going to St Ives, for that will lead to my other memory, which also seems to be my first memory, and in fact it is the most important of all my memories. If life has a base that it stands upon, if it is a bowl that one fills and fills and fills—then my bowl without a doubt stands upon this memory. It is of lying half asleep, half awake, in bed in the nursery at St Ives. It is of hearing the waves breaking, one, two, one, two, and sending a splash of water over the beach; and then breaking, one, two, one, two, behind a yellow blind. It is of hearing the blind draw its little acorn across the floor as the wind blew the blind out. It is of lying and hearing this splash and seeing this light, and feeling, it is almost impossible that I should be here; of feeling the purest ecstasy I can conceive.

I could spend hours trying to write that as it should be written, in order to give the feeling which is even at this moment very strong in me. But I should fail (unless I had some wonderful luck); I dare say I should only succeed in having the luck if I had begun by describing Virginia herself.

Here I come to one of the memoir writer's difficulties—one of the reasons why, though I read so many, so many are failures. They leave out the person to whom things happened. The reason is that it is so difficult to describe any human being. So they say: "This is what happened"; but they do not say what the person was like to whom it happened. And the events mean very little unless we know first to whom they happened. Who was I then? Adeline Virginia Stephen, the second daughter of Leslie and Julia Prinsep Stephen, born on 25th January 1882, descended from a great many people, some famous, others obscure; born into a large connection, born not of rich parents, but of well-to-do parents, born into a very communicative, literate, letter writing, visiting, articulate, late nineteenth century world; so that I could if I liked to take the trouble, write a great deal here not only about my mother and father but about uncles and aunts, cousins and friends. But I do not know how much of this, or what part of this, made me feel what I felt in the nursery at St Ives. I do not know how far I differ from other people. That is another memoir writer's difficulty. Yet to describe oneself truly one must have some standard of comparison; was I clever, stupid, good looking, ugly, passionate, cold—? Owing partly to the fact that I was never at school, never competed in any way with children of my own age, I have never been able to compare my gifts and defects with other people's. But of course there was one external reason for the intensity of this first impression: the impression of the waves and the acorn on the blind; the feeling, as I describe it sometimes to myself, of lying in a grape and seeing through a film of semi-transparent yellow—it was due partly to the many months we spent in London. The change of nursery was a great change. And there was the long train journey; and the excitement. I remember the dark; the lights; the stir of the going up to bed.

But to fix my mind upon the nursery—it had a balcony; there was a partition, but it joined the balcony of my father's and mother's bedroom. My mother would come out onto her balcony in a white dressing gown. There were passion flowers growing on the wall; they were great starry blossoms, with purple streaks, and large green buds, part empty, part full.

If I were a painter I should paint these first impressions in pale yellow, silver, and green. There was the pale yellow blind; the green sea; and the silver of the passion flowers. I should make a picture that was globular; semi-transparent. I should make a picture of curved petals; of shells; of things that were semi-transparent; I should make curved shapes, showing the light through, but not giving a clear outline. Everything would be large and dim; and what was seen would at the same time be heard; sounds would come through this petal or leaf—sounds indistinguishable from sights. Sound and sight seem to make equal parts of these first impressions. When I think of the early morning in bed I also hear the caw of rooks falling from a great height. The sound seems to fall through an elastic, gummy air; which holds it up; which prevents it from being sharp and distinct. The quality of the air above Talland House seemed to suspend sound, to let it sink down slowly, as if it were caught in a blue gummy veil. The rooks cawing is part of the waves breaking—one, two, one, two—and the splash as the wave drew back and then it gathered again, and I lay there half awake, half asleep, drawing in such ecstasy as I cannot describe.

The next memory—all these colour-and-sound memories hang together at St Ives—was much more robust; it was highly sensual. It was later. It still makes me feel warm; as if everything were ripe; humming; sunny; smelling so many smells at once; and all making a whole that even now makes me stop—as I stopped then going down to the beach; I stopped at the top to look down at the gardens. They were sunk beneath the road. The apples were on a level with one's head. The gardens gave off a murmur of bees; the apples were red and gold; there were also pink flowers; and grey and silver leaves. The buzz, the croon, the smell, all seemed to press voluptuously against some membrane; not to burst it; but to hum round one such a complete rapture of pleasure that I stopped, smelt; looked. But again I cannot describe that rapture. It was rapture rather than ecstasy.

The strength of these pictures—but sight was always then so much mixed with sound that picture is not the right word—the strength anyhow of these impressions makes me again digress. Those moments—in the nursery, on the road to the beach—can still be more real than the present moment. This I have just tested. For I got up and crossed the garden. Percy was digging the asparagus bed; Louie was shaking a mat in front of the bedroom door. But I was seeing them through the sight I saw here—the nursery and the road to the beach. At times I can go back to St Ives more completely than I can this morning. I can reach a state where I seem to be watching things happen as if I were there. That is, I suppose, that my memory supplies what I had forgotten, so that it seems as if it were happening independently, though I am really making it happen. In certain favourable moods, memories—what one has forgotten—come to the top. Now if this is so, is it not possible—I often wonder—that things we have felt with great intensity have an existence independent of our minds; are in fact still in existence? And if so, will it not be possible, in time, that some devices will be invented by which we can tap them? I see it—the past—as an avenue lying behind; a long ribbon of scenes, emotions. There at the end of the avenue still, are the garden and the nursery. Instead of remembering here a scene and there a sound, I shall fit a plug into the wall; and listen in to the past. I shall turn up August

1890. I feel that strong emotion must leave its trace; and it is only
a question of discovering how we can get ourselves again attached to
it, so that we shall be able to live our lives through from the start.

But the peculiarity of these two strong memories is that each was
very simple. I am hardly aware of myself, but only of the sensation.
I am only the container of the feeling of ecstasy, of the feeling of
rapture. Perhaps this is characteristic of all childhood memories; perhaps it accounts for their strength. Later we add to feelings much that
makes them more complex; and therefore less strong; or if not less
strong, less isolated, less complete. But instead of analysing this, here
is an instance of what I mean—my feeling about the looking-glass in
the hall.

There was a small looking-glass in the hall at Talland House. It had,
I remember, a ledge with a brush on it. By standing on tiptoe I could
see my face in the glass. When I was six or seven perhaps, I got into
the habit of looking at my face in the glass. But I only did this if I
was sure that I was alone. I was ashamed of it. A strong feeling of guilt
seemed naturally attached to it. But why was this so? One obvious
reason occurs to me—Vanessa and I were both what was called tom-
boys; that is, we played cricket, scrambled over rocks, climbed trees,
were said not to care for clothes and so on. Perhaps therefore to have
been found looking in the glass would have been against our tomboy
code. But I think that my feeling of shame went a great deal deeper.
I am almost inclined to drag in my grandfather—Sir James, who once
smoked a cigar, liked it, and so threw away his cigar and never smoked
another. I am almost inclined to think that I inherited a streak of the
puritan, of the Clapham Sect. At any rate, the looking-glass shame has
lasted all my life, long after the tomboy phase was over. I cannot now
powder my nose in public. Everything to do with dress—to be fitted,
to come into a room wearing a new dress—still frightens me; at least
makes me shy, self-conscious, uncomfortable. "Oh to be able to run,
like Julian Morrell, all over the garden in a new dress", I thought not
many years ago at Garsington; when Julian undid a parcel and put on
a new dress and scampered round and round like a hare. Yet feminin-
ity was very strong in our family. We were famous for our beauty—my
mother's beauty, Stella's beauty, gave me as early as I can remember,
pride and pleasure. What then gave me this feeling of shame, unless
it were that I inherited some opposite instinct? My father was spartan,

ascetic, puritanical. He had I think no feeling for pictures; no ear for music; no sense of the sound of words. This leads me to think that my—I would say "our" if I knew enough about Vanessa, Thoby and Adrian—but how little we know even about brothers and sisters—this leads me to think that my natural love for beauty was checked by some ancestral dread. Yet this did not prevent me from feeling ecstasies and raptures spontaneously and intensely and without any shame or the least sense of guilt, so long as they were disconnected with my own body. I thus detect another element in the shame which I had in being caught looking at myself in the glass in the hall. I must have been ashamed or afraid of my own body. Another memory, also of the hall, may help to explain this. There was a slab outside the dining room door for standing dishes upon. Once when I was very small Gerald Duckworth lifted me onto this, and as I sat there he began to explore my body. I can remember the feel of his hand going under my clothes; going firmly and steadily lower and lower. I remember how I hoped that he would stop; how I stiffened and wriggled as his hand approached my private parts. But it did not stop. His hand explored my private parts too. I remember resenting, disliking it—what is the word for so dumb and mixed a feeling? It must have been strong, since I still recall it. This seems to show that a feeling about certain parts of the body; how they must not be touched; how it is wrong to allow them to be touched; must be instinctive. It proves that Virginia Stephen was not born on the 25th January 1882, but was born many thousands of years ago; and had from the very first to encounter instincts already acquired by thousands of ancestresses in the past.

And this throws light not merely on my own case, but upon the problem that I touched on the first page; why it is so difficult to give any account of the person to whom things happen. The person is evidently immensely complicated. Witness the incident of the looking-glass. Though I have done my best to explain why I was ashamed of looking at my own face I have only been able to discover some possible reasons; there may be others; I do not suppose that I have got at the truth; yet this is a simple incident; and it happened to me personally; and I have no motive for lying about it. In spite of all this, people write what they call "lives" of other people; that is, they collect a number of events, and leave the person to whom it happened unknown. Let me add a dream; for it may refer to the incident of the looking-glass. I dreamt that I was looking in a glass when a horrible face—the face of an animal—suddenly showed over my shoulder. I cannot be sure if this was a dream, or if it happened. Was I looking in the glass one day when something in the background moved, and seemed to me alive? I cannot be sure. But I have always remembered the other face in the glass, whether it was a dream or a fact, and that it frightened me.

These then are some of my first memories. But of course as an account of my life they are misleading, because the things one does not remember are as important; perhaps they are more important. If I could remember one whole day I should be able to describe, superficially at least, what life was like as a child. Unfortunately, one only remembers what is exceptional. And there seems to be no reason why one thing is exceptional and another not. Why have I forgotten so many things that must have been, one would have thought, more memorable than what I do remember? Why remember the hum of bees in the garden going down to the beach, and forget completely being thrown naked by father into the sea? (Mrs Swanwick says she saw that happen.)

This leads to a digression, which perhaps may explain a little of my own psychology; even of other people's. Often when I have been writing one of my so-called novels I have been baffled by this same problem; that is, how to describe what I call in my private shorthand—"non-being". Every day includes much more non-being than being. Yesterday for example, Tuesday the 18th of April was [as] it happened a good day; above the average in "being". It was fine; I enjoyed writing these first pages; my head was relieved of the pressure of writing about Roger; I walked over Mount Misery and along the river; and save that the tide was out, the country, which I notice very closely always, was coloured and shaded as I like—there were the willows, I remember, all plumy and soft green and purple against the blue. I also read Chaucer with pleasure; and began a book—the memoirs of Madame de la Fayette—which interested me. These separate moments of being were however embedded in many more moments of non-being. I have already forgotten what Leonard and I talked about at lunch; and at tea; although it was a good day the goodness was embedded in a kind of nondescript cotton wool. This is always so. A great part of every day is not lived consciously. One

walks, eats, sees things, deals with what has to be done; the broken
vacuum cleaner; ordering dinner; writing orders to Mabel; washing;
cooking dinner; bookbinding. When it is a bad day the proportion of
non-being is much larger. I had a slight temperature last week; almost
the whole day was non-being. The real novelist can somehow convey
both sorts of being. I think Jane Austen can; and Trollope; perhaps
Thackeray and Dickens and Tolstoy. I have never been able to do
both. I tried—in *Night and Day;* and in *The Years.* But I will leave
the literary side alone for the moment.

As a child then, my days, just as they do now, contained a large
proportion of this cotton wool, this non-being. Week after week
passed at St Ives and nothing made any dint upon me. Then, for no
reason that I know about, there was a sudden violent shock; something happened so violently that I have remembered it all my life. I
will give a few instances. The first: I was fighting with Thoby on the
lawn. We were pommelling each other with our fists. Just as I raised
my fist to hit him, I felt: why hurt another person? I dropped my hand
instantly, and stood there, and let him beat me. I remember the
feeling. It was a feeling of hopeless sadness. It was as if I became aware
of something terrible; and of my own powerlessness. I slunk off alone,
feeling horribly depressed. The second instance was also in the garden
at St Ives. I was looking at the flower bed by the front door; "That
is the whole", I said. I was looking at a plant with a spread of leaves;
and it seemed suddenly plain that the flower itself was a part of the
earth; that a ring enclosed what was the flower; and that was the real
flower; part earth; part flower. It was a thought I put away as being
likely to be very useful to me later. The third case was also at St Ives.
Some people called Valpy had been staying at St Ives, and had left.
We were waiting at dinner one night, when somehow I overheard my
father or my mother say that Mr Valpy had killed himself. The next
thing I remember is being in the garden at night and walking on the
path by the apple tree. It seemed to me that the apple tree was
connected with the horror of Mr Valpy's suicide. I could not pass it.
I stood there looking at the grey-green creases of the bark—it was a
moonlit night—in a trance of horror. I seemed to be dragged down,
hopelessly, into some pit of absolute despair from which I could not
escape. My body seemed paralysed.

These are three instances of exceptional moments. I often tell them over, or rather they come to the surface unexpectedly. But now that for the first time I have written them down, I realise something that I have never realised before. Two of these moments ended in a state of despair. The other ended, on the contrary, in a state of satisfaction. When I said about the flower, "That is the whole", I felt that I had made a discovery. I felt that I had put away in my mind something that I should go back [to], to turn over and explore. It strikes me now that this was a profound difference. It was the difference in the first place between despair and satisfaction. This difference I think arose from the fact that I was quite unable to deal with the pain of discovering that people hurt each other; that a man I had seen had killed himself. The sense of horror held me powerless. But in the case of the flower I found a reason; and was thus able to deal with the sensation. I was not powerless. I was conscious—if only at a distance—that I should in time explain it. I do not know if I was older when I saw the flower than I was when I had the other two experiences. I only know that many of these exceptional moments brought with them a peculiar horror and a physical collapse; they seemed dominant; myself passive. This suggests that as one gets older one has a greater power through reason to provide an explanation; and that this explanation blunts the sledge-hammer force of the blow. I think this is true, because though I still have the peculiarity that I receive these sudden shocks, they are now always welcome; after the first surprise, I always feel instantly that they are particularly valuable. And so I go on to suppose that the shock-receiving capacity is what makes me a writer. I hazard the explanation that a shock is at once in my case followed by the desire to explain it. I feel that I have had a blow; but it is not, as I thought as a child, simply a blow from an enemy hidden behind the cotton wool of daily life; it is or will become a revelation of some order; it is a token of some real thing behind appearances; and I make it real by putting it into words. It is only by putting it into words that I make it whole; this wholeness means that it has lost its power to hurt me; it gives me, perhaps because by doing so I take away the pain, a great delight to put the severed parts together. Perhaps this is the strongest pleasure known to me. It is the rapture I get when in writing I seem to be discovering what belongs to what; making a scene come right; making a character come together. From this I reach what I might call a philosophy; at any rate it is a constant idea of mine; that behind the cotton wool is hidden a pattern; that we—I mean all human beings—are connected with this; that the whole world is a work of art; that we are parts of the work of art. *Hamlet* or a Beethoven quartet is the truth about this vast mass that we call the world. But there is no Shakespeare, there is no Beethoven; certainly and emphatically there is no God; we are the words; we are the music; we are the thing itself. And I see this when I have a shock.

This intuition of mine—it is so instinctive that it seems given to me, not made by me—has certainly given its scale to my life ever since I saw the flower in the bed by the front door at St Ives. If I were painting myself I should have to find some—rod, shall I say—something that would stand for the conception. It proves that one's life is not confined to one's body and what one says and does; one is living all the time in relation to certain background rods or conceptions. Mine is that there is a pattern hid behind the cotton wool. And this conception affects me every day. I prove this, now, by spending the morning writing, when I might be walking, running a shop, or learning to do something that will be useful if war comes. I feel that by writing I am doing what is far more necessary than anything else.

All artists I suppose feel something like this. It is one of the obscure elements in life that has never been much discussed. It is left out in almost all biographies and autobiographies, even of artists. Why did Dickens spend his entire life writing stories? What was his conception? I bring in Dickens partly because I am reading *Nicholas Nickleby* at the moment; also partly because it struck me, on my walk yesterday, that these moments of being of mine were scaffolding in the background; were the invisible and silent part of my life as a child. But in the foreground there were of course people; and these people were very like characters in Dickens. They were caricatures; they were very simple; they were immensely alive. They could be made with three strokes of the pen, if I could do it. Dickens owes his astonishing power to make characters alive to the fact that he saw them as a child sees them; as I saw Mr Wolstenholme; C. B. Clarke, and Mr Gibbs.

I name these three people because they all died when I was a child. Therefore they have never been altered. I see them exactly as I saw them then. Mr Wolstenholme was a very old gentleman who came every summer to stay with us. He was brown; he had a beard and very small eyes in fat cheeks; and he fitted into a brown wicker beehive chair as if it had been his nest. He used to sit in this beehive chair smoking and reading. He had only one characteristic—that when he ate plum tart he spurted the juice through his nose so that it made a purple stain on his grey moustache. This seemed enough to cause us perpetual delight. We called him "The Wooly One". By way of shading him a little I remember that we had to be kind to him because he was not happy at home; that he was very poor, yet once gave Thoby half a crown; that he had a son who was drowned in Australia; and I know too that he was a great mathematician. He never said a word all the time I knew him. But he still seems to me a complete character; and whenever I think of him I begin to laugh.

Mr Gibbs was perhaps less simple. He wore a tie ring; had a bald, benevolent head; was dry; neat; precise; and had folds of skin under his chin. He made father groan—"why can't you go—why can't you go?" And he gave Vanessa and myself two ermine skins, with slits down the middle out of which poured endless wealth—streams of silver. I also remember him lying in bed, dying; husky; in a night shirt; and showing us drawings by Retzsch. The character of Mr Gibbs also seems to me complete and amuses me very much.

As for C. B. Clarke, he was an old botanist; and he said to my father, "All you young botanists like Osmunda." He had an aunt aged eighty who went for a walking tour in the New Forest. That is all—that is all I have to say about these three old gentlemen. But how real they were! How we laughed at them! What an immense part they played in our lives!

One more caricature comes into my mind; though pity entered into this one. I am thinking of Justine Nonon. She was immensely old. Little hairs sprouted on her long bony chin. She was a hunchback; and walked like a spider, feeling her way with her long dry fingers from one chair to another. Most of the time she sat in the arm-chair beside the fire. I used to sit on her knee; and her knee jogged up and down; and she sang in a hoarse cracked voice "Ron ron ron—et plon plon plon—" and then her knee gave and I was tumbled onto the floor. She was French; she had been with the Thackerays. She only came to us on visits. She lived by herself at Shepherd's Bush; and used to bring Adrian a glass jar of honey. I got the notion that she was extremely poor; and it made me uncomfortable that she brought this honey, because I felt she did it by way of making her visit acceptable. She said too: "I have come in my carriage and pair"—which meant the red omnibus. For this too I pitied her; also because she began to wheeze; and the nurses said she would not live much longer; and soon she died. That is all I know about her; but I remember her as if she were a completely real person, with nothing left out, like the three old men.

[1939]

Almost like a
Split personality

GEORGE ORWELL

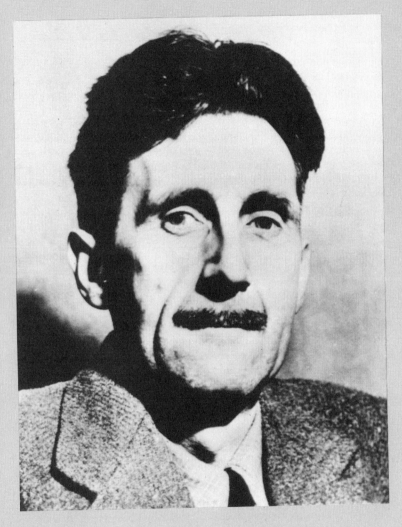

HBJ Photo

BORN AT MOTIHARI, BENGAL, in 1903, the son of a minor official in the Bengal Civil Service, George Orwell attended private schools in England on scholarships from the age of eight until he was graduated from Eton in 1921. But then, instead of going on to one of the universities as might have been expected, Orwell took the advice of a tutor who suggested that he "see something of the world" and joined the Indian Imperial Police. For five years he was a police officer in Burma, then resigned, as he said, "mainly because I could not go on any longer serving an imperialism which I had come to regard as very largely a racket."

For the next year and a half he lived in Paris on his savings and tried to write, but with little success. When his money ran out in the summer of 1929, he got his first taste of poverty as a *plongeur* (dishwasher) in a Paris restaurant, then as a tramp and day-laborer in London and the south of England. Indeed, being a tramp, sleeping in doss-houses, and eating hand-me-out meals so stimulated Orwell's imagination (and perhaps the psychic needs of an acute class-consciousness from having been a scholarship boy in exclusive schools) that even after he became a schoolteacher, and later a clerk in a London book shop, he continued to dress up in old clothes and go "on the bum" on weekends. In 1933 he published his first book, *Down and Out in Paris and London,* a vivid account of his experiences during the summer of 1929, and used instead of his real name, Eric Blair, the pseudonym "George Orwell." As with most other writers who have taken pen-names, the purpose was to keep a secret—in this case from his former Eton schoolmates: that he had once been "down and out." Though he published poetry and many book reviews during the next three years under his real name, he continued to use the name "Orwell" for his books (the novels *Burmese Days, A Clergyman's Daughter,* and *Keep the Aspidistra Flying*).

Between the summer of 1936 and the spring of 1937 Orwell underwent a great metamorphosis. Until then he had been a rather shabby, "serious"—but conventional—young poet on the fringes of the London literati, a very Gissing-like, unsuccessful writer, not at all interested in politics. But then a number of things happened. First, Victor Gollancz commissioned him to go to the north of England and observe the lives of the unemployed coal miners and to write a book about it, which the Left Book Club, a socialist organization, would publish *(The Road to Wigan Pier)*. Next, he got married, which meant he had to start earning a bit more money. Then John Lehmann invited him to submit something for a new magazine he was editing, and Orwell wrote his first real *essay* (as opposed to book review or reportage): he called it "Shooting an Elephant." And finally, in December, 1936, he left for the Spanish Civil War.

At the time that he arrived in Barcelona, Orwell was so naive about politics that he had only the vaguest notion which faction of the Left (the Republican, or Socialist, side) he wished to join. He was interested in the war mainly as a *war,* not as a battle of political ideologies. But his experiences over the next four months changed everything. To put it very simply, what Orwell discovered was that politics was all lies: that the Tory-dominated British press was distorting the truth about what was happening in Spain; and that the Soviets, who were presumably on the side of the workers, were in fact maneuvering to bring about a socialist defeat. As Orwell wrote many years later, "The Spanish war and other events in 1936–37 turned the scale and thereafter I knew where I stood. Every line of serious work that I have written since 1936 has been written, directly or indirectly, against totalitarianism and *for* democratic socialism, as I understand it." In April, 1937, Orwell was severely wounded while fighting on the Aragon front and was lucky to get out of Spain alive. When he got back to England he wrote the first of his important books, *Homage to Catalonia* (1938).

If the political events he observed in Spain were the turning point of Orwell's intellectual life, his near death might be called its psychological equivalent, for after 1936 Eric Blair vanished: no more poetry, no more *belles lettres* book reviews, and only one more conventional novel, *Coming Up for Air* (1939). "George Orwell" became George Orwell, a fiercely dedicated political journalist. But even that doesn't describe the writer who emerged from Spain, for Orwell was more than a mere journalist; he became a devil's advocate of twentieth-century liberalism, an iconoclast in the temples of socialism and communism. His last two books, *Animal Farm* (1945) and *1984* (1949), must be read not as novels nor even strictly as satires—though of course *Animal Farm* is a satire—but as Arguments in the service of truth and human freedom.

Orwell died of tuberculosis in 1950, a few months after finishing *1984*. Looking back over his work, the critic V. S. Pritchett declared that Orwell had been "the conscience of his generation," a claim one might examine by reading Orwell's *Collected Essays, Journalism and Letters,* published in 1968 in four. volumes.

Orwell was never a member of any political organization. Though he approved of many aspects of socialism, he was never a socialist. Though he defended the rights of the poor and oppressed, and occasionally (as in *1984*) sentimentalized their virtues, he never thought that their limited consciousness was the desired goal of man. Orwell believed in only one thing: honesty—or as he said in one of his essays, the "power of facing unpleasant facts." What he had discovered in Spain in 1937 was that objective truth could cease to exist, that the people who controlled the means of communication could—and *did*—alter it at will, and therefore, as his friend Arthur Koestler had said, history was dead. This, then, was Orwell's great perception, and it was his fear that this sort of "thought-control" was happening not only in the "totalitarian" countries but the "democracies" as well that underlay everything he wrote during the last thirteen years of his life.

As a writer, Orwell's rules were very simple: be clear, be concrete, and avoid all frills and mannerisms. But even these rules, as fine as they are, go only part way in explaining the particular forcefulness of his writing. To understand the rest, one must recall Joseph Conrad's credo: "My task, which I am trying to achieve is, by the power of the written word, to make you hear, to make you feel—it is, above all, to make you *see.*" Hearing, feeling, seeing—that is precisely what we are doing when we read George Orwell, and because of it we shall go on reading him for a long time to come.

A HANGING

It was in burma, a sodden morning of the rains. A sickly light, like yellow tinfoil, was slanting over the high walls into the jail yard. We were waiting outside the condemned cells, a row of sheds fronted with double bars, like small animal cages. Each cell measured about ten feet by ten and was quite bare within except for a plank bed and a pot for drinking water. In some of them brown silent men were squatting at the inner bars, with their blankets draped round them. These were the condemned men, due to be hanged within the next week or two.

One prisoner had been brought out of his cell. He was a Hindu, a puny wisp of a man, with a shaven head and vague liquid eyes. He had a thick, sprouting moustache, absurdly too big for his body, rather like the moustache of a comic man on the films. Six tall Indian warders were guarding him and getting him ready for the gallows. Two of them stood by with rifles and fixed bayonets, while the others handcuffed him, passed a chain through his handcuffs and fixed it to their belts, and lashed his arms tight to his sides. They crowded very close about him, with their hands always on him in a careful, caressing grip, as though all the while feeling him to make sure he was there. It was like men handling a fish which is still alive and may jump back into the water. But he stood quite unresisting, yielding his arms limply to the ropes, as though he hardly noticed what was happening.

Eight o'clock struck and a bugle call, desolately thin in the wet air, floated from the distant barracks. The superintendent of the jail, who was standing apart from the rest of us, moodily prodding the gravel with his stick, raised his head at the sound. He was an army doctor, with a gray toothbrush moustache and a gruff voice. "For God's sake hurry up, Francis," he said irritably. "The man ought to have been dead by this time. Aren't you ready yet?"

Francis, the head jailer, a fat Dravidian in a white drill suit and gold spectacles, waved his black hand. "Yes sir, yes sir," he bubbled. "All iss satisfactorily prepared. The hangman iss waiting. We shall proceed."

"Well, quick march, then. The prisoners can't get their breakfast till this job's over."

We set out for the gallows. Two warders marched on either side of the prisoner, with their rifles at the slope; two others marched close against him, gripping him by arm and shoulder, as though at once pushing and supporting him. The rest of us, magistrates and the like, followed behind. Suddenly, when we had gone ten yards, the procession stopped short without any order or warning. A dreadful thing had happened—a dog, come goodness knows whence, had appeared in the yard. It came bounding among us with a loud volley of barks, and leapt round us wagging its whole body, wild with glee at finding so many human beings together. It was a large woolly dog, half Airedale, half pariah. For a moment it pranced round us, and then, before anyone could stop it, it had made a dash for the prisoner and, jumping up, tried to lick his face. Everyone stood aghast, too taken aback even to grab at the dog.

"Who let that bloody brute in here?" said the superintendent angrily. "Catch it, someone!"

A warder, detached from the escort, charged clumsily after the dog, but it danced and gamboled just out of his reach, taking everything as part of the game. A young Eurasian jailer picked up a handful of gravel and tried to stone the dog away, but it dodged the stones and came after us again. Its yaps echoed from the jail walls. The prisoner, in the grasp of the two warders, looked on incuriously, as though this was another formality of the hanging. It was several minutes before someone managed to catch the dog. Then we put my handkerchief through its collar and moved off once more, with the dog still straining and whimpering.

It was about forty yards to the gallows. I watched the bare brown back of the prisoner marching in front of me. He walked clumsily with his bound arms, but quite steadily, with that bobbing gait of the Indian who never straightens his knees. At each step his muscles slid neatly into place, the lock of hair on his scalp danced up and down, his feet printed themselves on the wet gravel. And once, in spite of the men who gripped him by each shoulder, he stepped slightly aside to avoid a puddle on the path.

It is curious, but till that moment I had never realized what it means to destroy a healthy, conscious man. When I saw the prisoner

Beautiful
Paragraph #

step aside to avoid the puddle I saw the mystery, the unspeakable wrongness, of cutting a life short when it is in full tide. This man was not dying, he was alive just as we are alive. All the organs of his body were working—bowels digesting food, skin renewing itself, nails growing, tissues forming—all toiling away in solemn foolery. His nails would still be growing when he stood on the drop, when he was falling through the air with a tenth of a second to live. His eyes saw the yellow gravel and the gray walls, and his brain still remembered, foresaw, reasoned—reasoned even about puddles. He and we were a party of men walking together, seeing, hearing, feeling, understanding the same world; and in two minutes, with a sudden snap, one of us would be gone—one mind less, one world less.

The gallows stood in a small yard, separate from the main grounds of the prison, and overgrown with tall prickly weeds. It was a brick erection like three sides of a shed, with planking on top, and above that two beams and a crossbar with the rope dangling. The hangman, a gray-haired convict in the white uniform of the prison, was waiting beside his machine. He greeted us with a servile crouch as we entered. At a word from Francis the two warders, gripping the prisoner more closely than ever, half led half pushed him to the gallows and helped him clumsily up the ladder. Then the hangman climbed up and fixed the rope round the prisoner's neck.

We stood waiting, five yards away. The warders had formed in a rough circle round the gallows. And then, when the noose was fixed, the prisoner began crying out to his god. It was a high, reiterated cry of "Ram! Ram! Ram! Ram!" not urgent and fearful like a prayer or cry for help, but steady, rhythmical, almost like the tolling of a bell. The dog answered the sound with a whine. The hangman, still standing on the gallows, produced a small cotton bag like a flour bag and drew it down over the prisoner's face. But the sound, muffled by the cloth, still persisted, over and over again: "Ram! Ram! Ram! Ram! Ram!"

The hangman climbed down and stood ready, holding the lever. Minutes seemed to pass. The steady, muffled crying from the prisoner went on and on, "Ram! Ram! Ram!" never faltering for an instant. The superintendent, his head on his chest, was slowly poking the ground with his stick; perhaps he was counting the cries, allowing the prisoner a fixed number—fifty, perhaps, or a hundred. Everyone had changed color. The Indians had gone gray like bad coffee, and one or two of the bayonets were wavering. We looked at the lashed, hooded man on the drop, and listened to his cries—each cry another second of life; the same thought was in all our minds: oh, kill him quickly, get it over, stop that abominable noise!

Suddenly the superintendent made up his mind. Throwing up his head he made a swift motion with his stick. "Chalo!" he shouted almost fiercely.

There was a clanking noise, and then dead silence. The prisoner had vanished, and the rope was twisting on itself. I let go of the dog, and it galloped immediately to the back of the gallows; but when it got there it stopped short, barked, and then retreated into a corner of the yard, where it stood among the weeds, looking timorously out at us. We went round the gallows to inspect the prisoner's body. He was dangling with his toes pointed straight downward, very slowly revolving, as dead as a stone.

The superintendent reached out with his stick and poked the bare brown body; it oscillated slightly. "He's all right," said the superintendent. He backed out from under the gallows, and blew out a deep breath. The moody look had gone out of his face quite suddenly. He glanced at his wrist watch. "Eight minutes past eight. Well, that's all for this morning, thank God."

The warders unfixed bayonets and marched away. The dog, sobered and conscious of having misbehaved itself, slipped after them. We walked out of the gallows yard, past the condemned cells with their waiting prisoners, into the big central yard of the prison. The convicts, under the command of warders armed with lathis, were already receiving their breakfast. They squatted in long rows, each man holding a tin pannikin, while two warders with buckets marched round ladling out rice; it seemed quite a homely, jolly scene, after the hanging. An enormous relief had come upon us now that the job was done. One felt an impulse to sing, to break into a run, to snigger. All at once everyone began chattering gaily.

The Eurasian boy walking beside me nodded toward the way we had come, with a knowing smile: "Do you know, sir, our friend [he meant the dead man] when he heard his appeal had been dismissed, he pissed on the floor of his cell. From fright. Kindly take one of my cigarettes, sir. Do you not admire my new silver case, sir? From the boxwalah, two rupees eight annas. Classy European style."

Several people laughed—at what, nobody seemed certain.

Francis was walking by the superintendent, talking garrulously: "Well, sir, all hass passed off with the utmost satisfactoriness. It was all finished—flick! like that. It iss not always so—oah, no! I have known cases where the doctor wass obliged to go beneath the gallows and pull the prissoner's legs to ensure decease. Most disagreeable!"

"Wriggling about, eh? That's bad," said the superintendent.

"Ach, sir, it iss worse when they become refractory! One man, I recall, clung to the bars of hiss cage when we went to take him out. You will scarcely credit, sir, that it took six warders to dislodge him, three pulling at each leg. We reasoned with him. 'My dear fellow,' we said, 'think of all the pain and trouble you are causing to us!' But no, he would not listen! Ach, he wass very troublesome!"

I found that I was laughing quite loudly. Everyone was laughing. Even the superintendent grinned in a tolerant way. "You'd better all come out and have a drink," he said quite genially. "I've got a bottle of whisky in the car. We could do with it."

We went through the big double gates of the prison into the road. "Pulling at his legs!" exclaimed a Burmese magistrate suddenly, and burst into a loud chuckling. We all began laughing again. At that moment Francis' anecdote seemed extraordinarily funny. We all had a drink together, native and European alike, quite amicably. The dead man was a hundred yards away.

[1931]

SHOOTING AN ELEPHANT

In MOULMEIN, in lower Burma, I was hated by large numbers of people—the only time in my life that I have been important enough for this to happen to me. I was sub-divisional police officer of the town, and in an aimless, petty kind of way anti-European feeling was very bitter. No one had the guts to raise a riot, but if a European woman went through the bazaars alone somebody would probably spit betel juice over her dress. As a police officer I was an obvious target and was baited whenever it seemed safe to do so. When a nimble

Burman tripped me up on the football field and the referee (another Burman) looked the other way, the crowd yelled with hideous laughter. This happened more than once. In the end the sneering yellow faces of young men that met me everywhere, the insults hooted after me when I was at a safe distance, got badly on my nerves. The young Buddhist priests were the worst of all. There were several thousands of them in the town and none of them seemed to have anything to do except stand on street corners and jeer at Europeans.

All this was perplexing and upsetting. For at that time I had already made up my mind that imperialism was an evil thing and the sooner I chucked up my job and got out of it the better. Theoretically—and secretly, of course—I was all for the Burmese and all against their oppressors, the British. As for the job I was doing, I hated it more bitterly than I can perhaps make clear. In a job like that you see the dirty work of Empire at close quarters. The wretched prisoners huddling in the stinking cages of the lock-ups, the gray, cowed faces of the long-term convicts, the scarred buttocks of the men who had been flogged with bamboos—all these oppressed me with an intolerable sense of guilt. But I could get nothing into perspective. I was young and ill educated and I had had to think out my problems in the utter silence that is imposed on every Englishman in the East. I did not even know that the British Empire is dying, still less did I know that it is a great deal better than the younger empires that are going to supplant it. All I knew was that I was stuck between my hatred of the empire I served and my rage against the evil-spirited little beasts who tried to make my job impossible. With one part of my mind I thought of the British Raj as an unbreakable tyranny, as something clamped down, in *saecula saeculorum,* upon the will of prostrate peoples; with another part I thought that the greatest joy in the world would be to drive a bayonet into a Buddhist priest's guts. Feelings like these are the normal by-products of imperialism; ask any Anglo-Indian official, if you can catch him off duty.

One day something happened which in a roundabout way was enlightening. It was a tiny incident in itself; but it gave me a better glimpse than I had had before of the real nature of imperialism—the real motives for which despotic governments act. Early one morning the sub-inspector at a police station the other end of the town rang me up on the 'phone and said that an elephant was ravaging the

bazaar. Would I please come and do something about it? I did not
know what I could do, but I wanted to see what was happening and
I got on to a pony and started out. I took my rifle, an old .44
Winchester and much too small to kill an elephant, but I thought the
noise might be useful *in terrorem.* Various Burmans stopped me on the
way and told me about the elephant's doings. It was not, of course,
a wild elephant, but a tame one which had gone "must." It had been
chained up, as tame elephants always are when their attack of "must"
is due, but on the previous night it had broken its chain and escaped.
Its mahout, the only person who could manage it when it was in that
state, had set out in pursuit, but had taken the wrong direction and
was now twelve hours' journey away, and in the morning the elephant
had suddenly reappeared in the town. The Burmese population had
no weapons and were quite helpless against it. It had already destroyed somebody's bamboo hut, killed a cow and raided some fruit-
stalls and devoured the stock; also it had met the municipal rubbish
van and, when the driver jumped out and took to his heels, had turned
the van over and inflicted violences upon it.

The Burmese sub-inspector and some Indian constables were waiting for me in the quarter where the elephant had been seen. It was
a very poor quarter, a labyrinth of squalid bamboo huts, thatched
with palm-leaf, winding all over a steep hillside. I remember that it
was a cloudy, stuffy morning at the beginning of the rains. We began
questioning the people as to where the elephant had gone and, as
usual, failed to get any definite information. That is invariably the
case in the East; a story always sounds clear enough at a distance, but
the nearer you get to the scene of events the vaguer it becomes. Some
of the people said that the elephant had gone in one direction, some
said that he had gone in another, some professed not even to have
heard of any elephant. I had almost made up my mind that the whole
story was a pack of lies, when we heard yells a little distance away.
There was a loud, scandalized cry of "Go away, child! Go away this
instant!" and an old woman with a switch in her hand came round the
corner of a hut, violently shooing away a crowd of naked children.
Some more women followed, clicking their tongues and exclaiming;
evidently there was something that the children ought not to have
seen. I rounded the hut and saw a man's dead body sprawling in the
mud. He was an Indian, a black Dravidian coolie, almost naked, and

Writes more exactly by creating images

Description uses Concrete details

he could not have been dead many minutes. The people said that the elephant had come suddenly upon him round the corner of the hut, caught him with its trunk, put its foot on his back and ground him into the earth. This was the rainy season and the ground was soft, and his face had scored a trench a foot deep and a couple of yards long. He was lying on his belly with arms crucified and head sharply twisted to one side. His face was coated with mud, the eyes wide open, the teeth bared and grinning with an expression of unendurable agony. (Never tell me, by the way, that the dead look peaceful. Most of the corpses I have seen looked devilish.) The friction of the great beast's foot had stripped the skin from his back as neatly as one skins a rabbit. As soon as I saw the dead man I sent an orderly to a friend's house nearby to borrow an elephant rifle. I had already sent back the pony, not wanting it to go mad with fright and throw me if it smelt the elephant.

He sets it up in opposition to the others

The orderly came back in a few minutes with a rifle and five cartridges, and meanwhile some Burmans had arrived and told us that the elephant was in the paddy fields below, only a few hundred yards away. As I started forward practically the whole population of the quarter flocked out of the houses and followed me. They had seen the rifle and were all shouting excitedly that I was going to shoot the elephant. They had not shown much interest in the elephant when he was merely ravaging their homes, but it was different now that he was going to be shot. It was a bit of fun to them, as it would be to an English crowd; besides they wanted the meat. It made me vaguely uneasy. I had no intention of shooting the elephant—I had merely sent for the rifle to defend myself if necessary—and it is always unnerving to have a crowd following you. I marched down the hill, looking and feeling a fool, with the rifle over my shoulder and an ever-growing army of people jostling at my heels. At the bottom, when you got away from the huts, there was a metalled road and beyond that a miry waste of paddy fields a thousand yards across, not yet ploughed but soggy from the first rains and dotted with coarse grass. The elephant was standing eight yards from the road, his left side toward us. He took not the slightest notice of the crowd's approach. He was tearing up bunches of grass, beating them against his knees to clean them, and stuffing them into his mouth.

I had halted on the road. As soon as I saw the elephant I knew with perfect certainty that I ought not to shoot him. It is a serious matter to shoot a working elephant—it is comparable to destroying a huge and costly piece of machinery—and obviously one ought not to do it if it can possibly be avoided. And at that distance, peacefully eating, the elephant looked no more dangerous than a cow. I thought then and I think now that his attack of "must" was already passing off; in which case he would merely wander harmlessly about until the mahout came back and caught him. Moreover, I did not in the least want to shoot him. I decided that I would watch him for a little while to make sure that he did not turn savage again, and then go home.

But at that moment I glanced round at the crowd that had followed me. It was an immense crowd, two thousand at the least and growing every minute. It blocked the road for a long distance on either side. I looked at the sea of yellow faces above the garish clothes—faces all happy and excited over this bit of fun, all certain that the elephant was going to be shot. They were watching me as they would watch a conjurer about to perform a trick. They did not like me, but with the magical rifle in my hands I was momentarily worth watching. And suddenly I realized that I should have to shoot the elephant after all. The people expected it of me and I had got to do it; I could feel their two thousand wills pressing me forward, irresistibly. And it was at this moment, as I stood there with the rifle in my hands, that I first grasped the hollowness, the futility of the white man's dominion in the East. Here was I, the white man with his gun, standing in front of the unarmed native crowd—seemingly the leading actor of the piece; but in reality I was only an absurd puppet pushed to and fro by the will of those yellow faces behind. I perceived in this moment that when the white man turns tyrant it is his own freedom that he destroys. He becomes a sort of hollow, posing dummy, the conventionalized figure of a sahib. For it is the condition of his rule that he shall spend his life in trying to impress the "natives," and so in every crisis he has got to do what the "natives" expect of him. He wears a mask, and his face grows to fit it. I had got to shoot the elephant. I had committed myself to doing it when I sent for the rifle. A sahib has got to act like a sahib; he has got to appear resolute, to know his own mind and do definite things. To come all that way, rifle in hand, with two thousand people marching at my heels, and then to trail feebly away, having done nothing—no, that was impossible. The crowd would laugh at me.

And my whole life, every white man's life in the East, was one long struggle not to be laughed at.

But I did not want to shoot the elephant. I watched him beating his bunch of grass against his knees with that preoccupied grandmotherly air that elephants have. It seemed to me that it would be murder to shoot him. At that age I was not squeamish about killing animals, but I had never shot an elephant and never wanted to. (Somehow it always seems worse to kill a *large* animal.) Besides, there was the beast's owner to be considered. Alive, the elephant was worth at least a hundred pounds; dead, he would only be worth the value of his tusks, five pounds, possibly. But I had got to act quickly. I turned to some experienced-looking Burmans who had been there when we arrived, and asked them how the elephant had been behaving. They all said the same thing: he took no notice of you if you left him alone, but he might charge if you went too close to him.

It was perfectly clear to me what I ought to do. I ought to walk up to within, say, twenty-five yards of the elephant and test his behavior. If he charged, I could shoot; if he took no notice of me, it would be safe to leave him until the mahout came back. But also I knew that I was going to do no such thing. I was a poor shot with a rifle and the ground was soft mud into which one would sink at every step. If the elephant charged and I missed him, I should have about as much chance as a toad under a steam-roller. But even then I was not thinking particularly of my own skin, only of the watchful yellow faces behind. For at that moment, with the crowd watching me, I was not afraid in the ordinary sense, as I would have been if I had been alone. A white man mustn't be frightened in front of "natives"; and so, in general, he isn't frightened. The sole thought in my mind was that if anything went wrong those two thousand Burmans would see me pursued, caught, trampled on, and reduced to a grinning corpse like that Indian up the hill. And if that happened it was quite probable that some of them would laugh. That would never do. There was only one alternative. I shoved the cartridges into the magazine and lay down on the road to get a better aim.

The crowd grew very still, and a deep, low, happy sigh, as of people who see the theater curtain go up at last, breathed from innumerable throats. They were going to have their bit of fun after all. The rifle was a beautiful German thing with cross-hair sights. I did not then

So he shot the elephant after all B/C OF THE IMPERIALISM

know that in shooting an elephant one would shoot to cut an imaginary bar running from ear-hole to ear-hole. I ought, therefore, as the elephant was sideways on, to have aimed straight at his ear-hole; actually I aimed several inches in front of this, thinking the brain would be further forward.

When I pulled the trigger I did not hear the bang or feel the kick—one never does when a shot goes home—but I heard the devillish roar of glee that went up from the crowd. In that instant, in too short a time, one would have thought, even for the bullet to get there, a mysterious, terrible change had come over the elephant. He neither stirred, nor fell, but every line of his body had altered. He looked suddenly stricken, shrunken, immensely old, as though the frightful impact of the bullet had paralyzed him without knocking him down. At last, after what seemed a long time—it might have been five seconds, I dare say—he sagged flabbily to his knees. His mouth slobbered. An enormous senility seemed to have settled upon him. One could have imagined him thousands of years old. I fired again into the same spot. At the second shot he did not collapse but climbed with desperate slowness to his feet and stood weakly upright, with legs sagging and head drooping. I fired a third time. That was the shot that did for him. You could see the agony of it jolt his whole body and knock the last remnant of strength from his legs. But in falling he seemed for a moment to rise, for as his hind legs collapsed beneath him he seemed to tower upward like a huge rock toppling, his trunk reaching skyward like a tree. He trumpeted, for the first and only time. And then down he came, his belly toward me, with a crash that seemed to shake the ground even where I lay.

I got up. The Burmans were already racing past me across the mud. It was obvious that the elephant would never rise again, but he was not dead. He was breathing very rhythmically with long rattling gasps, his great mound of a side painfully rising and falling. His mouth was wide open—I could see far down into caverns of pale pink throat. I waited a long time for him to die, but his breathing did not weaken. Finally I fired my two remaining shots into the spot where I thought his heart must be. The thick blood welled out of him like red velvet, but still he did not die. His body did not even jerk when the shots hit him, the tortured breathing continued without a pause. He was dying, very slowly and in great agony, but in some world remote from me

where not even a bullet could damage him further. I felt that I had
got to put an end to that dreadful noise. It seemed dreadful to see the
great beast lying there, powerless to move and yet powerless to die,
and not even to be able to finish him. I sent back for my small rifle
and poured shot after shot into his heart and down his throat. They
seemed to make no impression. The tortured gasps continued as steadily as the ticking of a clock.

In the end I could not stand it any longer and went away. I heard
later that it took him half an hour to die. Burmans were bringing dahs
and baskets even before I left, and I was told they had stripped his
body almost to the bones by the afternoon.

Afterward, of course, there were endless discussions about the
shooting of the elephant. The owner was furious, but he was only an
Indian and could do nothing. Besides, legally I had done the right
thing, for a mad elephant has to be killed, like a mad dog, if its owner
fails to control it. Among the Europeans opinion was divided. The
older men said I was right, the younger men said it was a damn shame
to shoot an elephant for killing a coolie, because an elephant was
worth more than any damn Coringhee coolie. And afterward I was
very glad that the coolie had been killed; it put me legally in the right
and it gave me a sufficient pretext for shooting the elephant. I often
wondered whether any of the others grasped that I had done it solely
to avoid looking a fool.

He gave in to the will of the crowd

He thinks like an imperialist (that's the irony) last sentence ↑

[1936]

MARRAKECH

As THE CORPSE went past the flies left the restaurant table in a
cloud and rushed after it, but they came back a few minutes later.

The little crowd of mourners—all men and boys, no women—
threaded their way across the market-place between the piles of pome-
granates and the taxis and the camels, wailing a short chant over and
over again. What really appeals to the flies is that the corpses here are
never put into coffins, they are merely wrapped in a piece of rag and

carried on a rough wooden bier on the shoulders of four friends. When
the friends get to the burying-ground they hack an oblong hole a foot
or two deep, dump the body in it and fling over it a little of the
dried-up, lumpy earth, which is like broken brick. No gravestone, no
name, no identifying mark of any kind. The burying-ground is merely
a huge waste of hummocky earth, like a derelict building-lot. After a
month or two no one can even be certain where his own relatives are
buried.

When you walk through a town like this—two hundred thousand
inhabitants, of whom at least twenty thousand own literally nothing
except the rags they stand up in—when you see how the people live,
and still more how easily they die, it is always difficult to believe that
you are walking among human beings. All colonial empires are in
reality founded upon that fact. The people have brown faces—besides, there are so many of them! Are they really the same flesh as
yourself? Do they even have names? Or are they merely a kind of
undifferentiated brown stuff, about as individual as bees or coral
insects? They rise out of the earth, they sweat and starve for a few
years, and then they sink back into the nameless mounds of the
graveyard and nobody notices that they are gone. And even the graves
themselves soon fade back into the soil. Sometimes, out for a walk,
as you break your way through the prickly pear, you notice that it
is rather bumpy underfoot, and only a certain regularity in the bumps
tells you that you are walking over skeletons.

I was feeding one of the gazelles in the public gardens.

Gazelles are almost the only animals that look good to eat when
they are still alive, in fact, one can hardly look at their hindquarters
without thinking of mint sauce. The gazelle I was feeding seemed to
know that this thought was in my mind, for though it took the piece
of bread I was holding out it obviously did not like me. It nibbled
rapidly at the bread, then lowered its head and tried to butt me, then
took another nibble and then butted again. Probably its idea was that
if it could drive me away the bread would somehow remain hanging
in mid-air.

An Arab navvy working on the path nearby lowered his heavy hoe
and sidled towards us. He looked from the gazelle to the bread and
from the bread to the gazelle, with a sort of quiet amazement, as

though he had never seen anything quite like this before. Finally he
said shyly in French:

"*I* could eat some of that bread."

I tore off a piece and he stowed it gratefully in some secret place
under his rags. This man is an employee of the Municipality.

When you go through the Jewish quarters you gather some idea of
what the medieval ghettoes were probably like. Under their Moorish
rulers the Jews were only allowed to own land in certain restricted
areas, and after centuries of this kind of treatment they have ceased
to bother about overcrowding. Many of the streets are a good deal less
than six feet wide, the houses are completely windowless, and sore-
eyed children cluster everywhere in unbelievable numbers, like clouds
of flies. Down the centre of the street there is generally running a little
river of urine.

In the bazaar huge families of Jews, all dressed in the long black
robe and little black skull-cap, are working in dark fly-infested booths
that look like caves. A carpenter sits cross-legged at a prehistoric
lathe, turning chair-legs at lightning speed. He works the lathe with
a bow in his right hand and guides the chisel with his left foot, and
thanks to a lifetime of sitting in this position his left leg is warped out
of shape. At his side his grandson, aged six, is already starting on the
simpler parts of the job.

I was just passing the coppersmiths' booths when somebody noticed
that I was lighting a cigarette. Instantly, from the dark holes all
round, there was a frenzied rush of Jews, many of them old grandfa-
thers with flowing grey beards, all clamouring for a cigarette. Even a
blind man somewhere at the back of one of the booths heard a rumour
of cigarettes and came crawling out, groping in the air with his hand.
In about a minute I had used up the whole packet. None of these
people, I suppose, works less than twelve hours a day, and every one
of them looks on a cigarette as a more or less impossible luxury.

As the Jews live in self-contained communities they follow the same
trades as the Arabs, except for agriculture. Fruitsellers, potters, silver-
smiths, blacksmiths, butchers, leatherworkers, tailors, water-carriers,
beggars, porters—whichever way you look you see nothing but Jews.
As a matter of fact there are thirteen thousand of them, all living in
the space of a few acres. A good job Hitler isn't here. Perhaps he is

on his way, however. You hear the usual dark rumours about the Jews, not only from the Arabs but from the poorer Europeans.

"Yes, *mon vieux,* they took my job away from me and gave it to a Jew. The Jews! They're the real rulers of this country, you know. They've got all the money. They control the banks, finance—everything."

"But," I said, "isn't it a fact that the average Jew is a labourer working for about a penny an hour?"

"Ah, that's only for show! They're all moneylenders really. They're cunning, the Jews."

In just the same way, a couple of hundred years ago, poor old women used to be burned for witchcraft when they could not even work enough magic to get themselves a square meal.

All people who work with their hands are partly invisible, and the more important the work they do, the less visible they are. Still, a white skin is always fairly conspicuous. In northern Europe, when you see a labourer ploughing a field, you probably give him a second glance. In a hot country, anywhere south of Gibraltar or east of Suez, the chances are that you don't even see him. I have noticed this again and again. In a tropical landscape one's eye takes in everything except the human beings. It takes in the dried-up soil, the prickly pear, the palm-tree and the distant mountain, but it always misses the peasant hoeing at his patch. He is the same colour as the earth, and a great deal less interesting to look at.

It is only because of this that the starved countries of Asia and Africa are accepted as tourist resorts. No one would think of running cheap trips to the Distressed Areas. But where the human beings have brown skins their poverty is simply not noticed. What does Morocco mean to a Frenchman? An orange-grove or a job in government service. Or to an Englishman? Camels, castles, palm-trees, Foreign Legionnaires, brass trays and bandits. One could probably live here for years without noticing that for nine-tenths of the people the reality of life is an endless, back-breaking struggle to wring a little food out of an eroded soil.

Most of Morocco is so desolate that no wild animal bigger than a hare can live on it. Huge areas which were once covered with forest have turned into a treeless waste where the soil is exactly like broken-up brick. Nevertheless a good deal of it is cultivated, with frightful labour. Everything is done by hand. Long lines of women, bent double like inverted capital Ls, work their way slowly across the field, tearing up the prickly weeds with their hands, and the peasant gathering lucerne for fodder pulls it up stalk by stalk instead of reaping it, thus saving an inch or two on each stalk. The plough is a wretched wooden thing, so frail that one can easily carry it on one's shoulder, and fitted underneath with a rough iron spike which stirs the soil to a depth of about four inches. This is as much as the strength of the animals is equal to. It is usual to plough with a cow and a donkey yoked together. Two donkeys would not be quite strong enough, but on the other hand two cows would cost a little more to feed. The peasants possess no harrows, they merely plough the soil several times over in different directions, finally leaving it in rough furrows, after which the whole field has to be shaped with hoes into small oblong patches, to conserve water. Except for a day or two after the rare rainstorms there is never enough water. Along the edges of the fields channels are hacked out to a depth of thirty or forty feet to get at the tiny trickles which run through the subsoil.

Every afternoon a file of very old women passes down the road outside my house, each carrying a load of firewood. All of them are mummified with age and the sun, and all of them are tiny. It seems to be generally the case in primitive communities that the women, when they get beyond a certain age, shrink to the size of children. One day a poor old creature who could not have been more than four feet tall crept past me under a vast load of wood. I stopped her and put a five-sou piece (a little more than a farthing) into her hand. She answered with a shrill wail, almost a scream, which was partly gratitude but mainly surprise. I suppose that from her point of view, by taking any notice of her, I seemed almost to be violating a law of nature. She accepted her status as an old woman, that is to say as a beast of burden. When a family is travelling it is quite usual to see a father and a grown-up son riding ahead on donkeys, and an old woman following on foot, carrying the baggage.

But what is strange about these people is their invisibility. For several weeks, always at about the same time of day, the file of old women had hobbled past the house with their firewood, and though they had registered themselves on my eyeballs I cannot truly say that

I had seen them. Firewood was passing—that was how I saw it. It was only that one day I happened to be walking behind them, and the curious up-and-down motion of a load of wood drew my attention to the human being underneath it. Then for the first time I noticed the poor old earth-coloured bodies, bodies reduced to bones and leathery skin, bent double under the crushing weight. Yet I suppose I had not been five minutes on Moroccan soil before I noticed the overloading of the donkeys and was infuriated by it. There is no question that the donkeys are damnably treated. The Moroccan donkey is hardly bigger than a St. Bernard dog, it carries a load which in the British army would be considered too much for a fifteen-hands mule, and very often its pack-saddle is not taken off its back for weeks together. But what is peculiarly pitiful is that it is the most willing creature on earth, it follows its master like a dog and does not need either bridle or halter. After a dozen years of devoted work it suddenly drops dead, whereupon its master tips it into the ditch and the village dogs have torn its guts out before it is cold.

This kind of thing makes one's blood boil, whereas—on the whole—the plight of the human beings does not. I am not commenting, merely pointing to a fact. People with brown skins are next door to invisible. Anyone can be sorry for the donkey with its galled back, but it is generally owing to some kind of accident if one even notices the old woman under her load of sticks.

As the storks flew northward the Negroes were marching southward—a long, dusty column, infantry, screw-gun batteries and then more infantry, four or five thousand men in all, winding up the road with a clumping of boots and a clatter of iron wheels.

They were Senegalese, the blackest Negroes in Africa, so black that sometimes it is difficult to see whereabouts on their necks the hair begins. Their splendid bodies were hidden in reach-me-down khaki uniforms, their feet squashed into boots that looked like blocks of wood, and every tin hat seemed to be a couple of sizes too small. It was very hot and the men had marched a long way. They slumped under the weight of their packs and the curiously sensitive black faces were glistening with sweat.

As they went past a tall, very young Negro turned and caught my eye. But the look he gave me was not in the least the kind of look you

might expect. Not hostile, not contemptuous, not sullen, not even
inquisitive. It was the shy, wide-eyed Negro look, which actually is a
look of profound respect. I saw how it was. This wretched boy, who
is a French citizen and has therefore been dragged from the forest to
scrub floors and catch syphilis in garrison towns, actually has feelings
of reverence before a white skin. He has been taught that the white
race are his masters, and he still believes it.

But there is one thought which every white man (and in this connection it doesn't matter twopence if he calls himself a Socialist)
thinks when he sees a black army marching past. "How much longer
can we go on kidding these people? How long before they turn their
guns in the other direction?"

It was curious, really. Every white man there has this thought
stowed somewhere or other in his mind. I had it, so had the other
onlookers, so had the officers on their sweating chargers and the white
NCOs marching in the ranks. It was a kind of secret which we all knew
and were too clever to tell; only the Negroes didn't know it. And really
it was almost like watching a flock of cattle to see the long column,
a mile or two miles of armed men, flowing peacefully up the road,
while the great white birds drifted over them in the opposite direction,
glittering like scraps of paper.

[1939]

POLITICS AND THE ENGLISH LANGUAGE

MOST PEOPLE who bother with the matter at all would admit
that the English language is in a bad way, but it is generally assumed
that we cannot by conscious action do anything about it. Our civilization is decadent and our language—so the argument runs—must
inevitably share in the general collapse. It follows that any struggle
against the abuse of language is a sentimental archaism, like preferring
candles to electric light or hansom cabs to aeroplanes. Underneath
this lies the half-conscious belief that language is a natural growth and
not an instrument which we shape for our own purposes.

Now, it is clear that the decline of a language must ultimately have political and economic causes: it is not due simply to the bad influence of this or that individual writer. But an effect can become a cause, reinforcing the original cause and producing the same effect in an intensified form, and so on indefinitely. A man may take to drink because he feels himself to be a failure, and then fail all the more completely because he drinks. It is rather the same thing that is happening to the English language. It becomes ugly and inaccurate because our thoughts are foolish, but the slovenliness of our language makes it easier for us to have foolish thoughts. The point is that the process is reversible. Modern English, especially written English, is full of bad habits which spread by imitation and which can be avoided if one is willing to take the necessary trouble. If one gets rid of these habits one can think more clearly, and to think clearly is a necessary first step toward political regeneration: so that the fight against bad English is not frivolous and is not the exclusive concern of professional writers. I will come back to this presently, and I hope that by that time the meaning of what I have said here will have become clearer. Meanwhile, here are five specimens of the English language as it is now habitually written.

These five passages have not been picked out because they are especially bad—I could have quoted far worse if I had chosen—but because they illustrate various of the mental vices from which we now suffer. They are a little below the average, but are fairly representative samples. I number them so that I can refer back to them when necessary:

(1) I am not, indeed, sure whether it is not true to say that the Milton who once seemed not unlike a seventeenth-century Shelley had not become, out of an experience ever more bitter in each year, more alien [*sic*] to the founder of that Jesuit sect which nothing could induce him to tolerate.

Professor Harold Laski
(Essay in *Freedom of Expression*)

(2) Above all, we cannot play ducks and drakes with a native battery of idioms which prescribes such egregious collocations of vocables as the Basic *put up with* for *tolerate* or *put at a loss* for *bewilder*.

Professor Lancelot Hogben *(Interglossa)*

(3) On the one side we have the free personality: by definition it is not
neurotic, for it has neither conflict nor dream. Its desires, such as they
are, are transparent, for they are just what institutional approval keeps
in the forefront of consciousness; another institutional pattern would
alter their number and intensity; there is little in them that is natural,
irreducible, or culturally dangerous. But *on the other side,* the social
bond itself is nothing but the mutual reflection of these self-secure
integrities. Recall the definition of love. Is not this the very picture of
a small academic? Where is there a place in this hall of mirrors for either
personality or fraternity?

> Essay on psychology in *Politics* (New York)

(4) All the "best people" from the gentlemen's clubs, and all the frantic
fascist captains, united in common hatred of Socialism and bestial
horror of the rising tide of the mass revolutionary movement, have
turned to acts of provocation, to foul incendiarism, to medieval legends
of poisoned wells, to legalize their own destruction of proletarian organizations, and rouse the agitated petty-bourgeoisie to chauvinistic fer-
vor on behalf of the fight against the revolutionary way out of the crisis.

> Communist pamphlet

(5) If a new spirit *is* to be infused into this old country, there is one
thorny and contentious reform which must be tackled, and that is the
humanization and galvanization of the B.B.C. Timidity here will be-
speak canker and atrophy of the soul. The heart of Britain may be
sound and of strong beat, for instance, but the British lion's roar at
present is like that of Bottom in Shakespeare's *Midsummer Night's
Dream*—as gentle as any sucking dove. A virile new Britain cannot
continue indefinitely to be traduced in the eyes, or rather ears, of the
world by the effete languors of Langham Place, brazenly masquerading
as "standard English." When the Voice of Britain is heard at nine
o'clock, better far and infinitely less ludicrous to hear aitches honestly
dropped than the present priggish, inflated, inhibited, school-ma'amish
arch braying of blameless bashful mewing maidens!

> Letter in *Tribune*

Each of these passages has faults of its own, but, quite apart from
avoidable ugliness, two qualities are common to all of them. The first
is staleness of imagery; the other is lack of precision. The writer either
has a meaning and cannot express it, or he inadvertently says something else, or he is almost indifferent as to whether his words mean

anything or not. This mixture of vagueness and sheer incompetence is the most marked characteristic of modern English prose, and especially of any kind of political writing. As soon as certain topics are raised, the concrete melts into the abstract and no one seems able to think of turns of speech that are not hackneyed: prose consists less and less of *words* chosen for the sake of their meaning, and more and more of *phrases* tacked together like the sections of a prefabricated henhouse. I list below, with notes and examples, various of the tricks by means of which the work of prose-construction is habitually dodged:

Dying metaphors. A newly invented metaphor assists thought by evoking a visual image, while on the other hand a metaphor which is technically "dead" (e.g. *iron resolution*) has in effect reverted to being an ordinary word and can generally be used without loss of vividness. But in between these two classes there is a huge dump of worn-out metaphors which have lost all evocative power and are merely used because they save people the trouble of inventing phrases for themselves. Examples are: *Ring the changes on, take up the cudgels for, toe the line, ride roughshod over, stand shoulder to shoulder with, play into the hands of, no axe to grind, grist to the mill, fishing in troubled waters, on the order of the day, Achilles' heel, swan song, hotbed.* Many of these are used without knowledge of their meaning (what is a "rift," for instance?), and incompatible metaphors are frequently mixed, a sure sign that the writer is not interested in what he is saying. Some metaphors now current have been twisted out of their original meaning without those who use them ever being aware of the fact. For example, *toe the line* is sometimes written *tow the line.* Another example is *the hammer and the anvil,* now always used with the implication that the anvil gets the worst of it. In real life it is always the anvil that breaks the hammer, never the other way about: a writer who stopped to think what he was saying would be aware of this, and would avoid perverting the original phrase.

Operators or *verbal false limbs.* These save the trouble of picking out appropriate verbs and nouns, and at the same time pad each sentence with extra syllables which give it an appearance of symmetry. Characteristic phrases are *render inoperative, militate against,*

*make contact with, be subjected to, give rise to, give grounds for, have
the effect of, play a leading part (role) in, make itself felt, take effect,
exhibit a tendency to, serve the purpose of,* etc., etc. The key-note is
the elimination of simple verbs. Instead of being a single word, such
as *break, stop, spoil, mend, kill,* a verb becomes a *phrase,* made up of
a noun or adjective tacked on to some general-purpose verb such as
prove, serve, form, play, render. In addition, the passive voice is
wherever possible used in preference to the active, and noun constructions are used instead of gerunds *(by examination of* instead of *by
examining).* The range of verbs is further cut down by means of the
-ize and *de-* formations, and the banal statements are given an appearance of profundity by means of the *not un-* formation. Simple con-
junctions and prepositions are replaced by such phrases as *with
respect to, having regard to, the fact that, by dint of, in view of, in
the interests of, on the hypothesis that;* and the ends of sentences are
saved from anticlimax by such resounding commonplaces as *greatly
to be desired, cannot be left out of account, a development to be
expected in the near future, deserving of serious consideration,
brought to a satisfactory conclusion,* and so on and so forth.

Pretentious diction. Words like *phenomenon, element, individual*
(as noun), *objective, categorical, effective, virtual, basic, primary,
promote, constitute, exhibit, exploit, utilize, eliminate, liquidate,* are
used to dress up simple statement and give an air of scientific impar-
tiality to biased judgments. Adjectives like *epoch-making, epic, his-
toric, unforgettable, triumphant, age-old, inevitable, inexorable,
veritable,* are used to dignify the sordid processes of international
politics, while writing that aims at glorifying war usually takes on an
archaic color, its characteristic words being: *realm, throne, chariot,
mailed fist, trident, sword, shield, buckler, banner, jackboot, clarion.*
Foreign words and expressions such as *cul de sac, ancien régime, deus
ex machina, mutatis mutandis, status quo, gleichschaltung, weltan-
schauung,* are used to give an air of culture and elegance. Except for
the useful abbreviations *i.e., e.g.,* and *etc.,* there is no real need for any
of the hundreds of foreign phrases now current in English. Bad writers, and especially scientific, political, and sociological writers, are
nearly always haunted by the notion that Latin or Greek words are
grander than Saxon ones, and unnecessary words like *expedite, ame-*

liorate, predict, extraneous, deracinated, clandestine, subaqueous, and hundreds of others constantly gain ground from their Anglo-Saxon opposite numbers.* The jargon peculiar to Marxist writing *(hyena, hangman, cannibal, petty bourgeois, these gentry, lackey, flunkey, mad dog, White Guard,* etc.) consists largely of words and phrases translated from Russian, German, or French; but the normal way of coining a new word is to use a Latin or Greek root with the appropriate affix and, where necessary, the *-ize* formation. It is often easier to make up words of this kind *(deregionalize, impermissible, extra-marital, nonfragmentary* and so forth) than to think up the English words that will cover one's meaning. The result, in general, is an increase in slovenliness and vagueness.

Meaningless words. In certain kinds of writing, particularly in art criticism and literary criticism, it is normal to come across long passages which are almost completely lacking in meaning.† Words like *romantic, plastic, values, human, dead, sentimental, natural, vitality,* as used in art criticism, are strictly meaningless, in the sense that they not only do not point to any discoverable object, but are hardly ever expected to do so by the reader. When one critic writes, "The outstanding feature of Mr. X's work is its living quality," while another writes, "The immediately striking thing about Mr. X's work is its peculiar deadness," the reader accepts this as a simple difference of opinion. If words like *black* and *white* were involved, instead of the jargon words *dead* and *living,* he would see at once that language was being used in an improper way. Many political words are similarly abused. The word *Fascism* has now no meaning except in so far as it signifies "something not desirable." The words *democracy, socialism,*

---

*An interesting illustration of this is the way in which the English flower names which were in use till very recently are being ousted by Greek ones, *snapdragon* becoming *antirrhinum, forget-me-not* becoming *myosotis,* etc. It is hard to see any practical reason for this change of fashion: it is probably due to an instinctive turning away from the more homely word and a vague feeling that the Greek word is scientific.

†Example: "Comfort's catholicity of perception and image, strangely Whitmanesque in range, almost the exact opposite in aesthetic compulsion, continues to evoke that trembling atmospheric accumulative hinting at a cruel, an inexorably serene timelessness. . . . Wrey Gardiner scores by aiming at simple bull's-eyes with precision. Only they are not so simple, and through this contented sadness runs more than the surface bittersweet of resignation." *(Poetry Quarterly.)*

freedom, patriotic, realistic, justice, have each of them several different meanings which cannot be reconciled with one another. In the
case of a word like *democracy,* not only is there no agreed definition,
but the attempt to make one is resisted from all sides. It is almost
universally felt that when we call a country democratic we are prais-
ing it: consequently the defenders of every kind of régime claim that
it is a democracy, and fear that they might have to stop using the word
if it were tied down to any one meaning. Words of this kind are often
used in a consciously dishonest way. That is, the person who uses them
has his own private definition, but allows his hearer to think he means
something quite different. Statements like *Marshal Pétain was a true
patriot, The Soviet press is the freest in the world, The Catholic
Church is opposed to persecution,* are almost always made with intent
to deceive. Other words used in variable meanings, in most cases more
or less dishonestly, are: *class, totalitarian, science, progressive, reactionary, bourgeois, equality.*

Now that I have made this catalogue of swindles and perversions,
let me give another example of the kind of writing that they lead to.
This time it must of its nature be an imaginary one. I am going to
translate a passage of good English into modern English of the worst
sort. Here is a well-known verse from *Ecclesiastes:*

> I returned and saw under the sun, that the race is not to the swift, nor
> the battle to the strong, neither yet bread to the wise, nor yet riches
> to men of understanding, nor yet favor to men of skill; but time and
> chance happeneth to them all.

Here it is in modern English:

> Objective consideration of contemporary phenomena compels the con-
> clusion that success or failure in competitive activities exhibits no
> tendency to be commensurate with innate capacity, but that a consid-
> erable element of the unpredictable must invariably be taken into
> account.

This is a parody, but not a very gross one. Exhibit (3), above, for
instance, contains several patches of the same kind of English. It will
be seen that I have not made a full translation. The beginning and

ending of the sentence follow the original meaning fairly closely, but
in the middle the concrete illustrations—race, battle, bread—dissolve
into the vague phrase "success or failure in competitive activities."
This had to be so, because no modern writer of the kind I am discussing—no one capable of using phrases like "objective consideration of
contemporary phenomena"—would ever tabulate his thoughts in that
precise and detailed way. The whole tendency of modern prose is away
from concreteness. Now analyze these two sentences a little more
closely. The first contains forty-nine words but only sixty syllables,
and all its words are those of everyday life. The second contains
thirty-eight words of ninety syllables: eighteen of its words are from
Latin roots and one from Greek. The first sentence contains six vivid
images, and only one phrase ("time and chance") that could be called
vague. The second contains not a single fresh, arresting phrase, and
in spite of its ninety syllables it gives only a shortened version of the
meaning contained in the first. Yet without a doubt it is the second
kind of sentence that is gaining ground in modern English. I do not
want to exaggerate. This kind of writing is not yet universal, and
outcrops of simplicity will occur here and there in the worst-written
page. Still, if you or I were told to write a few lines on the uncertainty
of human fortunes, we should probably come much nearer to my
imaginary sentence than to the one from *Ecclesiastes.*

As I have tried to show, modern writing at its worst does not consist
in picking out words for the sake of their meaning and inventing
images in order to make the meaning clearer. It consists in gumming
together long strips of words which have already been set in order by
someone else, and making the results presentable by sheer humbug.
The attraction of this way of writing is that it is easy. It is easier—
even quicker, once you have the habit—to say *In my opinion it is not
an unjustifiable assumption that* than to say *I think.* If you use ready-
made phrases, you not only don't have to hunt about for words; you
also don't have to bother with the rhythms of your sentences, since
these phrases are generally so arranged as to be more or less euphoni-
ous. When you are composing in a hurry—when you are dictating to
a stenographer, for instance, or making a public speech—it is natural
to fall into a pretentious, Latinized style. Tags like *a consideration
which we should do well to bear in mind* or *a conclusion to which all
of us would readily assent* will save many a sentence from coming

down with a bump. By using stale metaphors, similes, and idioms, you save much mental effort, at the cost of leaving your meaning vague, not only for your reader but for yourself. This is the significance of mixed metaphors. The sole aim of a metaphor is to call up a visual image. When these images clash—as in *The Fascist octopus has sung its swan song, the jackboot is thrown into the melting pot*—it can be taken as certain that the writer is not seeing a mental image of the objects he is naming; in other words he is not really thinking. Look again at the examples I gave at the beginning of this essay. Professor Laski (1) uses five negatives in fifty-three words. One of these is superfluous, making nonsense of the whole passage, and in addition there is the slip—*alien* for akin—making further nonsense, and several avoidable pieces of clumsiness which increase the general vagueness. Professor Hogben (2) plays ducks and drakes with a battery which is able to write prescriptions, and, while disapproving of the everyday phrase *put up with,* is unwilling to look *egregious* up in the dictionary and see what it means; (3), if one takes an uncharitable attitude towards it, is simply meaningless: probably one could work out its intended meaning by reading the whole of the article in which it occurs. In (4), the writer knows more or less what he wants to say, but an accumulation of stale phrases chokes him like tea leaves blocking a sink. In (5), words and meaning have almost parted company. People who write in this manner usually have a general emotional meaning—they dislike one thing and want to express solidarity with another—but they are not interested in the detail of what they are saying. A scrupulous writer, in every sentence that he writes, will ask himself at least four questions, thus: What am I trying to say? What words will express it? What image or idiom will make it clearer? Is this image fresh enough to have an effect? And he will probably ask himself two more: Could I put it more shortly? Have I said anything that is avoidably ugly? But you are not obliged to go to all this trouble. You can shirk it by simply throwing your mind open and letting the ready-made phrases come crowding in. They will construct your sentences for you—even think your thoughts for you, to a certain extent—and at need they will perform the important service of partially concealing your meaning even from yourself. It is at this point that the special connection between politics and the debasement of language becomes clear.

In our time it is broadly true that political writing is bad writing. Where it is not true, it will generally be found that the writer is some kind of rebel, expressing his private opinions and not a "party line." Orthodoxy, of whatever color, seems to demand a lifeless, imitative style. The political dialects to be found in pamphlets, leading articles, manifestoes, White Papers and the speeches of undersecretaries do, of course, vary from party to party, but they are all alike in that one almost never finds in them a fresh, vivid, home-made turn of speech. When one watches some tired hack on the platform mechanically repeating the familiar phrases—*bestial atrocities, iron heel, blood-stained tyranny, free peoples of the world, stand shoulder to shoulder*—one often has a curious feeling that one is not watching a live human being but some kind of dummy: a feeling which suddenly becomes stronger at moments when the light catches the speaker's spectacles and turns them into blank discs which seem to have no eyes behind them. And this is not altogether fanciful. A speaker who uses that kind of phraseology has gone some distance towards turning himself into a machine. The appropriate noises are coming out of his larynx, but his brain is not involved as it would be if he were choosing his words for himself. If the speech he is making is one that he is accustomed to make over and over again, he may be almost unconscious of what he is saying, as one is when one utters the responses in church. And this reduced state of consciousness, if not indispensable, is at any rate favorable to political conformity.

In our time, political speech and writing are largely the defense of the indefensible. Things like the continuance of British rule in India, the Russian purges and deportations, the dropping of the atom bombs on Japan, can indeed be defended, but only by arguments which are too brutal for most people to face, and which do not square with the professed aims of political parties. Thus political language has to consist largely of euphemism, question-begging and sheer cloudy vagueness. Defenseless villages are bombarded from the air, the inhabitants driven out into the countryside, the cattle machine-gunned, the huts set on fire with incendiary bullets: this is called *pacification.* Millions of peasants are robbed of their farms and sent trudging along the roads with no more than they can carry: this is called *transfer of population* or *rectification of frontiers.* People are imprisoned for years without trial, or shot in the back of the neck or sent to die of scurvy in Arctic lumber camps: this is called *elimination of unreliable elements*. Such phraseology is needed if one wants to name things without calling up mental pictures of them. Consider for instance some comfortable English professor defending Russian totalitarianism. He cannot say outright, "I believe in killing off your opponents when you can get good results by doing so." Probably, therefore, he will say something like this:

"While freely conceding that the Soviet régime exhibits certain features which the humanitarian may be inclined to deplore, we must, I think, agree that a certain curtailment of the right to political opposition is an unavoidable concomitant of transitional periods, and that the rigors which the Russian people have been called upon to undergo have been amply justified in the sphere of concrete achievement."

The inflated style is itself a kind of euphemism. A mass of Latin words falls upon the facts like soft snow, blurring the outlines and covering up all the details. The great enemy of clear language is insincerity. When there is a gap between one's real and one's declared aims, one turns as it were instinctively to long words and exhausted idioms, like a cuttlefish squirting out ink. In our age there is no such thing as "keeping out of politics." All issues are political issues, and politics itself is a mass of lies, evasions, folly, hatred and schizophrenia. When the general atmosphere is bad, language must suffer. I should expect to find—this is a guess which I have not sufficient knowledge to verify—that the German, Russian and Italian languages have all deteriorated in the last ten or fifteen years, as a result of dictatorship.

But if thought corrupts language, language can also corrupt thought. A bad usage can spread by tradition and imitation, even among people who should and do know better. The debased language that I have been discussing is in some ways very convenient. Phrases like *a not unjustifiable assumption, leaves much to be desired, would serve no good purpose, a consideration which we should do well to bear in mind,* are a continuous temptation, a packet of aspirins always at one's elbow. Look back through this essay, and for certain you will find that I have again and again committed the very faults I am protesting against. By this morning's post I have received a pamphlet dealing with conditions in Germany. The author tells me that he "felt impelled" to write it. I open it at random, and here is almost the first sentence that I see: "[The Allies] have an opportunity not only of achieving a radical transformation of Germany's social and political structure in such a way as to avoid a nationalistic reaction in Germany itself, but at the same time of laying the foundations of a co-operative and unified Europe." You see, he "feels impelled" to write—feels, presumably, that he has something new to say—and yet his words, like cavalry horses answering the bugle, group themselves automatically into the familiar dreary pattern. This invasion of one's mind by ready-made phrases *(lay the foundations, achieve a radical transformation)* can only be prevented if one is constantly on guard against them, and every such phrase anaesthetizes a portion of one's brain.

I said earlier that the decadence of our language is probably curable. Those who deny this would argue, if they produced an argument at all, that language merely reflects existing social conditions, and that we cannot influence its development by any direct tinkering with words and constructions. So far as the general tone or spirit of a language goes, this may be true, but it is not true in detail. Silly words and expressions have often disappeared, not through any evolutionary process but owing to the conscious action of a minority. Two recent examples were *explore every avenue* and *leave no stone unturned,* which were killed by the jeers of a few journalists. There is a long list of flyblown metaphors which could similarly be got rid of if enough people would interest themselves in the job; and it should also be possible to laugh the *not un-* formation out of existence,* to reduce the amount of Latin and Greek in the average sentence, to drive out foreign phrases and strayed scientific words, and, in general, to make pretentiousness unfashionable. But all these are minor points. The defense of the English language implies more than this, and perhaps it is best to start by saying what it does *not* imply.

To begin with it has nothing to do with archaism, with the salvaging of obsolete words and turns of speech, or with the setting up of a "standard English" which must never be departed from. On the contrary, it is especially concerned with the scrapping of every word or idiom which has outworn its usefulness. It has nothing to do with

*One can cure oneself of the *not un-* formation by memorizing this sentence: *A not unblack dog was chasing a not unsmall rabbit across a not ungreen field.*

correct grammar and syntax, which are of no importance so long as one makes one's meaning clear, or with the avoidance of American-isms, or with having what is called a "good prose style." On the other hand it is not concerned with fake simplicity and the attempt to make written English colloquial. Nor does it even imply in every case preferring the Saxon word to the Latin one, though it does imply using the fewest and shortest words that will cover one's meaning. What is above all needed is to let the meaning choose the word, and not the other way about. In prose, the worst thing one can do with words is to surrender to them. When you think of a concrete object, you think wordlessly, and then, if you want to de-scribe the thing you have been visualizing you probably hunt about till you find the exact words that seem to fit it. When you think of something abstract you are more inclined to use words from the start, and unless you make a conscious effort to prevent it, the exist-ing dialect will come rushing in and do the job for you, at the ex-pense of blurring or even changing your meaning. Probably it is better to put off using words as long as possible and get one's mean-ing as clear as one can through pictures or sensations. Afterward one can choose—not simply *accept*—the phrases that will best cover the meaning, and then switch round and decide what impression one's words are likely to make on another person. This last effort of the mind cuts out all stale or mixed images, all prefabricated phrases, needless repetitions, and humbug and vagueness generally. But one can often be in doubt about the effect of a word or a phrase, and one needs rules that one can rely on when instinct fails. I think the following rules will cover most cases:

(i) Never use a metaphor, simile, or other figure of speech which you are used to seeing in print.

(ii) Never use a long word where a short one will do.

(iii) If it is possible to cut a word out, always cut it out.

(iv) Never use the passive where you can use the active.

(v) Never use a foreign phrase, a scientific word, or a jargon word if you can think of an everyday English equivalent.

(vi) Break any of these rules sooner than say anything outright barbarous.

These rules sound elementary, and so they are, but they demand a deep change of attitude in anyone who has grown used to writing in the style now fashionable. One could keep all of them and still write bad English, but one could not write the kind of stuff that I quoted in those five specimens at the beginning of this article.

I have not here been considering the literary use of language, but merely language as an instrument for expressing and not for concealing or preventing thought. Stuart Chase and others have come near to claiming that all abstract words are meaningless, and have used this as a pretext for advocating a kind of political quietism. Since you don't know what Fascism is, how can you struggle against Fascism? One need not swallow such absurdities as this, but one ought to recognize that the present political chaos is connected with the decay of language, and that one can probably bring about some improvement by starting at the verbal end. If you simplify your English, you are freed from the worst follies of orthodoxy. You cannot speak any of the necessary dialects, and when you make a stupid remark its stupidity will be obvious, even to yourself. Political language—and with variations this is true of all political parties, from Conservatives to Anarchists—is designed to make lies sound truthful and murder respectable, and to give an appearance of solidity to pure wind. One cannot change this all in a moment, but one can at least change one's own habits, and from time to time one can even, if one jeers loudly enough, send some worn-out and useless phrase—some *jackboot, Achilles' heel, hotbed, melting pot, acid test, veritable inferno,* or other lump of verbal refuse—into the dustbin where it belongs.

[1946]

WHY I WRITE
GEORGE ORWELL   *HE KNEW SOONER OR LATER HE'D BE WRITING*

FROM A VERY EARLY AGE, perhaps the age of five or six, I knew that when I grew up I should be a writer. Between the ages of about seventeen and twenty-four I tried to abandon this idea, but I did so with the consciousness that I was outraging my true nature and that sooner or later I should have to settle down and write books.

I was the middle child of three, but there was a gap of five years on either side, and I barely saw my father before I was eight. For this and other reasons I was somewhat lonely, and I soon developed disagreeable mannerisms which made me unpopular throughout my schooldays. I had the lonely child's habit of making up stories and holding conversations with imaginary persons, and I think from the very start my literary ambitions were mixed up with the feeling of being isolated and undervalued. I knew that I had a facility with words and a power of facing unpleasant facts, and I felt that this created a sort of private world in which I could get my own back for my failure in everyday life. Nevertheless the volume of serious—i.e. seriously intended—writing which I produced all through my childhood and boyhood would not amount to half a dozen pages. I wrote my first poem at the age of four or five, my mother taking it down to dictation. I cannot remember anything about it except that it was about a tiger and the tiger had "chair-like teeth"—a good enough phrase, but I fancy the poem was a plagiarism of Blake's "Tiger, Tiger". At eleven, when the war of 1914–18 broke out, I wrote a patriotic poem which was printed in the local newspaper, as was another, two years later, on the death of Kitchener. From time to time, when I was a bit older, I wrote bad and usually unfinished "nature poems" in the Georgian style. I also, about twice, attempted a short story which was a ghastly failure. That was the total of the would-be serious work that I actually set down on paper during all those years.

However, throughout this time I did in a sense engage in literary activities. To begin with there was the made-to-order stuff which I produced quickly, easily and without much pleasure to myself. Apart from school work, I wrote *vers d'occasion,* semicomic poems which I could turn out at what now seems to me astonishing speed—at fourteen I wrote a whole rhyming play, in imitation of Aristophanes, in about a week—and helped to edit school magazines, both printed and in manuscript. These magazines were the most pitiful burlesque stuff that you could imagine, and I took far less trouble with them than I now would with the cheapest journalism. But side by side with all this, for fifteen years or more, I was carrying out a literary exercise of a quite different kind: this was the making up of a continuous "story" about myself, a sort of diary existing only in the mind. I believe this is a common habit of children and adolescents. As a very small child I used to imagine that I was, say, Robin Hood, and picture myself as the hero of thrilling adventures, but quite soon my "story" ceased to be narcissistic in a crude way and became more and more a mere description of what I was doing and the things I saw. For minutes at a time this kind of thing would be running through my head: "He pushed the door open and entered the room. A yellow beam of sunlight, filtering through the muslin curtains, slanted on to the table, where a matchbox, half open, lay beside the inkpot. With his right hand in his pocket he moved across to the window. Down in the street a tortoiseshell cat was chasing a dead leaf," etc etc. This habit continued till I was about twenty-five, right through my non-literary years. Although I had to search, and did search, for the right words, I seemed to be making this descriptive effort almost against my will, under a kind of compulsion from outside. The "story" must, I suppose, have reflected the styles of the various writers I admired at different ages, but as far as I remember it always had the same meticulous descriptive quality.

When I was about sixteen I suddenly discovered the joy of mere words, i.e. the sounds and associations of words. The lines from *Paradise Lost*,

> So hee with difficulty and labour hard
> Moved on: with difficulty and labour hee,

which do not now seem to me so very wonderful, sent shivers down my backbone; and the spelling "hee" for "he" was an added pleasure. As for the need to describe things, I knew all about it already. So it is clear what kind of books I wanted to write, in so far as I could be said to want to write books at that time. I wanted to write enormous naturalistic novels with unhappy endings, full of detailed descriptions and arresting similes, and also full of purple passages in which words were used partly for the sake of their sound. And in fact my first completed novel, *Burmese Days*, which I wrote when I was thirty but projected much earlier, is rather that kind of book.

I give all this background information because I do not think one can assess a writer's motives without knowing something of his early

development. His subject matter will be determined by the age he
lives in—at least this is true in tumultuous, revolutionary ages like our
own—but before he ever begins to write he will have acquired an
emotional attitude from which he will never completely escape. It is
his job, no doubt, to discipline his temperament and avoid getting
stuck at some immature stage, or in some perverse mood: but if he
escapes from his early influences altogether, he will have killed his
impulse to write. Putting aside the need to earn a living, I think there
are four great motives for writing, at any rate for writing prose. They
exist in different degrees in every writer, and in any one writer the
proportions will vary from time to time, according to the atmosphere
in which he is living. They are:

His reason 4 writing political

1. Sheer egoism. Desire to seem clever, to be talked about, to be
remembered after death, to get your own back on grown-ups who
snubbed you in childhood, etc. etc. It is humbug to pretend that this
is not a motive, and a strong one. Writers share this characteristic with
scientists, artists, politicians, lawyers, soldiers, successful businessmen—in short, with the whole top crust of humanity. The great mass
of human beings are not acutely selfish. After the age of about thirty
they abandon individual ambition—in many cases, indeed, they almost abandon the sense of being individuals at all—and live chiefly
for others, or are simply smothered under drudgery. But there is also
the minority of gifted, wilful people who are determined to live their
own lives to the end, and writers belong in this class. Serious writers,
I should say, are on the whole more vain and self-centered than
journalists, though less interested in money.

2. Aesthetic enthusiasm. Perception of <u>beauty</u> in the external
world, or, on the other hand, in words and their right arrangement.
Pleasure in the impact of one sound on another, in the firmness of
good prose or the rhythm of a good story. Desire to share an experience which one feels is valuable and ought not to be missed. The
aesthetic motive is very feeble in a lot of writers, but even a pamphleteer or a writer of textbooks will have pet words and phrases which
appeal to him for non-utilitarian reasons; or he may feel strongly
about typography, width of margins, etc. Above the level of a railway
guide, no book is quite free from aesthetic considerations.

Love the beauty of words

3. Historical impulse. Desire to see things as they are, to find out
true facts and store them up for the use of posterity.

4. Political purpose—using the word "political" in the widest possible sense. Desire to push the world in a certain direction, to alter other people's idea of the kind of society that they should strive after. Once again, no book is genuinely free from political bias. The opinion that art should have nothing to do with politics is itself a political attitude.

It can be seen how these various impulses must war against one another, and how they must fluctuate from person to person and from time to time. By nature—taking your "nature" to be the state you have attained when you are first adult—I am a person in whom the first three motives would outweigh the fourth. In a peaceful age I might have written ornate or merely descriptive books, and might have remained almost unaware of my political loyalties. As it is I have been forced into becoming a sort of pamphleteer. First I spent five years in an unsuitable profession (the Indian Imperial Police, in Burma), and then I underwent poverty and the sense of failure. This increased my natural hatred of authority and made me for the first time fully aware of the existence of the working classes, and the job in Burma had given me some understanding of the nature of imperialism: but these experiences were not enough to give me an accurate political orientation. Then came Hitler, the Spanish civil war, etc. By the end of 1935 I had still failed to reach a firm decision. I remember a little poem that I wrote at that date, expressing my dilemma:

> A happy vicar I might have been
> Two hundred years ago,
> To preach upon eternal doom
> And watch my walnuts grow;
>
> But born, alas, in an evil time,
> I missed that pleasant haven,
> For the hair has grown on my upper lip
> And the clergy are all clean-shaven.
>
> And later still the times were good,
> We were so easy to please,
> We rocked our troubled thoughts to sleep
> On the bosoms of the trees.

All ignorant we dared to own
The joys we now dissemble;
The greenfinch on the apple bough
Could make my enemies tremble.

But girls' bellies and apricots,
Roach in a shaded stream,
Horses, ducks in flight at dawn,
All these are a dream.

It is forbidden to dream again;
We maim our joys or hide them;
Horses are made of chromium steel
And little fat men shall ride them.

I am the worm who never turned,
The eunuch without a harem;
Between the priest and the commissar
I walk like Eugene Aram;

And the commissar is telling my fortune
While the radio plays,
But the priest has promised an Austin Seven,
For Duggie always pays.

I dreamed I dwelt in marble halls,
And woke to find it true;
I wasn't born for an age like this;
Was Smith? Was Jones? Were you?

The Spanish war and other events in 1936–37 turned the scale and
thereafter I knew where I stood. Every line of serious work that I have
written since 1936 has been written, directly or indirectly, *against*
totalitarianism and *for* democratic Socialism, as I understand it. It
seems to me nonsense, in a period like our own, to think that one can
avoid writing of such subjects. Everyone writes of them in one guise
or another. It is simply a question of which side one takes and what
approach one follows. And the more one is conscious of one's political
bias, the more chance one has of acting politically without sacrificing
one's aesthetic and intellectual integrity.

What I have most wanted to do throughout the past ten years is

MOTIVATED BY HIS STRONG SENSE OF JUSTICE

to make political writing into an art. My starting point is always a feeling of partisanship, a sense of injustice. When I sit down to write a book, I do not say to myself, "I am going to produce a work of art." I write it because there is some lie that I want to expose, some fact to which I want to draw attention, and my initial concern is to get a hearing. But I could not do the work of writing a book, or even a long magazine article, if it were not also an aesthetic experience. Anyone who cares to examine my work will see that even when it is downright propaganda it contains much that a full-time politician would consider irrelevant. I am not able, and I do not want, completely to abandon the world-view that I acquired in childhood. So long as I remain alive and well I shall continue to feel strongly about prose style, to love the surface of the earth, and to take pleasure in solid objects and scraps of useless information. It is no use trying to suppress that side of myself. The job is to reconcile my ingrained likes and dislikes with the essentially public, non-individual activities that this age forces on all of us.

It is not easy. It raises problems of construction and of language, and it raises in a new way the problem of truthfulness. Let me give just one example of the cruder kind of difficulty that arises. My book about the Spanish civil war, *Homage to Catalonia,* is, of course, a frankly political book, but in the main it is written with a certain detachment and regard for form. I did try very hard in it to tell the whole truth without violating my literary instincts. But among other things it contains a long chapter, full of newspaper quotations and the like, defending the Trotskyists who were accused of plotting with Franco. Clearly such a chapter, which after a year or two would lose its interest for any ordinary reader, must ruin the book. A critic whom I respect read me a lecture about it. "Why did you put in all that stuff?" he said. "You've turned what might have been a good book into journalism." What he said was true, but I could not have done otherwise. I happened to know, what very few people in England had been allowed to know, that innocent men were being falsely accused. If I had not been angry about that I should never have written the book.

In one form or another this problem comes up again. The problem of language is subtler and would take too long to discuss. I will only say that of late years I have tried to write less picturesquely and more exactly. In any case I find that by the time you have perfected any style of writing, you have always outgrown it. *Animal Farm* was the first book in which I tried, with full consciousness of what I was doing, to fuse political purpose and artistic purpose into one whole. I have not written a novel for seven years, but I hope to write another fairly soon. It is bound to be a failure, every book is a failure, but I know with some clarity what kind of book I want to write.

Looking back through the last page or two, I see that I have made it appear as though my motives in writing were wholly public-spirited. I don't want to leave that as the final impression. All writers are vain, selfish and lazy, and at the very bottom of their motives there lies a mystery. Writing a book is a horrible, exhausting struggle, like a long bout of some painful illness. One would never undertake such a thing if one were not driven on by some demon whom one can neither resist nor understand. For all one knows that demon is simply the same instinct that makes a baby squall for attention. And yet it is also true that one can write nothing readable unless one constantly struggles to efface one's own personality. Good prose is like a window pane. I cannot say with certainty which of my motives are the strongest, but I know which of them deserve to be followed. And looking back through my work, I see that it is invariably where I lacked a *political* purpose that I wrote lifeless books and was betrayed into purple passages, sentences without meaning, decorative adjectives and humbug generally.

[1946]

E. B. WHITE

Photo: Donald E. Johnson

THE YOUNGEST OF SIX CHILDREN, E. B. White was born in Mt. Vernon, New York, on July 11, 1899. At the time, Mt. Vernon was still a small town—certainly not the beginning of suburbia that it is today—and White's father, who was prospering as a piano manufacturer, had moved his family up from Brooklyn because he thought Mt. Vernon would be a better place to raise children. As it turned out, it was almost perfect. Their house was large, the streets were shady, and the town was as peaceful as an upper-middle-class suburb could be at the turn of the century. "There was," White has written, describing their house, "an iron vase on the lawn and a copy of *Wet Days at Edgewood* on the library table." Years later, he recalled the things he did: "I rode my bicycle sitting backward on the handle bars, I made up poems, I played selections from *Aïda* on the piano. In winter, I tended goal in the hockey games on the frozen pond in the dell." To such idyllic pastimes was added, in 1905, a camp on one of the Belgrade lakes in Maine, and each August for many years thereafter the family went there for its summer vacation. Indeed, one gathers from his writings that there were few catastrophes in White's childhood more serious than hay fever, which recurred throughout his life. In 1917 he graduated from Mt. Vernon High School, and the following fall he entered Cornell University.

Unlike their cousins, the novelists, the American humorists of this century seem more or less to have taken to college, and White was no exception. He joined a fraternity, got gentlemanly marks in his courses, rode a motorcycle, and spent two months during his sophomore year as a private in the U.S. Army. (Enlisting only a few weeks before the Armistice, he got no farther than the campus drill field and faced no enemy worse than a flu epidemic, "which I met stoically with a bag of licorice drops.") His real interest, however, was writing, and in his senior year he was editor-in-chief of the *Cornell Daily Sun*.

After his graduation in 1921, White tried his hand for a while at various jobs in New York City, but was dissatisfied and restless. Then, in March of 1922, he and a friend decided to head west in White's Model T Ford. It was a leisurely trip, and when they arrived in Seattle six months later, White took a job as a reporter with the Seattle *Times*. But poetry, not journalism, was the thing he had his eye on in those days, and when the job fell through the following summer, it was with relief that he began looking around for something to do. What turned up was a steamer on its way to Alaska and Siberia, and White determined to go with it. With the last of his money he bought a one-way ticket as far as Skagway, and trusted that once on board he could get a job that would take him the full round trip. Luckily, he did, and that fall he returned to New York City.

For the next two years he worked in an advertising agency and tried to write poetry, but without much success. Then, in 1925, *The New Yorker* was founded, and very soon White was submitting poems and sketches. Harold Ross, the editor, was so impressed that he asked White to come to work, which he did, and for the next eleven years his wit and good sense did much to make the magazine the success that it was. He not only wrote many of the "Notes and Comments" that appeared in the "Talk of the Town," but also thought up the witty captions and taglines that turned normal space-fillers into capsule editorials on the absurdities of both man and the press. Even though most of his work during those years was unsigned, the recurrent style was unmistakable to anyone who read *The New Yorker* regularly. In 1929 White published his first two books: *The Lady Is Cold,* a collection of light verse, and *Is Sex Necessary?,* a spoof on scientific sex literature written in collaboration with his office mate, James Thurber.

In 1937, "desiring," he said, "to simplify my life," E. B. White left New York and moved his family to a salt water farm in North Brooklin, Maine. The following summer he began a regular monthly column for *Harper's Magazine* entitled "One Man's Meat," and it was soon apparent that an aspect of his character that had hitherto remained largely hidden was beginning to emerge. The essays that he sent down from Maine revealed a depth one wouldn't have expected from his earlier *New Yorker* pieces. The wit and clear sight into the nature of things were still there, but with a difference. No longer were they being exercised for the sake of cleverness alone—the thing one regrets about much of the work of Benchley, Sullivan, and even Thurber at times—but more seriously, as a means of revealing not merely man's absurdities, but his virtues as well. White, it turned out, could be as serious as he could be clever. Although *Quo Vadimus? or The Case for the Bicycle,* a collection of sketches that had appeared in *The New Yorker,* was published in 1939, the sort of humor that it contained was already a thing of the past. In 1943 he wrote the last of his columns for *Harper's* and returned to New York City, where he resumed the writing of *The New Yorker*'s editorial page. The maga-

zine's staff had been depleted by the war, and Ross had asked him
to help. A few years later he moved back to Maine and began writing
his "Letters from the East" (and other points of the compass) for *The
New Yorker.*

Altogether White wrote fifteen books and either edited or collaborated on four others. Two of the most charming are children's
stories that take their place alongside such modern classics as *The
Wind in the Willows* and the Pooh books: *Stuart Little* (1945) and
Charlotte's Web (1952). In 1941 he and his wife, Katharine S. White,
edited *A Subtreasury of American Humor,* and in 1959 he revised,
introduced, and wrote a chapter on style for a grammar handbook he
had used as a student at Cornell. To everyone's surprise, *The Elements
of Style,* by William Strunk, Jr., and E. B. White, became a national
best-seller. White's best essays appear in three collections: *One Man's
Meat* (1944), *The Second Tree from the Corner* (1954), and *The
Points of My Compass* (1962). In 1970 White published a third children's book, *The Trumpet of the Swan,* and in 1977 he was awarded
a Pulitzer Prize Special Citation in Letters for his lifetime's work. In
1985 he died, on his farm in Maine, at the age of eighty-six.

The themes that White came back to in essay after essay are, first,
that the natural is preferable to the artificial or mechanical, and, sec-
ondly, that even though time moves on apace and things constantly
change, the larger patterns of Nature are recurrent. The first idea is
generally presented as a lament for the past, and thus the imperceptive
reader often comes away with the impression that White is a nostalgic
reactionary. Read closely, however, the essays are quite clear in their
scorn for sentimentality, and whatever homage is paid the past proves
to be not a love for the simple and uncomplicated, but just the opposite, a love of the excitement and adventure that is inseparable from
physical hardships. As our material goods and comforts increase,
White would say, we lose touch with reality; we are dehumanized;
we become no better than the machine we created; indeed, worse
(see "The Hour of Letdown" in *The Second Tree from the Corner*).
Fortunately, however, there is always Nature, and no matter how
furiously we hack away at her, in the end she is victorious. These
beliefs, and the proof of his life, place White directly in the tradition
of his fellow New Englanders, Thoreau and Frost.

"With some writers," White wrote in *The Elements of Style,* "style
not only reveals the spirit of the man, it reveals his identity, as surely
as would his fingerprints." Then he added, a little later, "The approach
to style is by way of plainness, simplicity, orderliness, sincerity."
Taken together, the two statements—however simple they appear on

the surface—imply an extremely subtle attitude toward style. "How," one might ask, "am I to do both at the same time—be plain, simple, orderly, and sincere, and yet reveal the complexities of my identity?" No easy, practicable answer is given, for White knew that it is a problem that can be solved only by each solitary writer in his own unending struggle to make the words he sets down on paper approach the temper of his thought. But he does tell us two important things. The first is a belief: "The whole duty of a writer is to please and satisfy himself, and the true writer always plays to an audience of one." And the second is a method: "I write by ear, always with difficulty and seldom with any exact notion of what is taking place under the hood." In short, style, E. B. White would say, is a matter of character, intuition, faith, mystery . . . and hard work.

[Handwritten annotations in margins: "Father → son → Father = same Guy"; "Father → son"; "Conflict of the writer — roles of the writer of being a father 'n' a son —"; "transposition — change from place to place (4 paragraph)"; "PARADOXIAL There is no change CHANGE YES"]

ONCE MORE TO THE LAKE

ONE SUMMER, along about 1904, my father rented a camp on a lake in Maine and took us all there for the month of August. We all got ringworm from some kittens and had to rub Pond's Extract on our arms and legs night and morning, and my father rolled over in a canoe with all his clothes on; but outside of that the vacation was a success and from then on none of us ever thought there was any place in the world like that lake in Maine. We returned summer after summer— always on August 1st for one month. I have since become a salt-water man, but sometimes in summer there are days when the restlessness of the tides and the fearful cold of the sea water and the incessant wind which blows across the afternoon and into the evening makes me wish for the placidity of a lake in the woods. A few weeks ago this feeling got so strong I bought myself a couple of bass hooks and a spinner and returned to the lake where we used to go, for a week's fishing and to revisit old haunts.

I took along my son, who had never had any fresh water up his nose and who had seen lily pads only from train windows. On the journey over to the lake I began to wonder what it would be like. I wondered how time would have marred this unique, this holy spot—the coves and streams, the hills that the sun set behind, the camps and the paths behind the camps. I was sure that the tarred road would have found it out and I wondered in what other ways it would be desolated. It is strange how much you can remember about places like that once you allow your mind to return into the grooves which lead back. You remember one thing, and that suddenly reminds you of another thing. I guess I remembered clearest of all the early mornings, when the lake was cool and motionless, remembered how the bedroom smelled of the lumber it was made of and of the wet woods whose scent entered through the screen. The partitions in the camp were thin and did not extend clear to the top of the rooms, and as I was always the first up I would dress softly so as not to wake the others, and sneak out into the sweet outdoors and start out in the canoe, keeping close along the

Change → There used to BE 3 tRACKS
Now there are only 2 tRACKS upon
Once More to the Lake which they tRED [81
(tRANSPORTATION)

shore in the long shadows of the pines. I remembered being very careful never to rub my paddle against the gunwale for fear of disturbing the stillness of the cathedral.

The lake had never been what you would call a wild lake. There were cottages sprinkled around the shores, and it was in farming country although the shores of the lake were quite heavily wooded. Some of the cottages were owned by nearby farmers, and you would live at the shore and eat your meals at the farmhouse. That's what our family did. But although it wasn't wild, it was a fairly large and undisturbed lake and there were places in it which, to a child at least, seemed infinitely remote and primeval.

I was right about the tar: it led to within half a mile of the shore. But when I got back there, with my boy, and we settled into a camp near a farmhouse and into the kind of summertime I had known, I could tell that it was going to be pretty much the same as it had been before—I knew it, lying in bed the first morning, smelling the bedroom, and hearing the boy sneak quietly out and go off along the shore in a boat. I began to sustain the illusion that he was I, and therefore, by simple transposition, that I was my father. This sensation persisted, kept cropping up all the time we were there. It was not an entirely new feeling, but in this setting it grew much stronger. I seemed to be living a dual existence. I would be in the middle of some simple act, I would be picking up a bait box or laying down a table fork, or I would be saying something, and suddenly it would be not I but my father who was saying the words or making the gesture. It gave me a creepy sensation.

We went fishing the first morning. I felt the same damp moss covering the worms in the bait can, and saw the dragonfly alight on the tip of my rod as it hovered a few inches from the surface of the water. It was the arrival of this fly that convinced me beyond any doubt that everything was as it always had been, that the years were a mirage and there had been no years. The small waves were the same, chucking the rowboat under the chin as we fished at anchor, and the boat was the same boat, the same color green and the ribs broken in the same places, and under the floor-boards the same fresh-water leavings and debris—the dead helgramite, the wisps of moss, the rusty discarded fishhook, the dried blood from yesterday's catch. We stared silently at the tips of our rods, at the dragonflies that came and went.

[handwritten annotations: "Change OUTBOARD MOTORS IS NOW ANNOYING B/C I CAN CYLINDER is now 2 (technology)"]

I lowered the top of mine into the water, tentatively, pensively dis-
lodging the fly, which darted two feet away, poised, darted two feet
back, and came to rest again a little farther up the rod. There had
been no years between the ducking of this dragonfly and the other
one—the one that was part of memory. I looked at the boy, who was
silently watching his fly, and it was my hands that held his rod, my
eyes watching. I felt dizzy and didn't know which rod I was at the
end of.

We caught two bass, hauling them in briskly as though they were
mackerel, pulling them over the side of the boat in a business-like
manner without any landing net, and stunning them with a blow on
the back of the head. When we got back for a swim before lunch, the
lake was exactly where we had left it, the same number of inches from
the dock, and there was only the merest suggestion of a breeze. This
seemed an utterly enchanted sea, this lake you could leave to its own
devices for a few hours and come back to, and find that it had not
stirred, this constant and trustworthy body of water. In the shallows,
the dark, water-soaked sticks and twigs, smooth and old, were un-
dulating in clusters on the bottom against the clean ribbed sand, and
the track of the mussel was plain. A school of minnows swam by, each
minnow with its small individual shadow, doubling the attendance, so
clear and sharp in the sunlight. Some of the other campers were in
swimming, along the shore, one of them with a cake of soap, and the
water felt thin and clear and unsubstantial. Over the years there had
been this person with the cake of soap, this cultist, and here he was.
There had been no years.

Up to the farmhouse to dinner through the teeming, dusty field, the
road under our sneakers was only a two-track road. The middle track
was missing, the one with the marks of the hooves and the splotches
of dried, flaky manure. There had always been three tracks to choose
from in choosing which track to walk in; now the choice was narrowed
down to two. For a moment I missed terribly the middle alternative.
But the way led past the tennis court, and something about the way
it lay there in the sun reassured me; the tape had loosened along the
backline, the alleys were green with plantains and other weeds, and
the net (installed in June and removed in September) sagged in the
dry noon, and the whole place steamed with midday heat and hunger
and emptiness. There was a choice of pie for dessert, and one was

blueberry and one was apple, and the waitresses were the same country girls, there having been no passage of time, only the illusion of it
as in a dropped curtain—the waitresses were still fifteen; their hair had
been washed, that was the only difference—they had been to the
movies and seen the pretty girls with the clean hair.

Summertime, oh summertime, pattern of life indelible, the fade-
proof lake, the woods unshatterable, the pasture with the sweetfern
and the juniper forever and ever, summer without end; this was the
background, and the life along the shore was the design, the cottages
with their innocent and tranquil design, their tiny docks with the
flagpole and the American flag floating against the white clouds in the
blue sky, the little paths over the roots of the trees leading from camp
to camp and the paths leading back to the outhouses and the can of
lime for sprinkling, and at the souvenir counters at the store the
miniature birchbark canoes and the post cards that showed things
looking a little better than they looked. This was the American family
at play, escaping the city heat, wondering whether the newcomers in
the camp at the head of the cove were "common" or "nice," wondering whether it was true that the people who drove up for Sunday
dinner at the farmhouse were turned away because there wasn't
enough chicken.

It seemed to me, as I kept remembering all this, that those times
and those summers had been infinitely precious and worth saving.
There had been jollity and peace and goodness. The arriving (at the
beginning of August) had been so big a business in itself, at the railway
station the farm wagon drawn up, the first smell of the pine-laden air,
the first glimpse of the smiling farmer, and the great importance of
the trunks and your father's enormous authority in such matters, and
the feel of the wagon under you for the long ten-mile haul, and at the
top of the last long hill catching the first view of the lake after eleven
months of not seeing this cherished body of water. The shouts and
cries of the other campers when they saw you, and the trunks to be
unpacked, to give up their rich burden. (Arriving was less exciting
nowadays, when you sneaked up in your car and parked it under a tree
near the camp and took out the bags and in five minutes it was all
over, no fuss, no loud wonderful fuss about trunks.)

Peace and goodness and jollity. The only thing that was wrong now,
really, was the sound of the place, an unfamiliar nervous sound of the

outboard motors. This was the note that jarred, the one thing that would sometimes break the illusion and set the years moving. In those other summertimes all motors were inboard; and when they were at a little distance, the noise they made was a sedative, an ingredient of summer sleep. They were one-cylinder and two-cylinder engines, and some were make-and-break and some were jump-spark, but they all made a sleepy sound across the lake. The one-lungers throbbed and fluttered, and the twin-cylinder ones purred and purred, and that was a quiet sound too. But now the campers all had outboards. In the daytime, in the hot mornings, these motors made a petulant, irritable sound; at night, in the still evening when the afterglow lit the water, they whined about one's ears like mosquitoes. My boy loved our rented outboard, and his great desire was to achieve singlehanded mastery over it, and authority, and he soon learned the trick of choking it a little (but not too much), and the adjustment of the needle valve. Watching him I would remember the things you could do with the old one-cylinder engine with the heavy flywheel, how you could have it eating out of your hand if you got really close to it spiritually. Motor boats in those days didn't have clutches, and you would make a landing by shutting off the motor at the proper time and coasting in with a dead rudder. But there was a way of reversing them, if you learned the trick, by cutting the switch and putting it on again exactly on the final dying revolution of the flywheel, so that it would kick back against compression and begin reversing. Approaching a dock in a strong following breeze, it was difficult to slow up sufficiently by the ordinary coasting method, and if a boy felt he had complete mastery over his motor, he was tempted to keep it running beyond its time and then reverse it a few feet from the dock. It took a cool nerve, because if you threw the switch a twentieth of a second too soon you would catch the flywheel when it still had speed enough to go up past center, and the boat would leap ahead, charging bull-fashion at the dock.

We had a good week at the camp. The bass were biting well and the sun shone endlessly, day after day. We would be tired at night and lie down in the accumulated heat of the little bedrooms after the long hot day and the breeze would stir almost imperceptibly outside and the smell of the swamp drift in through the rusty screens. Sleep would come easily and in the morning the red squirrel would be on the roof,

CHANGE ► FROM Sasparilla etc to
Coca-Cola
(FOOD)

tapping out his gay routine. I kept remembering everything, lying in bed in the mornings—the small steamboat that had a long rounded stern like the lip of a Ubangi, and how quietly she ran on the moonlight sails, when the older boys played their mandolins and the girls sang and we ate doughnuts dipped in sugar, and how sweet the music was on the water in the shining night, and what it had felt like to think about girls then. After breakfast we would go up to the store and the things were in the same place—the minnows in a bottle, the plugs and spinners disarranged and pawed over by the youngsters from the boys' camp, the fig newtons and the Beeman's gum. Outside, the road was tarred and cars stood in front of the store. Inside, all was just as it had always been, except there was more Coca-Cola and not so much Moxie and root beer and birch beer and sarsaparilla. We would walk out with a bottle of pop apiece and sometimes the pop would backfire up our noses and hurt. We explored the streams, quietly, where the turtles slid off the sunny logs and dug their way into the soft bottom; and we lay on the town wharf and fed worms to the tame bass. Everywhere we went I had trouble making out which was I, the one walking at my side, the one walking in my pants.

One afternoon while we were there at that lake a thunderstorm came up. It was like the revival of an old melodrama that I had seen long ago with childish awe. The second-act climax of the drama of the electrical disturbance over a lake in America had not changed in any important respect. This was the big scene, still the big scene. The whole thing was so familiar, the first feeling of oppression and heat and a general air around camp of not wanting to go very far away. In midafternoon (it was all the same) a curious darkening of the sky, and a lull in everything that had made life tick; and then the way the boats suddenly swung the other way at their moorings with the coming of a breeze out of the new quarter, and the premonitory rumble. Then the kettle drums, then the snare, then the bass drum and cymbals, then crackling light against the dark, and the gods grinning and licking their chops in the hills. Afterward the calm, the rain steadily rustling in the calm lake, the return of light and hope and spirits, and the campers running out in joy and relief to go swimming in the rain, their bright cries perpetuating the deathless joke about how they were getting simply drenched, and the children screaming with delight at the new sensation of bathing in the rain, and the joke about getting drenched linking the generations in a strong indestructible chain. And the comedian who waded in carrying an umbrella.

When the others went swimming my son said he was going in too. He pulled his dripping trunks from the line where they had hung all through the shower, and wrung them out. Languidly, and with no thought of going in, I watched him, his hard little body, skinny and bare, saw him wince slightly as he pulled up around his vitals the small, soggy, icy garment. As he buckled the swollen belt suddenly my groin felt the chill of death.

[1941]

[handwritten annotations: He came to terms w/ his own mortality   HE RELIVES the moment   I don't understand the Ending   At I looking too hard?   HINTS OF CHANGE]

DEATH OF A PIG

I SPENT several days and nights in mid-September with an ailing pig and I feel driven to account for this stretch of time, more particularly since the pig died at last, and I lived, and things might easily have gone the other way round and none left to do the accounting. Even now, so close to the event, I cannot recall the hours sharply and am not ready to say whether death came on the third night or the fourth night. This uncertainty afflicts me with a sense of personal deterioration; if I were in decent health I would know how many nights I had sat up with a pig.

The scheme of buying a spring pig in blossomtime, feeding it through summer and fall, and butchering it when the solid cold weather arrives, is a familiar scheme to me and follows an antique pattern. It is a tragedy enacted on most farms with perfect fidelity to the original script. The murder, being premeditated, is in the first degree but is quick and skillful, and the smoked bacon and ham provide a ceremonial ending whose fitness is seldom questioned.

Once in a while something slips—one of the actors goes up in his lines and the whole performance stumbles and halts. My pig simply failed to show up for a meal. The alarm spread rapidly. The classic outline of the tragedy was lost. I found myself cast suddenly in the role of pig's friend and physician—a farcical character with an enema bag for a prop. I had a presentiment, the very first afternoon, that the play would never regain its balance and that my sympathies were now wholly with the pig. This was slapstick—the sort of dramatic treatment that instantly appealed to my old dachshund, Fred, who joined the vigil, held the bag, and, when all was over, presided at the interment. When we slid the body into the grave, we both were shaken to the core. The loss we felt was not the loss of ham but the loss of pig. He had evidently become precious to me, not that he represented a distant nourishment in a hungry time, but that he had suffered in a suffering world. But I'm running ahead of my story and shall have to go back.

My pigpen is at the bottom of an old orchard below the house. The pigs I have raised have lived in a faded building that once was an icehouse. There is a pleasant yard to move about in, shaded by an apple tree that overhangs the low rail fence. A pig couldn't ask for anything better—or none has, at any rate. The sawdust in the icehouse makes a comfortable bottom in which to root, and a warm bed. This sawdust, however, came under suspicion when the pig took sick. One of my neighbors said he thought the pig would have done better on new ground—the same principle that applies in planting potatoes. He said there might be something unhealthy about that sawdust, that he never thought well of sawdust.

It was about four o'clock in the afternoon when I first noticed that there was something wrong with the pig. He failed to appear at the trough for his supper, and when a pig (or a child) refuses supper a chill wave of fear runs through any household, or ice-household. After examining my pig, who was stretched out in the sawdust inside the building, I went to the phone and cranked it four times. Mr. Dameron answered. "What's good for a sick pig?" I asked. (There is never any identification needed on a country phone; the person on the other end knows who is talking by the sound of the voice and by the character of the question.)

"I don't know, I never had a sick pig," said Mr. Dameron, "but I can find out quick enough. You hang up and I'll call Henry."

Mr. Dameron was back on the line again in five minutes. "Henry says roll him over on his back and give him two ounces of castor oil or sweet oil, and if that doesn't do the trick give him an injection of soapy water. He says he's almost sure the pig's plugged up, and even if he's wrong, it can't do any harm."

I thanked Mr. Dameron. I didn't go right down to the pig, though.

I sank into a chair and sat still for a few minutes to think about my troubles, and then I got up and went to the barn, catching up on some odds and ends that needed tending to. Unconsciously I held off, for an hour, the deed by which I would officially recognize the collapse of the performance of raising a pig; I wanted no interruption in the regularity of feeding, the steadiness of growth, the even succession of days. I wanted no interruption, wanted no oil, no deviation. I just wanted to keep on raising a pig, full meal after full meal, spring into summer into fall. I didn't even know whether there were two ounces of castor oil on the place.

Shortly after five o'clock I remembered that we had been invited out to dinner that night and realized that if I were to dose a pig there was no time to lose. The dinner date seemed a familiar conflict: I move in a desultory society and often a week or two will roll by without my going to anybody's house to dinner or anyone's coming to mine, but when an occasion does arise, and I am summoned, something usually turns up (an hour or two in advance) to make all human intercourse seem vastly inappropriate. I have come to believe that there is in hostesses a special power of divination, and that they deliberately arrange dinners to coincide with pig failure or some other sort of failure. At any rate, it was after five o'clock and I knew I could put off no longer the evil hour.

When my son and I arrived at the pigyard, armed with a small bottle of castor oil and a length of clothesline, the pig had emerged from his house and was standing in the middle of his yard, listlessly. He gave us a slim greeting. I could see that he felt uncomfortable and uncertain. I had brought the clothesline thinking I'd have to tie him (the pig weighed more than a hundred pounds) but we never used it. My son reached down, grabbed both front legs, upset him quickly, and when he opened his mouth to scream I turned the oil into his throat—a pink, corrugated area I had never seen before. I had just time to read the label while the neck of the bottle was in his mouth. It said Puretest. The screams, slightly muffled by oil, were pitched in the hysterically high range of pigsound, as though torture were being carried out, but they didn't last long: it was all over rather suddenly, and, his legs released, the pig righted himself.

In the upset position the corners of his mouth had been turned down, giving him a frowning expression. Back on his feet again, he regained the set smile that a pig wears even in sickness. He stood his ground, sucking slightly at the residue of oil; a few drops leaked out of his lips while his wicked eyes, shaded by their coy little lashes, turned on me in disgust and hatred. I scratched him gently with oily fingers and he remained quiet, as though trying to recall the satisfaction of being scratched when in health, and seeming to rehearse in his mind the indignity to which he had just been subjected. I noticed, as I stood there, four or five small dark spots on his back near the tail end, reddish brown in color, each about the size of a housefly. I could not make out what they were. They did not look troublesome but at the same time they did not look like mere surface bruises or chafe marks. Rather they seemed blemishes of internal origin. His stiff white bristles almost completely hid them and I had to part the bristles with my fingers to get a good look.

Several hours later, a few minutes before midnight, having dined well and at someone else's expense, I returned to the pighouse with a flashlight. The patient was asleep. Kneeling, I felt his ears (as you might put your hand on the forehead of a child) and they seemed cool, and then with the light made a careful examination of the yard and the house for a sign that the oil had worked. I found none and went to bed.

We had been having an unseasonable spell of weather—hot, close days, with the fog shutting in every night, scaling for a few hours in midday, then creeping back again at dark, drifting in first over the trees on the point, then suddenly blowing across the fields, blotting out the world and taking possession of houses, men, and animals. Everyone kept hoping for a break, but the break failed to come. Next day was another hot one. I visited the pig before breakfast and tried to tempt him with a little milk in his trough. He just stared at it, while I made a sucking sound through my teeth to remind him of past pleasures of the feast. With very small, timid pigs, weanlings, this ruse is often quite successful and will encourage them to eat; but with a large, sick pig the ruse is senseless and the sound I made must have made him feel, if anything, more miserable. He not only did not crave food, he felt a positive revulsion to it. I found a place under the apple tree where he had vomited in the night.

At this point, although a depression had settled over me, I didn't suppose that I was going to lose my pig. From the lustiness of a healthy pig a man derives a feeling of personal lustiness; the stuff that goes into the trough and is received with such enthusiasm is an earnest of some later feast of his own, and when this suddenly comes to an end and the food lies stale and untouched, souring in the sun, the pig's imbalance becomes the man's vicariously, and life seems insecure, displaced, transitory.

As my own spirits declined, along with the pig's, the spirits of my vile old dachshund rose. The frequency of our trips down the footpath through the orchard to the pigyard delighted him, although he suffers greatly from arthritis, moves with difficulty, and would be bedridden if he could find anyone willing to serve him meals on a tray.

He never missed a chance to visit the pig with me, and he made many professional calls on his own. You could see him down there at all hours, his white face parting the grass along the fence as he wobbled and stumbled about, his stethoscope dangling—a happy quack, writing his villainous prescriptions and grinning his corrosive grin. When the enema bag appeared, and the bucket of warm suds, his happiness was complete, and he managed to squeeze his enormous body between the two lowest rails of the yard and then assumed full charge of the irrigation. Once, when I lowered the bag to check the flow, he reached in and hurriedly drank a few mouthfuls of the suds to test their potency. I have noticed that Fred will feverishly consume any substance that is associated with trouble—the bitter flavor is to his liking. When the bag was above reach, he concentrated on the pig and was everywhere at once, a tower of strength and inconvenience. The pig, curiously enough, stood rather quietly through this colonic carnival, and the enema, though ineffective, was not as difficult as I had anticipated.

I discovered, though, that once having given a pig an enema there is no turning back, no chance of resuming one of life's more stereotyped roles. The pig's lot and mine were inextricably bound now, as though the rubber tube were the silver cord. From then until the time of his death I held the pig steadily in the bowl of my mind; the task of trying to deliver him from his misery became a strong obsession. His suffering soon became the embodiment of all earthly wretchedness. Along toward the end of the afternoon, defeated in physicking, I phoned the veterinary twenty miles away and placed the case formally in his hands. He was full of questions, and when I casually mentioned the dark spots on the pig's back, his voice changed its tone.

"I don't want to scare you," he said, "but when there are spots, erysipelas has to be considered."

Together we considered erysipelas, with frequent interruptions from the telephone operator, who wasn't sure the connection had been established.

"If a pig has erysipelas can he give it to a person?" I asked.

"Yes, he can," replied the vet.

"Have they answered?" asked the operator.

"Yes, they have," I said. Then I addressed the vet again. "You better come over here and examine this pig right away."

"I can't come myself," said the vet, "but McFarland can come this evening if that's all right. Mac knows more about pigs than I do anyway. You needn't worry too much about the spots. To indicate erysipelas they would have to be deep hemorrhagic infarcts."

"Deep hemorrhagic what?" I asked.

"Infarcts," said the vet.

"Have they answered?" asked the operator.

"Well," I said, "I don't know what you'd call these spots, except they're about the size of a housefly. If the pig has erysipelas I guess I have it, too, by this time, because we've been very close lately."

"McFarland will be over," said the vet.

I hung up. My throat felt dry and I went to the cupboard and got a bottle of whiskey. Deep hemorrhagic infarcts—the phrase began fastening its hooks in my head. I had assumed that there could be nothing much wrong with a pig during the months it was being groomed for murder; my confidence in the essential health and endurance of pigs had been strong and deep, particularly in the health of pigs that belonged to me and that were part of my proud scheme. The awakening had been violent and I minded it all the more because I knew that what could be true of my pig could be true also of the rest of my tidy world. I tried to put this distasteful idea from me, but it kept recurring. I took a short drink of the whiskey and then, although I wanted to go down to the yard and look for fresh signs, I was scared to. I was certain I had erysipelas.

It was long after dark and the supper dishes had been put away when a car drove in and McFarland got out. He had a girl with him.

I could just make her out in the darkness—she seemed young and pretty. "This is Miss Owen," he said. "We've been having a picnic supper on the shore, that's why I'm late."

McFarland stood in the driveway and stripped off his jacket, then his shirt. His stocky arms and capable hands showed up in my flashlight's gleam as I helped him find his coverall and get zipped up. The rear seat of his car contained an astonishing amount of paraphernalia, which he soon overhauled, selecting a chain, a syringe, a bottle of oil, a rubber tube, and some other things I couldn't identify. Miss Owen said she'd go along with us and see the pig. I led the way down the warm slope of the orchard, my light picking out the path for them, and we all three climbed the fence, entered the pighouse, and squatted by the pig while McFarland took a rectal reading. My flashlight picked up the glitter of an engagement ring on the girl's hand.

"No elevation," said McFarland, twisting the thermometer in the light. "You needn't worry about erysipelas." He ran his hand slowly over the pig's stomach and at one point the pig cried out in pain.

"Poor piggledy-wiggledy!" said Miss Owen.

The treatment I had been giving the pig for two days was then repeated, somewhat more expertly, by the doctor, Miss Owen and I handing him things as he needed them—holding the chain that he had looped around the pig's upper jaw, holding the syringe, holding the bottle stopper, the end of the tube, all of us working in darkness and in comfort, working with the instinctive teamwork induced by emergency conditions, the pig unprotesting, the house shadowy, protecting, intimate. I went to bed tired but with a feeling of relief that I had turned over part of the responsibility of the case to a licensed doctor. I was beginning to think, though, that the pig was not going to live.

He died twenty-four hours later, or it might have been forty-eight—there is a blur in time here, and I may have lost or picked up a day in the telling and the pig one in the dying. At intervals during the last day I took cool fresh water down to him and at such times as he found the strength to get to his feet he would stand with head in the pail and snuffle his snout around. He drank a few sips but no more; yet it seemed to comfort him to dip his nose in water and bobble it about, sucking in and blowing out through his teeth. Much of the time, now, he lay indoors half buried in sawdust. Once, near the last, while I was attending him I saw him try to make a bed for himself but he lacked the strength, and when he set his snout into the dust he was unable to plow even the little furrow he needed to lie down in.

He came out of the house to die. When I went down, before going to bed, he lay stretched in the yard a few feet from the door. I knelt, saw that he was dead, and left him there: his face had a mild look, expressive neither of deep peace nor of deep suffering, although I think he had suffered a good deal. I went back up to the house and to bed, and cried internally—deep hemorrhagic intears. I didn't wake till nearly eight the next morning, and when I looked out the open window the grave was already being dug, down beyond the dump under a wild apple. I could hear the spade strike against the small rocks that blocked the way. Never send to know for whom the grave is dug, I said to myself, it's dug for thee. Fred, I well knew, was supervising the work of digging, so I ate breakfast slowly.

It was a Saturday morning. The thicket in which I found the gravediggers at work was dark and warm, the sky overcast. Here, among alders and young hackmatacks, at the foot of the apple tree, Lennie had dug a beautiful hole, five feet long, three feet wide, three feet deep. He was standing in it, removing the last spadefuls of earth while Fred patrolled the brink in simple but impressive circles, disturbing the loose earth of the mound so that it trickled back in. There had been no rain in weeks and the soil, even three feet down, was dry and powdery. As I stood and stared, an enormous earthworm which had been partially exposed by the spade at the bottom dug itself deeper and made a slow withdrawal, seeking even remoter moistures at even lonelier depths. And just as Lennie stepped out and rested his spade against the tree and lit a cigarette, a small green apple separated itself from a branch overhead and fell into the hole. Everything about this last scene seemed over-written—the dismal sky, the shabby woods, the imminence of rain, the worm (legendary bedfellow of the dead), the apple (conventional garnish of a pig).

But even so, there was a directness and dispatch about animal burial, I thought, that made it a more decent affair than human burial: there was no stopover in the undertaker's foul parlor, no wreath nor spray; and when we hitched a line to the pig's hind legs and dragged him swiftly from his yard, throwing our weight into the harness and leaving a wake of crushed grass and smoothed rubble over the dump,

ours was a businesslike procession, with Fred, the dishonorable pall-
bearer, staggering along in the rear, his perverse bereavement showing
in every seam in his face; and the post mortem performed handily and
swiftly right at the edge of the grave, so that the innards that had
caused the pig's death preceded him into the ground and he lay at last
resting squarely on the cause of his own undoing.

I threw in the first shovelful, and then we worked rapidly and
without talk, until the job was complete. I picked up the rope, made
it fast to Fred's collar (he is a notorious ghoul), and we all three filed
back up the path to the house, Fred bringing up the rear and holding
back every inch of the way, feigning unusual stiffness. I noticed that
although he weighed far less than the pig, he was harder to drag, being
possessed of the vital spark.

The news of the death of my pig traveled fast and far, and I received
many expressions of sympathy from friends and neighbors, for no one
took the event lightly and the premature expiration of a pig is, I soon
discovered, a departure which the community marks solemnly on its
calendar, a sorrow in which it feels fully involved. I have written this
account in penitence and in grief, as a man who failed to raise his pig,
and to explain my deviation from the classic course of so many raised
pigs. The grave in the woods is unmarked, but Fred can direct the
mourner to it unerringly and with immense good will, and I know he
and I shall often revisit it, singly and together, in seasons of reflection
and despair, on flagless memorial days of our own choosing.

[1948]

THE RING OF TIME

AFTER THE LIONS had returned to their cages, creeping angrily
through the chutes, a little bunch of us drifted away and into an open
doorway nearby, where we stood for a while in semidarkness, watching
a big brown circus horse go harumphing around the practice ring. His
trainer was a woman of about forty, and the two of them, horse and
woman, seemed caught up in one of those desultory treadmills of

afternoon from which there is no apparent escape. The day was hot, and we kibitzers were grateful to be briefly out of the sun's glare. The long rein, or tape, by which the woman guided her charge counterclockwise in his dull career formed the radius of their private circle, of which she was the revolving center; and she, too, stepped a tiny circumference of her own, in order to accommodate the horse and allow him his maximum scope. She had on a short-skirted costume and a conical straw hat. Her legs were bare and she wore high heels, which probed deep into the loose tanbark and kept her ankles in a state of constant turmoil. The great size and meekness of the horse, the repetitious exercise, the heat of the afternoon, all exerted a hypnotic charm that invited boredom; we spectators were experiencing a languor—we neither expected relief nor felt entitled to any. We had paid a dollar to get into the grounds, to be sure, but we had got our dollar's worth a few minutes before, when the lion trainer's whiplash had got caught around a toe of one of the lions. What more did we want for a dollar?

Behind me I heard someone say, "Excuse me, please," in a low voice. She was halfway into the building when I turned and saw her—a girl of sixteen or seventeen, politely threading her way through us onlookers who blocked the entrance. As she emerged in front of us, I saw that she was barefoot, her dirty little feet fighting the uneven ground. In most respects she was like any of two or three dozen showgirls you encounter if you wander about in the winter quarters of Mr. John Ringling North's circus, in Sarasota—cleverly proportioned, deeply browned by the sun, dusty, eager, and almost naked. But her grave face and the naturalness of her manner gave her a sort of quick distinction and brought a new note into the gloomy octagonal building where we had all cast our lot for a few moments. As soon as she had squeezed through the crowd, she spoke a word or two to the older woman, whom I took to be her mother, stepped to the ring, and waited while the horse coasted to a stop in front of her. She gave the animal a couple of affectionate swipes on his enormous neck and then swung herself aboard. The horse immediately resumed his rocking canter, the woman goading him on, chanting something that sounded like "Hop! Hop!"

In attempting to recapture this mild spectacle, I am merely acting as recording secretary for one of the oldest of societies—the society of those who, at one time or another, have surrendered, without even a show of resistance, to the bedazzlement of a circus rider. As a writing man, or secretary, I have always felt charged with the safekeeping of all unexpected items of worldly or unworldly enchantment, as though I might be held personally responsible if even a small one were to be lost. But it is not easy to communicate anything of this nature. The circus comes as close to being the world in microcosm as anything I know; in a way, it puts all the rest of show business in the shade. Its magic is universal and complex. Out of its wild disorder comes order; from its rank smell rises the good aroma of courage and daring; out of its preliminary shabbiness comes the final splendor. And buried in the familiar boasts of its advance agents lies the modesty of most of its people. For me the circus is at its best before it has been put together. It is at its best at certain moments when it comes to a point, as through a burning glass, in the activity and destiny of a single performer out of so many. One ring is always bigger than three. One rider, one aerialist, is always greater than six. In short, a man has to catch the circus unawares to experience its full impact and share its gaudy dream.

The ten-minute ride the girl took achieved—as far as I was concerned, who wasn't looking for it, and quite unbeknownst to her, who wasn't even striving for it—the thing that is sought by performers everywhere, on whatever stage, whether struggling in the tidal currents of Shakespeare or bucking the difficult motion of a horse. I somewhat got the idea she was just cadging a ride, improving a shining ten minutes in the diligent way all serious artists seize free moments to hone the blade of their talent and keep themselves in trim. Her brief tour included only elementary postures and tricks, perhaps because her warmup at this hour was unscheduled and the ring was not rigged for a real practice session. She swung herself off and on the horse several times, gripping his mane. She did a few knee-stands—or whatever they are called—dropping to her knees and quickly bouncing back up on her feet again. Most of the time she simply rode in a standing position, well aft on the beast, her hands hanging easily at her sides, her head erect, her straw-colored ponytail lightly brushing her shoulders, the blood of exertion showing faintly through the tan of her skin. Twice she managed a one-foot stance—a sort of ballet pose, with arms out-stretched. At one point the neck strap of her bathing suit broke and she went twice around the ring in the classic attitude of a woman making minor repairs to a garment. The fact that she was standing on the back of a moving horse while doing this invested the matter with a clownish significance that perfectly fitted the spirit of the circus—jocund, yet charming. She just rolled the strap into a neat ball and stowed it inside her bodice while the horse rocked and rolled beneath her in dutiful innocence. The bathing suit proved as self-reliant as its owner and stood up well enough without benefit of strap.

The richness of the scene was in its plainness, its natural condition—of horse, of ring, of girl, even to the girl's bare feet that gripped the bare back of her proud and ridiculous mount. The enchantment grew not out of anything that happened or was performed but out of something that seemed to go round and around and around with the girl, attending her, a steady gleam in the shape of a circle—a ring of ambition, of happiness, of youth. (And the positive pleasures of equilibrium under difficulties.) In a week or two, all would be changed, all (or almost all) lost: the girl would wear makeup, the horse would wear gold, the ring would be painted, the bark would be clean for the feet of the horse, the girl's feet would be clean for the slippers that she'd wear. All, all would be lost.

As I watched with the others, our jaws adroop, our eyes alight, I became painfully conscious of the element of time. Everything in the hideous old building seemed to take the shape of a circle, conforming to the course of the horse. The rider's gaze, as she peered straight ahead, seemed to be circular, as though bent by force of circumstance; then time itself began running in circles, and so the beginning was where the end was, and the two were the same, and one thing ran into the next and time went round and around and got nowhere. The girl wasn't so young that she did not know the delicious satisfaction of having a perfectly behaved body and the fun of using it to do a trick most people can't do, but she was too young to know that time does not really move in a circle at all. I thought: "She will never be as beautiful as this again"—a thought that made me acutely unhappy—and in a flash my mind (which is too much of a busybody to suit me) had projected her twenty-five years ahead, and she was now in the center of the ring, on foot, wearing a conical hat and high-heeled shoes, the image of the older woman, holding the long rein, caught in the treadmill of an afternoon long in the future. "She is at that enviable moment in life [I thought] when she believes she can go once around the ring, make one complete circuit, and at the end be exactly the same age as at the start." Everything in her movements, her expression, told you that for her the ring of time was perfectly formed, changeless, predictable, without beginning or end, like the ring in which she was travelling at this moment with the horse that wallowed under her. And then I slipped back into my trance, and time was circular again—time, pausing quietly with the rest of us, so as not to disturb the balance of a performer.

Her ride ended as casually as it had begun. The older woman stopped the horse, and the girl slid to the ground. As she walked toward us to leave, there was a quick, small burst of applause. She smiled broadly, in surprise and pleasure; then her face suddenly regained its gravity and she disappeared through the door.

It has been ambitious and plucky of me to attempt to describe what is indescribable, and I have failed, as I knew I would. But I have discharged my duty to my society; and besides, a writer, like an acrobat, must occasionally try a stunt that is too much for him. At any rate, it is worth reporting that long before the circus comes to town, its most notable performances have already been given. Under the bright lights of the finished show, a performer need only reflect the electric candle power that is directed upon him; but in the dark and dirty old training rings and in the makeshift cages, whatever light is generated, whatever excitement, whatever beauty, must come from original sources—from internal fires of professional hunger and delight, from the exuberance and gravity of youth. It is the difference between planetary light and the combustion of stars.

[1956]

ON A FLORIDA KEY

I AM WRITING this in a beach cottage on a Florida key. It is raining to beat the cars. The rollers from a westerly storm are creaming along the shore, making a steady boiling noise instead of the usual

intermittent slap. The Chamber of Commerce has drawn the friendly
blind against this ugliness and is busy getting out some advance notices of the style parade which is to be held next Wednesday at the
pavilion. The paper says cooler tomorrow.

The walls of my room are of matched boarding, applied horizontally
and painted green. On the floor is a straw mat. Under the mat is a layer
of sand that has been tracked into the cottage and has sifted through
the straw. I have thought some of taking the mat up and sweeping the
sand into a pile and removing it, but have decided against it. This is
the way keys form, apparently, and I have no particular reason to
interfere. On a small wooden base in one corner of the room is a gas
heater, supplied from a tank on the premises. This device can raise the
temperature of the room with great rapidity by converting the oxygen
of the air into heat. In deciding whether to light the heater or leave
it alone, one has only to choose whether he wants to congeal in a
well-ventilated room or suffocate in comfort. After a little practice,
a nice balance can be established—enough oxygen left to sustain life,
yet enough heat generated to prevent death from exposure.

On the west wall hangs an Indian rug, and to one edge of the rug
is pinned a button which carries the legend: Junior Programs Joop
Club. Built into the north wall is a cabinet made of pecky cypress. On
the top shelf are three large pine cones, two of them painted emerald-
green, the third painted brick-red. Also a gilded candlestick in the
shape of a Roman chariot. Another shelf holds some shells which, at
the expenditure of considerable effort on somebody's part, have been
made to look like birds. On the bottom shelf is a tiny toy collie, made
of rabbit fur, with a tongue of red flannel.

In the kitchenette just beyond where I sit is a gas stove and a small
electric refrigerator of an ancient vintage. The ice trays show deep
claw marks, where people have tried to pry them free, using can
openers and knives and screwdrivers and petulance. When the refrigerator snaps on it makes a noise which can be heard all through the
cottage and the lights everywhere go dim for a second and then return
to their normal brilliancy. This refrigerator contains the milk, the
butter, and the eggs for tomorrow's breakfast. More milk will arrive
in the morning, but I will save it for use on the morrow, so that every
day I shall use the milk of the previous day, never taking advantage
of the opportunity to enjoy perfectly fresh milk. This is a situation

which could be avoided if I had the guts to throw away a whole bottle
of milk, but nobody has that much courage in the world today. It is
a sin to throw away milk and we know it.

The water that flows from the faucets in the kitchen sink and in
the bathroom contains sulphur and is not good to drink. It leaves
deep-brown stains around the drains. Applied to the face with a
shaving brush, it feels as though fine sandpaper were being drawn
across your jowls. It is so hard and sulphurous that ordinary soap will
not yield to it, and the breakfast dishes have to be washed with a
washing powder known as Dreft.

On the porch of the cottage, each in a special stand, are two carboys
of spring water—for drinking, making coffee, and brushing teeth.
There is a deposit of two dollars on bottle and stand, and the water
itself costs fifty cents. Two rival companies furnish water to the
community, and I happened to get mixed up with both of them. Every
couple of days a man from one or the other of the companies shows
up and hangs around for a while, whining about the presence on my
porch of the rival's carboy. I have made an attempt to dismiss one
company and retain the other, but to accomplish it would require a
dominant personality and I haven't one. I have been surprised to see
how long it takes a man to drink up ten gallons of water. I should have
thought I could have done it in half the time it has taken me.

This morning I read in the paper of an old Negro, one hundred-and-
one years old, and he was boasting of the quantity of whiskey he had
drunk in his life. He said he had once worked in a distillery and they
used to give him half a gallon of whiskey a day to take home, which
kept him going all right during the week, but on weekends, he said,
he would have to buy a gallon extry, to tide him over till Monday.

In the kitchen cabinet is a bag of oranges for morning juice. Each
orange is stamped "Color Added." The dyeing of an orange, to make
it orange, is man's most impudent gesture to date. It is really an
appalling piece of effrontery, carrying the clear implication that Nature doesn't know what she is up to. I think an orange, dyed orange,
is as repulsive as a pine cone painted green. I think it is about as ugly
a thing as I have ever seen, and it seems hard to believe that here,
within ten miles, probably, of the trees that bore the fruit, I can't buy
an orange that somebody hasn't smeared with paint. But I doubt that
there are many who feel that way about it, because fraudulence has
become a national virtue and is well thought of in many circles. In the

last twenty-four hours, I see by this morning's paper, 136 cars of oranges have been shipped. There are probably millions of children today who have never seen a natural orange—only an artificially colored one. If they should see a natural orange they might think something had gone wrong with it.

There are two moving picture theaters in the town to which my key is attached by a bridge. In one of them colored people are allowed in the balcony. In the other, colored people are not allowed at all. I saw a patriotic newsreel there the other day which ended with a picture of the American flag blowing in the breeze, and the words: one nation indivisible, with liberty and justice for all. Everyone clapped, but I decided I could not clap for liberty and justice (for all) while I was in a theater from which Negroes had been barred. And I felt there were too many people in the world who think liberty and justice for all means liberty and justice for themselves and their friends. I sat there wondering what would happen to me if I were to jump up and say in a loud voice: "If you folks like liberty and justice so much, why do you keep Negroes from this theater?" I am sure it would have surprised everybody very much and it is the kind of thing I dream about doing but never do. If I had done it I suppose the management would have taken me by the arm and marched me out of the theater, on the grounds that it is disturbing the peace to speak up for liberty just as the feature is coming on. When a man is in the South he must do as the Southerners do; but although I am willing to call my wife "sugar" I am not willing to call a colored person a nigger.

Northerners are quite likely to feel that Southerners are bigoted on the race question, and Southerners almost invariably figure that Northerners are without any practical experience and therefore their opinions aren't worth much. The Jim Crow philosophy of color is unsatisfying to a Northerner, but is regarded as sensible and expedient to residents of towns where the Negro population is as large as or larger than the white. Whether one makes a practical answer or an idealistic answer to a question depends partly on whether one is talking in terms of one year, or ten years, or a hundred years. It is, in other words, conceivable that the Negroes of a hundred years from now will enjoy a greater degree of liberty if the present restrictions on today's Negroes are not relaxed too fast. But that doesn't get today's Negroes in to see Hedy Lamarr.

I have to laugh when I think about the sheer inconsistency of the

Southern attitude about color: the Negro barred from the movie house because of color, the orange with "color added" for its ultimate triumph. Some of the cities in this part of the State have fête days to commemorate the past and advertise the future, and in my mind I have been designing a float that I would like to enter in the parades. It would contain a beautiful Negro woman riding with the other bathing beauties and stamped with the magical words, Color Added.

In the cottage next door is a lady who is an ardent isolationist and who keeps running in and out with pamphlets, books, and marked-up newspapers, hoping to convince me that America should mind its own business. She tracks sand in, as well as ideas, and I have to sweep up after her two or three times a day.

Floridians are complaining this year that business is below par. They tell you that the boom in industry causes this unwholesome situation. When tycoons are busy in the North they have no time for sunning themselves, or even for sitting in a semitropical cottage in the rain. Miami is appropriating a few extra thousand dollars for its advertising campaign, hoping to lure executives away from the defense program for a few golden moments.

Although I am no archeologist, I love Florida as much for the remains of her unfinished cities as for the bright cabanas on her beaches. I love to prowl the dead sidewalks that run off into the live jungle, under the broiling sun of noon, where the cabbage palms throw their spiny shade across the stillborn streets and the creepers bind old curbstones in a fierce sensual embrace and the mocking birds dwell in song upon the remembered grandeur of real estate's purple hour. A boulevard which has been reclaimed by Nature is an exciting avenue; it breathes a strange prophetic perfume, as of some century still to come, when the birds will remember, and the spiders, and the little quick lizards that toast themselves on the smooth hard surfaces that once held the impossible dreams of men. Here along these bristling walks is a decayed symmetry in a living forest—straight lines softened by a kindly and haphazard Nature, pavements nourishing life with the beginnings of topsoil, the cracks in the walks possessed by root structures, the brilliant blossoms of the domesticated vine run wild, and overhead the turkey buzzard in the clear sky, on quiet wings, awaiting new mammalian death among the hibiscus, the yucca, the Spanish bayonet, and the palm. I remember the wonderful days and the tall dream of rainbow's end; the offices with the wall charts, the pins in the charts, the orchestras playing gently to prepare the soul of the wanderer for the mysteries of subdivision, the free bus service to the rainbow's beginning, the luncheon served on the little tables under the trees, the warm sweet air so full of the deadly contagion, the dotted line, the signature, and the premonitory qualms and the shadow of the buzzard in the wild wide Florida sky.

I love these rudimentary cities that were conceived in haste and greed and never rose to suffer the scarifying effects of human habitation, cities of not quite forgotten hopes, untouched by neon and by filth. And I love the beaches too, out beyond the cottage colony, where they are wild and free still, visited by the sandpipers that retreat before each wave, like children, and by an occasional hip-sprung farmwife hunting shells, or sometimes by a veteran digging for *Donax variabilis* to take back to his hungry mate in the trailer camp.

The sound of the sea is the most time-effacing sound there is. The centuries reroll in a cloud and the earth becomes green again when you listen, with eyes shut, to the sea—a young green time when the water and the land were just getting acquainted and had known each other for only a few billion years and the mollusks were just beginning to dip and creep in the shallows; and now man the invertebrate, under his ribbed umbrella, anoints himself with oil and pulls on his Polaroid glasses to stop the glare and stretches out his long brown body at ease upon a towel on the warm sand and listens.

The sea answers all questions, and always in the same way; for when you read in the papers the interminable discussions and the bickering and the prognostications and the turmoil, the disagreements and the fateful decisions and agreements and the plans and the programs and the threats and the counter threats, then you close your eyes and the sea dispatches one more big roller in the unbroken line since the beginning of the world and it combs and breaks and returns foaming and saying: "So soon?"

[1941]

THE ESSAYIST* E. B. White

THE ESSAYIST is a self-liberated man, sustained by the childish belief that everything he thinks about, everything that happens to him, is of general interest. He is a fellow who thoroughly enjoys his work, just as people who take bird walks enjoy theirs. Each new excursion of the essayist, each new "attempt," differs from the last and takes him into new country. This delights him. Only a person who is congenitally self-centered has the effrontery and the stamina to write essays.

There are as many kinds of essays as there are human attitudes or poses, as many essay flavors as there are Howard Johnson ice creams. The essayist arises in the morning and, if he has work to do, selects his garb from an unusually extensive wardrobe: he can pull on any sort of shirt, be any sort of person, according to his mood or his subject matter—philosopher, scold, jester, raconteur, confidant, pundit, devil's advocate, enthusiast. I like the essay, have always liked it, and even as a child was at work, attempting to inflict my young thoughts and experiences on others by putting them on paper. I early broke into print in the pages of *St. Nicholas.* I tend still to fall back on the essay form (or lack of form) when an idea strikes me, but I am not fooled about the place of the essay in twentieth-century American letters—it stands a short distance down the line. The essayist, unlike the novelist, the poet, and the playwright, must be content in his self-imposed role of second-class citizen. A writer who has his sights trained on the Nobel Prize or other earthly triumphs had best write a novel, a poem, or a play, and leave the essayist to ramble about, content with living a free life and enjoying the satisfactions of a somewhat undisciplined existence. (Dr. Johnson called the essay "an irregular, undigested piece"; this happy practitioner has no wish to quarrel with the good doctor's characterization.)

There is one thing the essayist cannot do, though—he cannot indulge himself in deceit or in concealment, for he will be found out in no time. Desmond MacCarthy, in his introductory remarks to the 1928 E. P. Dutton & Company edition of Montaigne, observes that

*An excerpt from White's "Foreword" to *Essays of E. B. White.*

Montaigne "had the gift of natural candour. . . ." It is the basic ingredient. And even the essayist's escape from discipline is only a partial escape: the essay, although a relaxed form, imposes its own disciplines, raises its own problems, and these disciplines and problems soon become apparent and (we all hope) act as a deterrent to anyone wielding a pen merely because he entertains random thoughts or is in a happy or wandering mood.

I think some people find the essay the last resort of the egoist, a much too self-conscious and self-serving form for their taste; they feel that it is presumptuous of a writer to assume that his little excursions or his small observations will interest the reader. There is some justice in their complaint. I have always been aware that I am by nature self-absorbed and egoistical; to write of myself to the extent I have done indicates a too great attention to my own life, not enough to the lives of others. I have worn many shirts, and not all of them have been a good fit. But when I am discouraged or downcast I need only fling open the door of my closet, and there, hidden behind everything else, hangs the mantle of Michel de Montaigne, smelling slightly of camphor.

[1977]

LEWIS THOMAS

A DISTINGUISHED MEDICAL RESEARCHER and administrator, dean of the School of Medicine at Yale University and author of over two hundred highly specialized papers in the fields of immunology and pathology, Dr. Lewis Thomas was invited in 1971 to write a monthly column for the *New England Journal of Medicine.* Given a free hand with everything but length (the column was limited to 1,200 words), he called it simply "Notes of a Biology-Watcher" and once a month, or thereabouts, presented a brief, personal overview of recent research or a current issue in the biological sciences. Hardly the sort of stuff to appeal to a wide audience, one would think. But Dr. Thomas wrote with such grace, wit, and wisdom, such clarity and *style,* that soon he had a following well beyond the medical profession. This led, in 1974, to the publication of twenty-nine of Dr. Thomas's columns in a book. To his great surprise *The Lives of a Cell* became a bestseller and was awarded the 1974 National Book Award for Arts and Letters.

Lewis Thomas was born in Flushing, New York, on November 25, 1913, the son of a general practitioner. After graduating from a private school in Manhattan, he entered Princeton University, intent on becoming a doctor; but exposure to the poetry of T. S. Eliot and Ezra Pound awakened his literary interests and he published poems in the college literary magazine. A course in advanced biology during his senior year drew him back to medicine as a career, but he continued to write. Graduating from Harvard Medical School in 1937, Thomas interned at Boston City Hospital. A poem written during that period was published in the *Atlantic Monthly.*

Following his residency at the Neurological Institute in New York City, Dr. Thomas was called into the navy in 1941. As a lieutenant commander doing research in tropical diseases, he took part in the invasion of Okinawa. (See Chapter 9, "Guam and Okinawa," of his autobiography, *The Youngest Science,* for a highly amusing description of this period.) In 1946 Thomas returned to the academic world of teaching and research, first at Johns Hopkins, then at Tulane and the University of Minnesota, moving steadily up through the academic ranks and into administration. From 1954 to 1969 Dr. Thomas was successively head of the Department of Pathology, director of University Hospital, and dean of the School of Medicine at New York University. Then he moved to Yale, where he became dean of the medical school. From 1973 to 1980 Dr. Thomas was president and chief executive officer of Memorial Sloan-Kettering Cancer Center in New York City, and now is its chancellor. Throughout this exceptional career Dr. Thomas has served on numerous scientific panels, committees, and commissions; he is a member of the National Academy of Sciences.

When Lewis Thomas took on the added responsibility of writing a column for the *New England Journal of Medicine* in 1971, it was clearly a labor of love, an opportunity to speak to his profession about the matters that most deeply concerned him. What these came down to was a highly optimistic view of the beneficent complexity of nature, a world of endless wonder that is strange beyond imagination, yet all to the good. "Most of the associations between the living things we know about are essentially cooperative ones, symbiotic in one degree or another. . . . Every creature is, in some degree, connected to and dependent on the rest."

Thomas took the phenomenon of symbiosis—the mutually beneficial relationship between organisms—for the title of his second collection of essays, *The Medusa and the Snail: More Notes of a Biology Watcher,* published in 1979. Bolder and wider-ranging in subject matter than *The Lives of a Cell,* it celebrates the diversity of life in terms at once serious and humorous, mystical and precise. Close scientific observation and the wildest flights of fancy are linked through subtle uses of paradox. In an essay on warts, Thomas wonders at the complex processes by which warts can be removed by hypnotic suggestion: "Not everyone believes this, but the evidence goes back a long way and is persuasive. Generations of internists and dermatologists, and their grandmothers for that matter, have been convinced of the phenomenon." In 1983 Dr. Thomas published *The Youngest Science,* an autobiography that traces the significant changes that have occurred in the practice of medicine and medical research during the twentieth century, and a third collection of essays, *Late Night Thoughts on Listening to Mahler's Ninth Symphony.*

As a stylist, Lewis Thomas writes in the great tradition of the informal essay. His manner is casual, offhand, spontaneous. In *The Youngest Science* he describes his initial efforts as an essayist:

> I tried outlining some ideas for essays, making lists of items I'd like to cover in each piece, organizing my thoughts in orderly sequences, and wrote several dreadful essays which I could not

bring myself to reread, and decided to give up being orderly. I changed the method to no method at all, picked out some suitable times late at night, usually on the weekend two days after I'd already passed the deadline, and wrote without outline or planning in advance, as fast as I could. This worked better, or at least was more fun, and I was able to get started.

Thomas's philosophic model is the preeminent sixteenth-century French essayist, Michel de Montaigne. In an essay entitled "Why Montaigne Is Not a Bore," Thomas describes Montaigne as he himself might be described: "He is, of course, a moralist and, like all the great moralists, also a humorist." Like Montaigne, Lewis Thomas is not an absolutist but only, he hopes, an ordinary man who tries to persuade you "of his ordinariness on every page. You cannot help but believe him in this; he is, above all else, an honest and candid man. And there is the marvel of his book: if Montaigne is an ordinary man, then what an encouragement, what a piece of work is, after all, an ordinary man!" Though Lewis Thomas would demur at any comparison to Montaigne, it is indeed that same quality one admires in him, and it is a quality one achieves only by careful attention to detail, whether looking through a microscope or applying pencil to paper.

DEATH IN THE OPEN

MOST OF THE DEAD ANIMALS you see on highways near the cities
are dogs, a few cats. Out in the countryside, the forms and coloring
of the dead are strange; these are the wild creatures. Seen from a car
window they appear as fragments, evoking memories of woodchucks,
badgers, skunks, voles, snakes, sometimes the mysterious wreckage of
a deer.

It is always a queer shock, part a sudden upwelling of grief, part
unaccountable amazement. It is simply astounding to see an animal
dead on a highway. The outrage is more than just the location; it is
the impropriety of such visible death, anywhere. You do not expect
to see dead animals in the open. It is the nature of animals to die alone,
off somewhere, hidden. It is wrong to see them lying out on the
highway; it is wrong to see them anywhere.

Everything in the world dies, but we only know about it as a kind
of abstraction. If you stand in a meadow, at the edge of a hillside, and
look around carefully, almost everything you can catch sight of is in
the process of dying, and most things will be dead long before you are.
If it were not for the constant renewal and replacement going on
before your eyes, the whole place would turn to stone and sand under
your feet.

There are some creatures that do not seem to die at all; they simply
vanish totally into their own progeny. Single cells do this. The cell
becomes two, then four, and so on, and after a while the last trace is
gone. It cannot be seen as death; barring mutation, the descendants
are simply the first cell, living all over again. The cycles of the slime
mold have episodes that seem as conclusive as death, but the withered
slug, with its stalk and fruiting body, is plainly the transient tissue of
a developing animal; the free-swimming amebocytes use this organ
collectively in order to produce more of themselves.

There are said to be a billion billion insects on the earth at any
moment, most of them with very short life expectancies by our standards. Someone has estimated that there are 25 million assorted in-

sects hanging in the air over every temperate square mile, in a column extending upward for thousands of feet, drifting through the layers of the atmosphere like plankton. They are dying steadily, some by being eaten, some just dropping in their tracks, tons of them around the earth, disintegrating as they die, invisibly.

Who ever sees dead birds, in anything like the huge numbers stipulated by the certainty of the death of all birds? A dead bird is an incongruity, more startling than an unexpected live bird, sure evidence to the human mind that something has gone wrong. Birds do their dying off somewhere, behind things, under things, never on the wing.

Animals seem to have an instinct for performing death alone, hidden. Even the largest, most conspicuous ones find ways to conceal themselves in time. If an elephant missteps and dies in an open place, the herd will not leave him there; the others will pick him up and carry the body from place to place, finally putting it down in some inexplicably suitable location. When elephants encounter the skeleton of an elephant out in the open, they methodically take up each of the bones and distribute them, in a ponderous ceremony, over neighboring acres.

It is a natural marvel. All of the life of the earth dies, all of the time, in the same volume as the new life that dazzles us each morning, each spring. All we see of this is the odd stump, the fly struggling on the porch floor of the summer house in October, the fragment on the highway. I have lived all my life with an embarrassment of squirrels in my backyard, they are all over the place, all year long, and I have never seen, anywhere, a dead squirrel.

I suppose it is just as well. If the earth were otherwise, and all the dying were done in the open, with the dead there to be looked at, we would never have it out of our minds. We can forget about it much of the time, or think of it as an accident to be avoided, somehow. But it does make the process of dying seem more exceptional than it really is, and harder to engage in at the times when we must ourselves engage.

In our way, we conform as best we can to the rest of nature. The obituary pages tell us of the news that we are dying away, while the birth announcements in finer print, off at the side of the page, inform us of our replacements, but we get no grasp from this of the enormity of scale. There are 3 billion of us on the earth, and all 3 billion must

be dead, on a schedule, within this lifetime. The vast mortality, involving something over 50 million of us each year, takes place in relative
secrecy. We can only really know of the deaths in our households, or
among our friends. These, detached in our minds from all the rest, we
take to be unnatural events, anomalies, outrages. We speak of our own
dead in low voices; struck down, we say, as though visible death can
only occur for cause, by disease or violence, avoidably. We send off
for flowers, grieve, make ceremonies, scatter bones, unaware of the
rest of the 3 billion on the same schedule. All of that immense mass
of flesh and bone and consciousness will disappear by absorption into
the earth, without recognition by the transient survivors.

Less than a half century from now, our replacements will have more
than doubled the numbers. It is hard to see how we can continue to
keep the secret, with such multitudes doing the dying. We will have
to give up the notion that death is catastrophe, or detestable, or
avoidable, or even strange. We will need to learn more about the
cycling of life in the rest of the system, and about our connection to
the process. Everything that comes alive seems to be in trade for
something that dies, cell for cell. There might be some comfort in the
recognition of synchrony, in the information that we all go down
together, in the best of company.

[1972]

ON NATURAL DEATH

THERE ARE so many new books about dying that there are now
special shelves set aside for them in bookshops, along with the health-
diet and home-repair paperbacks and the sex manuals. Some of them
are so packed with detailed information and step-by-step instructions
for performing the function that you'd think this was a new sort of
skill which all of us are now required to learn. The strongest impression the casual reader gets, leafing through, is that proper dying has
become an extraordinary, even an exotic experience, something only
the specially trained get to do.

Also, you could be led to believe that we are the only creatures capable of the awareness of death, that when all the rest of nature is being cycled through dying, one generation after another, it is a different kind of process, done automatically and trivially, more "natural," as we say.

An elm in our backyard caught the blight this summer and dropped stone dead, leafless, almost overnight. One weekend it was a normal-looking elm, maybe a little bare in spots but nothing alarming, and the next weekend it was gone, passed over, departed, taken. Taken is right, for the tree surgeon came by yesterday with his crew of young helpers and their cherry picker, and took it down branch by branch and carted it off in the back of a red truck, everyone singing.

The dying of a field mouse, at the jaws of an amiable household cat, is a spectacle I have beheld many times. It used to make me wince. Early in life I gave up throwing sticks at the cat to make him drop the mouse, because the dropped mouse regularly went ahead and died anyway, but I always shouted unaffections at the cat to let him know the sort of animal he had become. Nature, I thought, was an abomination.

Recently I've done some thinking about that mouse, and I wonder if his dying is necessarily all that different from the passing of our elm. The main difference, if there is one, would be in the matter of pain. I do not believe that an elm tree has pain receptors, and even so, the blight seems to me a relatively painless way to go even if there were nerve endings in a tree, which there are not. But the mouse dangling tail-down from the teeth of a gray cat is something else again, with pain beyond bearing, you'd think, all over his small body.

There are now some plausible reasons for thinking it is not like that at all, and you can make up an entirely different story about the mouse and his dying if you like. At the instant of being trapped and penetrated by teeth, peptide hormones are released by cells in the hypothalamus and the pituitary gland; instantly these substances, called endorphins, are attached to the surface of other cells responsible for pain perception; the hormones have the pharmacologic properties of opium; there is no pain. Thus it is that the mouse seems always to dangle so languidly from the jaws, lies there so quietly when dropped, dies of his injuries without a struggle. If a mouse could shrug, he'd shrug.

I do not know if this is true or not, nor do I know how to prove it if it is true. Maybe if you could get in there quickly enough and administer naloxone, a specific morphine antagonist, you could turn off the endorphins and observe the restoration of pain, but this is not something I would care to do or see. I think I will leave it there, as a good guess about the dying of a cat-chewed mouse, perhaps about dying in general.

Montaigne had a hunch about dying, based on his own close call in a riding accident. He was so badly injured as to be believed dead by his companions, and was carried home with lamentations, "all bloody, stained all over with the blood I had thrown up." He remembers the entire episode, despite having been "dead, for two full hours," with wonderment:

> It seemed to me that my life was hanging only by the tip of my lips. I closed my eyes in order, it seemed to me, to help push it out, and took pleasure in growing languid and letting myself go. It was an idea that was only floating on the surface of my soul, as delicate and feeble as all the rest, but in truth not only free from distress but mingled with that sweet feeling that people have who have let themselves slide into sleep. I believe that this is the same state in which people find themselves whom we see fainting in the agony of death, and I maintain that we pity them without cause. . . . In order to get used to the idea of death, I find there is nothing like coming close to it.

Later, in another essay, Montaigne returns to it:

> If you know not how to die, never trouble yourself; Nature will in a moment fully and sufficiently instruct you; she will exactly do that business for you; take you no care for it.

The worst accident I've ever seen was in Okinawa, in the early days of the invasion, when a jeep ran into a troop carrier and was crushed nearly flat. Inside were two young MPs, trapped in bent steel, both mortally hurt, with only their heads and shoulders visible. We had a conversation while people with the right tools were prying them free. Sorry about the accident, they said. No, they said, they felt fine. Is everyone else okay, one of them said. Well, the other one said, no hurry now. And then they died.

Pain is useful for avoidance, for getting away when there's time to get away, but when it is end game, and no way back, pain is likely to be turned off, and the mechanisms for this are wonderfully precise and quick. If I had to design an ecosystem in which creatures had to live off each other and in which dying was an indispensable part of living, I could not think of a better way to manage.

[1979]

ON CLONING A HUMAN BEING

IT IS now theoretically possible to recreate an identical creature from any animal or plant, from the DNA contained in the nucleus of any somatic cell. A single plant root-tip cell can be teased and seduced into conceiving a perfect copy of the whole plant; a frog's intestinal epithelial cell possesses the complete instructions needed for a new, same frog. If the technology were further advanced, you could do this with a human being, and there are now startled predictions all over the place that this will in fact be done, someday, in order to provide a version of immortality for carefully selected, especially valuable people.

The cloning of humans is on most of the lists of things to worry about from Science, along with behavior control, genetic engineering, transplanted heads, computer poetry, and the unrestrained growth of plastic flowers.

Cloning is the most dismaying of prospects, mandating as it does the elimination of sex with only a metaphoric elimination of death as compensation. It is almost no comfort to know that one's cloned, identical surrogate lives on, especially when the living will very likely involve edging one's real, now aging self off to the side, sooner or later. It is hard to imagine anything like filial affection or respect for a single, unmated nucleus; harder still to think of one's new, self-generated self as anything but an absolute, desolate orphan. Not to mention the complex interpersonal relationship involved in raising one's self from infancy, teaching the language, enforcing discipline, instilling good

Satire:
Literary
Genre that
aims to
improve
humanity
-n- its institutions
by holding
them up to
close
scrutiny

manners, and the like. How would you feel if you became an incorrigible juvenile delinquent by proxy, at the age of fifty-five?

The public questions are obvious. Who is to be selected, and on what qualifications? How to handle the risks of misused technology, such as self-determined cloning by the rich and powerful but socially objectionable, or the cloning by governments of dumb, docile masses for the world's work? What will be the effect on all the uncloned rest of us of human sameness? After all, we've accustomed ourselves through hundreds of millennia to the continual exhilaration of uniqueness; each of us is totally different, in a fundamental sense, from all the other four billion. Selfness is an essential fact of life. The thought of human nonselfness, precise sameness, is terrifying, when you think about it.

Well, don't think about it, because it isn't a probable possibility, not even as a long shot for the distant future, in my opinion. I agree that you might clone some people who would look amazingly like their parental cell donors, but the odds are that they'd be almost as different as you or me, and certainly more different than any of today's identical twins.

The time required for the experiment is only one of the problems, but a formidable one. Suppose you wanted to clone a prominent, spectacularly successful diplomat, to look after the Middle East problems of the distant future. You'd have to catch him and persuade him, probably not very hard to do, and extirpate a cell. But then you'd have to wait for him to grow up through embryonic life and then for at least forty years more, and you'd have to be sure all observers remained patient and unmeddlesome through his unpromising, ambiguous childhood and adolescence.

Moreover, you'd have to be sure of recreating his environment, perhaps down to the last detail. "Environment" is a word which really means people, so you'd have to do a lot more cloning than just the diplomat himself.

This is a very important part of the cloning problem, largely overlooked in our excitement about the cloned individual himself. You don't have to agree all the way with B. F. Skinner to acknowledge that the environment does make a difference, and when you examine what we really mean by the word "environment" it comes down to other human beings. We use euphemisms and jargon for this, like "social forces," "cultural influences," even Skinner's "verbal community," but what is meant is the dense crowd of nearby people who talk to, listen to, smile or frown at, give to, withhold from, nudge, push, caress, or flail out at the individual. No matter what the genome says, these people have a lot to do with shaping a character. Indeed, if all you had was the genome, and no people around, you'd grow a sort of vertebrate plant, nothing more.

So, to start with, you will undoubtedly need to clone the parents. No question about this. This means the diplomat is out, even in theory, since you couldn't have gotten cells from both his parents at the time when he was himself just recognizable as an early social treasure. You'd have to limit the list of clones to people already certified as sufficiently valuable for the effort, with both parents still alive. The parents would need cloning and, for consistency, their parents as well. I suppose you'd also need the usual informed-consent forms, filled out and signed, not easy to get if I know parents, even harder for grandparents.

But this is only the beginning. It is the whole family that really influences the way a person turns out, not just the parents, according to current psychiatric thinking. Clone the family.

Then what? The way each member of the family develops has already been determined by the environment set around him, and this environment is more people, people outside the family, schoolmates, acquaintances, lovers, enemies, car-pool partners, even, in special circumstances, peculiar strangers across the aisle on the subway. Find them, and clone them.

But there is no end to the protocol. Each of the outer contacts has his own surrounding family, and his and their outer contacts. Clone them all.

To do the thing properly, with any hope of ending up with a genuine duplicate of a single person, you really have no choice. You must clone the world, no less.

We are not ready for an experiment of this size, nor, I should think, are we willing. For one thing, it would mean replacing today's world by an entirely identical world to follow immediately, and this means no new, natural, spontaneous, random, chancy children. No children at all, except for the manufactured doubles of those now on the scene. Plus all those identical adults, including all of today's politicians, all seen double. It is too much to contemplate.

Moreover, when the whole experiment is finally finished, fifty years or so from now, how could you get a responsible scientific reading on the outcome? Somewhere in there would be the original clonee, probably lost and overworked, now well into middle age, but everyone around him would be precise duplicates of today's everyone. It would be today's same world, filled to overflowing with duplicates of today's people and their same, duplicated problems, probably all resentful at having had to go through our whole thing all over, sore enough at the clone to make endless trouble for him, if they found him.

And obviously, if the whole thing were done precisely right, they would still be casting about for ways to solve the problem of universal dissatisfaction, and sooner or later they'd surely begin to look around at each other, wondering who should be cloned for his special value to society, to get us out of all this. And so it would go, in regular cycles, perhaps forever.

I once lived through a period when I wondered what Hell could be like, and I stretched my imagination to try to think of a perpetual sort of damnation. I have to confess, I never thought of anything like this.

I have an alternative suggestion, if you're looking for a way out. Set cloning aside, and don't try it. Instead, go in the other direction. Look for ways to get mutations more quickly, new variety, different songs. Fiddle around, if you must fiddle, but never with ways to keep things the same, no matter who, not even yourself. Heaven, somewhere ahead, has got to be a change.

[1974]

THE TUCSON ZOO

SCIENCE GETS MOST of its information by the process of reductionism, exploring the details, then the details of the details, until all the smallest bits of the structure, or the smallest parts of the mechanism, are laid out for counting and scrutiny. Only when this is done can the investigation be extended to encompass the whole organism or the entire system. So we say.

Sometimes it seems that we take a loss, working this way. Much of today's public anxiety about science is the apprehension that we may forever be overlooking the whole by an endless, obsessive preoccupation with the parts. I had a brief, personal experience of this misgiving one afternoon in Tucson, where I had time on my hands and visited the zoo, just outside the city. The designers there have cut a deep pathway between two small artificial ponds, walled by clear glass, so when you stand in the center of the path you can look into the depths of each pool, and at the same time you can regard the surface. In one pool, on the right side of the path, is a family of otters; on the other side, a family of beavers. Within just a few feet from your face, on either side, beavers and otters are at play, underwater and on the surface, swimming toward your face and then away, more filled with life than any creatures I have ever seen before, in all my days. Except for the glass, you could reach across and touch them.

I was transfixed. As I now recall it, there was only one sensation in my head: pure elation mixed with amazement at such perfection. Swept off my feet, I floated from one side to the other, swiveling my brain, staring astounded at the beavers, then at the otters. I could hear shouts across my corpus callosum, from one hemisphere to the other. I remember thinking, with what was left in charge of my consciousness, that I wanted no part of the science of beavers and otters; I wanted never to know how they performed their marvels; I wished for no news about the physiology of their breathing, the coordination of their muscles, their vision, their endocrine systems, their digestive tracts. I hoped never to have to think of them as collections of cells. All I asked for was the full hairy complexity, then in front of my eyes, of whole, intact beavers and otters in motion.

It lasted, I regret to say, for only a few minutes, and then I was back in the late twentieth century, reductionist as ever, wondering about the details by force of habit, but not, this time, the details of otters and beavers. Instead, me. Something worth remembering had happened in my mind, I was certain of that; I would have put it somewhere in the brain stem; maybe this was my limbic system at work. I became a behavioral scientist, an experimental psychologist, an ethologist, and in the instant I lost all the wonder and the sense of being overwhelmed. I was flattened.

But I came away from the zoo with something, a piece of news about myself: I am coded, somehow, for otters and beavers. I exhibit instinctive behavior in their presence, when they are displayed close at hand behind glass, simultaneously below water and at the surface. I have receptors for this display. Beavers and otters possess a "releaser" for me, in the terminology of ethology, and the releasing was my experience. What was released? Behavior. What behavior? Standing, swiveling flabbergasted, feeling exultation and a rush of friendship. I could not, as the result of the transaction, tell you anything more about beavers and otters than you already know. I learned nothing new about them. Only about me, and I suspect also about you, maybe about human beings at large: we are endowed with genes which code out our reaction to beavers and otters, maybe our reaction to each other as well. We are stamped with stereotyped, unalterable patterns of response, ready to be released. And the behavior released in us, by such confrontations, is, essentially, a surprised affection. It is compulsory behavior and we can avoid it only by straining with the full power of our conscious minds, making up conscious excuses all the way. Left to ourselves, mechanistic and autonomic, we hanker for friends.

Everyone says, stay away from ants. They have no lessons for us; they are crazy little instruments, inhuman, incapable of controlling themselves, lacking manners, lacking souls. When they are massed together, all touching, exchanging bits of information held in their jaws like memoranda, they become a single animal. Look out for that. It is a debasement, a loss of individuality, a violation of human nature, an unnatural act.

Sometimes people argue this point of view seriously and with deep thought. Be individuals, solitary and selfish, is the message. Altruism, a jargon word for what used to be called love, is worse than weakness, it is sin, a violation of nature. Be separate. Do not be a social animal. But this is a hard argument to make convincingly when you have to depend on language to make it. You have to print up leaflets or publish books and get them bought and sent around, you have to turn up on television and catch the attention of millions of other human beings all at once, and then you have to say to all of them, all at once, all collected and paying attention: be solitary; do not depend on each other. You can't do this and keep a straight face.

Maybe altruism is our most primitive attribute, out of reach, beyond our control. Or perhaps it is immediately at hand, waiting to be released, disguised now, in our kind of civilization, as affection or friendship or attachment. I don't see why it should be unreasonable for all human beings to have strands of DNA coiled up in chromosomes, coding out instincts for usefulness and helpfulness. Usefulness may turn out to be the hardest test of fitness for survival, more important than aggression, more effective, in the long run, than grabbiness. If this is the sort of information biological science holds for the future, applying to us as well as to ants, then I am all for science.

One thing I'd like to know most of all: when those ants have made the Hill, and are all there, touching and exchanging, and the whole mass begins to behave like a single huge creature, and *thinks,* what on earth is that thought? And while you're at it, I'd like to know a second thing: when it happens, does any single ant know about it? Does his hair stand on end?

[1974]

THE IKS

THE SMALL TRIBE of Iks, formerly nomadic hunters and gatherers in the mountain valleys of northern Uganda, have become celebrities, literary symbols for the ultimate fate of disheartened, heartless mankind at large. Two disastrously conclusive things happened to them: the government decided to have a national park, so they were compelled by law to give up hunting in the valleys and become farmers on poor hillside soil, and then they were visited for two years by an anthropologist who detested them and wrote a book about them.

The message of the book is that the Iks have transformed themselves into an irreversibly disagreeable collection of unattached, brutish creatures, totally selfish and loveless, in response to the dismantling of their traditional culture. Moreover, this is what the rest of us are like in our inner selves, and we will all turn into Iks when the structure of our society comes all unhinged.

The argument rests, of course, on certain assumptions about the core of human beings, and is necessarily speculative. You have to agree in advance that man is fundamentally a bad lot, out for himself alone, displaying such graces as affection and compassion only as learned habits. If you take this view, the story of the Iks can be used to confirm it. These people seem to be living together, clustered in small, dense villages, but they are really solitary, unrelated individuals with no evident use for each other. They talk, but only to make ill-tempered demands and cold refusals. They share nothing. They never sing. They turn the children out to forage as soon as they can walk, and desert the elders to starve whenever they can, and the foraging children snatch food from the mouths of the helpless elders. It is a mean society.

They breed without love or even casual regard. They defecate on each other's doorsteps. They watch their neighbors for signs of misfortune, and only then do they laugh. In the book they do a lot of laughing, having so much bad luck. Several times they even laughed at the anthropologist, who found this especially repellent (one senses, between the lines, that the scholar is not himself the world's luckiest man). Worse, they took him into the family, snatched his food, defecated on his doorstep, and hooted dislike at him. They gave him two bad years.

It is a depressing book. If, as he suggests, there is only Ikness at the center of each of us, our sole hope for hanging on to the name of humanity will be in endlessly mending the structure of our society, and it is changing so quickly and completely that we may never find the threads in time. Meanwhile, left to ourselves alone, solitary, we will become the same joyless, zestless, untouching lone animals.

But this may be too narrow a view. For one thing, the Iks are extraordinary. They are absolutely astonishing, in fact. The anthropologist has never seen people like them anywhere, nor have I. You'd think, if they were simply examples of the common essence of mankind, they'd seem more recognizable. Instead, they are bizarre, anomalous. I have known my share of peculiar, difficult, nervous, grabby people, but I've never encountered any genuinely, consistently detestable human beings in all my life. The Iks sound more like abnormalities, maladies.

I cannot accept it. I do not believe that the Iks are representative of isolated, revealed man, unobscured by social habits. I believe their behavior is something extra, something laid on. This unremitting, compulsive repellence is a kind of complicated ritual. They must have learned to act this way; they copied it, somehow.

I have a theory, then. The Iks have gone crazy.

The solitary Ik, isolated in the ruins of an exploded culture, has built a new defense for himself. If you live in an unworkable society you can make up one of your own, and this is what the Iks have done. Each Ik has become a group, a one-man tribe on its own, a constituency.

Now everything falls into place. This is why they do seem, after all, vaguely familiar to all of us. We've seen them before. This is precisely the way groups of one size or another, ranging from committees to nations, behave. It is, of course, this aspect of humanity that has lagged behind the rest of evolution, and this is why the Ik seems so primitive. In his absolute selfishness, his incapacity to give anything away, no matter what, he is a successful committee. When he stands at the door of his hut, shouting insults at his neighbors in a loud harangue, he is city addressing another city.

Cities have all the Ik characteristics. They defecate on doorsteps, in rivers and lakes, their own or anyone else's. They leave rubbish. They detest all neighboring cities, give nothing away. They even build institutions for deserting elders out of sight.

Nations are the most Iklike of all. No wonder the Iks seem familiar. For total greed, rapacity, heartlessness, and irresponsibility there is nothing to match a nation. Nations, by law, are solitary, self-centered, withdrawn into themselves. There is no such thing as affection between nations, and certainly no nation ever loved another. They bawl insults from their doorsteps, defecate into whole oceans, snatch all the food, survive by detestation, take joy in the bad luck of others, celebrate the death of others, live for the death of others.

That's it, and I shall stop worrying about the book. It does not signify that man is a sparse, inhuman thing at his center. He's all right. It only says what we've always known and never had enough time to worry about, that we haven't yet learned how to stay human when assembled in masses. The Ik, in his despair, is acting out this failure, and perhaps we should pay closer attention. Nations have themselves become too frightening to think about, but we might learn some things by watching these people.

[1973]

HOW I BEGAN WRITING ESSAYS* LEWIS THOMAS

IN 1970, a symposium on "Inflammation" was held at Brook Lodge, somewhere outside Kalamazoo, sponsored by the Upjohn Company, which maintains the place as a conference center for meetings of university scientists. My assignment was to provide something called the keynote address, to precede about forty other papers by researchers, from all over, who were working on the phenomenon of inflammation. Since I had no way of knowing in advance what the papers would be about, I was free to say whatever I liked about the matter. I knew that the general drift of the papers would concern biochemical details of the defensive machinery in living tissues: the ways in which signals are exchanged between leukocytes and other cells in the presence of foreign invaders, mediators governing expansion and constriction of small blood vessels to regulate the passage of blood cells and various soluble components across the walls of capillaries and small veins, the clumping and sticking of leukocytes and platelets inside the vessels, all culminating in the Galenic signs of *rubor* (redness), *calor* (heat), *tumor* (swelling), and *dolor* (pain), the classical inflammatory reaction. This complicated chain of linked events, leading to the destruction and ejection of foreign material lodged in living tissue, was the topic at hand.

This kind of conference tends to be rather heavy going, and my talk was designed to lighten the proceedings at the outset by presenting a rather skewed view of inflammation. I thought of it, and still do, as an example of largely self-induced disease rather than pure defense, with all sorts of mutually incompatible, combative mechanisms turned loose at once, frequently resulting in more damage to the host than to the invader, a biological accident analogous to a multicar accident involving fire engines, ambulances, police cars, and tow trucks all colliding on a bridge.

The whole conference was recorded on tape by the sponsors, and several months later I received in the mail a pamphlet-sized reproduction of my talk, accompanied by a note saying that it was being sent round to the other participants. A day or so later I had a telephone

*An excerpt from Chapter 22 of *The Youngest Science*.

call from Franz Ingelfinger, the editor of the *New England Journal of Medicine.*

Ingelfinger said he had read the piece and liked it, parts of it anyway, although he didn't agree with all of it, and he wanted me to try writing some essays for the *Journal* in the same general style. The terms were attractive enough: I would have to write one essay each month, due on Thursday of the third week, no longer than the space of one *Journal* page (around a thousand words), on any topic I liked. There would be no pay, but in return he would promise that nobody would be allowed to edit an essay. They would print them or not, but not change them.

I could not say no. Not because of the *Journal*'s prestige or the opportunity to publish any idea I liked, but because I had been conditioned, long ago, to doing whatever Ingelfinger told me to do. Partly, this was a behaviorist reflex established by the contingencies of the Boston City Hospital internship. I had come to the service as the pup when Ingelfinger, who had graduated from Harvard a year earlier, was the Senior, nine months ahead of me and, therefore, my boss. Our relationship began, and continued, with him giving the orders and me carrying them out. But there was more to it. Going through the City Hospital internship in those days was something like combat on a disordered battlefield, and we became close friends. Ingelfinger was, among other things, a born teacher, and he set about teaching me everything he knew, from the moment I turned up on his ward in my new white suit. There were a great many small skills to be learned—how to put together a makeshift oxygen tent when the proper parts were missing, how to bring a new oxygen tank to a patient's bedside from the outer corridor where the things were stored (they were much too heavy to carry, and what you did was to tilt them over at exactly the right angle and then run down the ward behind them, sliding them along the waxed floor), how to wash out the stomach of someone in a coma, how to get a needle into an invisible vein, and so forth. Evenings we would sit around his room or mine, waiting for calls from the emergency room, playing records. Ingelfinger knew more about Mozart than I did, and couldn't stop teaching even then: he loved to put a record on, play it for a second or so, then lift the needle and challenge me to identify the phrase and its location. I was on duty Christmas Eve in 1937, and Ingelfinger was off, due in

the next morning at seven. It was a quiet night on the wards. I tacked
a note on his door to greet him, a Christmas card:

> Of Christmas joy I am the bringer.
> I bring good news to Ingelfinger.
> Though many turned in bed and cried,
> Nobody died, nobody died.

We had eighteen months together, and I came away with a deep
respect for his mind and character. After the internship, he went to
Philadelphia, I to New York, and in the years that followed we met
each other infrequently, once or twice a year, usually at the May
meetings of the Society for Clinical Investigation in Atlantic City.
Whenever we did meet we settled down to continue last year's conversation wherever we'd left off.

So, I told Ingelfinger I'd be glad to try writing the column for his
Journal, and began.

I had not written anything for fun since medical school and a couple
of years thereafter, except for occasional light verse and once in a
while a serious but not very clear or very good poem. Good bad verse
was what I was pretty good at. The only other writing I'd done was
scientific papers, around two hundred of them, composed in the re-
lentlessly flat style required for absolute unambiguity in every word,
hideous language as I read it today. The chance to break free of that
kind of prose, and to try the essay form, raised my spirits, but at the
same time worried me. I tried outlining some ideas for essays, making
lists of items I'd like to cover in each piece, organizing my thoughts
in orderly sequences, and wrote several dreadful essays which I could
not bring myself to reread, and decided to give up being orderly. I
changed the method to no method at all, picked out some suitable
times late at night, usually on the weekend two days after I'd already
passed the deadline, and wrote without outline or planning in advance, as fast as I could. This worked better, or at least was more fun,
and I was able to get started. I finished an essay called "The Lives of
a Cell," then one about the precautions against moon germs at the
time of the first moon landing, then several about the phenomenon
of symbiosis, and after six months I'd had six essays published and
thought that was enough. I wrote a letter to Ingelfinger, suggesting
that now it was probably time to stop—six essays seemed more of a

series than I'd planned, and perhaps the *Journal* would do well to drop the venture and start something new with someone else doing the writing. I got a letter back saying no, I had to keep it up, they were getting letters from readers expressing interest, and in case I had any doubts myself, I should know that even Lowell had telephoned Ingelfinger and said that the Thomas essays were not bad. Lowell was Dr. Francis Cabot Lowell, an intellectually austere Boston classmate of Ingelfinger's and a severe critic. If Lowell approved of the pieces I should surely keep them going.

After a while it became a kind of habit, and I continued writing with fair regularity for something over four years. One day I had a letter from Windsor, Canada, from Joyce Carol Oates, whom I had never met, telling me that a physician had shown her reprints of some of the essays; she advised me to think about collecting them for a book. I had received quite a lot of interesting mail about the essays, mostly from doctors and medical students, but the Oates letter was, and remains, the nicest letter in my files. I didn't see how the pieces could ever be made into a book, since they seemed to me quite unconnected with each other, but I was encouraged by her approval. A bit later, in 1973, I had notes from several publishing houses inquiring about the possibility of a book, but also letting me know that if I was interested in trying I would have to do a lot of rewriting and insert some new essays—"connecting pieces," they were called—in order for the thing to make sense. I was preoccupied in the dean's office at Yale, and wrote back that I couldn't manage the work. Then Elisabeth Sifton, an editor at The Viking Press, telephoned one morning to say that she would like to publish the essays as they were, no patching or connecting for me to do, and I said yes over the phone. They came out in 1974, titled for the first essay, *The Lives of a Cell.* It was the easiest of books to write, and I was surprised that it did well in the marketplace, especially pleased that its most active market was in university and medical school bookstores, which was what I'd hoped for. Having caught the habit, I kept on writing short essays, some for the *New England Journal,* some unpublished, and four years later there were enough for a second book, *The Medusa and the Snail.*

[1983]

PAUL FUSSELL

BORN IN PASADENA, CALIFORNIA, in 1924, Paul Fussell was raised, he says, "an upper-middle-class young gentleman." But combat duty in World War II changed all that: "I entered the war when I was nineteen, and I have been in it ever since. Melville's Ishmael says that a whale-ship was his Yale College and his Harvard. An infantry division was mine. . . ." Waking up one morning in a field covered with the bodies of German soldiers, Fussell says, "I suddenly knew I was not and never would be in a world that was reasonable or just." Henceforth he would view life with the detachment, irony, and occasional anger of a satirist.

Returning from the war, Fussell graduated from Pomona College in 1947 and—despite the whale-ship analogy—did indeed go to Harvard (M.A., 1949; Ph.D., 1952), where he studied eighteenth-century English literature. "The eighteenth century taught me how to appreciate satire, and the twentieth century taught me to perceive that it is worthy of satire." After a brief stint as an instructor at Connecticut College, Fussell joined the English department at Rutgers University in 1955. He taught at Rutgers for nearly thirty years, until he moved to the University of Pennsylvania in 1983, and that is where he still teaches.

During the 1960s Fussell wrote three outstanding scholarly books: *The Rhetorical World of Augustan Humanism: Ethics and Imagery from Swift to Burke* (1965); *Poetic Meter and Poetic Form* (1965); and *Samuel Johnson and the Life of Writing* (1971). But it wasn't until, he says, he got tired of writing what he was "supposed to write" and finally wrote about a subject he was deeply and emotionally interested in that Fussell discovered, in a sense, his true métier. *The Great War and Modern Memory* (1975), a brilliant analysis of the mythology of World War I as revealed in the literature it produced, derived much of its strength from Fussell's own traumatic experiences in World War II. Awarded both a National Book Award and the National Book Critics Circle Award for 1976, *The Great War and Modern Memory* has had a major influence on literary scholarship during the past decade, suggesting new insights into the interaction among reality, myth, and literature.

Encouraged by the success of *The Great War and Modern Mem-*

ory, Fussell has been writing essays on social, literary, and political subjects for such periodicals as *Harper's, Encounter,* and *The New Republic* ever since. In 1980 he published *Abroad: British Literary Traveling Between the Wars,* an analysis of the significance of travel after the "Great War" and some of the major British travel writers of the period. In 1982 Fussell published a collection of essays, *The Boy Scout Handbook and Other Observations;* the following year he produced an amusing satire of the American class system, *Class: A Guide Through the American Status System.* In 1990 Fussell published *Wartime: Understanding and Behavior in the Second World War.*

Aside from the great eighteenth-century satirists—Swift, Pope, and Johnson—the writer to whom Fussell attributes the greatest personal influence is Orwell:

> The motives Orwell talks about in his essay "Why I Write" overlap mine a lot. He says that he writes largely to correct what he sees as some public injustice or outrage or scandal. Writing is so hard, and I'm so lazy, I can't really motivate myself to move towards the typewriter unless I feel some strong impulse to right some wrong or to have my say about something that has annoyed me. . . . In *Abroad,* what annoyed me was the disappearance of real travel. In *The Great War and Modern Memory,* what annoyed me was people talking about body counts during the Vietnam War without any imagination of what that sort of thing meant. What I set out to chip away at in *Class* is the sort of middle-class American sense that you become a person by buying things, which is the basis of the whole country, after all, but which I find adolescent and stupid and backward and hopeless. Everything I've written, I think I've written because underneath I have sensed some annoyance at something and I've set out to try to oppose it.

As tough and committed as the foregoing statement is, Fussell is also an aristocrat, an epicure, and a sophisticate in the best sense of those terms, who can also say (as he does in the preface to *Abroad*) that he has

> dealt not just with books but with ships and trains, passport photographs and national borders and small French seaport towns, hotels and cafes and beach resorts, architecture ancient

and modern, food and drink, nude sunbathing, and sex, both procreative and recreational. I have dealt with icy trenches and sunny patios, West African and Brazilian chiggers, touts of all nations, suntan oil, oranges and palm trees, the symbolic status of weather, the psychology of the sense of place, the spatial dislocations characterizing "modern" writing, and the once indispensable vade mecums of Baedeker and Tauchnitz. . . . And I have not scrupled to include occasional personal reflections on travel, so that the book aspires at once to the condition of literary criticism, social and cultural history, and autobiography.

Paul Fussell became a teacher of literature, he says, because he hoped "that poetry and prose could save the world. . . ."—that world he had witnessed among the corpses of World War II. With such a goal, he must be as broad-ranging and inclusive as possible: "I am persuaded by the performance of George Orwell that literary, cultural, social, ethical, and political commentary can be virtually the same thing." It is a huge ambition—the ambition of civilization itself—and it makes reading Fussell stimulating indeed.

THE BOY SCOUT HANDBOOK

It's AMAZING how many interesting books humanistic criticism manages not to notice. Staring fixedly at its handful of teachable masterpieces, it seems content not to recognize that a vigorous literary-moral life constantly takes place just below (sometimes above) its vision. What a pity Lionel Trilling or Kenneth Burke never paused to examine the intersection of rhetoric and social motive among, say, the Knights of Columbus or the Elks. That these are their fellow citizens is less important than that the desires and rituals of these groups are desires and rituals, and thus of permanent social and psychological consequence. The culture of the Boy Scouts deserves this sort of look-in, especially since the right sort of people don't know much about it.

The right sort consists, of course, of liberal intellectuals. They have often gazed uneasily at the Boy Scout movement. After all, a general, the scourge of the Boers, invented it; Kipling admired it; the Hitler-jugend (and the Soviet Pioneers) aped it. If its insistence that there is a God has not sufficed to alienate the enlightened, its khaki uniforms, lanyards, salutes, badges, and flag-worship have seemed to argue incipient militarism, if not outright fascism. The movement has often seemed its own worst enemy. Its appropriation of Norman Rockwell as its official Apelles has not endeared it to those of exquisite taste. Nor has its cause been promoted by events like the TV appearance a couple of years ago of the Chief Pardoner, Gerald Ford, rigged out in scout neckerchief, assuring us from the teleprompter that a Scout is Reverent. Then there are the leers and giggles triggered by the very word "scoutmaster," which in knowing circles is alone sufficient to promise comic pederastic narrative. "*All* scoutmasters are homosexuals," asserted George Orwell, who also insisted that "*All* tobacconists are Fascists."

But anyone who imagines that the scouting movement is either sinister or stupid or funny should spend a few hours with the latest edition of *The Official Boy Scout Handbook* (1979). Social, cultural, and literary historians could attend to it profitably as well, for after *The Red Cross First Aid Manual, The World Almanac,* and the Gideon Bible, it is probably the best-known book in this country. Since the first edition in 1910, twenty-nine million copies have been read in bed by flashlight. The first printing of this ninth edition is 600,000. We needn't take too seriously the ascription of authorship to William ("Green Bar Bill") Hillcourt, depicted on the title page as an elderly gentleman bare-kneed in scout uniform and identified as Author, Naturalist, and World Scouter. He is clearly the Ann Page or Reddy Kilowatt of the movement, and although he's doubtless contributed to this handbook (by the same author is *Baden-Powell: The Two Lives of a Hero* [1965]), it bears all the marks of composition by committee, or "task force," as it's called here. But for all that, it's admirably written. And although a complex sentence is as rare as a reference to girls, the rhetoric of this new edition has made no compromise with what we are told is the new illiteracy of the young. The book assumes an audience prepared by a very good high-school education, undaunted by terms like *biosphere, ideology,* and *ecosystem.*

The pliability and adaptability of the scout movement explains its remarkable longevity, its capacity to flourish in a world dramatically different from its founder's. Like the Roman Catholic Church, the scout movement knows the difference between cosmetic and real change, and it happily embraces the one to avoid any truck with the other. Witness the new American flag patch, now worn at the top of the right sleeve. It betokens no access of jingoism or threat to a civilized internationalism. It simply conduces to dignity by imitating a similar affectation of police and fire departments in anarchic towns like New York City. The message of the flag patch is not "I am a fascist, straining to become old enough to purchase and wield guns." It is, rather, "I can be put to quasi-official use, and like a fireman or policeman I am trained in first aid and ready to help."

There are other innovations, none of them essential. The breeches of thirty years ago have yielded to trousers, although shorts are still in. The wide-brimmed army field hat of the First World War is a fixture still occasionally seen, but it is now augmented by headwear deriving from succeeding mass patriotic exercises: overseas caps and berets from World War II, and visor caps of the sort worn by General Westmoreland and sunbelt retirees. The scout handclasp has been

changed, perhaps because it was discovered in the context of the new
internationalism that the former one, in which the little finger was
separated from the other three on the right hand, transmitted inappropriate suggestions in the Third World. The handclasp is now the
normal civilian one, but given with the left hand. There's now much
less emphasis on knots than formerly; as if to signal this change, the
neckerchief is no longer religiously knotted at the tips. What used to
be known as artificial respiration ("Out goes the bad air, in comes the
good") has given way to "rescue breathing." The young are now being
familiarized with the metric system. Some bright empiric has discovered that a paste made of meat tenderizer is the best remedy for
painful insect stings. Constipation is not the bugbear it was a generation ago. And throughout there is a striking new lyricism. "Feel the
wind blowing through your hair," the scout is adjured, just as he is
exhorted to perceive that Being Prepared for life means learning "to
live happy" and—equally important—"to die happy." There's more
emphasis now on fun and less on duty; or rather, duty is validated
because, properly viewed, it is a pleasure. (If that sounds like advice
useful to grown-ups as well as to sprouts, you're beginning to get the
point.)

There are only two possible causes of complaint. The term "free
world" surfaces too often, although the phrase is mercifully uncapital-
ized. And the Deism is a bit insistent. The United States is defined as
a country "whose people believe in a supreme being." The words "In
God We Trust" on the coinage and currency are taken almost as a
constitutional injunction. The camper is told to carry along the
"Bible, Testament, or prayer book of your faith," even though, for
light backpacking, he is advised to leave behind air mattress, knife and
fork, and pancake turner. When the scout finds himself lost in the
woods, he is to "stay put and have faith that someone will find you."
In aid of this end, "Prayer will help." But the religiosity is so broad
that it's harmless. The words "your church" are followed always by
the phrase "or synagogue." The writers have done as well as they can
considering that they're saddled with the immutable twelve points of
Baden-Powell's Scout Law, stating unambiguously that "A Scout is
Reverent" and "faithful to his religious duties." But if "You have the
right to worship God in your own way," you must see to it that
"others retain their right to worship God in their way." Likewise, if

"you have the right to speak your mind without fear of prison or punishment," you must "ensure that right for others, even when you do not agree with them." If the book adheres to any politics, they can hardly be described as conservative; they are better described as slightly archaic liberal. It is broadly hinted that industrial corporations are prime threats to clean air and conservation. In every illustration depicting more than three boys, one is black. The section introducing the reader to some Great Americans pays respects not only to Franklin and Edison and John D. Rockefeller and Einstein; it also makes much of Walter Reuther and Samuel Gompers, as well as Harriet Tubman, Martin Luther King, and Whitney Young. There is a post-Watergate awareness that public officials must be watched closely. One's civic duties include the obligation to "keep up on what is going on around you" in order to "get involved" and "help change things that are not good."

Few books these days could be called compendia of good sense. This is one such, and its good sense is not merely about swimming safely and putting campfires "cold out." The good sense is psychological and ethical as well. Indeed, this handbook is among the very few remaining popular repositories of something like classical ethics, deriving from Aristotle and Cicero. Except for the handbook's adhesions to the motif of scenic beauty, it reads as if the Romantic movement had never taken place. The constant moral theme is the inestimable benefits of looking objectively outward and losing consciousness of self in the work to be done. To its young audience vulnerable to invitations to "trips" and trances and anxious self-absorption, the book calmly says: "Forget yourself." What a shame the psychobabblers of Marin County will never read it.

There is other invaluable advice, applicable to adults as well as to scouts. Some is practical, like "Never use flammable fluids to start a charcoal fire. They burn off fast, lighting only a little of the charcoal." Some is civic-moral: "Take a 2-hour walk where you live. Make a list of things that please you, another of things that should be improved." And then the kicker: "Set out to improve them." Some advice is even intellectual, and pleasantly uncompromising: "Reading trash all the time makes it impossible for anyone to be anything but a second-rate person." But the best advice is ethical: "Learn to think." "Gather knowledge." "Have initiative." "Respect the rights of others." Actually, there's hardly a better gauge for measuring the gross official misbehavior of the seventies than the ethics enshrined in this handbook. From its explicit ethics you can infer such propositions as "A scout does not tap his acquaintances' telephones," or "A scout does not bomb and invade a neutral country, and then lie about it," or "A scout does not prosecute war unless, as the Constitution provides, it has been declared by the Congress." Not to mention that because a scout is clean in thought, word, and deed, he does not, like Richard Nixon, designate his fellow citizens "shits" and then both record his filth and lie about the recordings ("A scout tells the truth").

Responding to Orwell's satiric analysis of "Boys' Weeklies" forty years ago, the boys' author Frank Richards, stigmatized by Orwell as a manufacturer of excessively optimistic and falsely wholesome stories, observed that "The writer for young people should . . . endeavor to give his young readers a sense of stability and solid security, because it is good for them, and makes for happiness and peace of mind." Even if it is true, as Orwell objects, that the happiness of youth is a cruel delusion, then, says Richards, "Let youth be happy, or as happy as possible. Happiness is the best preparation for misery, if misery must come. At least the poor kid will have had something." In the current world of Making It and Getting Away with It, there are not many books devoted to associating happiness with virtue. The shelves of the CIA and the State Department must be bare of them. "Horror swells around us like an oil spill," Terrence Des Pres said recently. "Not a day passes without more savagery and harm." He was commenting on Philip Hallie's *Lest Innocent Blood Be Shed,* an account of a whole French village's trustworthiness, loyalty, helpfulness, friendliness, courtesy, kindness, cheerfulness, and bravery in hiding scores of Jews during the Occupation. Des Pres concludes: "*Goodness.* When was the last time anyone used that word in earnest, without irony, as anything more than a doubtful cliché?" *The Official Boy Scout Handbook,* for all its focus on Axmanship, Backpacking, Cooking, First Aid, Flowers, Hiking, Map and Compass, Semaphore, Trees, and Weather, is another book about goodness. No home, and certainly no government office, should be without a copy. The generously low price of $3.50 is enticing, and so is the place on the back cover where you're invited to inscribe your name.

[1982]

APPEARANCE COUNTS

How is it that if you're sharp, you're generally able to estimate a person's class at a glance? What caste marks do you look for?

Good looks, first of all, distributed around the classes pretty freely, to be sure, but frequently a mark of high caste. Prudent natural selection is the reason, as Jilly Cooper perceives. She notes that if upper-class people marry downward, they tend to choose beauty only, and concludes: "In general, good-looking people marry up . . . and the insecure and ugly tend to marry down." Smiling is a class indicator— that is, not doing a lot of it. On the street, you'll notice that prole* women smile more, and smile wider, than those of the middle and upper classes. They like showing off their pretty dentures, for one thing, and for another, they're enmeshed in the "have a nice day" culture and are busy effusing a defensive optimism much of the time. And speaking of dentures, I witnessed recently an amazing perform-ance in which a prole man in a public place dropped his top plate into a position where he could thrust it forward with his tongue until, pink and yellow, it protruded an inch or so from his mouth. The intent seemed to be to "air" it. Now one simply can't imagine the middle or upper-middle classes doing that sort of thing, although you'd not be surprised to see an upper-class person, utterly careless of public opin-ion as he'd be, doing it.

Sheer height is a more trustworthy sign of class in England than everywhere, but classy people are seldom short and squat, even here. Regardless of one's height, having an ass that protrudes is low, as is having, or appearing to have, very little neck. The absence of neck is notable in Lawrence Welk, country-and-Western singers like Johnny Cash, and similar proles. If you're skeptical that looks give off class messages, in your imagination try conflating Roy Acuff with Averell Harriman, or Mayor Daley with George Bush. Or, for that matter, Minnie Pearl with Jackie Onassis.

Because 62 percent of Americans are overweight, a cheap way to

---

*In "Notes on Class" (1980) Fussell suggested that the traditional high, middle, and low classes be subdivided into nine; he positioned three levels of proletarians (hence, "prole") between the middle and lower classes.

achieve a sort of distinction is to be thin. This is the general aim of the top four classes, although the middle, because its work tends to be sedentary, has a terrible time abstaining from the potatoes. Destitutes and bottom-out-of-sights usually don't go around flaunting a lot of extra flesh, but seldom from choice. It's the three prole classes that get fat: fast foods and beer are two of the causes, but anxiety about slipping down a rung, resulting in nervous overeating, plays its part too, especially among high proles. Proles can rationalize their fat as an announcement of steady wages and the ability to eat out often: even "Going Out for Breakfast" is a thinkable operation for proles, if we believe they respond to the McDonald's TV ads the way they're conditioned to.

A recent magazine ad for a diet book aimed at proles stigmatizes a number of erroneous assumptions about weight, proclaiming with some inelegance that "They're All a Crock." Among vulgar errors thus rejected is the proposition that "All Social Classes Are Equally Overweight." The ad explains:

> Your weight is an advertisement of your social standing. A century ago, corpulence was a sign of success. But no more. Today it is the badge of the lower-middle class, where obesity is *four times* more prevalent than it is among the upper-middle and middle classes.

And not just four times more prevalent. Four times more visible, for flaunting obesity is a prole sign, as if the object were to offer maximum aesthetic offense to the higher classes and thus exact a form of revenge. Jonathan Raban, watching people at the Minnesota State Fair, was vouchsafed a spectacle suggesting calculated, vigorously intentional obesity:

> These farming families . . . were the descendants of hungry immigrants from Germany and Scandinavia. . . . Generation by generation, their families had eaten themselves into Americans. Now they all had the same figure: same broad bottom, same buddha belly, same neckless join between turkey-wattle chin and sperm-whale torso. The women had poured themselves into pink elasticized pantsuits; the men swelled against every seam and button of their plaid shirts and Dacron slacks.

And lest they not be sufficiently noticed, Raban reports, many of the men wore caps asking us to believe that, in opposition to the wisdom of the ages, "Happiness Is Being a Grandparent." Raban found himself so fascinated by U.S.A. fat that he proposes a Fatness Map, which would indicate that the fattest people live in areas where the immigration has been the most recent and "ancestral memories of hunger closest." On the other hand, "states . . . settled before 1776 would register least in the way of fatty tissue. Girth would generally increase from east to west and from south to north. The flab capital of the U.S.A. should be located somewhere in the triangle of Minnesota, Iowa, and the Dakotas."

We don't have to go all the way with Raban to perceive that there is an elite look in this country. It requires women to be thin, with a hairstyle dating back eighteen or twenty years or so. (The classiest women wear their hair for a lifetime in exactly the style they affected in college.) They wear superbly fitting dresses and expensive but always understated shoes and handbags, with very little jewelry. They wear scarves—these instantly betoken class, because they are useless except as a caste mark. Men should be thin. No jewelry at all. No cigarette case. Moderate-length hair, never dyed or tinted, which is a middle-class or high-prole sign, as the practice of President Reagan indicates. Never a hairpiece, a prole usage. (High and mid-proles call them *rugs, mats,* or *doilies.* Calling them *toops* is low-prole.) Both women's and men's elite looks are achieved by a process of rejection— of the current, the showy, the superfluous. Thus the rejection of fat by the elite. Michael Korda in his book *Success!* gets the point. "It pays," he finds, "to be thin."

But the elite rejection of the superfluous in no way implies a "minimal" look in clothes. Rather, "layering" is obligatory. As Alison Lurie says in *The Language of Clothes* (1981), "It has generally been true that the more clothes someone has on, the higher his or her status." And she goes on: "The recent fashion for 'layered' clothes may be related, as is sometimes claimed, to the energy shortage; it is also a fine way of displaying a large wardrobe."

The upper-middle-class woman will appear almost invariably in a skirt of gray flannel, Stuart plaid, or khaki; a navy-blue cardigan, which may be cable-stitched; a white blouse with Peter Pan collar; hose with flat shoes; hair preferably in a barrette. When it gets cold, she puts on a blue blazer, or, for business, a gray flannel suit. But the color toward which everything aspires is really navy. There will be lots of layering and a tendency to understate. The indispensable accessory will be a glasses case decorated with homemade needlepoint (an important caste mark: the needlepoint suggests hours of aimless leisure during which someone has worked on it—unthinkable for proles). If a woman does a lot of knitting for family and friends, chances are she's upper-middle-class. But if when she finishes a sweater she sews in a little label reading

> Handmade by Gertrude Willis

she's middle-class. If the label reads

> Hand-crafted by Gertrude Willis

she's high-prole.

If navy is the upper-middle-class color, purple is the prole equivalent, and it is scourged frequently by Barbara Blaes, wardrobe adviser to the Departments of Labor and Commerce as well as the CIA and the Food and Drug Administration. She gets $400 a day for rooting out prole garments from among women working in government departments. What she wants women to look like, as much as possible, is female men, in navy or gray tailored suits. Not, not assuredly, the pantsuit, especially not in purple, and especially not in purple polyester. That is the absolute bottom, the classic prole costume. It's right down there with another favorite prole getup, this one favored by the slender the way the pantsuit is by the obese. I refer to designer jeans worn with very high heels. This is a common outfit among newcomers to the suburbs who've not yet mastered the pseudo-prep, upper-middle look.

The purple polyester pantsuit offends two principles that determine class in clothes: the color principle and the organic-materials principle. Navy blue aside, colors are classier the more pastel or faded, and materials are classier the more they consist of anything that was once alive. That means wool, leather, silk, cotton, and fur. Only. All synthetic fibers are prole, partly because they're cheaper than natural ones, partly because they're not archaic, and partly because they're

entirely uniform and hence boring—you'll never find a bit of straw or
sheep excrement woven into an acrylic sweater. Veblen got the point
in 1899, speaking of mass-produced goods in general: "Machine-made
goods of daily use are often admired and preferred precisely on account of their excessive perfection by the vulgar and the underbred,
who have not given due thought to the punctilios of elegant consumption." (The organic principle also determines that in kitchens wood
is classier than Formica, and on the kitchen table a cotton cloth
"higher" than plastic or oilcloth.) So important for genuine upper-
middle-class standing is the total renunciation of artificial fibers that
the elite eye becomes skilled in detecting even, as *The Official Preppy
Handbook* has it, "a small percentage of polyester in an Oxford-cloth
shirt"—a sad middle-caste mark. The same invaluable book praises
young Caroline Kennedy unreservedly—"on technical points Prep-
pier than Mummy"—because "during four years at Harvard Square,
an unnatural fiber never went near her body." It somehow seems very
American and very late-twentieth-century—that is, very prole—that
we are now invited to buy bath towels, whose only office is to absorb
moisture, with their cotton, the sole absorbing fiber they contain,
carefully diluted by 12 percent Dacron polyester, to keep them from
absorbing so well.

But no one talks that way without risking rebuke from Mr. Fisher
A. Rhymes, Director of Public Affairs of the Man-Made Fiber Pro-
ducers Association, with headquarters in Washington, where it's in a
position to persuade the Army and Navy to introduce the maximum
number of man-made fibers not just into their towels but into their
mops and sponges as well. Mr. Rhymes stands ready at all times to
rebut calumnies, as he does in a recent letter to the *New York Times*
defending polyester against a fashion writer's strictures. "Polyester,"
he says, "in its many luxurious forms, is the most widely used fashion
fiber today." (Just what's wrong with it, of course, from the class point
of view.)

If you can gauge people's proximity to prole status by the color and
polyester content of their garments, legibility of their dress is another
sign. "Legible clothing" is Alison Lurie's useful term to designate
things like T-shirts or caps with messages on them you're supposed to
read and admire. The messages may be simple, like BUDWEISER or
HEINEKEN'S, or they may be complex and often lewd, like the one on

the girl's T-shirt: THE BEST PART IS INSIDE. When proles assemble to enjoy leisure, they seldom appear in clothing without words on it. As you move up the classes and the understatement principle begins to operate, the words gradually disappear, to be replaced, in the middle and upper-middle classes, by mere emblems, like the Lacoste alligator. Once, ascending further, you've left all such trademarks behind, you may correctly infer that you are entering the purlieus of the upper class itself. The same reason a T-shirt reading COKE'S THE REAL THING is prole determines that the necktie reading COUNTESS MARA is vulgar and middle-class.

There are psychological reasons why proles feel a need to wear legible clothing, and they are more touching than ridiculous. By wearing a garment reading SPORTS ILLUSTRATED or GATORADE or LESTER LANIN, the prole associates himself with an enterprise the world judges successful, and thus, for the moment, he achieves some importance. This is the reason why, at the Indianapolis Motor Speedway each May, you can see grown men walking around proud to wear silly-looking caps so long as they say GOODYEAR or VALVOLINE. Brand names today possess a totemistic power to confer distinction on those who wear them. By donning legible clothing you fuse your private identity with external commercial success, redeeming your insignificance and becoming, for the moment, somebody. For $27 you can send in to a post-office box in Holiday, Florida, and get a nylon jacket in blue, white, and orange that says, on the front, UNION 76. There are sizes for kids and ladies too. Just the thing for the picnic. And this need is not the proles' alone. Witness the T-shirts and carryalls stamped with the logo of *The New York Review of Books,* which convey the point "I read hard books," or printed with portraits of Mozart and Haydn and Beethoven, which assure the world, "I am civilized." The gold-plated blazer buttons displaying university seals affected by the middle class likewise identify the wearer with impressive brand names like the University of Indiana and Louisiana State.

The wearing of clothes either excessively new or excessively neat and clean also suggests that your social circumstances are not entirely secure. The upper and upper-middle classes like to appear in old clothes, as if to advertise how much of conventional dignity they can afford to throw away, as the men of these classes do also when they abjure socks while wearing loafers. Douglas Sutherland, in *The En-*

glish Gentleman (1980), is sound on the old-clothes principle. "Gentlemen," he writes, "may wear their suits until they are threadbare but they do so with considerable panache and it is evident to the most uncritical eye that they have been built by a good tailor." On the other hand, the middle class and the proles make much of new clothes, of course with the highest possible polyester content. The question of the class meaning of cleanliness is a tricky one, not as easy, perhaps, as Alison Lurie thinks. She finds cleanliness "a sign of status, since to be clean and neat always involves the expense of time and money." But laboring to present yourself scrupulously clean and neat suggests that you're worried about status slippage and that you care terribly what your audience thinks, both low signs. The perfect shirt collar, the too neatly tied necktie knot, the anxious overattention to dry cleaning—all betray the wimp. Or the nasty-nice. The deployment of the male bowtie is an illustration. If neatly tied, centered, and balanced, the effect is middle-class. When tied askew, as if carelessly or incompetently, the effect is upper-middle or even, if sufficiently inept, upper. The worst thing is being neat when, socially, you're supposed to be sloppy, or clean when you're supposed to be filthy. There's an analogy here with the excessively washed and polished automobile, almost infallibly a sign of prole ownership. Class people can afford to drive dirty cars. Just as, walking on the street, they're more likely to carry their business papers in tatty expanding files made of reddish-brown fiber, now fuzzy and sweat-stained, rather than in neat-looking attaché cases displaying lots of leather and brass, items that are a sad stigma of the middle class.

This principle of not-too-neat is crucial in men's clothing. Too careful means low—at least middle-class, perhaps prole. "Dear boy, you're almost too well dressed to be a gentleman," Neil Mackwood, author of *Debrett's In and Out* (1980), imagines an upper-class person addressing someone in the middle class, as if the speaker were implying that the addressee is not a gent but a model, a floorwalker, or an actor. "A now famous Hollywood actor," Vance Packard reports, "still reveals his lower . . . origins every time he sits down. He pulls up his trousers to preserve the crease." And King George IV is said to have observed of Robert Peel: "He's not a gentleman: he divides his coat-tails when he sits down."

The difference between high- versus low-caste effects in men's clothes is partly the result of the upper orders' being used to wearing suits, or at least jackets. As Lurie perceives, the suit "not only flatters the inactive, it deforms the laborious." (And the athletic or strenuously muscular: Arnold Schwarzenegger looks especially comic in a suit.) For this reason the suit—preferably the "dark suit"—was a prime weapon in the nineteenth-century war of the bourgeoisie against the proletariat. "The triumph of the . . . suit," says Lurie, "meant that the blue-collar man in his best clothes was at his worst in any formal confrontation with his 'betters.' " We can think of blacksmith Joe Gargary in Dickens's *Great Expectations,* dressed miserably to the nines for an appearance in the city, being patronized by the comfortably dressed Pip.

"This strategic disadvantage," Lurie goes on, "can still be seen in operation at local union-management confrontations, in the offices of banks and loan companies, and whenever a working-class man visits a government bureau." That's an illustration of John T. Molloy's general principle of the way men use clothing to convey class signals. When two men meet, he perceives, "One man's clothing is saying to the other man, 'I am more important than you are, please show respect'; or, 'I am your equal and expect to be treated as such'; or, 'I am not your equal and do not expect to be treated as such.' " For this reason, Molloy indicates, proles who want to rise must be extremely careful to affect "Northeastern establishment attire," which will mean that Brooks Brothers and J. Press will be their guides: "Business suits should be plain; no fancy or extra buttons; no weird color stitching; no flaps on the breast pocket; no patches on the sleeves; no belts in the back of the jacket; no leather ornamentation; no cowboy yokes. Never."

It's largely a matter of habit and practice, says C. Wright Mills in *The Power Elite* (1956): no matter where you live, he insists, "anyone with the money and the inclination can learn to be uncomfortable in anything but a Brooks Brothers suit." And, I would add, can learn to recoil from clothes with a glossy (middle-class) as opposed to a matte (upper-middle-class) finish. Middle-class clothes tend to err by excessive smoothness, to glitter a bit, to shine even before they're worn. Upper-middle clothes, on the other hand, lean to the soft, textured, woolly, nubby. Ultimately, the difference implies a difference between *city* and *country,* or labor and leisure, where *country* betokens not

decrepit dairy farms and bad schools but estates and horse-leisure.
Thus the popularity among the upper-middle class (and the would-be
upper-middle class, like members of Ivy university faculties) of the
tweed jacket. Country leisure is what it implies, not daily wage slavery
in the city.

The tweed jacket is indispensable to the upper-middle-class trick of
layering. A man signals that he's classy if, outdoors, he comes on in
a tweed jacket, with vest or sweater (or two), shirt, tie, long wool
scarf, and overcoat or raincoat. An analogy is with the upper-class
house, which has lots of different rooms for different purposes. Wearing one shirt over another—Oxford-cloth button-down over a turtleneck, for example—is upper-middle-class, and the shirt worn
underneath can even be a dress shirt (solid color is best) with its own
collar, a usage I've seen in warm weather on Madison Avenue in the
upper eighties. Since sweaters are practically obligatory for layering,
it's important to know that the classiest is the Shetland crew-neck
pullover, and in "Scottish" colors—heather and the like, especially
when a tieless Oxford-cloth shirt (palpably without artificial fibers)
just peeps over the top. Add a costly tweed jacket without shoulder
padding and no one can tell you're not upper-middle at least. The
V-neck sweater, designed to prove conclusively that you're wearing a
necktie, is for that reason middle-class or even high prole. It's hard
to believe that sometimes people tuck pullovers into the top of their
trousers, but I'm told they do. If this does happen, it's a very low sign.

The interpreter of men's class appearances can hardly do better
than study the costumes of the Presidents as they come and go. The
general principle here is that the two-button suit is more prole than
the three-button Eastern-establishment model. Most Presidents have
worn the two-button kind before, and when they assume the leadership of the Free World, they feel obliged to change, now affecting
three-button suits and resembling the Chairman of the Board of the
Chase Manhattan Bank. This is what made Richard Nixon look so
awkward most of the time. He was really comfortable in the sort of
Klassy Kut two-button suit you might wear if you were head of the
Savings & Loan Association of Whittier, California. His successor,
Gerald Ford, although brought up on the hick two-button model,
managed to wear the three-button job with some plausibility, being
more pliable and perhaps a faster study than Nixon. But he never

really pulled off the con, in features resembling as he did Joe Palooka rather than any known type of American aristocrat. James Earl Carter knew himself well enough to realize that he should reject two- and three-button suits alike, sticking to blue jeans and thus escaping criticism as one who aspires to the Establishment but fails.

Ronald Reagan, of course, doesn't need to affect the establishment style, sensing accurately that his lowbrow, God-fearing, intellect-distrusting constituency regards it as an affront (which, of course, to them it is). Reagan's style can be designated Los Angeles (or even Orange) County Wasp-Chutzpah. It registers the sense that if you stubbornly believe you're as good as educated and civilized people— i.e., those Eastern dudes—then you are. He is the perfect representative of the mind and soul of the Sun Belt. He favors, of course, the two-button suit with maximum shoulder padding and with a Truman-esque squared white handkerchief in the breast pocket, which makes him look, when he's dressed way up, like a prole setting off for church. Sometimes, for leisure activities (as he might express it), he affects the cowboy look, which, especially when one is aged, appeals mightily to the Sun Belt seniles. One hesitates even to speculate about the polyester levels of his outfits.

Indeed, Reagan violates virtually every canon of upper-class or even upper-middle-class presentation. The dyed hair is, as we've seen, an outrage, as is the rouge on the cheeks. (Will the President soon proceed to eye shadow and liner?) So is the white broadcloth shirt with its omnipresent hint of collar stays. (Anxiety about neatness.) The suit materials are scandalously bucolic middle-class: plaid, but never Glen plaid. The necktie is tied with a full Windsor knot, the favorite of sophisticated high-school boys everywhere. When after a press conference Dan Rather, not everyone's idea of a Preppy, comes on to "summarize" and try to make sense of the President's vagaries, his light-blue Oxford-cloth button-down and "regimental" tie make him, by contrast, look upper-middle-class. The acute student of men's class signals could virtually infer Reagan's politics of Midwestern small-town meanness from his getups, just as one might deduce Roosevelt's politics of aristocratic magnanimity from such classy accessories as his naval cape, pince-nez, and cigarette holder.

It's not just Ronald Reagan who violates all canons of gentlemanly attire. It's the conspicuous members of his "team" as well, like Al

Haig. (Even though he's no longer Secretary of State, he wants so much to be President that he's appropriately dealt with here.) It's cruel, of course, to demand that a soldier know anything about taste on those occasions when he's obliged to disguise himself as an ordinary person. (Although there's always the example of General George C. Marshall, who, after a lifetime of appearing in uniform, managed in mufti to wear the three-button, three-piece suit as if to the classy manner born.) Al Haig's class stigma is the gaping jacket collar, always a prole giveaway. Here, the collar of the jacket separates itself from the collar of the shirt and backs off and up an inch or so: the effect is that of a man coming apart. That this caste mark is without specifically reactionary political meaning is confirmed by a photograph of Richard Hoggart, the British radical critic and Labour Party enthusiast, used to promote a recent book of his: his jacket collar is gaping a full inch at the rear, ample indication that jacket gape afflicts the far left as well as the far right. What it betrays, indeed, is less the zealot than the stooge. Like the poor chap interviewed on TV recently by William F. Buckley. He was from Texas and wanted to censor school textbooks to repress, among other evils, *pro-mís-kitty.* (As gently as possible, Buckley corrected this mispronunciation of *promiscuity* so that the audience would know what the poor ass was talking about.) But even if the Texan had not, with complete confidence in his unaided powers, delivered repeatedly this prole mispronunciation, his perceptiveness and sensibility could have been inferred from the way his jacket collar gaped open *a full two inches.* Buckley's collar, of course, clung tightly to his neck and shoulders, turn and bow and bob as he might. And here I will reject all accusations that I am favoring the rich over the poor. The distinction I'm pointing to is not one between the tailored clothes of the fortunate and the store clothes of the others, for if you try you can get a perfectly fitting suit collar off the rack, or at least have it altered to fit snugly. The difference is in recognizing this as a class signal and not being aware of it as such. You've got to know that, as Douglas Sutherland says in *The English Gentleman,* almost the most important criterion in a suit worth wearing at all is "that it should fit well round the shoulders."

In addition to the gaping "Haig" or "stooge" jacket collar, there are two other low signals, visible usually when the subject is unjacketed, which instantly proclaim the wearer either middle-class or high-prole. They are, first, the nerd pack, and second, belt hangdowns of any kind. The nerd pack is that little plastic envelope, often with advertising on the outer flap, worn in the breast pocket of a shirt to prevent pens and pencils from soiling the acrylic. In the nerd-pack trade, it is called a "Pocket Protector." One mail-order catalog aimed at high proles assures you that your nerd pack can be personalized with a three-letter monogram. Nerd packs are favored by people obliged to simulate efficiency, like supermarket managers, or by people hoping to give the impression that their need to pull out a pen is virtually constant, like itinerant insurance salesmen.

Belt hangdowns, usually of real or fake leather, are another all but infallible signal of middle-classness or even outright prolehood. These vary from slide-rule cases, at the top, all the way down to dark-glasses cases, cigarette-pack holders "with Western hand-tooling," and—in a catalog—an "Eyeglass and Pen Holster: Deluxe Cowhide, Personalized with Your Initials." The term *holster* suggests the would-be macho implications of all these belt attachments. The fact that these hangdowns are usually high-prole indicates the social class of the low homosexuals who advertise their "sexual preferences" by wearing key rings on their belts, dangling from left or right, front or rear, as the case may be. One reason we may feel it difficult for an engineer ever to be upper-middle-class is that even in college he's begun this habitual daily wearing of belt hangdowns—if not slide rules or calculators, then low tools like geology picks and the like.

Imagine a man dressed in the summer costume appropriate for his work. He's wearing a short-sleeved white shirt (Dacron, largely), a necktie, dark trousers, and a nerd pack. He's a middle-class or high-prole clerk in a hardware store. Now notice: all you have to do to turn him into an "engineer" is to add one or more belt hangdowns and pop a white hardhat onto his head. Thus the social-class problems of engineers, uncertain always where they fit, whether with boss or worker, management or labor, the world of headwork or the world of handwork. And actually, anything attached to the belt, even if it doesn't ignominiously hang down, is a high-prole sign. Sunglasses, for example, in an artificial leather case. Rather than sport them on your belt, it's better even to let them dangle by the sidepiece from the top buttonhole of your shirt—a middle-class but at least not a prole habit.

If nerd packs and belt hangdowns instantly imply prole leanings, there are other signs almost as clear. When you're wearing a shirt with a sweater or jacket over it but omitting a necktie, what do you do with the shirt collar? Keeping all of it inside both sweater and jacket is upper- or upper-middle-class, partly, I suppose, because the effect is "careless" rather than "neat." On the other hand, displaying it spread out over the jacket collar, unless you're a member of the Israeli Knesset or teach at the Hebrew University, is flagrantly middle-class or prole—and may be even then. All you really have to know about this practice is that when out riding or otherwise got up in sports costume, the President favors it.

Shirts, indeed, are among the most class-eloquent garments, and there are countless ways you can lose caste through their agency. Wearing "white on white" is an easy way to drop to middle or high prole, while wearing a vest over a short-sleeved shirt or—like Ed Norton, in *The Honeymooners*—over a T-shirt will sink you to mid- or low prole. Sometimes one sees suspenders worn over a T-shirt, the equivalent of socks worn with sandals. In England especially, but also in Anglophile parts of the United States, these usages suggest that you're a middle-class secondary-school teacher of math or chemistry who, by appearing in his holiday garb, is secretly lusting for demotion to high prole.

Jewelry is another instant class-lowerer, like the enameled little Old Glory lapel pins worn by the insane and by cynical politicians working backward districts. When their ladies wear them with the colors picked out in rhinestones, the effect is even lower—deep-prole, shall we say. The general class rule about wristwatches is, the more "scientific," technological, and space-age, the lower. Likewise with the more "information" the watch is supposed to convey, like the time of day in Kuala Lumpur, the number of days elapsed in the year so far, or the current sign of the zodiac. Some upper-class devotees of the Cartier tank watch with the black lizard strap will argue that even a second hand compromises a watch's class, implying as it may the wearer's need for great accuracy, as if he were something like a professional timer of bus arrivals and departures. The other upper-class watch is the cheapest and simplest Timex, worn with a grosgrain-ribbon strap, changed often: black ones for formal wear are amusing. One prole mistake is to conceive cuff links classy, especially ones like

those in the wardrobe of Kurt Vonnegut's Billy Pilgrim, the optome-
trist hero of *Slaughterhouse-Five:* simulated Roman coins, quite large;
little roulette wheels that actually turn; and "another pair which had
a real thermometer in one and a real compass in the other." These
come close to the cuff links made of the "finest specimens of human
molars" which Meyer Wolfsheim in *The Great Gatsby* is proud to call
attention to.

Another significant social-class divide is the color of the raincoat.
After extensive and really quite impressive research, John T. Molloy
has discovered that in raincoat colors beige far outranks black, olive,
or dark blue. The black raincoat proves to be, indeed, a highly trustworthy prole sign. Thus Molloy exhorts his prole readers ambitious to
acquire an upper-middle-class look to equip themselves with beige
raincoats as soon as possible. The implication of beige, one supposes,
is that it advertises one's greater carelessness about the risk of stains:
there's a go-to-hell air about it that doesn't attend the prudent black
number. You will not be at all surprised now to hear that in *I Love
Lucy* the raincoat worn by Ricky Ricardo is black.

Go-to-hell in spirit also are the sports or playtime trousers which
identify the upper-middle class, especially the suburban branch. One
common type is white duck trousers with little green frogs embroidered all over them. A variation: light-green trousers, with dark-blue
embroidered whales. Or signal flags. Or bell buoys. Or lobsters. Or
anything genteel-marine, suggesting that the wearer has just strolled
a few steps away from his good-sized yacht. Thus also the class usefulness of Topsider shoes, the ones with the white soles "for gripping wet
decks." The same with windbreakers displaying lots of drawstrings.
The Chris-Craft mail-order catalog will show you the look to imitate,
but classes much below the upper middle should take warning that
they're unlikely to affect this yachtsman's look with much plausibility. A lot depends on a certain habitual carelessness in the carriage,
a quasi-windblown calculated sloppiness. It's almost impossible to
imitate, and you should have a long thin neck, too.

The topic of the class implications of men's neckties deserves a book
in itself. Here I can only sketch a few general principles. Skimpy as
its contribution of fabric to the total ensemble may be, the tie does
add to the effect of layering and for this reason if for no other is
identified with high status. But it must be said too that in the right

context omitting the tie entirely conveys the message that one is so classy—say, upper-class—as to be above all criticism, and that conventional canons of respectability don't apply. The necktie's association with responsibility, good employeeship, and other presumed attributes of the obedient middle class is well documented by an experiment conducted by Molloy. He had a series of men interviewed for good jobs. Some wore ties, others did not. "Invariably," he found,

> those men who wore their ties to interviews were offered jobs; those without them were turned down. And in one almost incredible situation, the interviewer . . . was made so uncomfortable by the applicant's lack of a tie that he gave the man $6.50, told him to go out and buy a tie, put it on, and then come back to complete the interview. He still didn't get the job.

The same suggestion that the necktie is an important marker of the division between the middle and the prole classes emerges from another of Molloy's experiments, this one performed at the horrible Port Authority Bus Terminal in New York, a traditional locus of every imaginable vice, menace, and outrage. He himself posed as a middle-class man who had left his wallet home and had somehow to get back to the suburbs. At the rush hour, he tried to borrow 75 cents for his bus fare, the first hour wearing a suit but no tie, the second hour properly dressed, tie and all. "In the first hour," he reports, "I made $7.23, but in the second, with my tie on, I made $26, and one man even gave me extra money for a newspaper."

The principle that clothing moves lower in status the more legible it becomes applies to neckties with a vengeance. The ties worn by the top classes eschew the more obvious forms of verbal or even too crudely symbolic statement, relying on stripes, amoeba-like foulard blobs, or small dots to make the point that the wearer possesses too much class to care to specify right out in front what it's based on. (This illustrates the privacy principle, or the principle of mind-your-own-little-disgusting-middle-class-business, a customary element of the aristocratic stance.) Small white dots against a dark background, perhaps the most conservative tie possible, are favored both by uppers and upper-middles and, defensively, by those nervous about being thought low, coarse, drunken, or cynical, like journalists and TV news readers and sportscasters, and by those whose fiduciary honor must be thought beyond question, like the trust officers working for the better metropolitan banks.

Moving down from stripes, blobs, or dots, we come to necktie patterns with a more overt and precise semiotic function. Some, designed to announce that the upper-middle-class wearer is a sport, will display diagonal patterns of little flying pheasants, or small yachts, signal flags, and sextants. ("I hunt and own a yacht. Me rich and sporty!") Just below these are the "milieu" patterns, designed to celebrate the profession of the wearer and to congratulate him on having so fine a profession. These are worn either by insecure members of the upper-middle class (like surgeons) or by members of the middle class aspiring to upper-middle status (like accountants). Thus a tie covered with tiny caduceuses proclaims "Hot damn! I am a physician." (Significantly, there is no milieu tie pattern for dentists.) Little scales signify "I am a lawyer." Musical notes: "I have something to do with music." Dollar signs, or money bags: a stockbroker, banker, perhaps a wildly successful plastic surgeon, or a lottery winner. I've even seen one tie with a pattern of little jeeps, whose meaning I've found baffling, for surely if you were a *driver* in any of our wars you'd not be likely to announce it. Other self-congratulatory patterns like little whales or dolphins or seals can suggest that you love nature and spend a lot of time protecting it and are thus a fine person. Any of these milieu ties can be alternated with the "silk rep" model striped with the presumed colors of British (never, *never* German, French, Italian, Spanish, Portuguese, or White Russian) regiments, clubs, or universities.

As we move further down the class hierarchy, actual words begin to appear on ties, and these are meant to be commented on by viewers. One such exhibitionist artifact is the Grandfather's Tie in dark blue with grandchildren's names hand-painted on it, diagonally, in white. Imagine the conversations that ensue when you wear it! Another kind reads "I'd rather be sailing," "skiing," etc., and these can also be effective underminers of privacy—"conversation-starters," and thus useful adjuncts to comfy middle-class status, in the tradition of expecting neighbors to drop in without warning.

Some ties down in this stratum affect great cleverness, reading "Thank God It's Friday" or "Oh Hell, It's Monday"; and a way to get a chuckle out of your audience and at the same time raise your class a bit is to have these sentiments abbreviated on your tie with yachting signal flags. At the bottom of the middle class, just before it turns to high prole, we encounter ties depicting large flowers in brilliant colors, or simply bright "artistic" splotches. The message is frequently "I'm a merry dog." These wearers are the ones Molloy is addressing when, discussing neckties, he warns, "Avoid purple under all circumstances."

Further down still, where questions of yacht ownership or merry doghood are too preposterous to be claimed even on a necktie, we come upon the high- or mid-prole "bola" tie, a woven or leather thong with a slide (often of turquoise or silver), affected largely by retired persons residing in Sun Belt places like New Mexico. Like any other sort of tie, this one makes a statement, saying: "Despite appearances, I'm really as good as you are, and my 'necktie,' though perhaps unconventional, is really better than your traditional tie, because it suggests the primitive and therefore the unpretentious, pure, and virtuous." Says the bola, "The person wearing me is a child of nature, even though actually eighty years old." Like many things bought by proles, these bola ties can be very expensive, especially when the slide is made of precious metal or displays "artwork." The point again is that money, although important, is not always the most important criterion of class. Below the bola wearers, at the very bottom, stand the low proles, the destitute, and the bottom-out-of-sight, who never wear a tie, or wear one—and one is all they own—so rarely that the day is memorable for that reason. Down here, the tie is an emblem of affectation and even effeminacy, and you can earn a reputation for being la-di-da by appearing in one, as if you thought yourself better than other people. One prole wife says of her spouse: "I'm going to bury my husband in his T-shirt if the undertaker will allow it."

Today, hats, because of their rarity, present an easier class problem than neckties. Since the felt fedora went out, upper-middle-class people can wear only the equivalent of parody hats—"Russian" fur, the L. L. Bean "Irish" tweed hat favored by Senator Pat Moynihan, or the floppy white fishing or tennis hat popular among the top classes despite its being favored by Franklin D. Roosevelt. Class accrues to hats now only as they declare themselves to be frivolous accessories. To take any hat seriously is to descend. Especially such novelty hats as the brown-or-black-dyed rabbit-fur fedoras affected in the early 1980s by the middle class in the Northeast and upper Midwest, who sought, at once, respectability and a touch of dash. Another hat that had considerable success with the same class was the dark-blue visored "Greek fisherman's cap" as merchandised through *The New Yorker.* When worn, this item was designed to state, "I've been to Greece and am thus well-to-do, rich enough to fly long distances on Olympic Airlines, as well as adventurous enough to relish exotic things like retsina, taramasalata, etc." But the problem with this headwear was its proletarian associations, which became even more egregious when it began appearing in versions made of black leather. Actually, only six things can be made of black leather without causing class damage to the owner: belts, shoes, handbags, gloves, camera cases, and dog leashes.

There once was a time, when Czar Nicholas and King George V wore yachting caps, when visors did not convey instant prole signals, as they do now, associated as they are not just with Greek fishermen but with workmen, soldiers, chauffeurs, policemen, railway personnel, and baseball players. Proles take to visor caps instinctively, which accounts for the vast popularity among them of what we must call simply the prole cap. This is the "baseball" cap made largely of plastic meshwork in primary colors (red, blue, yellow) with, in the rear, an open space crossed by a strap for self-adjustment: "One Size Fits All [Proles]." Regardless of the precise style of the prole cap, it seems crucial that it be ugly. It's the male equivalent of the purple acrylic slacks worn by the prole's wife, and like all items of clothing, it says something. It says to those whose expensive educations have persuaded them that the ideal of dignity is the Piazza San Marco or the Parthenon or that the ideal of the male head derives from Michelangelo's *David* or the Adam of the Sistine Chapel: "I'm as good as you are." The little strap at the rear is the significant prole feature because it demeans the buyer and user, making him do the work formerly thought the obligation of the seller, who used to have to stock numerous sizes. It's like such other prole features of the contemporary scene as the jet plane and the supermarket, where convenience for the seller is disguised by publicity and fraud to pass for convenience for the buyer. To achieve even greater ugliness, the prole will sometimes wear his cap back to front. This places the strap in full view transecting the wearer's forehead, as if pride in the one-size-fits-all gadget were motivating him to display the cap's "technology" and his own command of it. President Reagan wore a prole cap while in performance once atop a tractor in Peoria. It looked natural. And any lingering uncertainty about the class meaning of the prole cap can be resolved by a glance at the upper-middle-class L. L. Bean catalog, which, while offering all sorts of headgear, draws the line at the plastic prole cap, although it does go so far as to offer one in suede. Next to the T-shirt, the prole cap is probably the favorite place for the display of language, running all the way from rudenesses like UP YOURS to gentilities like CAROLINA TOOL AND ENGINEERING CO., BALDWIN FILTERS, or PARK'S SAUSAGES. Tom Carvel's prole ice-cream-franchise holders wear prole caps with CARVEL on the front.

One might think that with the prole cap one has reached the nadir in men's headgear. But no: there are one or two steps down even from it. One is the version of the prole cap into whose visor attached plastic sun-glass lenses fold up. And below even this stooge item is the Sun-brella Hat. This erects itself on little stilts from a headband and opens and closes like an umbrella. It is some twenty inches wide, and the gores between the ribs are usually red and white. It is thoroughly "modern," the sort of idea that would occur to someone only in the latter days of the twentieth century.

Which brings up the whole matter of archaism and top-class taste. We've already seen that organic materials like wool and wood outrank man-made, like nylon and Formica, and in that superiority lurks the principle of archaism as well, nylon and Formica being nothing if not up-to-date. There seems a general agreement, even if often unconscious, that archaism confers class. Thus the middle class's choice of "colonial" or "Cape Cod" houses. Thus one reason Britain and Europe still, to Americans, have class. Thus one reason why inheritance and "old money" are such important class principles. Thus the practice among top-out-of-sight and upper classes of costuming their servants in some archaic livery, even such survivals as the white apron on the maid or, on the butler, a striped vest. It's a way of implying that the money goes back a considerable time, and that one retains the preferences and habits one learned very long ago.

What Veblen specified as the leisure class's "veneration of the archaic" shows itself everywhere: in the popularity among the upper-middle class of attending opera and classical ballet; of sending its issue to single-sex prep schools, because more unregenerate and old-style than coed ones; of traveling to view antiquities in Europe and the Middle East; of studying the "humanities" instead of, say, electrical engineering, since the humanities involve the past and studying them usually results in elegiac emotions. Even the study of law has about it this attractive aura of archaism: there's all that dog Latin, and the "cases" must all be rooted in the past. Classy people never deal with the future. That's for vulgarians like traffic engineers, planners, and inventors. Speaking of the sophisticated TV viewer's love of old black-and-white films, British critic Peter Conrad comments, "Style for us is whatever's perished, outmoded, lost." Since the upper orders possess archaism as their very own class principle—even their devotion to old clothes signals their retrograde sentiment—what can the lower orders do but fly to the new, not just to sparkling new garments but to cameras and electronic apparatus and stereo sets and trick watches and electric kitchens and video games?

As Russell Lynes perceived in *The Tastemakers,* despite the façade of modernity a corporation erects to impress the proles, behind the scenes the upper business classes cleave to flagrantly archaic effects. "If you will visit Lever House in New York," he writes,

> the sheer glass box that sits handsomely on Park Avenue to house the offices of Lever Brothers, you will find that the higher the echelon the more old-fashioned the surroundings. The public front is one of daring modernity. The offices of the clerks and department managers are in the functional tradition. But when you reach the offices of top management you will find that there are open fireplaces and chandeliers with an Early American flavor.... If you will visit the executive dining room of the J. Walter Thompson Company ... you will find yourself in what appears to be a Cape Cod house furnished with Windsor chairs and rag rugs. It has wooden casement windows.

As all salesmen recognize, if you're selling something it's better for your social class to be selling something archaic—like real wine or unpasteurized cheese or bread without preservatives or Renaissance art objects or rare books. Selling something old, indeed, almost re-

deems the class shame of selling anything at all. Even trading in real
sponges is class-preferable to trading in artificial ones, a fact permit-
ting us to appreciate the way the organic and archaic finally fuse into
one classy thing.

  It is in part because Britain has seen better days that Anglophilia
is so indispensable an element in upper-class taste, in clothes, literature, allusion, manners, and ceremony. The current irony of the Anglophilic class motif will not escape us. In the nineteenth century,
with Britain commanding much of the world, it would seem natural
for snobs to ape British usages. Snobs still do, but not because Britain
is powerful but because Britain is feeble. To acquire and display
British goods shows how archaic you are, and so validates upper- and
upper-middle-class standing. Thus tartan skirts for women, Shetland
sweaters, Harris tweeds, Burberrys, "regimental" neckties. A general
American male assumption among classes above high prole is that to
be "well dressed" you should look as much as possible like a British
gentleman as depicted in movies about fifty years ago. One reason
riding lessons are vouchsafed the young of the top classes is that the
socially best outfits and accessories are imported from England. Top-
class food resembles British, being bland and mushy, with little taste
and no chances taken. The upper-middle-class Sunday dinner is often
indistinguishable from its British counterpart: roast, with potatoes
and two veg. Being the American ambassador to the Court of St.
James's is still felt to confer upper-class status, even if you're really
Walter Annenberg. It's not like being ambassador to Sri Lanka or
Venezuela.
  Deeply engraved on the American consciousness is the superstition,
abundantly visible in the Gothic flourishes of our university architec-
ture, that institutions of the higher learning are the more authentic
the more they allude to their two great British originals. Thus a low
mail-order degree mill in Glendale, California, searching for a name
for itself that will attract maximum prole bucks, comes up with—
Kensington University. But it's when you move north from the prole
and middle classes and approach the upper-middle that you begin to
get overpowering whiffs of Mother England, which smells like expensive old leather bindings, Jeyes's fluid, and tar soap. You realize that
in the upper-middle class are people who actually believe that Oxford
and Cambridge are better, rather than just older, than Harvard and

Yale—and the University of Michigan, for that matter. Examining the upper-middle class, you find people who, despite their normal proud resistance to advertising, believe that Schweppes club soda is better than White Rock. You meet people whose dinner tables ring not just with passing references to the royal family but with prolonged earnest dissertations about Charles and Lady Di and Margaret and Anne and Andrew and little Prince William.

And the appeal of Anglophilia to even the middle class should never be underestimated. I say this on the evidence of a correspondence I once had with a friend of mine, a "developer" or mass house contractor who built whole new towns at once. Having run out of names for his streets, he solicited my help. (I was living in Knightsbridge at the time.) He asked me to supply him with an alphabetical list of classy— that is, British—street names that would attract the eminently middle-class buyers of his houses. Knowing how important this was for the self-respect and even mental health of his clients, I sent him a list immediately, which started like this:

Albemarle
Berkeley
Cavendish
Devonshire
Exeter
Fanshawe, etc.

All he had to do was add such terminations as

Street
Court
Circle
Way
Lane (as in Park "Lane")
Grove

and his house-buyers would be spared the shame of living on McGillicutty Street or Bernstein Boulevard or Guappo Terrace. When I reached the end of the alphabet—passing through Landsdowne and Montpelier and Osborne and Priory—I couldn't resist "Windsor" for W, and today there's some poor puzzled fellow wondering why success is so slow in arriving, since for years he's been residing at 221 Windsor Close instead of living on West Broad Street. New terrible jumped-up places like Houston are quick to surround themselves with tract suburbs bearing the most egregious British names, like these (which actually are parts of Houston):

> Nottingham Oaks
> Afton Oaks
> Inverness Forest
> Sherwood Forest (!)
> Braes Manor
> Meredith Manor

There's even a Shamrock Manor, hardly Anglo and only very doubtfully classy, but Houston's so far from Boston that perhaps no one will catch on. It all reminds one a bit of poor Dr. Herman ("Hy") Tarnower, done to death by his upper-middle girlfriend, who hoped to disguise his vulgarity by strewing his waiting room with British periodicals.

The same sense that if it's British it must have class prompts those who change their names to opt for Anglophilic sounds. No one would change from Poshenitz to Gamberini, but all would change from Horowitz to Howe. And if you merchandise tasteless little blobs of dough, you can sell billions of them by calling them "English" muffins.

[1983]

MY WAR

I RECOGNIZE that . . . I have given the Second World War a bad press, rejecting all attempts to depict it as a sensible proceeding or to mitigate its cruelty and swinishness. I have rubbed the reader's nose in some very noisome materials—corpses, maddened dogs, deserters and looters, pain, Auschwitz, weeping, scandal, cowardice, mistakes and defeats, sadism, hangings, horrible wounds, fear and panic. When-

ever I deliver this unhappy view of the war, especially w
pass it through a protective screen of irony, I hear fr
readers. Speaking of my observations on the photograph
sailor on his ruined gunmount, for example, a woman fr
finds me "callous," and focusing on my remarks about the photograph
of the German soldiers engaged in hanging the partisan boy and girl,
she says,

> As the daughter of survivors of the Holocaust, it is beyond my compre-
> hension how Mr. Fussell can ramble on about the "respectability" and
> "normality" of the Germans . . . while a young girl hangs from a rope
> and a young boy, his hands bound behind his back, waits to be hanged.
> While this photograph should elicit pathos and anger at seeing young
> lives being so cruelly blotted out, Mr. Fussell is concerned about the
> "almost frivolous touch" of the "two colored decorative rope, sugges-
> tive of a bathrobe cord or gift tie."

In short, my approach has been "insensitive": I have demonstrated
an "overwhelming deficiency in human compassion." Another
reader, who I suspect has had as little empirical contact with the
actualities of war face-to-face as the correspondent from Brooklyn,
found the same essay "black and monstrous" and concluded that
the magazine publishing it "disgraced itself." It seems like the old
story of punishing the messenger for bringing bad news. But one has
always known that irony has a hard time of it in this country, especially irony reflecting some skepticism about the human instincts for
reason and virtue.

How did I pick up this dark, ironical, flip view of the war? Why do
I enjoy exhibiting it? The answer is that I contracted it in the infantry, and I suspect I embraced it with special vigor once I found how
it annoyed people who had not fought at close quarters in terrible
weather and shot people to death and been hit by a shell from a
German gun. My view of the war is a form of revenge. Indeed, the
careful reader will have discerned in all the essays in this book a
speaker who is really a pissed-off infantryman, disguised as a literary
and cultural commentator. He is embittered that the Air Corps had
beds to sleep in, that Patton's Third Army got all the credit, that
non-combatants of the Medical Administrative and Quartermaster

Corps wore the same battle-stars as he, that soon after the war the "enemy" he had labored to destroy had been re-armed by his own government and positioned to oppose one of his old Allies. "We broke our ass for nothin'," says Sergeant Croft in *The Naked and The Dead.* These are this speaker's residual complaints while he is affecting to be annoyed primarily by someone's bad writing or slipshod logic or lazy editing or pretentious ideas. As Louis Simpson says, "The war made me a foot-soldier for the rest of my life," and after any war foot-soldiers are touchy.

My war is virtually synonymous with my life. I entered the war when I was nineteen, and I have been in it ever since. Melville's Ishmael says that a whale-ship was his Yale College and his Harvard. An infantry division was mine, the 103rd, whose dispirited personnel wore a colorful green and yellow cactus on their left shoulders. These hillbillies and Okies, drop-outs and used-car salesmen and petty criminals were my teachers and friends.

How did an upper-middle-class young gentleman find himself in so unseemly a place? Why wasn't he in the Navy, at least, or in the OSS or Air Corps administration or editing the *Stars and Stripes* or being a general's aide? The answer is comic: at the age of twenty I found myself leading forty riflemen over the Vosges Mountains and watching them torn apart by German artillery and machine-guns because when I was sixteen, in junior college, I was fat and flabby, with feminine tits and a big behind. For years the thing I'd hated most about school was gym, for there I was obliged to strip and shower communally. Thus I chose to join the R.O.T.C. (infantry, as it happened) because that was a way to get out of gym, which meant you never had to take off your clothes and invite—indeed, compel—ridicule. You rationalized by noting that this was 1939 and that a little "military training" might not, in the long run, be wasted. Besides, if you worked up to be a cadet officer, you got to wear a Sam Browne belt, from which depended a nifty saber.

When I went on to college, it was natural to continue my technique for not exposing my naked person, and luckily my college had an infantry R.O.T.C. unit, where I was welcomed as something of an experienced hand. This was in 1941. When the war began for the United States, college students were solicited by various "programs" of the navy and marine corps and coast guard with plans for transforming them into officers. But people enrolled in the R.O.T.C. unit were felt to have committed themselves already. They had opted for the infantry, most of them all unaware, and that's where they were going to stay. Thus while shrewder friends were enrolling in Navy V-1 or signing up for the pacific exercises of the Naval Japanese Language Program or the Air Corps Meteorological Program, I signed up for the Infantry Enlisted Reserve Corps, an act guaranteeing me one extra semester in college before I was called. After basic training, advancement to officer training was promised, and that seemed a desirable thing, even if the crossed rifles on the collar did seem to betoken some hard physical exertion and discomfort—marching, sleeping outdoors, that sort of thing. But it would help "build you up," and besides officers, even in the Infantry, got to wear those wonderful pink trousers and receive constant salutes.

It was such imagery of future grandeur that in spring, 1943, sustained me through eighteen weeks of basic training in 100-degree heat at dreary Camp Roberts, California, where to toughen us, it was said, water was forbidden from 8:00 A.M. to 5:00 P.M. ("water discipline," this was called). Within a few weeks I'd lost all my flab and with it the whole ironic "reason" I found myself there at all. It was abundantly clear already that "infantry" had been a big mistake: it was not just stupid and boring and bloody, it was athletic, and thus not at all for me. But supported by vanity and pride I somehow managed to march thirty-five miles and tumble through the obstacle course, and a few months later I found myself at the Infantry School, Fort Benning, Georgia, where, training to become an officer, I went through virtually the same thing over again. As a Second Lieutenant of Infantry I "graduated" in the spring of 1944 and was assigned to the 103rd Division at Camp Howze, Texas, the local equivalent of Camp Roberts, only worse: Roberts had white-painted two-storey clapboard barracks, Howze one-storey tar-paper shacks. But the heat was the same, and the boredom, and the local whore-culture, and the hillbilly songs:

> Who's that gal with the red dress on?
> Some folks call her Dinah.
> She stole my heart away,
> Down in Carolina.

The 103rd Division had never been overseas, and all the time I was putting my rifle platoon through its futile exercises we were being prepared for the invasion of southern France, which followed the landings in Normandy. Of course we didn't know this, and assumed from the training ("water discipline" again) that we were destined for the South Pacific. There were some exercises involving towed gliders that seemed to portend nothing at all but self-immolation, we were so inept with these devices. In October, 1944, we were all conveyed by troop transports to Marseilles.

It was my first experience of abroad, and my life-long affair with France dates from the moment I first experienced such un-American phenomena as: formal manners and a respect for the language; a well-founded skepticism; the pollarded plane trees on the Av. R. Schuman; the red wine and real bread; the *pissoirs* in the streets; the international traffic signs and the visual public language hinting a special French understanding of things: *Hôtel de Ville, Defense d'afficher;* the smell of Turkish tobacco when one has been brought up on Virginia and Burley. An intimation of what we might be opposing was supplied by the aluminum Vichy coinage. On one side, a fasces and *Etat Français.* No more Republic. On the other, *Liberté, Egalité, Fraternité* replaced by *Travail* (as in *Arbeit Macht Frei*), *Famille,* and *Patrie* (as in *Vaterland*). But before we had time to contemplate all this, we were moving rapidly northeast. After a truck ride up the Rhone Valley, still pleasant with girls and flowers and wine, our civilized period came to an abrupt end. On the night of November 11 (nice irony there) we were introduced into the line at St. Dié, in Alsace.

We were in "combat." I find the word embarrassing, carrying as it does false chivalric overtones (as in "single combat"). But synonyms are worse: *fighting* is not accurate, because much of the time you are being shelled, which is not fighting but suffering; *battle* is too high and remote; *in action* is a euphemism suited more to dire telegrams than description. "Combat" will have to do, and my first hours of it I recall daily, even now. They fueled, and they still fuel, my view of things.

Everyone knows that a night relief is among the most difficult of infantry maneuvers. But we didn't know it, and in our innocence we expected it to go according to plan. We and the company we were replacing were cleverly and severely shelled: it was as if the Germans a few hundred feet away could see us in the dark and through the thick pine growth. When the shelling finally stopped, at about midnight, we realized that, although near the place we were supposed to be, until daylight we would remain hopelessly lost. The order came down to stop where we were, lie down among the trees, and get some sleep. We would finish the relief at first light. Scattered over several hundred yards, the two hundred and fifty of us in F Company lay down in a darkness so thick we could see nothing at all. Despite the . terror of our first shelling (and several people had been hit), we slept as soundly as babes. At dawn I awoke, and what I saw all around were numerous objects I'd miraculously not tripped over in the dark. These objects were dozens of dead German boys in greenish-gray uniforms, killed a day or two before by the company we were relieving. If darkness had hidden them from us, dawn disclosed them with open eyes and greenish-white faces like marble, still clutching their rifles and machine-pistols in their seventeen-year-old hands, fixed where they had fallen. (For the first time I understood the German phrase for the war-dead: *die Gefallenen*.) Michelangelo could have made something beautiful out of these forms, in the *Dying Gaul* tradition, and I was startled to find that in a way I couldn't understand, at first they struck me as beautiful. But after a moment, no feeling but shock and horror. My adolescent illusions, largely intact to that moment, fell away all at once, and I suddenly knew I was not and never would be in a world that was reasonable or just. The scene was less apocalyptic than shabbily ironic: it sorted so ill with modern popular assumptions about the idea of progress and attendant improvements in public health, social welfare, and social justice. To transform guiltless boys into cold marble after passing them through unbearable fear and humiliation and pain and contempt seemed to do them an interesting injustice. I decided to ponder these things. In 1917, shocked by the Battle of the Somme and recovering from neurasthenia, Wilfred Owen was reading a life of Tennyson. He wrote his mother: "Tennyson, it seems, was always a great child. So should I have been but for Beaumont Hamel." So should I have been but for St. Dié.

After that, one day was much like another: attack at dawn, run and fall and crawl and sweat and worry and shoot and be shot at and cower from mortar shells, always keeping up a jaunty carriage in front of one's platoon; and at night, "consolidate" the objective, usually another hill, sometimes a small town, and plan the attack for the next morning. Before we knew it we'd lost half the company, and we all realized then that for us there would be no way out until the war ended but sickness, wounds, or oblivion. And the war would end only as we pressed our painful daily advance. Getting it over was our sole motive. Yes, we knew about the Jews. But our skins seemed to us more valuable at the time.

The word for the German defense all along was clever, a word that never could have been applied to our procedures. It was my first experience, to be repeated many times in later years, of the cunning ways of Europe versus the blunter ways of the New World. Although manned largely by tired thirty-year-old veterans (but sharp enough to have got out of Normandy alive), old men, and crazy youths, the German infantry was officered superbly, and their defense, which we experienced for many months, was disciplined and orderly. My people would have run, or at least "snaked off." But the Germans didn't, until the very end. Their uniforms were a scandal—rags and beat-up boots and unauthorized articles—but somehow they held together. Nazis or not, they did themselves credit. Lacking our lavish means, they compensated by patience and shrewdness. Not until well after the war did I discover that many times when they unaccountably located us hidden in deep woods and shelled us accurately, they had done so by inferring electronically the precise positions of the radios over which we innocently conversed.

As the war went on, the destruction of people became its sole means. I felt sorry for the Germans I saw killed in quantity every-where—along the roads, in cellars, on roof-tops—for many reasons. They were losing, for one thing, and their deaths meant nothing, though they had been persuaded that resistance might "win the war." And they were so pitifully dressed and accoutered: that was touching. Boys with raggedy ad hoc uniforms and *Panzerfausts* and too few comrades. What were they doing? They were killing themselves; and for me, who couldn't imagine being killed, for people my age voluntarily to get themselves killed caused my mouth to drop open.

Irony describes the emotion, whatever it is, occasioned by perceiving some great gulf, half-comic, half-tragic, between what one expects and what one finds. It's not quite "disillusion," but it's adjacent to it. My experience in the war was ironic because my innocence before had prepared me to encounter in it something like the same reasonableness that governed prewar life. This, after all, was the tone dominating the American relation to the war: talk of "the future," allotments and bond purchases carefully sent home, hopeful fantasies of "the postwar world." I assumed, in short, that everyone would behave according to the clear advantages offered by reason. I had assumed that in war, like chess, when you were beaten you "resigned"; that when outnumbered and outgunned you retreated; that when you were surrounded you surrendered. I found out differently, and with a vengeance. What I found was people obeying fatuous and murderous "orders" for no reason I could understand, killing themselves because someone "told them to," prolonging the war when it was hopelessly lost because— because it was unreasonable to do so. It was my introduction to the shakiness of civilization. It was my first experience of the profoundly irrational element, and it made ridiculous all talk of plans and preparations for the future and goodwill and intelligent arrangements. Why did the red-haired young German machine-gunner firing at us in the woods not go on living—marrying, going to university, going to the beach, laughing, smiling—but keep firing long after he had made his point, and require us to kill him with a grenade?

Before we knew it it was winter, and the winter in 1944–1945 was the coldest in Europe for twenty-five years. For the ground troops conditions were unspeakable, and even the official history admits the disaster, imputing the failure to provide adequate winter clothing— analogous to the similar German oversight when the Russian winter of 1941–1942 surprised the planners—to optimism, innocence, and "confidence":

> Confidence born of the rapid sweep across Europe in the summer of 1944 and the conviction on the part of many that the successes of Allied arms would be rewarded by victory before the onset of winter contributed to the unpreparedness for winter combat.

The result of thus ignoring the injunction "Be Prepared" was 64,008 casualties from "cold injury"—not wounds but pneumonia and trench-foot. The official history sums up: "This constitutes more than four 15,000-man divisions. Approximately 90 percent of cold casualties involved riflemen and there were about 4,000 riflemen per infantry division. Thus closer to 13 divisions were critically disabled for combat." We can appreciate those figures by recalling that the invasion of Normandy was initially accomplished by only six divisions (nine if we add the airborne). Thus crucial were little things like decent mittens and gloves, fur-lined parkas, thermal underwear—all of which any normal peacetime hiker or skier would demand as protection against prolonged exposure. But "the winter campaign in Europe was fought by most combat personnel in a uniform that did not give proper protection": we wore silly long overcoats, right out of the nineteenth century; thin field jackets, designed to convey an image of manliness at Fort Bragg; and dress wool trousers. We wore the same shirts and huddled under the same blankets as Pershing's troops in the expedition against Pancho Villa in 1916. Of the 64,008 who suffered "cold injury" I was one. During February, 1945, I was back in various hospitals for a month with pneumonia. I told my parents it was flu.

That month away from the line helped me survive for four weeks more but it broke the rhythm and, never badly scared before, when I returned to the line early in March I found for the first time that I was terrified, unwilling to take the chances which before had seemed rather sporting. My month of safety had renewed my interest in survival, and I was psychologically and morally ill-prepared to lead my platoon in the great Seventh Army attack of March 15, 1945. But lead it I did, or rather push it, staying as far in the rear as was barely decent. And before the day was over I had been severely rebuked by a sharp-eyed lieutenant-colonel who threatened court martial if I didn't pull myself together. Before that day was over I was sprayed with the contents of a soldier's torso when I was lying behind him and he knelt to fire at a machine-gun holding us up: he was struck in the heart, and out of the holes in the back of his field jacket flew little clouds of tissue, blood, and powdered cloth. Near him another man raised himself to fire, but the machine-gun caught him in the mouth, and as he fell he looked back at me with surprise, blood and teeth dribbling out onto the leaves. He was one to whom early on I had given the Silver Star for heroism, and he didn't want to let me down.

As if in retribution for my cowardice, in the late afternoon, near Engwiller, Alsace, clearing a woods full of Germans cleverly dug in, my platoon was raked by shells from an 88, and I was hit in the back and leg by shell fragments. They felt like red-hot knives going in, but I was as interested in the few quiet moans, like those of a hurt child drifting off to sleep, of my thirty-seven-year-old platoon sergeant— we'd been together since Camp Howze—killed instantly by the same shell. We were lying together, and his immediate neighbor on the other side, a lieutenant in charge of a section of heavy machine-guns, was killed instantly too. And my platoon was virtually wiped away. I was in disgrace, I was hurt, I was clearly expendable—while I lay there the supply sergeant removed my issue wristwatch to pass on to my replacement—and I was twenty years old.

I bore up all right while being removed from "the field" and passed back through the first-aid stations where I was known. I was deeply on morphine, and managed brave smiles as called for. But when I got to the evacuation hospital thirty miles behind the lines and was coming out from the anesthetic of my first operation, all my affectations of control collapsed, and I did what I'd wanted to do for months. I cried, noisily and publicly, and for hours. I was the scandal of the ward. There were lots of tears back there: in the operating room I saw a nurse dissolve in shoulder-shaking sobs when a boy died with great stertorous gasps on the operating table she was attending. That was the first time I'd seen anyone cry in the whole European Theater of Operations, and I must have cried because I felt that there, out of "combat," tears were licensed. I was crying because I was ashamed and because I'd let my men be killed and because my sergeant had been killed and because I recognized as never before that he might have been me and that statistically if in no other way he was me, and that I had been killed too. But ironically I had saved my life by almost losing it, for my leg wound providentially became infected, and by the time it was healed and I was ready for duty again, the European war was over, and I journeyed back up through a silent Germany to re-join my reconstituted platoon "occupying" a lovely Tyrolean valley near Innsbruck. For the infantry there was still the Japanese war to sweat out, and I was destined for it, despite the dramatic gash in my leg. But thank God the Bomb was dropped while I was on my way there, with the result that I can write this.

That day in mid-March that ended me was the worst of all for F Company. We knew it was going to be bad when it began at dawn, just like an episode from the First World War, with an hour-long artillery preparation and a smoke-screen for us to attack through.

What got us going and carried us through was the conviction that, suffer as we might, we were at least "making history." But we didn't even do that. Liddell Hart's 766-page *History of the Second World War* never heard of us. It mentions neither March 15th nor the 103rd Infantry Division. The only satisfaction history has offered is the evidence that we caused Josef Goebbels some extra anxiety. The day after our attack he entered in his log under "Military Situation":

> In the West the enemy has now gone over to the attack in the sector between Saarbrücken and Hagenau in addition to the previous flash-points. . . . His objective is undoubtedly to drive in our front on the Saar and capture the entire region south of the Moselle and west of the Rhine.

And he goes on satisfyingly: "Mail received testifies to a deep-seated lethargy throughout the German people degenerating almost into hopelessness. There is very sharp criticism of the . . . entire national leadership." One reason: "The Moselle front is giving way." But a person my age I met thirty years later couldn't believe that there was still any infantry fighting in France in the spring of 1945, and puzzled by my dedicating a book of mine to my dead platoon sergeant with the date March 15, 1945, confessed that he couldn't figure out what had happened to him.

To become disillusioned you must earlier have been illusioned. Evidence of the illusions suffered by the youth I was is sadly available in the letters he sent, in unbelievable profusion, to his parents. They radiate a terrible naïveté, together with a pathetic disposition to be pleased in the face of boredom and, finally, horror. The young man had heard a lot about the importance of "morale" and ceaselessly labored to sustain his own by sustaining his addressees'. Thus: "We spent all of Saturday on motor maintenance," he writes from Fort Benning; "a very interesting subject." At Benning he believes all he's told and fails to perceive that he's being prepared for one thing only, and that a nasty, hazardous job, whose performers on the line have a life expectancy of six weeks. He assures his parents: "I can get all sorts of assignments from here: . . . Battalion staff officer, mess officer, rifle platoon leader, weapons platoon leader, company executive officer, communications officer, motor officer, etc." (Was it an instinct for protecting himself from a truth half-sensed that made him bury *rifle platoon leader* in the middle of this list?) Like a bright schoolboy, he is pleased when grown-ups tell him he's done well. "I got a compliment on my clean rifle tonight. The lieutenant said, 'Very good.' I said, 'Thank you, sir.' " His satisfaction in making Expert Rifleman is touching; it is "the highest possible rating," he announces. And although he is constantly jokey, always on the lookout for what he terms "laffs," he seems to have no sense of humor:

> We're having a very interesting week . . . , taking up the carbine, automatic rifle, rifle grenade, and the famous "bazooka." We had the bazooka today, and it was very enjoyable, although we could not fire it because of lack of ammunition.

He has the most impossible standards of military excellence, and he enlists his critical impulse in the service of optimistic self-deception. Appalled by the ineptitude of the 103rd Division in training, he writes home: "As I told you last time, this is a very messed up division. It will never go overseas as a unit, and is now serving mainly as a replacement training center, disguised as a combat division."

Because the image of himself actually leading troops through bullets and shellfire is secretly unthinkable, fatuous hope easily comes to his assistance. In August, 1944, with his division preparing to ship abroad, he asserts that the Germans seem to be "on their last legs." Indeed, he reports, "bets are being made . . . that the European war will be over in six weeks." But October finds him on the transport heading for the incredible, and now he "expects," he says, that "this war will end some time in November or December," adding, "I feel very confident and safe." After the epiphanies of the line in November and December, he still entertains hopes for an early end, for the Germans are rational people, and what rational people would persist in immolating themselves once it's clear that they've lost the war? "This *can't* last much longer," he finds.

The letters written during combat are full of requests for food packages from home, and interpretation of this obsession is not quite as simple as it seems. The C and K rations were tedious, to be sure, and as readers of *All Quiet on the Western Front* and *The Middle*

Parts of Fortune know, soldiers of all times and places are fixated on food. But how explain this young man's requests for "fantastic items" like gherkins, olives, candy-coated peanuts (the kind "we used to get out of slot-machines at the beach"), cans of chili and tamales, cashew nuts, devilled ham, and fig pudding? The lust for a little swank is the explanation, I think, the need for some exotic counterweight to the uniformity, the dullness, the lack of point and distinction he sensed everywhere. These items also asserted an unbroken contact with home, and a home defined as the sort of place fertile not in corned-beef hash and meat-and-vegetable stew but gum drops and canned chicken. In short, an upper-middle-class venue.

Upper-middle-class too, I suspect, is the unimaginative cruelty of some of these letters, clear evidence of arrested emotional development. "Period" anti-Semitic remarks are not infrequent, and they remain unrebuked by any of his addressees. His understanding of the American South (he's writing from Georgia) can be gauged from his remark, "Everybody down here is illiterate." In combat some of his bravado is a device necessary to his emotional survival, but some bespeaks a genuine insensitivity:

Feb. 1, 1945

Dear Mother and Dad:

Today is the division's 84th consecutive day on line. The average is 90–100 days, although one division went 136 without being relieved. . . .

This house we're staying in used to be the headquarters of a local German Motor Corps unit, and it's full of printed matter, uniforms, propaganda, and pictures of Der Führer. I am not collecting any souveniers [*sic*], although I have had ample opportunity to pick up helmets, flags, weapons, etc. The only thing I have kept is a Belgian pistol, which one German was carrying who was unfortunate enough to walk right into my platoon. That is the first one I had the job of shooting. I have kept the pistol as a souvenier of my first Kraut.

It is odd how hard one becomes after a little bit of this stuff, but it gets to be more like killing mad dogs than people. . . .

Love to all,
Paul.

The only comfort I can take today in contemplating these letters is the ease with which their author can be rationalized as a stranger. Even the handwriting is not now my own. There are constant shows of dutifulness to parents, and even grandparents, and mentions of churchgoing, surely anomalous in a leader of assault troops. Parental approval is indispensable: "This week I was 'Class A Agent Officer' for Co. F, paying a $6000 payroll without losing a cent! I felt very proud of myself!" And the complacency! The twittiness! From hospital, where for a time he's been in an enlisted men's ward: "Sometimes I enjoy being with the men just as much as associating with the officers." (*Associating* is good.) The letter-writer is more pretentious than literate ("Alright," "thank's," "curiousity"), and his taste is terrible. He is thrilled to read Bruce Barton's *The Man Nobody Knows* ("It presents Christ in a very human light"), Maugham's *The Summing Up,* and the short stories of Erskine Caldwell. Even his often-sketched fantasies of the postwar heaven are grimly conventional: he will get married (to whom?); he will buy a thirty-five-foot sloop and live on it; he will take a year of non-serious literary graduate study at Columbia; he will edit a magazine for yachtsmen. He seems unable to perceive what is happening, constantly telling his addressee what will please rather than what he feels. He was never more mistaken than when he assured his parents while recovering from his wounds, "Please try not to worry, as no permanent damage has been done."

But the shock of these wounds and the long period recovering from them seem to have matured him a tiny bit, and some of his last letters from the hospital suggest that one or two scales are beginning to fall from his eyes:

One of the most amazing things about this war is the way the bizarre and unnatural become the normal after a short time. Take this hospital and its atmosphere: after a long talk with him, an eighteen-year-old boy without legs seems like the *normal* eighteen-year-old. You might even be surprised if a boy of the same age should walk in on both his legs. He would seem the freak and the object of pity. It is easy to imagine, after seeing some of these men, that *all* young men are arriving on this planet with stumps instead of limbs.

The same holds true with life at the front. The same horrible unreal-

ness that is so hard to describe. . . . I think I'll have to write a book
about all this some time.

But even here, he can't conclude without reverting to cliché and
twirpy optimism:

> Enough for this morning. I'm feeling well and I'm very comfortable,
> and the food is improving. We had chicken and ice cream yesterday!

He has not read Swift yet, but in the vision of the young men with
their stumps there's perhaps a hint that he's going to. And indeed,
when he enrolled in graduate school later, the first course he was
attracted to was "Swift and Pope." And ever since he's been trying
to understand satire, and even to experiment with it himself.

It was in the army that I discovered my calling. I hadn't known that
I was a teacher, but I found I could explain things: the operation of
flamethrowers, map-reading, small-arms firing, "field sanitation." I
found I could "lecture" and organize and make things clear. I could
start at the beginning of a topic and lead an audience to the end. When
the war was over, being trained for nothing useful, I naturally fell into
the course which would require largely a mere continuation of this act.
In becoming a college teacher of literature I was aware of lots of
company: thousands of veterans swarmed to graduate schools to study
literature, persuaded that poetry and prose could save the world, or
at least help wash away some of the intellectual shame of the years
we'd been through. From this generation came John Berryman and
Randall Jarrell and Delmore Schwartz and Saul Bellow and Louis
Simpson and Richard Wilbur and John Ciardi and William Meredith
and all the others who, afire with the precepts of the New Criticism,
embraced literature, and the teaching of it, as a quasi-religious obligation.

To this day I tend to think of all hierarchies, especially the academic one, as military. The undergraduate students, at the "bottom,"
are the recruits and draftees, privates all. Teaching assistants and
graduate students are the non-coms, with grades (only officers have
"ranks") varying according to seniority: a G-4 is more important than
a G-1, etc. Instructors, where they still exist, are the Second and First

Lieutenants, and together with the Assistant Professors (Captains) comprise the company-grade officers. When we move up to the tenured ranks, Associate Professors answer to field-grade officers, Majors and Colonels. Professors are Generals, beginning with Brigadier— that's a newly promoted one. Most are Major Generals, and upon retirement they will be advanced to Lieutenant-General ("Professor Emeritus"). The main academic administration is less like a higher authority in the same structure than an adjacent echelon, like a group of powerful congressmen, for example, or people from the Judge Advocate's or Inspector General's departments. The Board of Trustees, empowered to make professorial appointments and thus confer academic ranks and privileges, is the equivalent of the President of the United States, who signs commissions very like Letters of Academic Appointment: "Reposing special trust and confidence in the . . . abilities of ———, I do appoint him," etc. It is not hard to see also that the military principle crudely registered in the axiom Rank Has Its Privileges operates in academic life, where there are plums to be plucked like frequent leaves of absence, single-occupant offices, light teaching loads, and convenient, all-weather parking spaces.

I think this generally unconscious way of conceiving of the academic hierarchy is common among people who went to graduate school immediately after the war, and who went on the G.I. Bill. Perhaps many were attracted to university teaching as a postwar profession because in part they felt they understood its mechanisms already. Thus their ambitiousness, their sense that if to be a First Lieutenant is fine, to work up to Lieutenant-General is wonderful. And I suspect that their conception of instruction is still, like mine, tinged with Army. I think all of us of that vintage feel uneasy with forms of teaching which don't recognize a clear hierarchy—team-teaching, for example, or even the seminar, which assumes the fiction that leader and participants possess roughly equal knowledge and authority. For students (that is, enlisted men) to prosecute a rebellion, as in the 1960's and early 70's, is tantamount to mutiny, an offense, as the Articles of War indicate, "to be punished by death, or such other punishment as a court-martial shall direct." I have never been an enthusiast for The Movement.

In addition to remaining rank-conscious, I persist in the army habit of exact personnel classification. For me, everyone still has an invisible "spec number" indicating what his job is or what he's supposed to be doing. Thus a certain impatience with people of ambiguous identity, or worse, people who don't seem to do anything, like self-proclaimed novelists and poets who generate no apprehensible product. These seem to me the T-5's of the postwar world, mere Technicians Fifth Grade, parasites, drones, noncombatants.

Twenty years after the First World War Siegfried Sassoon reports that he was still having dreams about it, dreams less of terror than of obligation. He dreams that

> the War is still going on and I have got to return to the Front. I complain bitterly to myself because it hasn't stopped yet. I am worried because I can't find my active-service kit. I am worried because I have forgotten how to be an officer. I feel that I can't face it again, and sometimes I burst into tears and say, "It's no good, I can't do it." But I know that I can't escape going back, and search frantically for my lost equipment.

That's uniquely the dream of a junior officer. I had such dreams too, and mine persisted until about 1960, when I was thirty-six, past re-call age.

Those who actually fought on the line in the war, especially if they were wounded, constitute an in-group forever separate from those who did not. Praise or blame does not attach: rather, there is the accidental possession of a special empirical knowledge, a feeling of a mysterious shared ironic awareness manifesting itself in an instinctive skepticism about pretension, publicly enunciated truths, the vanities of learning, and the pomp of authority. Those who fought know a secret about themselves, and it's not very nice. As Frederick Manning said in 1929, remembering 1914–1918: "War is waged by men; not by beasts, or by gods. It is a peculiarly human activity. To call it a crime against mankind is to miss at least half its significance; it is also the punishment of a crime."

And now that those who fought have grown much older, we must wonder at the frantic avidity with which we struggled then to avoid death, digging our foxholes like madmen, running from danger with

burning lungs and pounding hearts. What, really, were we so frightened of? Sometimes now the feeling comes over us that Housman's
lines which in our boyhood we thought attractively cynical are really
just:

> Life, to be sure, is nothing much to lose;
> But young men think it is, and we were young.

[1982]

CAROL BLY

Milkweed Editions

BORN IN 1930, Carol Bly grew up in Minnesota and North Carolina, attended a fashionable boarding school in New England, graduated from Wellesley College, and spent a year in graduate school at the University of Minnesota. During the next twenty-odd years she and her husband, the poet Robert Bly, put out a series of small, influential literary magazines *(The Fifties, The Sixties,* and *The Seventies)*. She did all the things an energetic, educated, civic-minded citizen might do: helped found an arts center, served on the local Chamber of Commerce, did volunteer work for her church.

In 1973 Bly began writing a series of "letters"—as she called them—for the magazines *Preview* and *Minnesota Monthly,* published by Minnesota Public Radio (which also produced the radio show "A Prairie Home Companion"). In part celebrations of midwestern rural life (see "Getting Tired" and "Great Snows"), the main purpose of Bly's essays is to criticize the stultifying repression of feeling in rural America, and how that inevitably leads to moral lassitude. In the prologue to *Letters from the Country* she puts it all very simply and directly: "The problem of people's not feeling is very serious." Bly wants her readers to "wake up," to live passionately, to take their lives more seriously, to replace reverence for "sacred cows" with courageous thought. In an essay called "The Way Out of Small-Town Niceness and Loneliness," she writes with sharp sarcasm:

> Very nice Midwestern women tell their children constantly to (1) be nice; (2) think nice things; (3) and if you can't say something nice don't say anything at all.
>
> We have more socially mute people in the Midwest than other sections have.

In 1981 Carol Bly's essays were published under the title *Letters from the Country.* She has also published short stories in *The New Yorker, American Review, Ploughshares,* and *The Best American Short Stories, 1983;* her short stories came out in a collection titled *Backbone* in 1985. Three of the stories in *Backbone* were made into the movie *Rachel River,* released on "American Playhouse" in 1989. Bly has also published several pamphlets written for special occasions or groups: *Soil and Survival* (with Nancy Paddock and Joe Paddock) for the Sierra Club (1986); *Bad Government and Silly Literature* (1986); and *Small Towns: A Close Second Look at a Very Good Place* (1987). After teaching English at the University of Minnesota and at Hamline University, in 1990 Bly was named Benedict Distinguished Professor of English at Carleton College, Northfield, Minnesota.

Carol Bly's literary career didn't begin until she was in her forties, and she was fifty-one when her first book was published. By then she had married, raised four children, and divorced. She represents a new kind of writer, not "literary" in the same sense that Virginia Woolf and Joan Didion are literary; not as sophisticated as they, nor as detached; a writer, rather, who is motivated primarily by the idea that through writing she can perhaps change things. Carol Bly ends her last essay with a direct statement to her reader:

> This is my last Letter from the Country. That is why it is so shrill. Gadflies are always looking out a chance to be shrill anyway, so I jumped to this one and have shouted my favorite hope: that we can educate children not to be problem solvers but to be madly expressive all their lives.

And that is the sort of writer Carol Bly is. She is conscientious; she writes with great conviction about matters that concern her; she writes with integrity, honesty, and style; she writes for the man on the barstool at the VFW lounge more than for the literary critic; and those who read her are perhaps changed a little by that experience.

GETTING TIRED

THE MEN have left a gigantic 6600 combine a few yards from our grove, at the edge of the stubble. For days it was working around the farm; we heard it on the east, later on the west, and finally we could see it grinding back and forth over the windrows on the south. But now it has been simply squatting at the field's edge, huge, tremendously still, very professional, slightly dangerous.

We all have the correct feelings about this new combine: this isn't the good old farming where man and soil are dusted together all day; this isn't farming a poor man can afford, either, and therefore it further threatens his hold on the American "family farm" operation. We have been sneering at this machine for days, as its transistor radio, amplified well over the engine roar, has been grinding up our silence, spreading a kind of shrill ghetto evening all over the farm.

But now it is parked, and after a while I walk over to it and climb up its neat little John Deere-green ladder on the left. Entering the big cab up there is like coming up into a large ship's bridge on visitors' day—heady stuff to see the inside workings of a huge operation like the Queen Elizabeth II. On the other hand I feel left out, being only a dumbfounded passenger. The combine cab has huge windows flaring wider at the top; they lean forward over the ground, and the driver sits so high behind the glass in its rubber moldings it is like a movie-set spaceship. He has obviously come to dominate the field, whether he farms it or not.

The value of the 66 is that it can do anything, and to change it from a combine into a cornpicker takes one man about half an hour, whereas most machine conversions on farms take several men a half day. It frees its owner from a lot of monkeying.

Monkeying, in city life, is what little boys do to clocks so they never run again. In farming it has two quite different meanings. The first is small side projects. You monkey with poultry, unless you're a major egg handler. Or you monkey with ducks or geese. If you have a very small milk herd, and finally decide that prices plus state regulations don't make your few Holsteins worthwhile, you "quit monkeying with them." There is a hidden dignity in this word: it precludes mention of money. It lets the wife of a very marginal farmer have a conversation with a woman who may be helping her husband run fifteen hundred acres. "How you coming with those geese?" "Oh, we've been real disgusted. We're thinking of quitting monkeying with them." It saves her having to say, "We lost our shirts on those darn geese."

The other meaning of monkeying is wrestling with and maintaining machinery, such as changing heads from combining to cornpicking. Farmers who cornpick the old way, in which the corn isn't shelled automatically during picking in the field but must be elevated to the top of a pile by belt and then shelled, put up with some monkeying.

Still, cornpicking and plowing is a marvelous time of the year on farms; one of the best autumns I've had recently had a few days of fieldwork in it. We were outside all day, from six in the morning to eight at night—coming in only for noon dinner. We ate our lunches on a messy truck flatbed. (For city people who don't know it: *lunch* isn't a noon meal; it is what you eat out of a black lunch pail at 9 A.M. and 3 P.M. If you offer a farmer a cup of coffee at 3:30 P.M. he or she is likely to say, "No thanks, I've already had lunch.") There were four of us hired to help—a couple to plow, Celia (a skilled farmhand who worked steady for our boss), and me. Lunch was always two sandwiches of white commercial bread with luncheon meat, and one very generous piece of cake-mix cake carefully wrapped in Saran Wrap. (I never found anyone around here self-conscious about using Saran Wrap when the Dow Chemical Company was also making napalm.)

It was very pleasant on the flatbed, squinting out over the yellow picked cornstalks—each time we stopped for lunch, a larger part of the field had been plowed black. We fell into the easy psychic habit of farmworkers: admiration of the boss. "Ja, I see he's buying one of those big 4010s," someone would say. We always perked up at inside information like that. Or "Ja," as the woman hired steady told us, "he's going to plow the home fields first this time, instead of the other way round." We temporary help were impressed by that, too. Then, with real flair, she brushed a crumb of luncheon meat off her jeans, the way you would make sure to flick a gnat off spotless tennis whites.

It is the true feminine touch to brush a crumb off pants that are encrusted with Minnesota Profile A heavy loam, many swipes of SAE 40 oil, and grain dust.

All those days, we never tired of exchanging information on how *he* was making out, what *he* was buying, whom *he* was going to let drive the new tractor, and so on. There is always something to talk about with the other hands, because farming is genuinely absorbing. It has the best quality of work: nothing else seems real. And everyone doing it, even the cheapest helpers like me, can see the layout of the whole—from spring work, to cultivating, to small grain harvest, to cornpicking, to fall plowing.

The second day I was promoted from elevating corncobs at the corn pile to actual plowing. Hour after hour I sat up there on the old Alice, as she was called (an Allis-Chalmers WC that looked rusted from the Flood). You have to sit twisted part way around, checking that the plowshares are scouring clean, turning over and dropping the dead crop and soil, not clogging. For the first two hours I was very political. I thought about what would be good for American farming—stronger marketing organizations, or maybe a law like the Norwegian Odal law, preventing the breaking up of small farms or selling them to business interests. Then the sun got high, and each time I reached the headlands area at the field's end I dumped off something else, now my cap, next my jacket, finally my sweater.

Since the headlands are the last to be plowed, they serve as a field road until the very end. There are usually things parked there—a pickup or a corn trailer—and things dumped—my warmer clothing, our afternoon lunch pails, a broken furrow wheel someone picked up.

By noon I'd dropped all political interest, and was thinking only: how unlike this all is to Keats's picture of autumn, a "season of mists and mellow fruitfulness." This gigantic expanse of horizon, with everywhere the easy growl of tractors, was simply teeming with extrovert energy. It wouldn't calm down for another week, when whoever was lowest on the totem pole would be sent out to check a field for dropped parts or to drive away the last machines left around.

The worst hours for all common labor are the hours after noon dinner. Nothing is inspiring then. That is when people wonder how they ever got stuck in the line of work they've chosen for life. Or they wonder where the cool Indian smoke of secrets and messages began to vanish from their marriage. Instead of plugging along like a cheerful

beast working for me, the Allis now smelled particularly gassy. To stay
awake I froze my eyes onto an indented circle in the hood around the
gas cap. Someone had apparently knocked the screw cap fitting down
into the hood, so there was a moat around it. In this moat some
overflow gas leapt in tiny waves. Sometimes the gas cap was a castle,
this was the moat; sometimes it was a nuclear-fission plant, this was
the horrible hot-water waste. Sometimes it was just the gas cap on the
old Alice with the spilt gas bouncing on the hot metal.

Row after row. I was stupefied. But then around 2:30 the shadows
appeared again, and the light, which had been dazing and white, grew
fragile. The whole prairie began to gather itself for the cool evening. All
of a sudden it was wonderful to be plowing again, and when I came to
the field end, the filthy jackets and the busted furrow wheel were just
benign mistakes: that is, if it chose to, the jacket could be a church
robe, and the old wheel could be something with some pride to it, like a
helm. And I felt the same about myself: instead of being someone with a
half interest in literature and a half interest in farming doing a half-
decent job plowing, I could have been someone desperately needed in
Washington or Zurich. I drank my three o'clock coffee joyously, and
traded the other plowman a Super-Valu cake-mix lemon cake slice for a
Holsum baloney sandwich because it had garlic in it.

By seven at night we had been plowing with headlights for an hour.
I tried to make up games to keep going, on my second wind, on my
third wind, but labor is labor after the whole day of it; the mind
refuses to think of ancestors. It refuses to pretend the stalks marching
up to the right wheel in the spooky light are men-at-arms, or to
imagine a new generation coming along. It doesn't care. Now the
Republicans could have announced a local meeting in which they
would propose a new farm program whereby every farmer owning less
than five hundred acres must take half price for his crop, and every
farmer owning more than a thousand acres shall receive triple price
for his crop, and I was so tired I wouldn't have shown up to protest.

A million hours later we sit around in a daze at the dining-room
table, and nobody says anything. In low, courteous mutters we ask for
the macaroni hotdish down this way, please. Then we get up in ones
and twos and go home. Now the farm help are all so tired we *are* a
little like the various things left out on the headlands—some tools, a
jacket, someone's thermos top—used up for that day. Thoughts won't
even stick to us any more.

Such tiredness must be part of farmers' wanting huge machinery like the Deere 6600. That tiredness that feels so good to the occasional laborer and the athlete is disturbing to a man destined to it eight months of every year. But there is a more hidden psychology in the issue of enclosed combines versus open tractors. It is this: one gets too many impressions on the open tractor. A thousand impressions enter as you work up and down the rows: nature's beauty or nature's stubbornness, politics, exhaustion, but mainly the feeling that all this repetition—last year's cornpicking, this year's cornpicking, next year's cornpicking—is taking up your lifetime. The mere repetition reveals your eventual death.

When you sit inside a modern combine, on the other hand, you are so isolated from field, sky, all the real world, that the brain is dulled. You are not sensitized to your own mortality. You aren't sensitive to anything at all.

This must be a common choice of our mechanical era: to hide from life inside our machinery. If we can hide from life in there, some idiotic part of the psyche reasons, we can hide from death in there as well.

[1973]

GREAT SNOWS

> How strange to think of giving up all ambition!
> Suddenly I see with such clear eyes
> The white flake of snow
> That has just fallen in the horse's mane.
> "Watering the Horse," by Robert Bly,
> Silence in the Snowy Fields

IT IS sometimes mistakenly thought by city people that grown-ups don't love snow. They think only children who haven't got to shovel it love snow, or only people like the von Fürstenburgs and their friends who get to go skiing in exotic places and will never backslope a roadside in all their lives: that is a mistake. The fact is that most country or small-town Minnesotans love snow. They relish snow in large inconvenient storms; they like the excesses of it, they like the threat of it, the endless work of it, the glamour of it.

Before a storm, Madison is full of people excitedly laying in food stocks for the three-day blow. People lay in rather celebratory food, too. Organic-food parents get chocolate for the children; weight watchers lay in macaroni and Sara Lee cakes; recently converted vegetarians backslide to T-bones. People hang around the large Super-Valu window and keep a tough squinty-eyed watch on the storm progress with a lot of gruff, sensible observations (just like Houston Control talking to the moon, very much on top of it all) like "Ja, we need this for spring moisture . . ." or "Ja, it doesn't look like letting up at all . . ." or "Ja, you can see where it's beginning to drift up behind the VFW." The plain pleasure of it is scarcely hidden.

That is before the storm. Then the town empties out as the farmers and their families take their stocks home before U.S. 75, Minnesota 40, and Lac Qui Parle 19 close up. During the storm itself heroism is the routine attitude. I remember once when the phone was out, before all the telephone lines went underground, and the power was off, our neighbor came lightly in his huge pack boots across the drift top, high up from our house level, like an upright black ant, delicately choosing his footing over the hard-slung and paralyzed snow waves. He looked as if he were walking across a frozen North Atlantic. He had come over to see if we were O.K. It was before snowmobiles, at −40 degrees a welcome gesture.

Then right after a storm we all go back uptown because we have to see how the town has filled. The streets are walled ten and eleven feet high. If they had had underground parking ramps in the pyramids this is what they'd have looked like, white-painted, and we crawl between the neatly carved clean walls. The horrible snow buildup is a point of pride. In 1969 a fine thing happened: the county of Lac Qui Parle imported a couple of gigantic snow-removal machines from Yellowstone Park. It cost several thousand dollars to get those monsters here; when they arrived our heavy, many-layered, crusted snow broke the machines—they couldn't handle it. With glittering eyes we sent them back to Yellowstone Park.

Snowdrifts in the bad years, as in 1969, force us to dump garbage and nonburnables ever nearer the house, until finally in March there is a semicircle of refuse nearly at the front door. Even the German shepherd lowers his standards; the snow around the doghouse entrance is unspeakable.

If one has any kind of luck one garners comfort from great weather, but if there is some anxious and unresolved part of one's inner life, snowfall and certainly snowboundness can make it worse. During the winter of 1968–69, the three doctors of our town prescribed between two and three times as much tranquilizing medicine as usual. And Robert Frost, despite being one of the best snow poets going, has an odd, recurring fretfulness about snow:

> The woods are lovely, dark and deep,
> But I have promises to keep

What promises? To whom? If we think about it it sounds moralistic and self-denying—a moral showing-off in some way. The nervousness is stronger, though, in "Desert Places":

> Snow falling and night falling fast, oh, fast
> In a field I looked into going past,
> And the ground almost covered smooth in snow,
> But a few weeds and stubble showing last.
>
> The woods around it have it—it is theirs.
> All animals are smothered in their lairs.
> I am too absent-spirited to count;
> The loneliness includes me unawares.

I am struck by the malaise of the word *absent-spirited.* It must mean—this joy in snow or fretfulness in snow—that whatever is providential and coming to each of us from within is sped the faster by snowfall.

Being out in a blizzard is not lovely. Nature then feels worse than inimical; it feels simply impersonal. It isn't that, like some goddess in Homer, she wants to grab and freeze your body in her drifts; it is that you can be taken and still the wind will keep up its regular blizzard whine and nothing has made a difference. In February of 1969 the fuel men couldn't get through for weeks; one midnight my husband and I had to transfer oil from a drum behind an old shed to our house tank.

We did this in cans, load after load, crawling on all fours and rolling
in the ravines between the drifts. It had some nice moments: every
ten minutes or so we'd meet behind the old shed, when one returned
an empty can and the other was coming away with a full one, and we'd
crouch in the scoured place, leaning over the nasty, rusted, infuriat-
ingly slow spigot of the oil tank there. Looking at each other, we saw
we had that impersonal aspect of snow-covered people. It was peculiar
to think that anyone behind those freezing, melting, refreezing eye-
brows ever objected to an act of Congress or ever loved a summer
woods or memorized the tenor to anything by Christopher Tye. Back
inside, our job done, still cold and rough-spoken, still walking like
bears, we studied the children in their beds.

To us in Minnesota a blizzard in itself is of no practical good, but
it is interesting how useful blizzards can be. Ordinary snowfall, not
moved into deep-packed areas by wind, runs off too quickly in the
spring and can't be controlled for good use. The *Proceedings of the
American Society of Civil Engineers* has essay after essay on uses of
Rocky Mountain snowmelt. Twenty-five hundred years ago, and
possibly even earlier, the Persians used deep-drifted snow for irrigation. They built their *qanats.* Qanats are brick-walled tunnels running from the snowfields of the Elburz and other mountain ranges of
Iran to villages fifteen or twenty miles away. At a point in the
mountains' water table still higher than the land level of the
parched miles and miles to be irrigated, the arched brick tunnels
were carefully sloped to keep the water moving. The "mother well"
was 200 feet deep and deeper. These 22,000 tunnels (there were
30,000 in 1960 but 8,000 were not in working condition) had air-
shafts for fresh air and maintenance access every 50 to 60 yards.
Darius took the qanat technique to Egypt in the 5th century B.C.
Nothing could have been cultivated in three-fourths of the now-
irrigated fields of Iran without the ancient qanats. Persia was the
originator of melons, cucumbers, and pears.

This is just to give an idea of mankind's long use of heavily drifted
snow. Since we don't *use* blizzards in western Minnesota, the question
lingers: why the pleasure in great weather? As with children in thunderstorms, I think we all have a secret affair of long standing with the
other face of things. Children want the parents and the police and the
other irritating powers to have their measure taken; they want a

change of justice; but it goes further: they have a secret affection for bad weather.

Storms, what is more, force us to look at nature closely, and that is never boring. All meetings of the Business Improvement Association and the Countryside Council and the play rehearsal committees stop in a blizzard. It is a help. Two things make nature lovely to people, I think: enforced, extended leisure in a natural place—which storms give us out here; and second, planning our own lives instead of just following along. The moment, for example, that someone finally decides not to take the promising job offered by Reserve Mining, for example, or the moment someone decides not to pad a travel-expense account at the Ramada is a moment in which ice and snow and bare trunks look better, less happenstance, less pointless. C. S. Lewis goes very far: he claims that the fact that we all agree on what is meant by *good* or *holy* (that is, no one thinks robbery or despoiling the land or depriving the poor is good) indicates that goodness and holiness are actually a normal, planned part of our universe—perfectly natural to the species. He would not be surprised at all to see snow on a horse's mane all the better for having just worked out an ethical decision.

[1975]

QUIETLY THINKING OVER
THINGS AT CHRISTMAS

THE WINTER SOLSTICE is the ancient season of joining spirit and animal. In the old dances, people dressed as animals, the Morris men holding deer's heads before their faces and carrying a hobbyhorse for the Abbots Bromley horn dance; and a wren was hunted and killed, to make way for the new king. Swedish children, in fact, still think of Staffan (St. Stephen) as the patron saint of horses; in their archaic, beautiful carol *"Staffan var en stålledrang!"* St. Stephen has two red ponies, two white ponies, and one dappled. He is set upon and murdered in the forest, and his body arrives home on horseback. We don't celebrate Christ's resurrection at Christmas because that is the *part-*

ing of body and spirit; we celebrate His birth, the *joining* of body and spirit. It is a terrific season in Minnesota: children left free to grow inward are remarkably dreamy from late October through Twelfth Night to the dullness of late January.

Then how doubly cruel that our Midwest society operates to deprive huge segments of the populace of quiet thinking for themselves, especially at Christmastime. Thousands are brought up to be respectful of this or that sacred subject—family life, church activity, Christmastime, motherhood, the office of the American presidency. Any sacred cow is a curse in that it must be taken as a whole—its core, its history, and its aura, all in one. It is taboo to separate sacred subjects into their parts and say, this two-thirds is okay, this one-third is rot. Whenever a *whole* subject is sacred, we cannot think about it quietly. And, if we are not allowed quiet thought, the lie somewhere in the subject begins to grow inside us, and we feel the lie and become frenetic in our efforts to suppress it, and then we become distrustful of other people because they might wake up the part that is lie. We become addicted to not "rocking the boat."

When we think about it, we notice that rocking the boat—the greatest anathema in small-town life—consists nearly entirely of dividing a subject into its components and treating the several components differently one from the other. For example, when people in Madison began speaking of Nixon's crookedness, several of our town leaders remarked that they wished "they'd just drop the whole Watergate thing" before the United States was "blown wide open." I thought that was very interesting, because it meant that Nixon could not be taken as one component of the nation; the society, the presidency, the national polity and psyche, all apparently were felt to be welded together and would either survive or be "blown wide open" together. Yet we know the reverse is true: when you take a rotten potato out of the barrel, in good time, you save the barrel, you don't "blow it wide open." In other words, there is a sanity in treating parts of anything separately.

It is considered rocking the boat to say that the Lutheran Church is a drag, although we all know it is a drag; yet it is very likely that if the hypocritical and heartless elements of church life were brought out into the open, like Watergate, truth and some new strength for reform might well race in and fill the spaces.

It is rocking the boat to find that a city council has floated a crooked bond issue on a building, for example; yet we all know that every time such corruption is exposed it has helped, not destroyed, the town. The businessmen who remained honest throughout are brought closer together.

Or to take a small instance: it is rocking the boat to read Eliot's "Journey of the Magi" at Christmas to a rural study club because Christmas is a "joyous family season" and Eliot is frank, full of solitude, and "very different." He reminds us of a part of Christmas that is like death, and that Christmas presages death. Here is a poem of Auden's which is quiet and thoughtful; it doesn't break new ground—its strength is in its taking up *part* of Christmas instead of trying, frenetically, to be enthusiastic about the whole:

> There are enough
> Left-overs to do, warmed-up, for the rest of the week—
> Not that we have much appetite, having drunk such a lot,
> Stayed up so late, attempted—quite unsuccessfully—
> To love all our relatives, and in general
> Grossly overestimated our powers. Once again
> As in previous years we have seen the actual Vision and failed
> To do more than entertain it as an agreeable
> Possibility, once again we have sent Him away
> Begging though to remain His disobedient servant,
> The promising child who cannot keep His word for long.

This is quiet, and absorbing, in comparison to the frantic uplift and clean bounce of *Christmas Ideals* magazine. It is cruel to condition people against reading such poems as Eliot's or Auden's.

Inexperience with quiet thought has another side effect in Minnesota: a residual, rather habitual chill between men and women. This is the way it seems to work. Nearly all of us women feel it our job to keep up civilization; we have an ancient conviction that if we don't keep it up the men will ease backward through evolution, with their socks and their hauteur, the way Poland Chinas turn back into wild boars with such frightening speed. So if we believe that Christmas's character as a "joyous season" and "a family time" is a civilizing notion, we feel constrained to uphold it. A part of us says Yes, but why are we frenetic and miserable at Christmas then? and why is the suicide rate so high at Christmas?

The answer must be in the components of Christmas—two-thirds may be joyous family material, but at least one-third must be introversion and contemplation and animal celebration: julebokking* isn't an accident! We "horse around" during the days of Christmas; it is the season of horses and mischief. But Midwest housewives aren't free to do mischief! Or to consider this sacred subject in its components. So they are stuck, still sitting cold in church circle meetings saying, "Christmas is a joyous family time," feeling the partial lie of it. Meanwhile, the husband also suffers from the lie. Because he is likely not to be so conditioned to passivity as his wife, he fights the lie. He goes down to the VFW lounge or somewhere, somewhere dark and damned and against the pious tone of the town, and the hell with it: he is going to do some serious drinking; that is, he is going to recover, somehow, feelings he has repressed.

I've seen a certain expression in men's faces in places like VFW lounges, but only recently have I understood this look: it is a look of deliberate *intelligence.* You have all the rest as well, of course—the boorish leaning over the carelessly mixed drinks, the beastly canned music, the spasmodic, loud, halting conversations, which some idiot at intervals contrives to liven up with a joke by which Norway, Poland, or Israel is the loser—there is all that, of course—but there is a very common expression of true cunning and a will to see straight: the men's eyes stare and look bald. I now understand that look to mean that they have come to recover suppressed knowledge which their wives or their town won't let them uncover elsewhere, not for a moment. They have come to say the damned things: all our leaders in Washington are a bunch of bad-language nouns, and big businessmen who have control of everything have bad-language verbed the country, and this being conned into buying presents is a lot of collective bad-language noun, and in family life—in raising kids—a human being is somehow partially bad-language past participled by raising a family at all. All this is an attempt to recognize the bad fraction of sacred wholes.

If the men could succeed in recognizing that, they would win for themselves the old joy of *quietly thinking about things.* What hap-

---

*Julebokking—Christmas joking, the Norwegian equivalent of the horsing around with fools' masses, etc.

pens, however, is that the man returns home, excited by the shadow
material that has been seen and said—he drives home really excited.
The sodium-lighted main street and the crescent-shaped pile of
plowed snow around a car that wasn't moved off before the plow came
by and the gritted railroad tracks at the level crossing—all this feels
like his own country and he is intact, in a glittering, frantic way. It
is what is called having had a pretty good drunk. Then he arrives home
and his wife, whether she spent the evening with him or waited at
home, is snapped into her civilization-upholding stance. A drunk,
idol-smashing man is a threat to civilization: he will uncover the
one-third sacred subject she tries to suppress under family cheer; he
will force her into *thought* instead of *reverence.* In a word, she is
terrified. She snaps at him. And he is so vulnerable because his spirit
is freed and has climbed outward nearly to his skin—in fact, it is
nearly on his surface. He wants to go on considering truths here,
truths there, he wants to give just desserts to this evildoer and that
evildoer, and he wants to remark that such-and-such a wretched
failure around town really has a good side to him, by God! He wants
to consider things in their components. So, when his wife snaps at him
in her pain, she attacks part of his spiritual life.

She has no idea what a stunning blow it is. All his quiet judgments
leak back down through the great crack in him, before they ever had
a chance to become genuine, quiet, thought-out and talked-about
judgments; it has all poured down back through the crack as water
drops with lightning speed into a fissure in the earth, vanishing, and
then the crack itself closes, and he is locked out of his soul again for
a while. A dull anger lies over the earth of him now, like a dust cloud
above all these movings; as he and his wife glide around the living
room, putting out lights near the nonflammable tree, the dull anger
in him paws over toward her. Either everything is sacred (the point
she stuck at) or everything is a big bunk (the point he had arrived at)
and they don't evolve beyond that with each other.

If we are producing this scene over and over in our countryside we
have a very mean side to our society. Perhaps we can work up a
community of cures for that part of Minnesota life which isn't so
lovely; I want to make two suggestions here. First, let us start teaching
that women need not be positive about sacred occasions; they may be
thinkers and pessimists. Second, let us start teaching that whenever

something new or something old is to be discussed it should be discussed in its parts, severally. Not, then: How did you like the concert? but, Which part of the concert did you like least? which most? This will increase the accuracy of people's remarks. A trendy question that is going around in Minnesota now is the identity issue that hit the East Coast in the late 1950s: "Who am I? My God, I've got to have a clear sense of who I am!" It is astonishing that people should expect to identify the whole *I*, to come up with one answer. Any answer given to such a question is bound to contain a lie in it which will ferment anxiety, just as we see the anxiety in individual men and women suffering from sacred-cowism. Nearly any answer ought to be, I think: it is one-third this way, one-third that way, and there is a third I don't understand yet.

There is a casual relaxation in not pronouncing on whole subjects. If the women of the Midwest could learn to be casual instead of pious, they could drop those defenses; they could entertain one-third pessimism on countless subjects, which would make possible thoughtful conversation with each other and men. They could release themselves and men from lip service to family life and motherhood and the holiness of being together all the time: they could stop *upholding* this value and that value and just comment together. Then the men, in turn, could use their own homes instead of the VFW lounge to explore unconscious material. I think it would help tremendously, because when you go to the VFW-lounge sort of place you tend to turn *all* to bunk—which is only the flip side of holding *all* sacred. The end result of that syndrome is the Dean Martin show, in which every single decent thing there is, from animal life to the United States Senate, even the private life of Senator Humphrey, is compulsively attacked with the intent of reducing it to trash. That is self-hatred, not quiet thought.

Viewing things in their component parts makes reform possible, too. If "the whole country's going to the dogs" you can't reform anything, but if one-third of the country is going to the dogs, you can decide precisely *which* third (or other fraction) and work to get it out. We can't fire the whole CIA; we could work at eliminating all those who conspired to ruin Allende, for example.

It is interesting that the Southern white woman is conditioned, much as is the Midwestern woman, to be cheerful and extroverted, and to honor sacred cows while a young woman. But then there comes a significant difference: In middle age the Southerner is expected to change roles: she becomes an accurate commenter on human nature, rich in earthy metaphor even, the one who cuts through falseness— even a *femme horrible*. It must be a terrific relief! And there is a playfulness to it, which no one can say the Lutheran Church encourages here. Our women, and men often, are stuck upholding sacred cows until their fifties and sixties. I have been working with senior citizens recently, and I have noticed with interest and surprise that at seventy and seventy-five Midwestern women who have been conventional do finally get free of positive thinking and upholding institutions, and they can become the most marvelous sharers of this or that tough truth—and they gain the singular playfulness that goes with not lying to oneself any more.

When a frank and quiet person like that *does* praise something finally, it isn't the perfunctory flagwaving kind of thing at all; when a free person comments on Christ's being made man at Christmas, for example, the effect is not the frantic theology of habitual liars.

[1974]

OUR CLASS SYSTEM

*Landmarks are disappearing rapidly. Why should I fret over the
loss of a raw-boned farmhouse on a bleak hillside, or an obsolete
schoolhouse back in a grove? Because they are cairns and buoys
by which we circumnavigate the social landscape. Without them
we will never know where we are—or who.*
                    Newell Searle, Assistant Director,
                    Minnesota Humanities Commission

ONCE I WAS LOST in Paris. I had got away from the Seine, on the Left Bank, and eventually came to the Place de Saint Sulpice, named for the church in its center. All round the square were small and large shops selling devotional statuary—not hundreds but thousands of plasticine Virgins and Josephs and Marys, donkeys visiting Christ, the sheep and the Wise Men, shepherds. Those I handled were white, ready to be painted by the buyer or perhaps to be left white for the effect of purity. I saw little attempt by the sculptors to *start where the people are*—that convincing approach of grantsmen and teachers.

These figures started, rather, in some dreamhouse of Western religions. Animals, men, son of God—all were refined, all pure white; the people had the high foreheads of Norman and Breton Frenchmen. There was no nonsense about the Wise Men's having had to ride camels or sleep several nights in these robes. These camels did not bite, and unlike Eliot's, were not refractory. As I looked at the thousands of figures (for there were several shop windows full of them), I realized that the villages the Wise Men passed through were full of latent theologians and apparently we who buy figures for our crêches are latent theologians, too—even those of us who buy the worst offenders, the tiny Veronicas with bloody veils and the youths that look like Shattuck boys with daubs of red spots on palms and feet, or the Virgins for some reason placed in tiny Coldstream sentry boxes. Parisians call all such devotional crockery *saint sulpice,* since so much of it is sold around that church.

What is the good of *saint sulpice?* The good of it is that whoever thought up the idea of a crêche at all, who was likely St. Francis of Assisi, had heart to know that *starting where the people are* is at best useless. What we all care for is what we yearn to be—not what or where we seem to be. Any art, even *saint sulpice,* that reminds us of what we yearn to be is a help.

I was reminded of the little religious statues one weekend in March of this past year. I had driven across southern Minnesota to give a talk. Like other speakers, I rehearsed in the car. I gave my talk to the steering wheel (aloud) and made up the questions and fielded them, answering those I could, asking for help from the imaginary audience for those I couldn't. At three o'clock in the afternoon I checked into the motel room reserved for me, and went over the whole talk again. At seven I went and gave the talk. It wasn't much good.

There are so many ways to give an indifferent talk despite all one's efforts! In any event, I had that experience. It is embarrassing to do a dumb job of something and be paid generously for it and have it received kindly. I didn't sleep very well that night. The man in the room next to mine was pretty sick most of the night. He thumped around his room a lot, and sometimes he was sick at one end of it, and sometimes at the other. He did not quiet down until three o'clock in the morning. At six I got up and left.

As I was turning the key in my car door, I saw there was the most wonderful March frost all over everything. It was very slight. It lay slick and lacy on the motel turn-around and on Minnesota 19. Its fragile tails lay along the oak branches. In the rear side window of my car I saw my reflection and I looked all right: no one could see that this person had taken pay for a dull speech and then hadn't slept very well.

Just then the man from next door came out to start his car. He too looked all right—groomed and brisk. He looked a little formalized, the way the ill do when they have sluiced their faces and mean to keep their troubles to themselves. He even looked like an ad for our species: Reliable Human Being with Sensibility, Moral Substance, Experienced in Idealistic Projects: Inquire Within. No one could guess he had been sick all over his motel room all night and had infuriated his neighbor and possibly did for a living nothing more numinous than designing comic-strip layouts for appliance retailers. He and I both looked very nice, and as I drove away in the cold, fine morning, Minnesota looked wonderful.

I drove a long time before stopping for breakfast because for some reason I got to thinking of those unimpressive little crêche figures I'd once seen in Paris. The image of them kept coming to mind. At last I understood that the whited look of Blue Earth County must have done it—or the idealized look which two tired, not very successful human beings had managed to achieve. So it struck me: no matter how mediocre people's recent record, they still wish to recognize the part of themselves that is like the stiff little crêche figures—the part that is astir with symbol.

It follows that when the symbolic past is destroyed in our landscape it is not just the sensitive who lose by it: we all do. We had better know that hungover salesmen and mediocre speakers have very good dreams of humanity in them—everybody must have—and therefore the gradual takeover of corrugated bins, alas so much cheaper and faster to put up than our 1940s barns, and the takeover of highway sprawl, and the heartless pushing over and burning of farmstead groves are damaging to the inner life not just of conscious Minnesotans like Newell Searle of the Humanities Commission, who see landscape as buoys marking things far under the surface, but to everyone.

Unfortunately people who work hard at saving the Minnesota landscape tend to think they are saving its beauty for themselves and for others equally sensitive to beauty. Beyond that, in their view of things, lie the coarse masses who drop the gum wrappers into Minnetonka and the Brule. In their view, there are the very few hardpressed good guys losing the landscape to a plethora of bad guys. Their view is a luxury. To save the past and present beauty of Minnesota we shall have to give up that very view, which Americans hold dear. We shall have to give up our kind of class system.

I do not mean our social class system, through which one can wander however one likes, upward or downward. Anyone can gradually learn to call women women instead of ladies, or to polish bare wood instead of laying broadloom, or to call one's people parents instead of folks—or do whatever's wanted. All those class markings are no problem to anyone; what is serious is that underneath all that, and underneath our pointing at British snobbery, we have a strongbox class lockup that I find disgusting. Its basic premise is: some people have an ethical or an aesthetic nature and others simply haven't. It is a lie, a lie which sits at table right next to a truth which is that some people are conscious of their ethical or aesthetic nature; others are unconscious of it. But everybody has it.

For everyone fretting aloud over the loss of "a raw-boned farmhouse on a bleak hillside" there are others who experience the same deprivation but so unconsciously that it shows only as undifferentiated despondency. Even the smiling drinker, easing himself heavily between boothback and table in the VFW lounge, is offended and frightened by the wrecking of the Minnesota landscape. He is offended, that is, with that fraction of his daily conscious thought not already absorbed by response to financial squeeze. He perceives wreckage of fishing lakes as an enemy, all right, but this enemy is only 3 percent (or so) of the total host lined up against him: the nearest enemy soldiery are economic pressure, boredom, lack of leisure, daily discourtesies given and received simply because no one taught an alternative to them.

Let's imagine a soldier dug in on Anzio beachhead, with the German emplacements very close and very high above the American positions, and then tell that soldier that four kilometers behind the high ground some boys have laid two-by-fours across the road with twenty-penny nails sticking up along them, so that when the U.S. supply trucks try to advance they will get flats. Then if you ask the soldier, "Do you feel threatened by those little boys? They are your natural enemy, you know!" the soldier can't take you seriously: visible before him are all those gray helmets. It is something the same with the VFW drinker. If he appears not to be taking up for conservation of the woods, it is not necessarily that he is insensitive to beauty. He scarcely has time, he is so pressed upon by other things. It is a psychological parallel to a soldier's already having to point a rifle in too many directions.

Further, natural beauty is a low priority with nearly all of us. We may grieve for the vanishing past or despoiled present beauty; we may acknowledge that reminders—like well-loved farm sites—incline us to spirit, but we can only occasionally be roused on the subject; whether taught it in the VFW or the Episcopal church or the Countryside Council, the fact is we have been taught that economic reality is important, and psychic reality is at its best a luxury consideration, and at its usual worst, slaver.

Of course Minnesotans will continue staging fights to preserve our landscape—and not just those showing up at Spring Hill conferences called Partners for a Livable Minnesota, but Minnesotans by the hundreds. Their efforts will be useful only if they abandon the notion that some people don't need symbol and beauty. When a class system operates in the *psyche* then it has arrived at full depravity. Surely the worst use of *saint sulpice* is preferable to deciding out of hand that some people haven't holy insides and holy needs.

[1978]

GROWING UP EXPRESSIVE

LOVE, DEATH, the cruelty of power, and time's curve past the stars are what children want to look at. For convenience's sake, let's say these are the four most vitally touching things in life. Little children ask questions about them with relish. Children, provided they are still little enough, have no eye to doing any problem solving about love or death or injustice or the universe; they are simply interested. I've noticed that as we read aloud literature to them, about Baba Yaga, and Dr. Doolittle, and Ivan and the Firebird, and Rat and Mole, children are not only interested, they are prepared to be vitally touched by the great things of life. If you like the phrase, they are what some people call "being as a little child." Another way of looking at it is to say that in our minds we have two kinds of receptivity to life going on all the time: first, being vitally touched and enthusiastic (grateful, enraged, puzzled—but, at all events, *moved*) and, second, having a will to solve problems.

Our gritty society wants and therefore deliberately trains problem solvers, however, not mystics. We teach human beings to keep themselves conscious only of problems that *can* conceivably be solved. There must be no hopeless causes. Now this means that some subjects, of which death and sexual love come to mind straight off, should be kept at as low a level of consciousness as possible. Both resist problem solving. A single-minded problem solver focuses his consciousness, of course, on problems to be solved, but even he realizes there is a concentric, peripheral band of other material around the problems. This band appears to him as "issues." He is not interested in these issues for themselves; he sees them simply as impacting on the problems. He will allow us to talk of love, death, injustice, and eternity— he may even encourage us to do so because his group-dynamics training advises him to let us have our say, thus dissipating our willfulness—but his heart is circling, circling, looking for an opening to *wrap up* these "issues" so he can return attention to discrete, solvable problems. For example, a physician who has that mentality does not wish to be near dying patients very much. They are definitely not a solvable problem. If he is wicked, he will regard them as a present issue

with impact on a future problem: then he will order experimentation
done on them during their last weeks with us. It means his ethic is
toward the healing process only, but not toward the dying person. His
ethic is toward problem solving, not toward wonder. He will feel quite
conscientious while doing the experiments on the dying patient, because he feels he is saving lives of future patients.

To return to little children for a second: they simply like to contemplate life and death. So our difficulty, in trying to educate adults so
they will be balanced but enthusiastic, is to keep both streams going—
the problem solving, which seems to be the mental genius of our
species, and the fearless contemplation of gigantic things, the spiritual
genius of our species.

The problem-solving mentality is inculcated no less in art and
English classes than in mathematics and science. Its snake oil is hope
of success: by setting very small topics in front of people, for which
it is easy for them to see the goals, the problems, the solutions, their
egos are not threatened. They feel hopeful of being effective. Therefore, to raise a generation of problem solvers, you encourage them to
visit the county offices (as our sixth-grade teachers do) and you lead
them to understand that this is citizenship. You carefully do not
suggest that citizenship also means comparatively complex and hopeless activities like Amnesty International's pressure to get prisoners
in far places released or at least no longer tortured. Small egos are
threatened by huge, perhaps insoluble problems. Therefore, one feeds
the small ego confidence by setting before it dozens and dozens of very
simple situations. The ego is nourished by feeling it understands the
relationship between the county recorder's office and the county trea-
surer's office; in later life, when young people find a couple of sticky
places in county government, they will confidently work at smoothing
them. How very different an experience such problem solving is from
having put before one the spectacle of the United States' various
stances and activities with respect to germ warfare. Educators regularly steer off all interest in national and international government to
one side, constantly feeding our rural young people on questions to
which one can hope for answers on a short timeline. We do not ask
them to exercise that muscle which bears the weight of vast considerations—such as cruelty in large governments. By the time the average
rural Minnesotan is eighteen, he or she expects to stay in cheerful
places, devote some time to local government and civic work, and

"win the little ones." Rural young people have a repertoire of pejorative language for hard causes: "opening that keg of worms," "no end to that once you get into it," "don't worry—you can't do anything about that from where you are," "we could go on about that forever!" They are right, of course: we could, and our species, at its most cultivated, does go on forever about love, death, power, time, the universe. But some of us, alas, have been conditioned by eighteen fashionably to despise those subjects because there are no immediate answers to all the questions they ask us.

The other way we negatively reinforce any philosophical bent in children is to pretend we don't see the content in their artwork. We comment only on the technique, in somewhat the same way you can scarcely get a comment on rural preachers' sermon content: the response is always, He does a good (or bad) job of speaking. "Well, but what did he say?" "Oh, he talked really well. The man can preach!"

The way to devalue the content of a child's painting is to say, "Wow, you sure can paint!" The average art teacher in Minnesota is at pains to find something to say to the third grader's painting of a space machine with complicated, presumably electronic equipment in it. Here is the drawing in words: A man is sitting at some controls. Outside his capsule, fire is flying from emission points on his ship toward another spaceship at right, hitting it. Explosions are coming out of its side and tail. What is an art teacher to do with this? Goodness knows. So he or she says, "My goodness, I can see there's a lot of action there!" It is said in a deliberately encouraging way but anyone can hear under the carefully supportive comment: "A lot of work going into nothing but more TV-inspired violence." One might as well have told the child, "Thank you for sharing."

I once attended a regional writers' group at which a young poet wrote about his feelings of being a single parent and trying to keep his sanity as he cared for his children. In his poem, he raced up the staircase, grabbed a gun, and shot the clock. When he finished reading it aloud to us, someone told him, "I certainly am glad you shared with us. I'd like to really thank you for sharing."

If we are truly serious about life we are going to have to stop thanking people for sharing. It isn't enough response to whatever has been offered. It is half ingenuous, and sometimes it is insincere, and often it is patronizing. It is the *dictum excrementi* of our decade.

I would like to keep in mind for a moment the art works described

above: the child's painting of a spaceship assaulting another spaceship, and the harrowed father's racing up the staircase and shooting
the clock. Here is a third. It is a twelve-year-old's theme for English
class.

They were their four days and nights before anyone found them. It was
wet and cold down there. As little kids at the orphanage, they had been
beaten every night until they could scarcely make it to bed. Now they
were older. Duane and Ellen leaned together. "I love you forever," she
told him. He asked her, "Even though my face is marked from getting
scarlett fever and polio and small pox and newmonya and they
wouldn't take decent care of me, not call the doctor or anything, so
the marks will always be on me?" "You know I love you," Ellen told
him. "You know that time they tortured me for information and I was
there but I didn't talk and later I found out it was your uncle who did
it. I didn't talk because I remembered the American flag." Just then
they heard someone shout, "Anyone alive down there in this mess?"
You see a bomb had gone off destroying a entire U.S.A. city where they
lived. Duane had lived with his cruel uncle who took him out of the
orphanage to get cheap labor and Ellen lived at a boardinghouse where
there were rats that ate pages of her diary all the time. Now they both
looked up and shouted "We're here!" A head appeared at the top of
the well into which they had fallen or they would of been in 6,500
pieces like all the other men and ladies even pregnant ones and little
kids in that town. Now this head called down, "Oh—a boy and a girl!"
then the head explained it was going for a ladder and ropes and it
ducked away and where it had been they saw the beginnings of stars
for that night, the stars still milky in front of the bright blue because
the sky wasn't dark enough yet to show them up good.

The English teacher will typically comment on this story by observ-
ing that the spelling is uneven, and adjectives get used as adverbs. In
rural Minnesota (if not elsewhere) an English teacher can spend every
class hour on adjectives used as adverbs: it is meat and potatoes to
a nag. But when we discuss spelling, syntax, and adverbs, we are
talking method, not content. The child notices that nothing is said of
the story's *plot*. No one remarks on the *feelings* in it. Now if this
happens every time a child hands in fiction or a poem, the child will
realize by the time he reaches twelfth grade that meaning or feelings
are not worth anything, that "mechanics" (note the term) are all that
matter.

It is rare for a public school English teacher to comment on a child's
content unless the material is *factual*. Minnesota teachers encourage
writing booklets about the state, themes on ecology and county government, on how Dad strikes the field each autumn, on how Mom
avoids open-kettle canning because the USDA advises against it. In
this way, our children are conditioned to regard writing as problem
solving instead of contemplation, as routine thinking instead of imaginative inquiry.

How can we manage it otherwise?

I would like to suggest some questions we can ask children about
their artwork which will encourage them to grow up into lovers, lobby
supporters, and Amnesty International members, instead of only
township officers and annual protestors against daylight saving time.
Let us gather all the elements of the three artworks presented in this
Letter: the little boy's spaceship-war painting, the young divorced
father's narrative poem, and the twelve-year-old girl's story of love in
a well. We have a set of images before us, then:

Man directing spaceship fire
Another aircraft being obliterated
Staircase, man shooting a clock; children
Cruel orphanage
Torture
Last survivors of a decimated city

Let us, instead of lending the great sneer to these images, be respectful
of them. It may help to pretend the painting is by Picasso, that
Flaubert wrote the father/clock scene, and that Tolstoy wrote the
well story. It helps to remember that Picasso felt the assault of historical events on us—like Guernica; Flaubert, as skillfully as Dostoyevsky
and with less self-pity, was an observer of violent detail; and the
Tolstoy who wrote *Resurrection* or the scene of Pierre's imprisonment
in *War and Peace* would turn to the well/love story without qualm.

We know we would never say to Picasso, Flaubert, or Tolstoy,
"Why don't you draw something you know about from everyday life?
Why don't you write about something you know about? You say Anna
was smashed beneath a train? Thank you for sharing!"

The fact is that a child's feelings about orphanages and torture and
love are things that he does know about. They are psychic realities

inside him, and when he draws them, he is drawing something from everyday life. Sometimes they are from his night life of dreaming, but in any event they are images of passion and he is drawing from his genuine if garbled experience. A few years ago there was a stupid movement to discourage children's reading of Grimms' fairy tales. Later, with a more sophisticated psychology, we learned that the stepmother who is hostile and overweening is a reality to all children; the cutting-off of the hero's right hand and replacing of it with a hand of silver is a reality to all children. Spaceships, witches' gingerbread houses, orphanages, being the last two people to survive on earth—all these are part of the inner landscape, something children know about. Therefore, in examining their artwork, we need better sets of questions to ask them. Young people who are not repressed are going to lay their wild stuff in front of adults (hoping for comment of some kind, praise if possible) until the sands of life are run, so we had better try to be good at responding to them. And unless we want to raise drones suitable only for conveyor-belt shifts, we had better be at least half as enthusiastic as when they tell us, Mama, I got the mowing finished.

Here are some questions to ask our young artist. How much of that electronic equipment is used for firepower and how much just to run the ship? After the other spaceship is blown up and the people in it are dead, what will this man do? Will he go home somewhere? Were the stars out that night? You said he'll go home to his parents. Did the other man have parents? How soon will that man's parents find out that his spaceship was destroyed? Could you draw in the stars? You said they were out—could you draw them into the picture some way? but don't ruin anything you've got in there now. Also, that wire you said ran to the solar plates, will you darken it so it shows better? Don't change it—just make it clearer. Yes—terrific! Can you see the planet where the other man would have returned to if he had lived till morning?

The young father's story: There is an obvious psychic complication to this story: the violence in his shooting out the clock face is gratuitous, and the plea for attention on the part of the author directed at the reader is glaring: clock faces as psychological symbols are in the public domain. Anyone who tells a friend (or a group of strangers) I am going to shoot up a clock face at 11 P.M. is asking for psychological attention. In a civil world, to ask is to receive, so if we are civilized we have to pay attention and ask the young author: Why does the father in the story blast the clock? And, when he replies, we have to ask some more. If there was ever an instance in which it was O.K. to say, "Thanks for sharing," this is not it.

I should like to add that this will be especially difficult for rural teachers because the traditional country way to treat any kind of mental problem is to stare it down. It didn't happen. I didn't hear that insane thing you just said, and you know you don't really hate your mother. What nice parent would shoot a clock? We uniformly do what Dr. Vaillant in *Adaptations to Life* would call a denial adaptation. It takes a brave questioner when the young person brings in a crazy story.

The well/love story: Did you know there really are such orphanages? There are orphanages where the children have to get up at four-thirty to work in the dairy, and the girls work hours and hours in the kitchens, and the children's growth is stunted. Did you make the girl so brave on purpose? Were they a lucky couple or an unlucky couple, or is that the sort of a question you can't ask? You made a point of telling us they'd been through a lot of hardship. What would it have been like for them if they hadn't? Do you want to talk about what blew up the city? Did you imagine yourself in the well?

Those are not brilliant questions; they are simply respectful, because the art works described are concerned with death by violence; cruelty by institutions; treachery by relations; bravery (or cowardice—either one is important); sexual love, either despite or encouraged by dreadful circumstances.

They are some of the subjects in *War and Peace,* in Dürer's etchings, paintings, and woodcuts, and in *Madame Bovary.*

It is a moot question in my mind which of two disciplines will be the more useful in helping people stay vitally touched by the Great Things: psychology might do it—and English literature in high school might do it (instruction on the college level is generally so dutiful to methodology that it seems a lost cause to me. "How did D. H. Lawrence foreshadow this event?" and "What metaphors does Harold Rosenberg use in his discussion of Action Painting?" are the questions of technocrats, not preservers of spirit. It is as if we got home from church and the others said, "How was church?" "We had Eucharist," we tell them. "Well, how was it?" they ask. "Pretty good," we reply. "Bishop Anderson was there. He held the chalice eight inches above the rail so no one spilled, then he turned and wiped the chalice after each use so no germs were passed along. People who had already communed returned to their benches using the north aisle so there was no bottlenecking at the chancel.")

I don't think churches will be helpful in preserving the mystical outlook as long as they see life and death as a *problem*—a problem of salvation—with a solution to be worked at. Churches have an axe to grind. They might take the father running up the staircase to be an impact subject: they would wish to use their program to solve his problem. Churchmen often appear to be companionable counselors, but the appearance is largely manner and habit. Under the manner, the clergyman's mindset is nearly always to see a disturbed or grieving person's imagery as *the issues*. From there, he swings into psychological problem solving.

I would like to commend this responsibility to our English teachers: that they help our children preserve pity, happiness, and grief inside themselves. They can enhance those feelings by having young children both write and draw pictures. They can be very enthusiastic about the children's first drawings of death in the sky. Adults, particularly mature ones who have *not* got children in school at the moment, should make it clear that we expect this of English teachers and that we don't give a damn if LeRoy and Merv never in their lives get the sentence balance of past conditional and perfect subjunctive clauses right. We need to protect some of the Things Invisible inside LeRoy and Merv and the rest of us.

This is my last Letter from the Country. That is why it is so shrill. Gadflies are always looking out a chance to be shrill anyway, so I jumped to this one and have shouted my favorite hope: that we can educate children not to be problem solvers but to be madly expressive all their lives.

[1979]

JOAN DIDION

JOAN DIDION WAS BORN in Sacramento, California, on December 5, 1934, a fifth-generation descendant of pioneers who had helped settle the Sacramento Valley in the 1840s. In her autobiographical essays she frequently points out how different Sacramento is from the California most people think of—Hollywood, freeways, a rootless population. Sacramento has always been farming country, and Didion's ancestors were landowners, their politics conservative, their religion Episcopal. She grew up in a world where the middle-class values of character, morality, and economy were firmly established.

During World War II her family was temporarily uprooted as they followed her father, an officer in the air corps, to air bases around the country, celebrating "makeshift Christmases in rented rooms." With the end of the war they returned to Sacramento and a settled life again, where there were "teacups hand-painted with cabbage roses" and they visited "the great-aunts on Sundays." After graduating from the local high school, Didion went to the University of California at Berkeley (A.B., 1956) and from there to New York, where she was an associate feature editor at *Vogue* for seven years. (As a senior at Berkeley she had won *Vogue*'s *Prix de Paris.*) In 1964 she married John Gregory Dunne, a writer for *Time,* and a few months later they left New York for Los Angeles, intending to stay only six months; it was one of those leaves of absence from frustrating security that writers often take in order to see if they can make it on their own, just writing.

Fortunately, within a year Didion and Dunne had both established freelance associations with *The Saturday Evening Post,* and by the end of 1966 they shared a regular *Post* column entitled "Points West." (They have also collaborated on the screenplays for *The Panic in Needle Park, A Star is Born,* and *True Confessions.*) In 1968 Didion published *Slouching Towards Bethlehem,* a collection of her essays from the *Post* and other magazines, and she began receiving serious attention from literary critics. (An earlier novel, *Run River,* 1963, written while she was at *Vogue,* had gone largely unnoticed.) What critics admired in *Slouching Towards Bethlehem* were Didion's economical style, her candidness, and the intense clarity with which she reported some of the most grotesque aspects of life in America in the late sixties.

In 1970 Joan Didion published *Play It as It Lays,* a novel of apocalyptic vision reminiscent of Nathanael West's *The Day of the Locust.*
A depressing tale of abortion, divorce, and suicide in Hollywood and
Las Vegas, *Play It as It Lays* is also, in the end, a story of survival:
despite all that happens to her, the central character, Maria Wyeth,
does not give up. As she says at the end, "I know what 'nothing'
means, and keep on playing." *Play It as It Lays* was nominated for the
1970 National Book Award in Fiction.

In her third novel, *A Book of Common Prayer* (1977), Didion again
portrays a woman who attempts to survive a catastrophic life. Charlotte Douglas, like Maria Wyeth, lacks heroic qualities; she is shallow,
foolish, weak. Coming out of a protected, monied background, she is
not prepared to deal with a world that is deceptively evil. And yet
again, in the novel's moral complexity, Charlotte Douglas ends up
being a deeply sympathetic character and a hero of sorts: she survives.

In 1979 a second collection of essays, *The White Album,* was
published. Again creating vivid images of personal and cultural break-
down, Didion writes with painful honesty about the difficulty of maintaining a sense of meaningful purpose in a fragmented world. In an
essay entitled "On the Morning After the Sixties" she explains the
difference between the private values of her own generation and the
collective beliefs of young people in the late sixties and early seventies: "If I could believe that going to a barricade would affect man's
fate in the slightest I would go to that barricade, and often wish that
I could, but I would be less than honest to say that I expect to happen
on such a happy ending."

In the essay "Why I Write" Didion says she "can bring . . . no
reports from any other front" than the very private one of the writer
in "the act of writing." Yet in 1982 she went to the "front" (as it is)
in El Salvador and brought back the most harrowing account of the
troubles occurring there. Three long essays appeared in *The New York
Review of Books* in October 1982 and later formed the bulk of her
book *Salvador* (1983). In 1984 she published her fourth novel, *Democracy* (borrowing the title of a political satire written by Henry
Adams in 1880). An exploration of the "dislocations" that have occurred in American life during the last twenty years, *Democracy*
examines the relationships between money, political life, and the mass
media as experienced by a woman, Inez Christian Victor, whose
husband is a United States Senator who aspires to be President.

Joan Didion's style is one of ellipses and vivid images, often put into
paradoxical juxtapositions. She is simultaneously candid in her revela-

tions of her personal life, and private. Her effects are often achieved
as much by what she leaves out as what she includes. In an interview
in *The Paris Review,* she revealed that the two writers who have had
the greatest influence on her are Ernest Hemingway and Henry
James—a stylistic paradox if ever there was one. It is perhaps easier
to think of her style as *cinematic*—that is, deriving its power largely
from a rapid "cutting" between vivid images. It is a style to which
many readers today can respond more easily than the rhetorical ca-
dences of the past.

GOODBYE TO ALL THAT

How many miles to Babylon?
Three score miles and ten—
Can I get there by candlelight?
Yes, and back again—
If your feet are nimble and light
You can get there by candlelight.

IT IS EASY to see the beginnings of things, and harder to see the ends. I can remember now, with a clarity that makes the nerves in the back of my neck constrict, when New York began for me, but I cannot lay my finger upon the moment it ended, can never cut through the ambiguities and second starts and broken resolves to the exact place on the page where the heroine is no longer as optimistic as she once was. When I first saw New York I was twenty, and it was summertime, and I got off a DC-7 at the old Idlewild temporary terminal in a new dress which had seemed very smart in Sacramento but seemed less smart already, even in the old Idlewild temporary terminal, and the warm air smelled of mildew and some instinct, programmed by all the movies I had ever seen and all the songs I had ever heard sung and all the stories I had ever read about New York, informed me that it would never be quite the same again. In fact it never was. Some time later there was a song on all the jukeboxes on the upper East Side that went "but where is the schoolgirl who used to be me," and if it was late enough at night I used to wonder that. I know now that almost everyone wonders something like that, sooner or later and no matter what he or she is doing, but one of the mixed blessings of being twenty and twenty-one and even twenty-three is the conviction that nothing like this, all evidence to the contrary notwithstanding, has ever happened to anyone before.

Of course it might have been some other city, had circumstances been different and the time been different and had I been different, might have been Paris or Chicago or even San Francisco, but because I am talking about myself I am talking here about New York. That first night I opened my window on the bus into town and watched for the skyline, but all I could see were the wastes of Queens and the big signs that said MIDTOWN TUNNEL THIS LANE and then a flood of summer rain (even that seemed remarkable and exotic, for I had come out of the West where there was no summer rain), and for the next three days I sat wrapped in blankets in a hotel room air-conditioned to 35° and tried to get over a bad cold and a high fever. It did not occur to me to call a doctor, because I knew none, and although it did occur to me to call the desk and ask that the air conditioner be turned off, I never called, because I did not know how much to tip whoever might come—was anyone ever so young? I am here to tell you that someone was. All I could do during those three days was talk long-distance to the boy I already knew I would never marry in the spring. I would stay in New York, I told him, just six months, and I could see the Brooklyn Bridge from my window. As it turned out the bridge was the Triborough, and I stayed eight years.

In retrospect it seems to me that those days before I knew the names of all the bridges were happier than the ones that came later, but perhaps you will see that as we go along. Part of what I want to tell you is what it is like to be young in New York, how six months can become eight years with the deceptive ease of a film dissolve, for that is how those years appear to me now, in a long sequence of sentimental dissolves and old-fashioned trick shots—the Seagram Building fountains dissolve into snowflakes, I enter a revolving door at twenty and come out a good deal older, and on a different street. But most particularly I want to explain to you, and in the process perhaps to myself, why I no longer live in New York. It is often said that New York is a city for only the very rich and the very poor. It is less often said that New York is also, at least for those of us who came there from somewhere else, a city for only the very young.

I remember once, one cold bright December evening in New York, suggesting to a friend who complained of having been around too long that he come with me to a party where there would be, I assured him with the bright resourcefulness of twenty-three, "new faces." He laughed literally until he choked, and I had to roll down the taxi window and hit him on the back. "New faces," he said finally, "don't tell me about *new faces*." It seemed that the last time he had gone

to a party where he had been promised "new faces," there had been
fifteen people in the room, and he had already slept with five of the
women and owed money to all but two of the men. I laughed with him,
but the first snow had just begun to fall and the big Christmas trees
glittered yellow and white as far as I could see up Park Avenue and
I had a new dress and it would be a long while before I would come
to understand the particular moral of the story.

It would be a long while because, quite simply, I was in love with
New York. I do not mean "love" in any colloquial way, I mean that
I was in love with the city, the way you love the first person who ever
touches you and never love anyone quite that way again. I remember
walking across Sixty-second Street one twilight that first spring, or the
second spring, they were all alike for a while. I was late to meet
someone but I stopped at Lexington Avenue and bought a peach and
stood on the corner eating it and knew that I had come out of the
West and reached the mirage. I could taste the peach and feel the soft
air blowing from a subway grating on my legs and I could smell lilac
and garbage and expensive perfume and I knew that it would cost
something sooner or later—because I did not belong there, did not
come from there—but when you are twenty-two or twenty-three, you
figure that later you will have a high emotional balance, and be able
to pay whatever it costs. I still believed in possibilities then, still had
the sense, so peculiar to New York, that something extraordinary
would happen any minute, any day, any month. I was making only
$65 or $70 a week then ("Put yourself in Hattie Carnegie's hands,"
I was advised without the slightest trace of irony by an editor of the
magazine for which I worked), so little money that some weeks I had
to charge food at Bloomingdale's gourmet shop in order to eat, a fact
which went unmentioned in the letters I wrote to California. I never
told my father that I needed money because then he would have sent
it, and I would never know if I could do it by myself. At that time
making a living seemed a game to me, with arbitrary but quite inflexi-
ble rules. And except on a certain kind of winter evening—six-thirty
in the Seventies, say, already dark and bitter with a wind off the river,
when I would be walking very fast toward a bus and would look in
the bright windows of brownstones and see cooks working in clean
kitchens and imagine women lighting candles on the floor above and
beautiful children being bathed on the floor above that—except on

nights like those, I never felt poor; I had the feeling that if I needed money I could always get it. I could write a syndicated column for teenagers under the name "Debbi Lynn" or I could smuggle gold into India or I could become a $100 call girl, and none of it would matter. Nothing was irrevocable; everything was within reach. Just around every corner lay something curious and interesting, something I had never before seen or done or known about. I could go to a party and meet someone who called himself Mr. Emotional Appeal and ran The Emotional Appeal Institute or Tina Onassis Blandford or a Florida cracker who was then a regular on what he called "the Big C," the Southampton–El Morocco circuit ("I'm well-connected on the Big C, honey," he would tell me over collard greens on his vast borrowed terrace), or the widow of the celery king of the Harlem market or a piano salesman from Bonne Terre, Missouri, or someone who had already made and lost two fortunes in Midland, Texas. I could make promises to myself and to other people and there would be all the time in the world to keep them. I could stay up all night and make mistakes, and none of it would count.

You see I was in a curious position in New York: it never occurred to me that I was living a real life there. In my imagination I was always there for just another few months, just until Christmas or Easter or the first warm day in May. For that reason I was most comfortable in the company of Southerners. They seemed to be in New York as I was, on some indefinitely extended leave from wherever they belonged, disinclined to consider the future, temporary exiles who always knew when the flights left for New Orleans or Memphis or Richmond or, in my case, California. Someone who lives always with a plane schedule in the drawer lives on a slightly different calendar. Christmas, for example, was a difficult season. Other people could take it in stride, going to Stowe or going abroad or going for the day to their mothers' places in Connecticut; those of us who believed that we lived somewhere else would spend it making and canceling airline reservations, waiting for weatherbound flights as if for the last plane out of Lisbon in 1940, and finally comforting one another, those of us who were left, with the oranges and mementos and smoked-oyster stuffings of childhood, gathering close, colonials in a far country.

Which is precisely what we were. I am not sure that it is possible for anyone brought up in the East to appreciate entirely what New York, the idea of New York, means to those of us who came out of the West and the South. To an Eastern child, particularly a child who has always had an uncle on Wall Street and who has spent several hundred Saturdays first at F. A. O. Schwarz and being fitted for shoes at Best's and then waiting under the Biltmore clock and dancing to Lester Lanin, New York is just a city, albeit *the* city, a plausible place for people to live. But to those of us who came from places where no one had heard of Lester Lanin and Grand Central Station was a Saturday radio program, where Wall Street and Fifth Avenue and Madison Avenue were not places at all but abstractions ("Money," and "High Fashion," and "The Hucksters"), New York was no mere city. It was instead an infinitely romantic notion, the mysterious nexus of all love and money and power, the shining and perishable dream itself. To think of "living" there was to reduce the miraculous to the mundane; one does not "live" at Xanadu.

In fact it was difficult in the extreme for me to understand those young women for whom New York was not simply an ephemeral Estoril but a real place, girls who bought toasters and installed new cabinets in their apartments and committed themselves to some reasonable future. I never bought any furniture in New York. For a year or so I lived in other people's apartments; after that I lived in the Nineties in an apartment furnished entirely with things taken from storage by a friend whose wife had moved away. And when I left the apartment in the Nineties (that was when I was leaving everything, when it was all breaking up) I left everything in it, even my winter clothes and the map of Sacramento County I had hung on the bedroom wall to remind me who I was, and I moved into a monastic four-room floor-through on Seventy-fifth Street. "Monastic" is perhaps misleading here, implying some chic severity; until after I was married and my husband moved some furniture in, there was nothing at all in those four rooms except a cheap double mattress and box springs, ordered by telephone the day I decided to move, and two French garden chairs lent me by a friend who imported them. (It strikes me now that the people I knew in New York all had curious and self-defeating sidelines. They imported garden chairs which did not sell very well at Hammacher Schlemmer or they tried to market hair straighteners in Harlem or they ghosted exposés of Murder Incorporated for Sunday supplements. I think that perhaps none of us was very serious, *engagé* only about our most private lives.)

All I ever did to that apartment was hang fifty yards of yellow theatrical silk across the bedroom windows, because I had some idea that the gold light would make me feel better, but I did not bother to weight the curtains correctly and all that summer the long panels of transparent golden silk would blow out the windows and get tangled and drenched in the afternoon thunderstorms. That was the year, my twenty-eighth, when I was discovering that not all of the promises would be kept, that some things are in fact irrevocable and that it had counted after all, every evasion and every procrastination, every mistake, every word, all of it.

   That is what it was all about, wasn't it? Promises? Now when New York comes back to me it comes in hallucinatory flashes, so clinically detailed that I sometimes wish that memory would effect the distortion with which it is commonly credited. For a lot of the time I was in New York I used a perfume called *Fleurs de Rocaille,* and then *L'Air du Temps,* and now the slightest trace of either can short-circuit my connections for the rest of the day. Nor can I smell Henri Bendel jasmine soap without falling back into the past, or the particular mixture of spices used for boiling crabs. There were barrels of crab boil in a Czech place in the Eighties where I once shopped. Smells, of course, are notorious memory stimuli, but there are other things which affect me the same way. Blue-and-white striped sheets. Vermouth cassis. Some faded nightgowns which were new in 1959 or 1960, and some chiffon scarves I bought about the same time.

   I suppose that a lot of us who have been young in New York have the same scenes on our home screens. I remember sitting in a lot of apartments with a slight headache about five o'clock in the morning. I had a friend who could not sleep, and he knew a few other people who had the same trouble, and we would watch the sky lighten and have a last drink with no ice and then go home in the early morning light, when the streets were clean and wet (had it rained in the night? we never knew) and the few cruising taxis still had their headlights on and the only color was the red and green of traffic signals. The White Rose bars opened very early in the morning; I recall waiting in one of them to watch an astronaut go into space, waiting so long that at the moment it actually happened I had my eyes not on the television screen but on a cockroach on the tile floor. I liked the bleak branches above Washington Square at dawn, and the monochromatic flatness of Second Avenue, the fire escapes and the grilled storefronts peculiar and empty in their perspective.

It is relatively hard to fight at six-thirty or seven in the morning, without any sleep, which was perhaps one reason we stayed up all night, and it seemed to me a pleasant time of day. The windows were shuttered in that apartment in the Nineties and I could sleep a few hours and then go to work. I could work then on two or three hours' sleep and a container of coffee from Chock Full O' Nuts. I liked going to work, liked the soothing and satisfactory rhythm of getting out a magazine, liked the orderly progression of four-color closings and two-color closings and black-and-white closings and then The Product, no abstraction but something which looked effortlessly glossy and could be picked up on a newsstand and weighed in the hand. I liked all the minutiae of proofs and layouts, liked working late on the nights the magazine went to press, sitting and reading *Variety* and waiting for the copy desk to call. From my office I could look across town to the weather signal on the Mutual of New York Building and the lights that alternately spelled out TIME and LIFE above Rockefeller Plaza; that pleased me obscurely, and so did walking uptown in the mauve eight o'clocks of early summer evenings and looking at things, Lowestoft tureens in Fifty-seventh Street windows, people in evening clothes trying to get taxis, the trees just coming into full leaf, the lambent air, all the sweet promises of money and summer.

Some years passed, but I still did not lose that sense of wonder about New York. I began to cherish the loneliness of it, the sense that at any given time no one need know where I was or what I was doing. I liked walking, from the East River over to the Hudson and back on brisk days, down around the Village on warm days. A friend would leave me the key to her apartment in the West Village when she was out of town, and sometimes I would just move down there, because by that time the telephone was beginning to bother me (the canker, you see, was already in the rose) and not many people had that number. I remember one day when someone who did have the West Village number came to pick me up for lunch there, and we both had hangovers, and I cut my finger opening him a beer and burst into tears, and we walked to a Spanish restaurant and drank Bloody Marys and *gazpacho* until we felt better. I was not then guilt-ridden about spending afternoons that way, because I still had all the afternoons in the world.

And even that late in the game I still liked going to parties, all
parties, bad parties, Saturday-afternoon parties given by recently
married couples who lived in Stuyvesant Town, West Side parties
given by unpublished or failed writers who served cheap red wine and
talked about going to Guadalajara, Village parties where all the guests
worked for advertising agencies and voted for Reform Democrats,
press parties at Sardi's, the worst kinds of parties. You will have
perceived by now that I was not one to profit by the experience of
others, that it was a very long time indeed before I stopped believing
in new faces and began to understand the lesson in that story, which
was that it is distinctly possible to stay too long at the Fair.

I could not tell you when I began to understand that. All I know
is that it was very bad when I was twenty-eight. Everything that was
said to me I seemed to have heard before, and I could no longer listen.
I could no longer sit in little bars near Grand Central and listen to
someone complaining of his wife's inability to cope with the help while
he missed another train to Connecticut. I no longer had any interest
in hearing about the advances other people had received from their
publishers, about plays which were having second-act trouble in Philadelphia, or about people I would like very much if only I would come
out and meet them. I had already met them, always. There were
certain parts of the city which I had to avoid. I could not bear upper
Madison Avenue on weekday mornings (this was a particularly inconvenient aversion, since I then lived just fifty or sixty feet east of
Madison), because I would see women walking Yorkshire terriers and
shopping at Gristede's, and some Veblenesque gorge would rise in my
throat. I could not go to Times Square in the afternoon, or to the New
York Public Library for any reason whatsoever. One day I could not
go into a Schrafft's; the next day it would be Bonwit Teller.
I hurt the people I cared about, and insulted those I did not. I cut
myself off from the one person who was closer to me than any other.
I cried until I was not even aware when I was crying and when I was
not, cried in elevators and in taxis and in Chinese laundries, and when
I went to the doctor he said only that I seemed to be depressed, and
should see a "specialist." He wrote down a psychiatrist's name and
address for me, but I did not go.
Instead I got married, which as it turned out was a very good thing

to do but badly timed, since I still could not walk on upper Madison Avenue in the mornings and still could not talk to people and still cried in Chinese laundries. I had never before understood what "despair" meant, and I am not sure that I understand now, but I understood that year. Of course I could not work. I could not even get dinner with any degree of certainty, and I would sit in the apartment on Seventy-fifth Street paralyzed until my husband would call from his office and say gently that I did not have to get dinner, that I could meet him at Michael's Pub or at Toots Shor's or at Sardi's East. And then one morning in April (we had been married in January) he called and told me that he wanted to get out of New York for a while, that he would take a six-month leave of absence, that we would go somewhere.

It was three years ago that he told me that, and we have lived in Los Angeles since. Many of the people we knew in New York think this a curious aberration, and in fact tell us so. There is no possible, no adequate answer to that, and so we give certain stock answers, the answers everyone gives. I talk about how difficult it would be for us to "afford" to live in New York right now, about how much "space" we need. All I mean is that I was very young in New York, and that at some point the golden rhythm was broken, and I am not that young any more. The last time I was in New York was in a cold January, and everyone was ill and tired. Many of the people I used to know there had moved to Dallas or had gone on Antabuse or had bought a farm in New Hampshire. We stayed ten days, and then we took an afternoon flight back to Los Angeles, and on the way home from the airport that night I could see the moon on the Pacific and smell jasmine all around and we both knew that there was no longer any point in keeping the apartment we still kept in New York. There were years when I called Los Angeles "the Coast," but they seem a long time ago.

[1967]

ON GOING HOME

I AM HOME for my daughter's first birthday. By "home" I do not mean the house in Los Angeles where my husband and I and the baby live, but the place where my family is, in the Central Valley of California. It is a vital although troublesome distinction. My husband likes my family but is uneasy in their house, because once there I fall into their ways, which are difficult, oblique, deliberately inarticulate, not my husband's ways. We live in dusty houses ("D-U-S-T," he once wrote with his finger on surfaces all over the house, but no one noticed it) filled with mementos quite without value to him (what could the Canton dessert plates mean to him? how could he have known about the assay scales, why should he care if he did know?), and we appear to talk exclusively about people we know who have been committed to mental hospitals, about people we know who have been booked on drunk-driving charges, and about property, particularly about property, land, price per acre and C-2 zoning and assessments and freeway access. My brother does not understand my husband's inability to perceive the advantage in the rather common real-estate transaction known as "sale-leaseback," and my husband in turn does not understand why so many of the people he hears about in my father's house have recently been committed to mental hospitals or booked on drunk-driving charges. Nor does he understand that when we talk about sale-leasebacks and right-of-way condemnations we are talking in code about the things we like best, the yellow fields and the cottonwoods and the rivers rising and falling and the mountain roads closing when the heavy snow comes in. We miss each other's points, have another drink and regard the fire. My brother refers to my husband, in his presence, as "Joan's husband." Marriage is the classic betrayal.

Or perhaps it is not any more. Sometimes I think that those of us who are now in our thirties were born into the last generation to carry the burden of "home," to find in family life the source of all tension and drama. I had by all objective accounts a "normal" and a "happy" family situation, and yet I was almost thirty years old before I could talk to my family on the telephone without crying after I had hung up. We did not fight. Nothing was wrong. And yet some nameless anxiety colored the emotional charges between me and the place that I came from. The question of whether or not you could go home again was a very real part of the sentimental and largely literary baggage with which we left home in the fifties; I suspect that it is irrelevant to the children born of the fragmentation after World War II. A few weeks ago in a San Francisco bar I saw a pretty young girl on crystal take off her clothes and dance for the cash prize in an "amateur-topless" contest. There was no particular sense of moment about this, none of the effect of romantic degradation, of "dark journey," for which my generation strived so assiduously. What sense could that girl possibly make of, say, *Long Day's Journey into Night?* Who is beside the point?

That I am trapped in this particular irrelevancy is never more apparent to me than when I am home. Paralyzed by the neurotic lassitude engendered by meeting one's past at every turn, around every corner, inside every cupboard, I go aimlessly from room to room. I decide to meet it head-on and clean out a drawer, and I spread the contents on the bed. A bathing suit I wore the summer I was seventeen. A letter of rejection from *The Nation,* an aerial photograph of the site for a shopping center my father did not build in 1954. Three teacups hand-painted with cabbage roses and signed "E.M.," my grandmother's initials. There is no final solution for letters of rejection from *The Nation* and teacups hand-painted in 1900. Nor is there any answer to snapshots of one's grandfather as a young man on skis, surveying around Donner Pass in the year 1910. I smooth out the snapshot and look into his face, and do and do not see my own. I close the drawer, and have another cup of coffee with my mother. We get along very well, veterans of a guerrilla war we never understood.

Days pass. I see no one. I come to dread my husband's evening call, not only because he is full of news of what by now seems to me our remote life in Los Angeles, people he has seen, letters which require attention, but because he asks what I have been doing, suggests uneasily that I get out, drive to San Francisco or Berkeley. Instead I drive across the river to a family graveyard. It has been vandalized since my last visit and the monuments are broken, overturned in the dry grass. Because I once saw a rattlesnake in the grass I stay in the car and listen to a country-and-Western station. Later I drive with my

father to a ranch he has in the foothills. The man who runs his cattle
on it asks us to the roundup, a week from Sunday, and although I
know that I will be in Los Angeles I say, in the oblique way my family
talks, that I will come. Once home I mention the broken monuments
in the graveyard. My mother shrugs.

I go to visit my great-aunts. A few of them think now that I am
my cousin, or their daughter who died young. We recall an anecdote
about a relative last seen in 1948, and they ask if I still like living in
New York City. I have lived in Los Angeles for three years, but I say
that I do. The baby is offered a horehound drop, and I am slipped a
dollar bill "to buy a treat." Questions trail off, answers are abandoned,
the baby plays with the dust motes in a shaft of afternoon sun.

It is time for the baby's birthday party: a white cake, strawberry-
marshmallow ice cream, a bottle of champagne saved from another
party. In the evening, after she has gone to sleep, I kneel beside the
crib and touch her face, where it is pressed against the slats, with
mine. She is an open and trusting child, unprepared for and unaccus-
tomed to the ambushes of family life, and perhaps it is just as well that
I can offer her little of that life. I would like to give her more. I would
like to promise her that she will grow up with a sense of her cousins
and of rivers and of her great-grandmother's teacups, would like to
pledge her a picnic on a river with fried chicken and her hair un-
combed, would like to give her *home* for her birthday, but we live
differently now and I can promise her nothing like that. I give her a
xylophone and a sundress from Madeira, and promise to tell her a
funny story.

[1967]

ON MORALITY

As it happens I am in Death Valley, in a room at the Enterprise
Motel and Trailer Park, and it is July, and it is hot. In fact it is 119°.
I cannot seem to make the air conditioner work, but there is a small
refrigerator, and I can wrap ice cubes in a towel and hold them against

the small of my back. With the help of the ice cubes I have been trying to think, because *The American Scholar* asked me to, in some abstract way about "morality," a word I distrust more every day, but my mind veers inflexibly toward the particular.

Here are some particulars. At midnight last night, on the road in from Las Vegas to Death Valley Junction, a car hit a shoulder and turned over. The driver, very young and apparently drunk, was killed instantly. His girl was found alive but bleeding internally, deep in shock. I talked this afternoon to the nurse who had driven the girl to the nearest doctor, 185 miles across the floor of the Valley and three ranges of lethal mountain road. The nurse explained that her husband, a talc miner, had stayed on the highway with the boy's body until the coroner could get over the mountains from Bishop, at dawn today. "You can't just leave a body on the highway," she said. "It's immoral."

It was one instance in which I did not distrust the word, because she meant something quite specific. She meant that if a body is left alone for even a few minutes on the desert, the coyotes close in and eat the flesh. Whether or not a corpse is torn apart by coyotes may seem only a sentimental consideration, but of course it is more: one of the promises we make to one another is that we will try to retrieve our casualties, try not to abandon our dead to the coyotes. If we have been taught to keep our promises—if, in the simplest terms, our upbringing is good enough—we stay with the body, or have bad dreams.

I am talking, of course, about the kind of social code that is sometimes called, usually pejoratively, "wagon-train morality." In fact that is precisely what it is. For better or worse, we are what we learned as children: my own childhood was illuminated by graphic litanies of the grief awaiting those who failed in their loyalties to each other. The Donner-Reed Party, starving in the Sierra snows, all the ephemera of civilization gone save that one vestigial taboo, the provision that no one should eat his own blood kin. The Jayhawkers, who quarreled and separated not far from where I am tonight. Some of them died in the Funerals and some of them died down near Badwater and most of the rest of them died in the Panamints. A woman who got through gave the Valley its name. Some might say that the Jayhawkers were killed by the desert summer, and the Donner Party by the mountain winter, by circumstances beyond control; we were taught instead that they had somewhere abdicated their responsibilities, somehow breached their primary loyalties, or they would not have found themselves helpless in the mountain winter or the desert summer, would not have given way to acrimony, would not have deserted one another, would not have *failed.* In brief, we heard such stories as cautionary tales, and they still suggest the only kind of "morality" that seems to me to have any but the most potentially mendacious meaning.

You are quite possibly impatient with me by now; I am talking, you want to say, about a "morality" so primitive that it scarcely deserves the name, a code that has as its point only survival, not the attainment of the ideal good. Exactly. Particularly out here tonight, in this country so ominous and terrible that to live in it is to live with antimatter, it is difficult to believe that "the good" is a knowable quantity. Let me tell you what it is like out here tonight. Stories travel at night on the desert. Someone gets in his pickup and drives a couple of hundred miles for a beer, and he carries news of what is happening, back wherever he came from. Then he drives another hundred miles for another beer, and passes along stories from the last place as well as from the one before; it is a network kept alive by people whose instincts tell them that if they do not keep moving at night in the desert they will lose all reason. Here is a story that is going around the desert tonight: over across the Nevada line, sheriff's deputies are diving in some underground pools, trying to retrieve a couple of bodies known to be in the hole. The widow of one of the drowned boys is over there; she is eighteen, and pregnant, and is said not to leave the hole. The divers go down and come up, and she just stands there and stares into the water. They have been diving for ten days but have found no bottom to the caves, no bodies and no trace of them, only the black 90° water going down and down and down, and a single translucent fish, not classified. The story tonight is that one of the divers has been hauled up incoherent, out of his head, shouting—until they got him out of there so that the widow could not hear—about water that got hotter instead of cooler as he went down, about light flickering through the water, about magma, about underground nuclear testing. That is the tone stories take out here, and there are quite a few of them. And it is more than the stories alone. Across the road at the Faith Community Church a couple of dozen old people, come here to live in trailers and die in the sun, are holding a prayer sing. I cannot hear them and do not want to. What I can hear are occasional coyotes and a constant chorus of "Baby the Rain Must Fall" from the jukebox in the Snake Room next door, and if I were also to hear those dying voices, those Midwestern voices drawn to this lunar country for some unimaginable atavistic rites, *rock of ages cleft for me,* I think I would lose my own reason. Every now and then I imagine I hear a rattlesnake, but my husband says that it is a faucet, a paper rustling, the wind. Then he stands by a window, and plays a flashlight over the dry wash outside.

What does it mean? It means nothing manageable. There is some sinister hysteria in the air out here tonight, some hint of the monstrous perversion to which any human idea can come. "I followed my own conscience." "I did what I thought was right." How many madmen have said it and meant it? How many murderers? Klaus Fuchs said it, and the men who committed the Mountain Meadows Massacre said it, and Alfred Rosenberg said it. And, as we are rotely and rather presumptuously reminded by those who would say it now, Jesus said it. Maybe we have all said it, and maybe we have been wrong. Except on that most primitive level—our loyalties to those we love—what could be more arrogant than to claim the primacy of personal conscience? ("Tell me," a rabbi asked Daniel Bell when he said, as a child, that he did not believe in God, "Do you think God cares?") At least some of the time, the world appears to me as a painting by Hieronymous Bosch; were I to follow my conscience then, it would lead me out onto the desert with Marion Faye, out to where he stood in *The Deer Park* looking east to Los Alamos and praying, as if for rain, that it would happen: *". . . let it come and clear the rot and the stench and the stink, let it come for all of everywhere, just so it comes and the world stands clear in the white dead dawn."*

Of course you will say that I do not have the right, even if I had the power, to inflict that unreasonable conscience upon you; nor do I want you to inflict your conscience, however reasonable, however enlightened, upon me. ("We must be aware of the dangers which lie in our most generous wishes," Lionel Trilling once wrote. "Some paradox of our nature leads us, when once we have made our fellow men the objects of our enlightened interest, to go on to make them the objects of our pity, then of our wisdom, ultimately of our coer-

cion.") That the ethic of conscience is intrinsically insidious seems
scarcely a revelatory point, but it is one raised with increasing infre-
quency; even those who do raise it tend to *segue* with troubling
readiness into the quite contradictory position that the ethic of conscience is dangerous when it is "wrong," and admirable when it is
"right."

You see I want to be quite obstinate about insisting that we have
no way of knowing—beyond that fundamental loyalty to the social
code—what is "right" and what is "wrong," what is "good" and what
"evil." I dwell so upon this because the most disturbing aspect of
"morality" seems to me to be the frequency with which the word now
appears; in the press, on television, in the most perfunctory kinds of
conversation. Questions of straightforward power (or survival) politics, questions of quite indifferent public policy, questions of almost
anything: they are all assigned these factitious moral burdens. There
is something facile going on, some self-indulgence at work. Of course
we would all like to "believe" in something, like to assuage our private
guilts in public causes, like to lose our tiresome selves; like, perhaps,
to transform the white flag of defeat at home into the brave white
banner of battle away from home. And of course it is all right to do
that; that is how, immemorially, things have gotten done. But I think
it is all right only so long as we do not delude ourselves about what
we are doing, and why. It is all right only so long as we remember that
all the *ad hoc* committees, all the picket lines, all the brave signatures
in *The New York Times,* all the tools of agitprop straight across the
spectrum, do not confer upon anyone any *ipso facto* virtue. It is all
right only so long as we recognize that the end may or may not be
expedient, may or may not be a good idea, but in any case has nothing
to do with "morality." Because when we start deceiving ourselves into
thinking not that we want something or need something, not that it
is a pragmatic necessity for us to have it, but that it is a *moral
imperative* that we have it, then is when we join the fashionable
madmen, and then is when the thin whine of hysteria is heard in the
land, and then is when we are in bad trouble. And I suspect we are
already there.

[1965]

AT THE DAM

SINCE THE AFTERNOON in 1967 when I first saw Hoover Dam, its image has never been entirely absent from my inner eye. I will be talking to someone in Los Angeles, say, or New York, and suddenly the dam will materialize, its pristine concave face gleaming white against the harsh rusts and taupes and mauves of that rock canyon hundreds or thousands of miles from where I am. I will be driving down Sunset Boulevard, or about to enter a freeway, and abruptly those power transmission towers will appear before me, canted vertiginously over the tailrace. Sometimes I am confronted by the intakes and sometimes by the shadow of the heavy cable that spans the canyon and sometimes by the ominous outlets to unused spillways, black in the lunar clarity of the desert light. Quite often I hear the turbines. Frequently I wonder what is happening at the dam this instant, at this precise intersection of time and space, how much water is being released to fill downstream orders and what lights are flashing and which generators are in full use and which just spinning free.

I used to wonder what it was about the dam that made me think of it at times and in places where I once thought of the Mindanao Trench, or of the stars wheeling in their courses, or of the words *As it was in the beginning, is now and ever shall be, world without end, amen.* Dams, after all, are commonplace: we have all seen one. This particular dam had existed as an idea in the world's mind for almost forty years before I saw it. Hoover Dam, showpiece of the Boulder Canyon project, the several million tons of concrete that made the Southwest plausible, the *fait accompli* that was to convey, in the innocent time of its construction, the notion that mankind's brightest promise lay in American engineering.

Of course the dam derives some of its emotional effect from precisely that aspect, that sense of being a monument to a faith since misplaced. "They died to make the desert bloom," reads a plaque dedicated to the 96 men who died building this first of the great high dams, and in context the worn phrase touches, suggests all of that trust in harnessing resources, in the meliorative power of the dynamo, so central to the early Thirties. Boulder City, built in 1931 as the construction town for the dam, retains the ambience of a model city, a new town, a toy triangular grid of green lawns and trim bungalows, all fanning out from the Reclamation building. The bronze sculptures at the dam itself evoke muscular citizens of a tomorrow that never came, sheaves of wheat clutched heavenward, thunderbolts defied. Winged Victories guard the flagpole. The flag whips in the canyon wind. An empty Pepsi-Cola can clatters across the terrazzo. The place is perfectly frozen in time.

But history does not explain it all, does not entirely suggest what makes that dam so affecting. Nor, even, does energy, the massive involvement with power and pressure and the transparent sexual overtones to that involvement. Once when I revisited the dam I walked through it with a man from the Bureau of Reclamation. For a while we trailed behind a guided tour, and then we went on, went into parts of the dam where visitors do not generally go. Once in a while he would explain something, usually in that recondite language having to do with "peaking power," with "outages" and "dewatering," but on the whole we spent the afternoon in a world so alien, so complete and so beautiful unto itself that it was scarcely necessary to speak at all. We saw almost no one. Cranes moved above us as if under their own volition. Generators roared. Transformers hummed. The gratings on which we stood vibrated. We watched a hundred-ton steel shaft plunging down to that place where the water was. And finally we got down to that place where the water was, where the water sucked out of Lake Mead roared through thirty-foot penstocks and then into thirteen-foot penstocks and finally into the turbines themselves. "Touch it," the Reclamation man said, and I did, and for a long time I just stood there with my hands on the turbine. It was a peculiar moment, but so explicit as to suggest nothing beyond itself.

There was something beyond all that, something beyond energy, beyond history, something I could not fix in my mind. When I came up from the dam that day the wind was blowing harder, through the canyon and all across the Mojave. Later, toward Henderson and Las Vegas, there would be dust blowing, blowing past the Country-Western Casino FRI & SAT NITES and blowing past the Shrine of Our Lady of Safe Journey STOP & PRAY, but out at the dam there was no dust, only the rock and the dam and a little greasewood and a few garbage cans, their tops chained, banging against a fence. I walked across the marble star map that traces a sidereal revolution of the equinox and fixes forever, the Reclamation man had told me, for all time and for all people who can read the stars, the date the dam was dedicated. The star map was, he had said, for when we were all gone and the dam was left. I had not thought much of it when he said it, but I thought of it then, with the wind whining and the sun dropping behind a mesa with the finality of a sunset in space. Of course that was the image I had seen always, seen it without quite realizing what I saw, a dynamo finally free of man, splendid at last in its absolute isolation, transmitting power and releasing water to a world where no one is.

[1970]

ON KEEPING A NOTEBOOK

" 'THAT WOMAN ESTELLE,' " the note reads, " 'is partly the reason why George Sharp and I are separated today.' *Dirty crepe-de-Chine wrapper, hotel bar, Wilmington RR, 9:45 A.M. August Monday morning.*"

Since the note is in my notebook, it presumably has some meaning to me. I study it for a long while. At first I have only the most general notion of what I was doing on an August Monday morning in the bar of the hotel across from the Pennsylvania Railroad station in Wilmington, Delaware (waiting for a train? missing one? 1960? 1961? why Wilmington?), but I do remember being there. The woman in the dirty crepe-de-Chine wrapper had come down from her room for a beer, and the bartender had heard before the reason why George Sharp and she were separated today. "Sure," he said, and went on mopping the floor. "You told me." At the other end of the bar is a girl. She is talking, pointedly, not to the man beside her but to a cat lying in the triangle of sunlight cast through the open door. She is wearing a plaid silk dress from Peck & Peck, and the hem is coming down.

Here is what it is: the girl has been on the Eastern Shore, and now she is going back to the city, leaving the man beside her, and all she can see ahead are the viscous summer sidewalks and the 3 A.M. long-distance calls that will make her lie awake and then sleep drugged through all the steaming mornings left in August (1960? 1961?). Because she must go directly from the train to lunch in New York, she wishes that she had a safety pin for the hem of the plaid silk dress, and she also wishes that she could forget about the hem and the lunch and stay in the cool bar that smells of disinfectant and malt and make friends with the woman in the crepe-de-Chine wrapper. She is afflicted by a little self-pity, and she wants to compare Estelles. That is what that was all about.

Why did I write it down? In order to remember, of course, but exactly what was it I wanted to remember? How much of it actually happened? Did any of it? Why do I keep a notebook at all? It is easy to deceive oneself on all those scores. The impulse to write things down is a peculiarly compulsive one, inexplicable to those who do not share it, useful only accidentally, only secondarily, in the way that any compulsion tries to justify itself. I suppose that it begins or does not begin in the cradle. Although I have felt compelled to write things down since I was five years old, I doubt that my daughter ever will, for she is a singularly blessed and accepting child, delighted with life exactly as life presents itself to her, unafraid to go to sleep and unafraid to wake up. Keepers of private notebooks are a different breed altogether, lonely and resistant rearrangers of things, anxious malcontents, children afflicted apparently at birth with some presentiment of loss.

My first notebook was a Big Five tablet, given to me by my mother with the sensible suggestion that I stop whining and learn to amuse myself by writing down my thoughts. She returned the tablet to me a few years ago; the first entry is an account of a woman who believed herself to be freezing to death in the Arctic night, only to find, when day broke, that she had stumbled onto the Sahara Desert, where she would die of the heat before lunch. I have no idea what turn of a five-year-old's mind could have prompted so insistently "ironic" and exotic a story, but it does reveal a certain predilection for the extreme which has dogged me into adult life; perhaps if I were analytically inclined I would find it a truer story than any I might have told about

Donald Johnson's birthday party or the day my cousin Brenda put
Kitty Litter in the aquarium.

So the point of my keeping a notebook has never been, nor is it now,
to have an accurate factual record of what I have been doing or
thinking. That would be a different impulse entirely, an instinct for
reality which I sometimes envy but do not possess. At no point have
I ever been able successfully to keep a diary; my approach to daily
life ranges from the grossly negligent to the merely absent, and on
those few occasions when I have tried dutifully to record a day's
events, boredom has so overcome me that the results are mysterious
at best. What is this business about "shopping, typing piece, dinner
with E, depressed"? Shopping for what? Typing what piece? Who is
E? Was this "E" depressed, or was I depressed? Who cares?

In fact I have abandoned altogether that kind of pointless entry;
instead I tell what some would call lies. "That's simply not true," the
members of my family frequently tell me when they come up against
my memory of a shared event. "The party was *not* for you, the spider
was *not* a black widow, *it wasn't that way at all.*" Very likely they
are right, for not only have I always had trouble distinguishing between what happened and what merely might have happened, but I
remain unconvinced that the distinction, for my purposes, matters.
The cracked crab that I recall having for lunch the day my father
came home from Detroit in 1945 must certainly be embroidery,
worked into the day's pattern to lend verisimilitude; I was ten years
old and would not now remember the cracked crab. The day's events
did not turn on cracked crab. And yet it is precisely that fictitious crab
that makes me see the afternoon all over again, a home movie run all
too often, the father bearing gifts, the child weeping, an exercise in
family love and guilt. Or that is what it was to me. Similarly, perhaps
it never did snow that August in Vermont; perhaps there never were
flurries in the night wind, and maybe no one else felt the ground
hardening and summer already dead even as we pretended to bask in
it, but that was how it felt to me, and it might as well have snowed,
could have snowed, did snow.

How it felt to me: that is getting closer to the truth about a
notebook. I sometimes delude myself about why I keep a notebook,
imagine that some thrifty virtue derives from preserving everything

observed. See enough and write it down, I tell myself, and then some
morning when the world seems drained of wonder, some day when I
am only going through the motions of doing what I am supposed to
do, which is write—on that bankrupt morning I will simply open my
notebook and there it will all be, a forgotten account with accumulated interest, paid passage back to the world out there: dialogue
overheard in hotels and elevators and at the hatcheck counter in
Pavillon (one middle-aged man shows his hat check to another and
says, "That's my old football number"); impressions of Bettina Ap-
theker and Benjamin Sonnenberg and Teddy ("Mr. Acapulco")
Stauffer; careful *aperçus* about tennis bums and failed fashion models
and Greek shipping heiresses, one of whom taught me a significant
lesson (a lesson I could have learned from F. Scott Fitzgerald, but
perhaps we all must meet the very rich for ourselves) by asking, when
I arrived to interview her in her orchid-filled sitting room on the
second day of a paralyzing New York blizzard, whether it was snowing
outside.

I imagine, in other words, that the notebook is about other people.
But of course it is not. I have no real business with what one stranger
said to another at the hatcheck counter in Pavillon; in fact I suspect
that the line "That's my old football number" touched not my own
imagination at all, but merely some memory of something once read,
probably "The Eighty-Yard Run." Nor is my concern with a woman
in a dirty crepe-de-Chine wrapper in a Wilmington bar. My stake is
always, of course, in the unmentioned girl in the plaid silk dress.
Remember what it was to be me: that is always the point.

It is a difficult point to admit. We are brought up in the ethic that
others, any others, all others, are by definition more interesting than
ourselves; taught to be diffident, just this side of self-effacing. ("You're
the least important person in the room and don't forget it," Jessica
Mitford's governess would hiss in her ear on the advent of any social
occasion; I copied that into my notebook because it is only recently
that I have been able to enter a room without hearing some such
phrase in my inner ear.) Only the very young and the very old may
recount their dreams at breakfast, dwell upon self, interrupt with
memories of beach picnics and favorite Liberty lawn dresses and the
rainbow trout in a creek near Colorado Springs. The rest of us are

expected, rightly, to affect absorption in other people's favorite dresses, other people's trout.

And so we do. But our notebooks give us away, for however dutifully we record what we see around us, the common denominator of all we see is always, transparently, shamelessly, the implacable "I." We are not talking here about the kind of notebook that is patently for public consumption, a structural conceit for binding together a series of graceful *pensées;* we are talking about something private, about bits of the mind's string too short to use, an indiscriminate and erratic assemblage with meaning only for its maker.

And sometimes even the maker has difficulty with the meaning. There does not seem to be, for example, any point in my knowing for the rest of my life that, during 1964, 720 tons of soot fell on every square mile of New York City, yet there it is in my notebook, labeled "FACT." Nor do I really need to remember that Ambrose Bierce liked to spell Leland Stanford's name "£eland $tanford" or that "smart women almost always wear black in Cuba," a fashion hint without much potential for practical application. And does not the relevance of these notes seem marginal at best?:

> In the basement museum of the Inyo County Courthouse in Independence, California, sign pinned to a mandarin coat: "This MANDARIN COAT was often worn by Mrs. Minnie S. Brooks when giving lectures on her TEAPOT COLLECTION."

> Redhead getting out of car in front of Beverly Wilshire Hotel, chinchilla stole, Vuitton bags with tags reading:

> MRS LOU FOX
>
> HOTEL SAHARA
>
> VEGAS

Well, perhaps not entirely marginal. As a matter of fact, Mrs. Minnie S. Brooks and her MANDARIN COAT pull me back into my own childhood, for although I never knew Mrs. Brooks and did not visit Inyo County until I was thirty, I grew up in just such a world, in houses cluttered with Indian relics and bits of gold ore and ambergris and the souvenirs my Aunt Mercy Farnsworth brought back from the

Orient. It is a long way from that world to Mrs. Lou Fox's world,
where we all live now, and is it not just as well to remember that?
Might not Mrs. Minnie S. Brooks help me to remember what I am?
Might not Mrs. Lou Fox help me to remember what I am not?

But sometimes the point is harder to discern. What exactly did I
have in mind when I noted down that it cost the father of someone
I know $650 a month to light the place on the Hudson in which he
lived before the Crash? What use was I planning to make of this line
by Jimmy Hoffa: "I may have my faults, but being wrong ain't one
of them"? And although I think it interesting to know where the girls
who travel with the Syndicate have their hair done when they find
themselves on the West Coast, will I ever make suitable use of it?
Might I not be better off just passing it on to John O'Hara? What is
a recipe for sauerkraut doing in my notebook? What kind of magpie
keeps this notebook? *"He was born the night the Titanic went down."*
That seems a nice enough line, and I even recall who said it, but is
it not really a better line in life than it could ever be in fiction?
But of course that is exactly it: not that I should ever use the line,
but that I should remember the woman who said it and the afternoon
I heard it. We were on her terrace by the sea, and we were finishing
the wine left from lunch, trying to get what sun there was, a California
winter sun. The woman whose husband was born the night the *Titanic*
went down wanted to rent her house, wanted to go back to her
children in Paris. I remember wishing that I could afford the house,
which cost $1,000 a month. "Someday you will," she said lazily.
"Someday it all comes." There in the sun on her terrace it seemed easy
to believe in someday, but later I had a low-grade afternoon hangover
and ran over a black snake on the way to the supermarket and was
flooded with inexplicable fear when I heard the checkout clerk explaining to the man ahead of me why she was finally divorcing her
husband. "He left me no choice," she said over and over as she
punched the register. "He has a little seven-month-old baby by her,
he left me no choice." I would like to believe that my dread then was
for the human condition, but of course it was for me, because I wanted
a baby and did not then have one and because I wanted to own the
house that cost $1,000 a month to rent and because I had a hangover.
It all comes back. Perhaps it is difficult to see the value in having

one's self back in that kind of mood, but I do see it; I think we are well advised to keep on nodding terms with the people we used to be, whether we find them attractive company or not. Otherwise they turn up unannounced and surprise us, come hammering on the mind's door at 4 A.M. of a bad night and demand to know who deserted them, who betrayed them, who is going to make amends. We forget all too soon the things we thought we could never forget. We forget the loves and the betrayals alike, forget what we whispered and what we screamed, forget who we were. I have already lost touch with a couple of people I used to be; one of them, a seventeen-year-old, presents little threat, although it would be of some interest to me to know again what it feels like to sit on a river levee drinking vodka-and-orange-juice and listening to Les Paul and Mary Ford and their echoes sing "How High the Moon" on the car radio. (You see I still have the scenes, but I no longer perceive myself among those present, no longer could even improvise the dialogue.) The other one, a twenty-three-year-old, bothers me more. She was always a good deal of trouble, and I suspect she will reappear when I least want to see her, skirts too long, shy to the point of aggravation, always the injured party, full of recriminations and little hurts and stories I do not want to hear again, at once saddening me and angering me with her vulnerability and ignorance, an apparition all the more insistent for being so long banished.

It is a good idea, then, to keep in touch, and I suppose that keeping in touch is what notebooks are all about. And we are all on our own when it comes to keeping those lines open to ourselves: your notebook will never help me, nor mine you. *"So what's new in the whiskey business?"* What could that possibly mean to you? To me it means a blonde in a Pucci bathing suit sitting with a couple of fat men by the pool at the Beverly Hills Hotel. Another man approaches, and they all regard one another in silence for a while. "So what's new in the whiskey business?" one of the fat men finally says by way of welcome, and the blonde stands up, arches one foot and dips it in the pool, looking all the while at the cabaña where Baby Pignatari is talking on the telephone. That is all there is to that, except that several years later I saw the blonde coming out of Saks Fifth Avenue in New York with her California complexion and a voluminous mink coat. In the harsh wind that day she looked old and irrevocably tired to me, and even the skins in the mink coat were not worked the way they were doing them that year, not the way she would have wanted them done, and there is the point of the story. For a while after that I did not like to look in the mirror, and my eyes would skim the newspapers and pick out only the deaths, the cancer victims, the premature coronaries, the suicides, and I stopped riding the Lexington Avenue IRT because I noticed for the first time that all the strangers I had seen for years—the man with the seeing-eye dog, the spinster who read the classified pages every day, the fat girl who always got off with me at Grand Central—looked older than they once had.

It all comes back. Even that recipe for sauerkraut: even that brings it back. I was on Fire Island when I first made that sauerkraut, and it was raining, and we drank a lot of bourbon and ate the sauerkraut and went to bed at ten, and I listened to the rain and the Atlantic and felt safe. I made the sauerkraut again last night and it did not make me feel any safer, but that is, as they say, another story.

[1966]

WHY I WRITE Joan Didion

OF COURSE I stole the title for this talk from George Orwell. One reason I stole it was that I like the sound of the words: *Why I Write.* There you have three short unambiguous words that share a sound, and the sound they share is this:

I

I

I

In many ways writing is the act of saying *I,* of imposing oneself upon other people, of saying *listen to me, see it my way, change your mind.* It's an aggressive, even a hostile act. You can disguise its aggressiveness all you want with veils of subordinate clauses and qualifiers and tentative subjunctives, with ellipses and evasions—with the whole manner of intimating rather than claiming, of alluding rather than stating—but there's no getting around the fact that setting words on paper is the tactic of a secret bully, an invasion, an imposition of the writer's sensibility on the reader's most private space.

I stole the title not only because the words sounded right but because they seemed to sum up, in a no-nonsense way, all I have to tell you. Like many writers I have only this one "subject," this one "area": the act of writing. I can bring you no reports from any other front. I may have other interests: I am "interested," for example, in marine biology, but I don't flatter myself that you would come out to hear me talk about it. I am not a scholar. I am not in the least an intellectual, which is not to say that when I hear the word "intellectual" I reach for my gun, but only to say that I do not think in abstracts. During the years when I was an undergraduate at Berkeley I tried, with a kind of hopeless late-adolescent energy, to buy some temporary visa into the world of ideas, to forge for myself a mind that could deal with the abstract.

In short I tried to think. I failed. My attention veered inexorably back to the specific, to the tangible, to what was generally considered, by everyone I knew then and for that matter have known since, the peripheral. I would try to contemplate the Hegelian dialectic and would find myself concentrating instead on a flowering pear tree outside my window and the particular way the petals fell on my floor. I would try to read linguistic theory and would find myself wondering instead if the lights were on in the bevatron up the hill. When I say that I was wondering if the lights were on in the bevatron you might immediately suspect, if you deal in ideas at all, that I was registering the bevatron as a political symbol, thinking in shorthand about the military-industrial complex and its role in the university community, but you would be wrong. I was only wondering if the lights were on in the bevatron, and how they looked. A physical fact.

I had trouble graduating from Berkeley, not because of this inability to deal with ideas—I was majoring in English, and I could locate the house-and-garden imagery in *The Portrait of a Lady* as well as the next person, "imagery" being by definition the kind of specific that got my attention—but simply because I had neglected to take a course in Milton. For reasons which now sound baroque I needed a degree by the end of that summer, and the English department finally agreed, if I would come down from Sacramento every Friday and talk

about the cosmology of *Paradise Lost,* to certify me proficient in
Milton. I did this. Some Fridays I took the Greyhound bus, other
Fridays I caught the Southern Pacific's City of San Francisco on the
last leg of its transcontinental trip. I can no longer tell you whether
Milton put the sun or the earth at the center of his universe in
Paradise Lost, the central question of at least one century and a topic
about which I wrote 10,000 words that summer, but I can still recall
the exact rancidity of the butter in the City of San Francisco's dining
car, and the way the tinted windows on the Greyhound bus cast the
oil refineries around Carquinez Straits into a grayed and obscurely
sinister light. In short my attention was always on the periphery, on
what I would see and taste and touch, on the butter, and the Greyhound bus. During those years I was traveling on what I knew to be
a very shaky passport, forged papers: I knew that I was no legitimate
resident in any world of ideas. I knew I couldn't think. All I knew then
was what I couldn't do. All I knew then was what I wasn't, and it took
me some years to discover what I was.

Which was a writer.

By which I mean not a "good" writer or a "bad" writer but simply
a writer, a person whose most absorbed and passionate hours are spent
arranging words on pieces of paper. Had my credentials been in order
I would never have become a writer. Had I been blessed with even
limited access to my own mind there would have been no reason to
write. I write entirely to find out what I'm thinking, what I'm looking
at, what I see and what it means. What I want and what I fear. Why
did the oil refineries around Carquinez Straits seem sinister to me in
the summer of 1956? Why have the night lights in the bevatron
burned in my mind for twenty years? *What is going on in these
pictures in my mind?*

When I talk about pictures in my mind I am talking, quite specifically, about images that shimmer around the edges. There used to be
an illustration in every elementary psychology book showing a cat
drawn by a patient in varying stages of schizophrenia. This cat had
a shimmer around it. You could see the molecular structure breaking
down at the very edges of the cat: the cat became the background and
the background the cat, everything interacting, exchanging ions. People on hallucinogens describe the same perception of objects. I'm not
a schizophrenic, nor do I take hallucinogens, but certain images do

shimmer for me. Look hard enough, and you can't miss the shimmer. It's there. You can't think too much about these pictures that shimmer. You just lie low and let them develop. You stay quiet. You don't talk to many people and you keep your nervous system from shorting out and you try to locate the cat in the shimmer, the grammar in the picture.

Just as I meant "shimmer" literally I mean "grammar" literally. Grammar is a piano I play by ear, since I seem to have been out of school the year the rules were mentioned. All I know about grammar is its infinite power. To shift the structure of a sentence alters the meaning of that sentence, as definitely and inflexibly as the position of a camera alters the meaning of the object photographed. Many people know about camera angles now, but not so many know about sentences. The arrangement of the words matters, and the arrangement you want can be found in the picture in your mind. The picture dictates the arrangement. The picture dictates whether this will be a sentence with or without clauses, a sentence that ends hard or a dying-fall sentence, long or short, active or passive. The picture tells you how to arrange the words and the arrangement of the words tells you, or tells me, what's going on in the picture. *Nota bene:*

It tells you.

You don't tell it.

Let me show you what I mean by pictures in the mind. I began *Play It as It Lays* just as I have begun each of my novels, with no notion of "character" or "plot" or even "incident." I had only two pictures in my mind, more about which later, and a technical intention, which was to write a novel so elliptical and fast that it would be over before you noticed it, a novel so fast that it would scarcely exist on the page at all. About the pictures: the first was of white space. Empty space. This was clearly the picture that dictated the narrative intention of the book—a book in which anything that happened would happen off the page, a "white" book to which the reader would have to bring his or her own bad dreams—and yet this picture told me no "story," suggested no situation. The second picture did. This second picture was of something actually witnessed. A young woman with long hair and a short white halter dress walks through the casino at the Riviera in Las Vegas at one in the morning. She crosses the casino alone and picks up a house telephone. I watch her because I have heard her paged, and recognize her name: she is a minor actress I see around Los Angeles from time to time, in places like Jax and once in a gynecologist's office in the Beverly Hills Clinic, but have never met. I know nothing about her. Who is paging her? Why is she here to be paged? How exactly did she come to this? It was precisely this moment in Las Vegas that made *Play It as It Lays* begin to tell itself to me, but the moment appears in the novel only obliquely, in a chapter which begins:

> Maria made a list of things she would never do. She would never: walk through the Sands or Caesar's alone after midnight. She would never: ball at a party, do S-M unless she wanted to, borrow furs from Abe Lipsey, deal. She would never: carry a Yorkshire in Beverly Hills.

That is the beginning of the chapter and that is also the end of the chapter, which may suggest what I meant by "white space."

I recall having a number of pictures in my mind when I began the novel I just finished, *A Book of Common Prayer.* As a matter of fact one of these pictures was of that bevatron I mentioned, although I would be hard put to tell you a story in which nuclear energy figured. Another was a newspaper photograph of a hijacked 707 burning on the desert in the Middle East. Another was the night view from a room in which I once spent a week with paratyphoid, a hotel room on the Colombian coast. My husband and I seemed to be on the Colombian coast representing the United States of America at a film festival (I recall invoking the name "Jack Valenti" a lot, as if its reiteration could make me well), and it was a bad place to have fever, not only because my indisposition offended our hosts but because every night in this hotel the generator failed. The lights went out. The elevator stopped. My husband would go to the event of the evening and make excuses for me and I would stay alone in this hotel room, in the dark. I remember standing at the window trying to call Bogotá (the telephone seemed to work on the same principle as the generator) and watching the night wind come up and wondering what I was doing eleven degrees off the equator with a fever of 103. The view from that window definitely figures in *A Book of Common Prayer,* as does the burning 707, and yet none of these pictures told me the story I needed.

The picture that did, the picture that shimmered and made these other images coalesce, was the Panama airport at 6 A.M. I was in this airport only once, on a plane to Bogotá that stopped for an hour to refuel, but the way it looked that morning remained superimposed on everything I saw until the day I finished *A Book of Common Prayer*. I lived in that airport for several years. I can still feel the hot air when I step off the plane, can see the heat already rising off the tarmac at 6 A.M. I can feel my skirt damp and wrinkled on my legs. I can feel the asphalt stick to my sandals. I remember the big tail of a Pan American plane floating motionless down at the end of the tarmac. I remember the sound of a slot machine in the waiting room. I could tell you that I remember a particular woman in the airport, an American woman, a *norteamericana,* a thin *norteamericana* about 40 who wore a big square emerald in lieu of a wedding ring, but there was no such woman there.

I put this woman in the airport later. I made this woman up, just as I later made up a country to put the airport in, and a family to run the country. This woman in the airport is neither catching a plane nor meeting one. She is ordering tea in the airport coffee shop. In fact she is not simply "ordering" tea but insisting that the water be boiled, in front of her, for twenty minutes. Why is this woman in this airport? Why is she going nowhere, where has she been? Where did she get that big emerald? What derangement, or disassociation, makes her believe that her will to see the water boiled can possibly prevail?

> She had been going to one airport or another for four months, one could see it, looking at the visas on her passport. All those airports where Charlotte Douglas's passport had been stamped would have looked alike. Sometimes the sign on the tower would say "Bienvenidos" and sometimes the sign on the tower would say "Bienvenue," some places were wet and hot and others dry and hot, but at each of these airports the pastel concrete walls would rust and stain and the swamp off the runway would be littered with the fuselages of cannibalized Fairchild F-227's and the water would need boiling.
>
> "I knew why Charlotte went to the airport even if Victor did not.
> "I knew about airports."

These lines appear about halfway through *A Book of Common Prayer,* but I wrote them during the second week I worked on the book, long before I had any idea where Charlotte Douglas had been or why she went to airports. Until I wrote these lines I had no character called "Victor" in mind: the necessity for mentioning a name, and the name "Victor," occurred to me as I wrote the sentence. *I knew why Charlotte went to the airport* sounded incomplete. *I knew why Charlotte went to the airport even if Victor did not* carried a little more narrative drive. Most important of all, until I wrote these lines I did not know who "I" was, who was telling the story. I had intended until that moment that the "I" be no more than the voice of the author, a 19th-century omniscient narrator. But there it was:

> "I knew why Charlotte went to the airport even if Victor did not.
> "I knew about airports."

This "I" was the voice of no author in my house. This "I" was someone who not only knew why Charlotte went to the airport but also knew someone called "Victor." Who was Victor? Who was this narrator? Why was this narrator telling me this story? Let me tell you one thing about why writers write: had I known the answer to any of these questions I would never have needed to write a novel.

[1976]

ALICE WALKER

Jim Marshall

ALICE WALKER WAS BORN in Eatonton, Georgia, on February 9, 1944, the eighth child of Willie Lee and Minnie Lou Walker, black sharecroppers. In many of her essays Walker documents the harshness of their life in those days, the "hard work in the fields, the shabby houses, the evil greedy men who worked my father to death and almost broke the courage" of her mother, and of how "on hot Saturday afternoons of my childhood I gazed longingly through the window of the corner drugstore where white youngsters sat on stools in air-conditioned comfort and drank Cokes and nibbled ice-cream cones." And yet, looking back on her childhood, she also recalls "neighborly kindness and sustaining love" and "the Georgia countryside where I fished and swam and walked through fields of black-eyed Susans."

Early in her teens Alice Walker began seeing the world beyond Eatonton, spending her summers in Boston with older brothers and sisters who had already moved north. In 1961 she was awarded a scholarship to attend Spelman College in Atlanta, and the following summer was selected to attend a World Youth Peace Festival in Helsinki, Finland. It was also during her freshman year at Spelman that she heard Dr. Martin Luther King, Jr., for the first time: "I have often thought that if it had not been for . . . Dr. King, I would have come of age believing in nothing and no one. As it was, my life, like that of millions of black young Southerners, seemed to find its beginning and its purpose at the precise moment I first heard him speak." In the summer of 1963 she rode a bus from Boston to Washington to sit "perched on the limb of a tree far from the Lincoln Center" while Dr. King delivered his eloquent "I Have a Dream" speech to hundreds of thousands of Freedom Marchers.

In 1964, disillusioned with the conservative, middle-class values she found at Spelman, Walker transferred to Sarah Lawrence College, and it was there, during an intense week of writing in the winter of her senior year, that she wrote her first book of poems. "Each morning, the poems finished during the night were stuffed under Muriel Rukeyser's door—her classroom was an old gardener's cottage in the middle of the campus. Then I would hurry back to my room to write some more. I didn't care what she did with the poems. I only knew I wanted someone to read them as if they were new leaves sprouting from an old tree." What Muriel Rukeyser, a distinguished poet, did with the poems was to send them to her agent, who gave them to an editor at a major publishing house, who immediately accepted them for publication. Alice Walker had just turned twenty-one.

Following her graduation from Sarah Lawrence in 1965, Walker went back to Georgia for the summer to register black voters, then returned north to attend the Bread Loaf Writers' Conference on a scholarship. She took a job with the New York City Welfare Department, but left in 1967 when she won a writing fellowship from the Ingram Merrill Foundation. By now her stories and essays were beginning to appear in magazines and anthologies (such as *Voices of the Revolution* and *The Best Short Stories by Negro Writers from 1899 to the Present,* both published in 1967), and she was awarded a residency at The MacDowell Colony, an artists' retreat.

That same year, 1967, she married Mel Leventhal, a young lawyer, and they moved to Jackson, Mississippi, where Leventhal prosecuted the Jackson school-desegregation cases. As "the only interracial, married, home-owning couple in Mississippi," their life in Jackson was one of constant taunts and threats: "All the while," Walker has written, "there was the fear that my young husband would not return from one of his trips to visit his clients in the Mississippi backwoods." Though Walker was also involved with the civil rights movement—working in the Head Start program, teaching black studies at Jackson State College—she does not consider herself to have been a "true activist." Rather, she says that she "sat in a book-lined study and wrote" and "when I was working well and the poems and stories grew, I had no time to think of" social and political issues. During the late sixties and early seventies she wrote her first novel, *The Third Life of George Copeland* (1970); her second poetry collection, *Revolutionary Petunias and Other Poems* (1973); her first collection of short stories, *In Love and Trouble: Stories of Black Women* (1973); and a biography of Langston Hughes for young readers.

In 1971, needing "a change from Mississippi," Alice Walker moved to Boston with her infant daughter and spent the next year-and-a-half supported by a fellowship from the Radcliffe Institute and teaching part-time at Wellesley College and the Boston campus of the University of Massachusetts. Returning to Mississippi in 1973—ten years after the March on Washington—Walker found that since most of the civil rights battles had been won, the new black middle class—"the very class that owes its new affluence to the Movement"—had "abandoned itself to the pursuit of cars, expensive furniture, large houses, and the finest Scotch," and "now refuses to support the organizations that made its success possible, and has retreated from its concern for black people who are poor." Disillusioned, Walker and Leventhal left Mississippi and moved to Brooklyn, where he now sued racist landlords and she wrote an elegiac novel about the Movement (*Meridian,* 1976).

In 1974 Alice Walker began a long association with *Ms.* magazine when it published her essay "In Search of Our Mothers' Gardens." Focusing on the neglect and mistreatment of black women throughout history, Walker became a leading spokesperson for black feminism, and coined a word to describe the characteristics of such a person: *womanist.* (See *In Search of Our Mothers' Gardens,* 1983.) In 1976 Walker and Leventhal were divorced.

By 1979 her next novel began forming itself in her mind: she speaks of her characters "trying to contact me, to speak *through* me." But being "country people," they "refused even to visit" her in New York. So Walker disposed of the house she had only three months earlier bought and moved west to California, settling finally in the countryside north of San Francisco, in a place that "looked a lot like the town in Georgia most of them were from." And there they came freely, and the novel flowed. *The Color Purple* was published in 1982 and won both the Pulitzer Prize and American Book Award for fiction in 1983. The quality that most distinguishes *The Color Purple* is the voice of its narrator, Celie, and the other characters who speak through her; and even though the things that happen to them are tragic, the voices are joyous. And that is the same quality one finds in Alice Walker's own voice, and which raises it above polemics, despite the gravity of her subject matter.

In 1989 Walker published *The Temple of My Familiar,* a mythological narrative that presents an unorthodox view of race, gender, and human history.

THE CIVIL RIGHTS MOVEMENT: WHAT GOOD WAS IT?

SOMEONE SAID RECENTLY to an old black lady from Mississippi, whose legs had been badly mangled by local police who arrested her for "disturbing the peace," that the Civil Rights Movement was dead, and asked, since it was dead, what she thought about it. The old lady replied, hobbling out of his presence on her cane, that the Civil Rights Movement was like herself, "if it's dead, it shore ain't ready to lay down!"

This old lady is a legendary freedom fighter in her small town in the Delta. She has been severely mistreated for insisting on her rights as an American citizen. She has been beaten for singing Movement songs, placed in solitary confinement in prisons for talking about freedom, and placed on bread and water for praying aloud to God for her jailers' deliverance. For such a woman the Civil Rights Movement will never be over as long as her skin is black. It also will never be over for twenty million others with the same "affliction," for whom the Movement can never "lay down," no matter how it is killed by the press and made dead and buried by the white American public. As long as one black American survives, the struggle for equality with other Americans must also survive. This is a debt we owe to those blameless hostages we leave to the future, our children.

Still, white liberals and deserting Civil Rights sponsors are quick to justify their disaffection from the Movement by claiming that it is all over. "And since it is over," they will ask, "would someone kindly tell me what has been gained by it?" They then list statistics supposedly showing how much more advanced segregation is now than ten years ago—in schools, housing, jobs. They point to a gain in conservative politicians during the last few years. They speak of ghetto riots and of the survey that shows that most policemen are admittedly too anti-Negro to do their jobs in ghetto areas fairly and effectively. They speak of every area that has been touched by the Civil Rights Movement as somehow or other going to pieces.

They rarely talk, however, about human attitudes among Negroes that have undergone terrific changes just during the past seven to ten years (not to mention all those years when there was a Movement and only the Negroes knew about it). They seldom speak of changes in personal lives because of the influence of people in the Movement. They see general failure and few, if any, individual gains.

They do not understand what it is that keeps the Movement from "laying down" and Negroes from reverting to their former *silent* second-class status. They have apparently never stopped to wonder why it is always the white man—on his radio and in his newspaper and on his television—who says that the Movement is dead. If a Negro were audacious enough to make such a claim, his fellows might hanker to see him shot. The Movement is dead to the white man because it no longer interests him. And it no longer interests him because he can afford to be uninterested: he does not have to live by it, with it, or for it, as Negroes must. He can take a rest from the news of beatings, killings, and arrests that reach him from North and South—if his skin is white. Negroes cannot now and will never be able to take a rest from the injustices that plague them, for they—not the white man—are the target.

Perhaps it is naïve to be thankful that the Movement "saved" a large number of individuals and gave them something to live for, even if it did not provide them with everything they wanted. (Materially, it provided them with precious little that they wanted.) When a movement awakens people to the possibilities of life, it seems unfair to frustrate them by then denying what they had thought was offered. But what was offered? What was promised? What was it all about? What good did it do? Would it have been better, as some have suggested, to leave the Negro people as they were, unawakened, unallied with one another, unhopeful about what to expect for their children in some future world?

I do not think so. If knowledge of my condition is all the freedom I get from a "freedom movement," it is better than unawareness, forgottenness, and hopelessness, the existence that is like the existence of a beast. Man only truly lives by knowing; otherwise he simply performs, copying the daily habits of others, but conceiving nothing of his creative possibilities as a man, and accepting someone else's superiority and his own misery.

When we are children, growing up in our parents' care, we await the spark from the outside world. Sometimes our parents provide it—if we are lucky—sometimes it comes from another source far from home. We sit, paralyzed, surrounded by our anxiety and dread, hoping we will not have to grow up into the narrow world and ways we see about us. We are hungry for a life that turns us on; we yearn for a knowledge of living that will save us from our innocuous lives that resemble death. We look for signs in every strange event; we search for heroes in every unknown face.

It was just six years ago that I began to be alive. I had, of course, been living before—for I am now twenty-three—but I did not really know it. And I did not know it because nobody told me that I—a pensive, yearning, typical high-school senior, but Negro—existed in the minds of others as I existed in my own. Until that time my mind was locked apart from the outer contours and complexion of my body as if it and the body were strangers. The mind possessed both thought and spirit—I wanted to be an author or a scientist—which the color of the body denied. I had never seen myself and existed as a statistic exists, or as a phantom. In the white world I walked, less real to them than a shadow; and being young and well hidden among the slums, among people who also did not exist—either in books or in films or in the government of their own lives—I waited to be called to life. And, by a miracle, I was called.

There was a commotion in our house that night in 1960. We had managed to buy our first television set. It was battered and over-priced, but my mother had gotten used to watching the afternoon soap operas at the house where she worked as maid, and nothing could satisfy her on days when she did not work but a continuation of her "stories." So she pinched pennies and bought a set.

I remained listless throughout her "stories," tales of pregnancy, abortion, hypocrisy, infidelity, and alcoholism. All these men and women were white and lived in houses with servants, long staircases that they floated down, patios where liquor was served four times a day to "relax" them. But my mother, with her swollen feet eased out of her shoes, her heavy body relaxed in our only comfortable chair, watched each movement of the smartly coiffed women, heard each word, pounced upon each innuendo and inflection, and for the duration of these "stories" she saw herself as one of them. She placed herself in every scene she saw, with her braided hair turned blond, her two hundred pounds compressed into a sleek size-seven dress, her rough dark skin smooth and *white.* Her husband became "dark and handsome," talented, witty, urbane, charming. And when she turned to look at my father sitting near her in his sweat shirt with his smelly feet raised on the bed to "air," there was always a tragic look of surprise on her face. Then she would sigh and go out to the kitchen looking lost and unsure of herself. My mother, a truly great woman who raised eight children of her own and half a dozen of the neighbors' without a single complaint, was convinced that she did not exist compared to "them." She subordinated her soul to theirs and became a faithful and timid supporter of the "Beautiful White People." Once she asked me, in a moment of vicarious pride and despair, if I didn't think that "they" were "jest naturally smarter, prettier, better." My mother asked this: a woman who never got rid of any of her children, never cheated on my father, was never a hypocrite if she could help it, and never even tasted liquor. She could not even bring herself to blame "them" for making her believe what they wanted her to believe: that if she did not look like them, think like them, be sophisticated and corrupt-for-comfort's-sake like them, she was a nobody. Black was not a color on my mother; it was a shield that made her invisible.

Of course, the people who wrote the soap-opera scripts always made the Negro maids in them steadfast, trusty, and wise in a home-remedial sort of way; but my mother, a maid for nearly forty years, never once identified herself with the scarcely glimpsed black servant's face beneath the ruffled cap. Like everyone else, in her day-dreams at least, she thought she was free.

Six years ago, after half-heartedly watching my mother's soap operas and wondering whether there wasn't something more to be asked of life, the Civil Rights Movement came into my life. Like a good omen for the future, the face of Dr. Martin Luther King, Jr., was the first black face I saw on our new television screen. And, as in a fairy tale, my soul was stirred by the meaning for me of his mission—at the time he was being rather ignominiously dumped into a police van for having led a protest march in Alabama—and I fell in love with the sober and determined face of the Movement. The singing of "We Shall Overcome"—that song betrayed by nonbelievers in it—rang for the first time in my ears. The influence that my mother's soap operas might have had on me became impossible. The life of Dr. King, seeming bigger and more miraculous than the man himself, because of all he had done and suffered, offered a pattern of strength and sincerity I felt I could trust. He had suffered much because of his simple belief in nonviolence, love, and brotherhood. Perhaps the majority of men could not be reached through these beliefs, but because Dr. King kept trying to reach them in spite of danger to himself and his family, I saw in him the hero for whom I had waited so long.

What Dr. King promised was not a ranch-style house and an acre of manicured lawn for every black man, but jail and finally freedom. He did not promise two cars for every family, but the courage one day for all families everywhere to walk without shame and unafraid on their own feet. He did not say that one day it will be us chasing prospective buyers out of our prosperous well-kept neighborhoods, or in other ways exhibiting our snobbery and ignorance as all other ethnic groups before us have done; what he said was that we had a right to live anywhere in this country we chose, and a right to a meaningful well-paying job to provide us with the upkeep of our homes. He did not say we had to become carbon copies of the white American middle class; but he did say we had the right to become whatever we wanted to become.

Because of the Movement, because of an awakened faith in the newness and imagination of the human spirit, because of "black and white together"—for the first time in our history in some human relationship on and off TV—because of the beatings, the arrests, the hell of battle during the past years, I have fought harder for my life and for a chance to be myself, to be something more than a shadow or a number, than I had ever done before in my life. Before, there had seemed to be no real reason for struggling beyond the effort for daily bread. Now there was a chance at that other that Jesus meant when He said we could not live by bread alone.

I have fought and kicked and fasted and prayed and cursed and cried myself to the point of existing. It has been like being born again, literally. Just "knowing" has meant everything to me. Knowing has pushed me out into the world, into college, into places, into people.

Part of what existence means to me is knowing the difference between what I am now and what I was then. It is being capable of looking after myself intellectually as well as financially. It is being able to tell when I am being wronged and by whom. It means being awake

to protect myself and the ones I love. It means being a part of the
world community, and being *alert* to which part it is that I have
joined, and knowing how to change to another part if that part does
not suit me. To know is to exist: to exist is to be involved, to move
about, to see the world with my own eyes. This, at least, the Movement has given me.

The hippies and other nihilists would have me believe that it is all
the same whether the people in Mississippi have a movement behind
them or not. Once they have their rights, they say, they will run all
over themselves trying to be just like everybody else. They will be well
fed, complacent about things of the spirit, emotionless, and without
that marvelous humanity and "soul" that the Movement has seen
them practice time and time again. "What has the Movement done,"
they ask, "with the few people it has supposedly helped?" "Got them
white-collar jobs, moved them into standardized ranch houses in
white neighborhoods, given them nondescript gray flannel suits?"
"What are these people now?" they ask. And then they answer themselves, "Nothings!"

I would find this reasoning—which I have heard many, many times
from hippies and nonhippies alike—amusing if I did not also consider
it serious. For I think it is a delusion, a cop-out, an excuse to disassoci-
ate themselves from a world in which they feel too little has been
changed or gained. The real question, however, it appears to me, is
not whether poor people will adopt the middle-class mentality once
they are well fed; rather, it is whether they will ever be well fed enough
to be able to choose whatever mentality they think will suit them. The
lack of a movement did not keep my mother from *wishing* herself
bourgeois in her daydreams.

There is widespread starvation in Mississippi. In my own state of
Georgia there are more hungry families than Lester Maddox would
like to admit—or even see fed. I went to school with children who ate
red dirt. The Movement has prodded and pushed some liberal senators
into pressuring the government for food so that the hungry may eat.
Food stamps that were two dollars and out of the reach of many
families not long ago have been reduced to fifty cents. The price is still
out of the reach of some families, and the government, it seems to a
lot of people, could spare enough free food to feed its own people. It
angers people in the Movement that it does not; they point to the

billions in wheat we send free each year to countries abroad. Their government's slowness while people are hungry, its unwillingness to believe that there are Americans starving, its stingy cutting of the price of food stamps, make many Civil Rights workers throw up their hands in disgust. But they do not give up. They do not withdraw into the world of psychedelia. They apply what pressure they can to make the government give away food to hungry people. They do not plan so far ahead in their disillusionment with society that they can see these starving families buying identical ranch-style houses and sending their snobbish children to Bryn Mawr and Yale. They take first things first and try to get them fed.

They do not consider it their business, in any case, to say what kind of life the people they help must lead. How one lives is, after all, one of the rights left to the individual—when and if he has opportunity to choose. It is not the prerogative of the middle class to determine what is worthy of aspiration. There is also every possibility that the middle-class people of tomorrow will turn out ever so much better than those of today. I even know some middle-class people of today who are not *all* bad.

I think there are so few Negro hippies because middle-class Negroes, although well fed, are not careless. They are required by the treacherous world they live in to be clearly aware of whoever or whatever might be trying to do them in. They are middle class in money and position, but they cannot afford to be middle class in complacency. They distrust the hippie movement because they know that it can do nothing for Negroes as a group but "love" them, which is what all paternalists claim to do. And since the only way Negroes can survive (which they cannot do, unfortunately, on love alone) is with the support of the group, they are wisely wary and stay away.

A white writer tried recently to explain that the reason for the relatively few Negro hippies is that Negroes have built up a "super-cool" that cracks under LSD and makes them have a "bad trip." What this writer doesn't guess at is that Negroes are needing drugs less than ever these days for any kind of trip. While the hippies are "tripping," Negroes are going after power, which is so much more important to their survival and their children's survival than LSD and pot.

Everyone would be surprised if the Israelis ignored the Arabs and

took up "tripping" and pot smoking. In this country we are the
Israelis. Everybody who can do so would like to forget this, of course.
But for us to forget it for a minute would be fatal. "We Shall Over-
come" is just a song to most Americans, *but we must do it.* Or die.

What good was the Civil Rights Movement? If it had just given this
country Dr. King, a leader of conscience, for once in our lifetime, it
would have been enough. If it had just taken black eyes off white
television stories, it would have been enough. If it had fed one starving
child, it would have been enough.

If the Civil Rights Movement is "dead," and if it gave us nothing
else, it gave us each other forever. It gave some of us bread, some of
us shelter, some of us knowledge and pride, all of us comfort. It gave
us our children, our husbands, our brothers, our fathers, as men
reborn and with a purpose for living. It broke the pattern of black
servitude in this country. It shattered the phony "promise" of white
soap operas that sucked away so many pitiful lives. It gave us history
and men far greater than Presidents. It gave us heroes, selfless men
of courage and strength, for our little boys and girls to follow. It gave
us hope for tomorrow. It called us to life.

Because we live, it can never die.

[1967]

BROTHERS AND SISTERS

WE LIVED on a farm in the South in the fifties, and my brothers,
the four of them I knew (the fifth had left home when I was three
years old), were allowed to watch animals being mated. This was not
unusual; nor was it considered unusual that my older sister and I were
frowned upon if we even asked, innocently, what was going on. One
of my brothers explained the mating one day, using words my father
had given him: "The bull is getting a little something on his stick,"
he said. And he laughed. "What stick?" I wanted to know. "Where
did he get it? How did he pick it up? Where did he put it?" All my
brothers laughed.

I believe my mother's theory about raising a large family of five boys and three girls was that the father should teach the boys and the mother teach the girls the facts, as one says, of life. So my father went around talking about bulls getting something on their sticks and she went around saying girls did not need to know about such things. They were "womanish" (a very bad way to be in those days) if they asked.

The thing was, watching the matings filled my brothers with an aimless sort of lust, as dangerous as it was unintentional. They knew enough to know that cows, months after mating, produced calves, but they were not bright enough to make the same connection between women and their offspring.

Sometimes, when I think of my childhood, it seems to me a particularly hard one. But in reality, everything awful that happened to me didn't seem to happen to *me* at all, but to my older sister. Through some incredible power to negate my presence around people I did not like, which produced invisibility (as well as an ability to appear mentally vacant when I was nothing of the kind), I was spared the humiliation she was subjected to, though at the same time, I felt every bit of it. It was as if she suffered for my benefit, and I vowed early in my life that none of the things that made existence so miserable for her would happen to me.

The fact that she was not allowed at official matings did not mean she never saw any. While my brothers followed my father to the mating pens on the other side of the road near the barn, she stationed herself near the pigpen, or followed our many dogs until they were in a mating mood, or, failing to witness something there, she watched the chickens. On a farm it is impossible *not* to be conscious of sex, to wonder about it, to dream . . . but to whom was she to speak of her feelings? Not to my father, who thought all young women perverse. Not to my mother, who pretended all her children grew out of stumps she magically found in the forest. Not to me, who never found anything wrong with this lie.

When my sister menstruated she wore a thick packet of clean rags between her legs. It stuck out in front like a penis. The boys laughed at her as she served them at the table. Not knowing any better, and because our parents did not dream of actually *discussing* what was

going on, she would giggle nervously at herself. I hated her for gig-
gling, and it was at those times I would think of her as dim-witted.
She never complained, but she began to have strange fainting fits
whenever she had her period. Her head felt as if it were splitting, she
said, and everything she ate came up again. And her cramps were so
severe she could not stand. She was forced to spend several days of
each month in bed.

My father expected all of his sons to have sex with women. "Like
bulls," he said, "a man *needs* to get a little something on his stick."
And so, on Saturday nights, into town they went, chasing the girls.
My sister was rarely allowed into town alone, and if the dress she wore
fit too snugly at the waist, or if her cleavage dipped too far below her
collarbone, she was made to stay home.

"But why can't I go too," she would cry, her face screwed up with
the effort not to wail.

"They're boys, your brothers, *that's* why they can go."

Naturally, when she got the chance, she responded eagerly to boys.
But when this was discovered she was whipped and locked up in her
room.

I would go in to visit her.

"Straight Pine," she would say, "you don't know what it *feels* like
to want to be loved by a man."

"And if this is what you get for feeling like it I never will," I said,
with—I hoped—the right combination of sympathy and disgust.

"Men smell so good," she would whisper ecstatically. "And when
they look into your eyes, you just melt."

Since they were so hard to catch, naturally she thought almost any
of them terrific.

"Oh, that Alfred!" she would moon over some mediocre, square-
headed boy, "he's so *sweet!*" And she would take his ugly picture out
of her bosom and kiss it.

My father was always warning her not to come home if she ever
found herself pregnant. My mother constantly reminded her that
abortion was a sin. Later, although she never became pregnant, her
period would not come for months at a time. The painful symptoms,
however, never varied or ceased. She fell for the first man who loved
her enough to beat her for looking at someone else, and when I was
still in high school, she married him.

My fifth brother, the one I never knew, was said to be different from the rest. He had not liked matings. He would not watch them. He thought the cows should be given a choice. My father had disliked him because he was soft. My mother took up for him. "Jason is just tender-hearted," she would say in a way that made me know he was her favorite; "he takes after me." It was true that my mother cried about almost anything.

Who was this oldest brother? I wondered.

"Well," said my mother, "he was someone who always loved you. Of course he was a great big boy when you were born and out working on his own. He worked on a road gang building roads. Every morning before he left he would come in the room where you were and pick you up and give you the biggest kisses. He used to look at you and just smile. It's a pity you don't remember him."

I agreed.

At my father's funeral I finally "met" my oldest brother. He is tall and black with thick gray hair above a young-looking face. I watched my sister cry over my father until she blacked out from grief. I saw my brothers sobbing, reminding each other of what a great father he had been. My oldest brother and I did not shed a tear between us. When I left my father's grave he came up and introduced himself. "You don't ever have to walk alone," he said, and put his arms around me.

One out of five ain't *too* bad, I thought, snuggling up.

But I didn't discover until recently his true uniqueness: He is the only one of my brothers who assumes responsibility for all his children. The other four all fathered children during those Saturday-night chases of twenty years ago. Children—my nieces and nephews whom I will probably never know—they neither acknowledge as their own, provide for, or even see.

It was not until I became a student of women's liberation ideology that I could understand and forgive my father. I needed an ideology that would define his behavior in context. The black movement had given me an ideology that helped explain his colorism (he *did* fall in love with my mother partly because she was so light; he never denied it). Feminism helped explain his sexism. I was relieved to know his sexist behavior was not something uniquely his own, but, rather, an imitation of the behavior of the society around us.

All partisan movements add to the fullness of our understanding of society as a whole. They never detract; or, in any case, one must not allow them to do so. Experience adds to experience. "The more things the better," as O'Connor and Welty both have said, speaking, one of marriage, the other of Catholicism.

I desperately needed my father and brothers to give me male models I could respect, because white men (for example; being particularly handy in this sort of comparison)—whether in films or in person— offered man as dominator, as killer, and always as hypocrite.

My father failed because he copied the hypocrisy. And my brothers—except for one—never understood they must represent half the world to me, as I must represent the other half to them.

A story / Representation of how society Affected her life & how she grew up & the family affects the passion her.

[1975]

BEAUTY: WHEN THE OTHER DANCER IS THE SELF

IT IS A BRIGHT SUMMER DAY in 1947. My father, a fat, funny man with beautiful eyes and a subversive wit, is trying to decide which of his eight children he will take with him to the county fair. My mother, of course, will not go. She is knocked out from getting most of us ready: I hold my neck stiff against the pressure of her knuckles as she hastily completes the braiding and then beribboning of my hair.

My father is the driver for the rich old white lady up the road. Her name is Miss Mey. She owns all the land for miles around, as well as the house in which we live. All I remember about her is that she once offered to pay my mother thirty-five cents for cleaning her house, raking up piles of her magnolia leaves, and washing her family's clothes, and that my mother—she of no money, eight children, and a chronic earache—refused it. But I do not think of this in 1947. I am two and a half years old. I want to go everywhere my daddy goes. I am excited at the prospect of riding in a car. Someone has told me fairs are fun. That there is room in the car for only three of us doesn't faze me at all. Whirling happily in my starchy frock, showing off my biscuit-polished patent-leather shoes and lavender socks, tossing my head in a way that makes my ribbons bounce, I stand, hands on hips, before my father. "Take me, Daddy," I say with assurance; "I'm the prettiest!"

Later, it does not surprise me to find myself in Miss Mey's shiny black car, sharing the back seat with the other lucky ones. Does not surprise me that I thoroughly enjoy the fair. At home that night I tell the unlucky ones all I can remember about the merry-go-round, the man who eats live chickens, and the teddy bears, until they say: that's enough, baby Alice. Shut up now, and go to sleep.

It is Easter Sunday, 1950. I am dressed in a green, flocked, scalloped-hem dress (handmade by my adoring sister, Ruth) that has its own smooth satin petticoat and tiny hot-pink roses tucked into each scallop. My shoes, new T-strap patent leather, again highly biscuit-polished. I am six years old and have learned one of the longest Easter speeches to be heard that day, totally unlike the speech I said when I was two: "Easter lilies/pure and white/blossom in/the morning light." When I rise to give my speech I do so on a great wave of love and pride and expectation. People in the church stop rustling their new crinolines. They seem to hold their breath. I can tell they admire my dress, but it is my spirit, bordering on sassiness (womanishness), they secretly applaud.

"That girl's a little *mess*," they whisper to each other, pleased.

Naturally I say my speech without stammer or pause, unlike those who stutter, stammer, or, worst of all, forget. This is before the word "beautiful" exists in people's vocabulary, but "Oh, isn't she the *cutest* thing!" frequently floats my way. "And got so much sense!" they gratefully add . . . for which thoughtful addition I thank them to this day.

It was great fun being cute. But then, one day, it ended.

I am eight years old and a tomboy. I have a cowboy hat, cowboy boots, checkered shirt and pants, all red. My playmates are my brothers, two and four years older than I. Their colors are black and green, the only difference in the way we are dressed. On Saturday nights we

all go to the picture show, even my mother; Westerns are her favorite
kind of movie. Back home, "on the ranch," we pretend we are Tom
Mix, Hopalong Cassidy, Lash LaRue (we've even named one of our
dogs Lash LaRue); we chase each other for hours rustling cattle, being
outlaws, delivering damsels from distress. Then my parents decide to
buy my brothers guns. These are not "real" guns. They shoot "BBs,"
copper pellets my brothers say will kill birds. Because I am a girl, I
do not get a gun. Instantly I am relegated to the position of Indian.
Now there appears a great distance between us. They shoot and shoot
at everything with their new guns. I try to keep up with my bow and
arrows.

One day while I am standing on top of our makeshift "garage"—
pieces of tin nailed across some poles—holding my bow and arrow and
looking out toward the fields, I feel an incredible blow in my right eye.
I look down just in time to see my brother lower his gun.

Both brothers rush to my side. My eye stings, and I cover it with
my hand. "If you tell," they say, "we will get a whipping. You don't
want that to happen, do you?" I do not. "Here is a piece of wire,"
says the older brother, picking it up from the roof; "say you stepped
on one end of it and the other flew up and hit you." The pain is
beginning to start. "Yes," I say. "Yes, I will say that is what happened." If I do not say this is what happened, I know my brothers
will find ways to make me wish I had. But now I will say anything
that gets me to my mother.

Confronted by our parents we stick to the lie agreed upon. They
place me on a bench on the porch and I close my left eye while they
examine the right. There is a tree growing from underneath the porch
that climbs past the railing to the roof. It is the last thing my right
eye sees. I watch as its trunk, its branches, and then its leaves are
blotted out by the rising blood.

I am in shock. First there is intense fever, which my father tries to
break using lily leaves bound around my head. Then there are chills:
my mother tries to get me to eat soup. Eventually, I do not know how,
my parents learn what has happened. A week after the "accident"
they take me to see a doctor. "Why did you wait so long to come?"
he asks, looking into my eye and shaking his head. "Eyes are sympathetic," he says. "If one is blind, the other will likely become blind
too."

This comment of the doctor's terrifies me. But it is really how I look that bothers me most. Where the BB pellet struck there is a glob of whitish scar tissue, a hideous cataract, on my eye. Now when I stare at people—a favorite pastime, up to now—they will stare back. Not at the "cute" little girl, but at her scar. For six years I do not stare at anyone, because I do not raise my head.

Years later, in the throes of a mid-life crisis, I ask my mother and sister whether I changed after the "accident." "No," they say, puzzled. "What do you mean?"

What do I mean?

I am eight, and, for the first time, doing poorly in school, where I have been something of a whiz since I was four. We have just moved to the place where the "accident" occurred. We do not know any of the people around us because this is a different county. The only time I see the friends I knew is when we go back to our old church. The new school is the former state penitentiary. It is a large stone building, cold and drafty, crammed to overflowing with boisterous, ill-disciplined children. On the third floor there is a huge circular imprint of some partition that has been torn out.

"What used to be here?" I ask a sullen girl next to me on our way past it to lunch.

"The electric chair," says she.

At night I have nightmares about the electric chair, and about all the people reputedly "fried" in it. I am afraid of the school, where all the students seem to be budding criminals.

"What's the matter with your eye?" they ask, critically.

When I don't answer (I cannot decide whether it was an "accident" or not), they shove me, insist on a fight.

My brother, the one who created the story about the wire, comes to my rescue. But then brags so much about "protecting" me, I become sick.

After months of torture at the school, my parents decide to send me back to our old community, to my old school. I live with my grandparents and the teacher they board. But there is no room for Phoebe, my cat. By the time my grandparents decide there *is* room, and I ask for my cat, she cannot be found. Miss Yarborough, the boarding teacher, takes me under her wing, and begins to teach me to play the piano. But soon she marries an African—a "prince," she says—and is whisked away to his continent.

At my old school there is at least one teacher who loves me. She is the teacher who "knew me before I was born" and bought my first baby clothes. It is she who makes life bearable. It is her presence that finally helps me turn on the one child at the school who continually calls me "one-eyed bitch." One day I simply grab him by his coat and beat him until I am satisfied. It is my teacher who tells me my mother is ill.

My mother is lying in bed in the middle of the day, something I have never seen. She is in too much pain to speak. She has an abscess in her ear. I stand looking down on her, knowing that if she dies, I cannot live. She is being treated with warm oils and hot bricks held against her cheek. Finally a doctor comes. But I must go back to my grandparents' house. The weeks pass but I am hardly aware of it. All I know is that my mother might die, my father is not so jolly, my brothers still have their guns, and I am the one sent away from home.

"You did not change," they say.

Did I imagine the anguish of never looking up?

I am twelve. When relatives come to visit I hide in my room. My cousin Brenda, just my age, whose father works in the post office and whose mother is a nurse, comes to find me. "Hello," she says. And then she asks, looking at my recent school picture, which I did not want taken, and on which the "glob," as I think of it, is clearly visible, "You still can't see out of that eye?"

"No," I say, and flop back on the bed over my book.

That night, as I do almost every night, I abuse my eye. I rant and rave at it, in front of the mirror. I plead with it to clear up before morning. I tell it I hate and despise it. I do not pray for sight. I pray for beauty.

"You did not change," they say.

I am fourteen and baby-sitting for my brother Bill, who lives in Boston. He is my favorite brother and there is a strong bond between us. Understanding my feelings of shame and ugliness he and his wife take me to a local hospital, where the "glob" is removed by a doctor named O. Henry. There is still a small bluish crater where the scar tissue was, but the ugly white stuff is gone. Almost immediately I become a different person from the girl who does not raise her head. Or so I think. Now that I've raised my head I win the boyfriend of my dreams. Now that I've raised my head I have plenty of friends. Now that I've raised my head classwork comes from my lips as faultlessly as Easter speeches did, and I leave high school as valedictorian, most popular student, and *queen,* hardly believing my luck. Ironically, the girl who was voted most beautiful in our class (and was) was later shot twice through the chest by a male companion, using a "real" gun, while she was pregnant. But that's another story in itself. Or is it?

"You did not change," they say.

It is now thirty years since the "accident." A beautiful journalist comes to visit and to interview me. She is going to write a cover story for her magazine that focuses on my latest book. "Decide how you want to look on the cover," she says. "Glamorous, or whatever."

Never mind "glamorous," it is the "whatever" that I hear. Suddenly all I can think of is whether I will get enough sleep the night before the photography session: if I don't, my eye will be tired and wander, as blind eyes will.

At night in bed with my lover I think up reasons why I should not appear on the cover of a magazine. "My meanest critics will say I've sold out," I say. "My family will now realize I write scandalous books."

"But what's the real reason you don't want to do this?" he asks.

"Because in all probability," I say in a rush, "my eye won't be straight."

"It will be straight enough," he says. Then, "Besides, I thought you'd made your peace with that."

And I suddenly remember that I have.

I remember:

I am talking to my brother Jimmy, asking if he remembers anything unusual about the day I was shot. He does not know I consider that day the last time my father, with his sweet home remedy of cool lily leaves, chose me, and that I suffered and raged inside because of this. "Well," he says, "all I remember is standing by the side of the highway with Daddy, trying to flag down a car. A white man stopped, but when Daddy said he needed somebody to take his little girl to the doctor, he drove off."

I remember:

I am in the desert for the first time. I fall totally in love with it. I am so overwhelmed by its beauty, I confront for the first time, consciously, the meaning of the doctor's words years ago: "Eyes are sympathetic. If one is blind, the other will likely become blind too." I realize I have dashed about the world madly, looking at this, looking at that, storing up images against the fading of the light. *But I might have missed seeing the desert!* The shock of that possibility—and gratitude for over twenty-five years of sight—sends me literally to my knees. Poem after poem comes—which is perhaps how poets pray.

ON SIGHT

I am so thankful I have seen
The Desert
And the creatures in the desert
And the desert Itself.

The desert has its own moon
Which I have seen
With my own eye.
There is no flag on it.

Trees of the desert have arms
All of which are always up
That is because the moon is up
The sun is up
Also the sky
The stars
Clouds
None with flags.

If there *were* flags, I doubt
the trees would point.
Would you?

But mostly, I remember this:

I am twenty-seven, and my baby daughter is almost three. Since her birth I have worried about her discovery that her mother's eyes are different from other people's. Will she be embarrassed? I think. What will she say? Every day she watches a television program called "Big Blue Marble." It begins with a picture of the earth as it appears from the moon. It is bluish, a little battered-looking, but full of light, with whitish clouds swirling around it. Every time I see it I weep with love, as if it is a picture of Grandma's house. One day when I am putting Rebecca down for her nap, she suddenly focuses on my eye. Something inside me cringes, gets ready to try to protect myself. All children are cruel about physical differences, I know from experience, and that they don't always mean to be is another matter. I assume Rebecca will be the same.

But no-o-o-o. She studies my face intently as we stand, her inside and me outside her crib. She even holds my face maternally between her dimpled little hands. Then, looking every bit as serious and lawyerlike as her father, she says, as if it may just possibly have slipped my attention: "Mommy, there's a *world* in your eye." (As in, "Don't be alarmed, or do anything crazy.") And then, gently, but with great interest: "Mommy, where did you *get* that world in your eye?"

For the most part, the pain left then. (So what, if my brothers grew up to buy even more powerful pellet guns for their sons and to carry real guns themselves. So what, if a young "Morehouse man" once nearly fell off the steps of Trevor Arnett Library because he thought my eyes were blue.) Crying and laughing I ran to the bathroom, while Rebecca mumbled and sang herself off to sleep. Yes indeed, I realized, looking into the mirror. There *was* a world in my eye. And I saw that it was possible to love it: that in fact, for all it had taught me of shame and anger and inner vision, I *did* love it. Even to see it drifting out of orbit in boredom, or rolling up out of fatigue, not to mention floating back at attention in excitement (bearing witness, a friend has called it), deeply suitable to my personality, and even characteristic of me.

That night I dream I am dancing to Stevie Wonder's song "Always" (the name of the song is really "As," but I hear it as "Always"). As I dance, whirling and joyous, happier than I've ever been in my life, another bright-faced dancer joins me. We dance and kiss each other and hold each other through the night. The other dancer has obviously come through all right, as I have done. She is beautiful, whole and free. And she is also me.

[1983]

IN SEARCH OF
OUR MOTHERS' GARDENS

*I described her own nature and temperament. Told how they
needed a larger life for their expression. . . . I pointed out that
in lieu of proper channels, her emotions had overflowed into
paths that dissipated them. I talked, beautifully I thought, about
an art that would be born, an art that would open the way for
women the likes of her. I asked her to hope, and build up an inner
life against the coming of that day. . . . I sang, with a strange
quiver in my voice, a promise song.*

Jean Toomer, "Avey," *Cane*

THE POET speaking to a prostitute who falls asleep while he's
talking—

When the poet Jean Toomer walked through the South in the early
twenties, he discovered a curious thing: black women whose spirituality was so intense, so deep, so *unconscious,* that they were themselves
unaware of the richness they held. They stumbled blindly through
their lives: creatures so abused and mutilated in body, so dimmed and
confused by pain, that they considered themselves unworthy even of
hope. In the selfless abstractions their bodies became to the men who
used them, they became more than "sexual objects," more even than
mere women: they became "Saints." Instead of being perceived as
whole persons, their bodies became shrines: what was thought to be
their minds became temples suitable for worship. These crazy Saints
stared out at the world, wildly, like lunatics—or quietly, like suicides;
and the "God" that was in their gaze was as mute as a great stone.

Who were these Saints? These crazy, loony, pitiful women?

Some of them, without a doubt, were our mothers and grandmothers.

In the still heat of the post-Reconstruction South, this is how they
seemed to Jean Toomer: exquisite butterflies trapped in an evil honey,
toiling away their lives in an era, a century, that did not acknowledge

them, except as "the *mule* of the world." They dreamed dreams that no one knew—not even themselves, in any coherent fashion—and saw visions no one could understand. They wandered or sat about the countryside crooning lullabies to ghosts, and drawing the mother of Christ in charcoal on courthouse walls.

They forced their minds to desert their bodies and their striving spirits sought to rise, like frail whirlwinds from the hard red clay. And when those frail whirlwinds fell, in scattered particles, upon the ground, no one mourned. Instead, men lit candles to celebrate the emptiness that remained, as people do who enter a beautiful but vacant space to resurrect a God.

Our mothers and grandmothers, some of them: moving to music not yet written. And they waited.

They waited for a day when the unknown thing that was in them would be made known; but guessed, somehow in their darkness, that on the day of their revelation they would be long dead. Therefore to Toomer they walked, and even ran, in slow motion. For they were going nowhere immediate, and the future was not yet within their grasp. And men took our mothers and grandmothers, "but got no pleasure from it." So complex was their passion and their calm.

To Toomer, they lay vacant and fallow as autumn fields, with harvest time never in sight: and he saw them enter loveless marriages, without joy; and become prostitutes, without resistance; and become mothers of children, without fulfillment.

For these grandmothers and mothers of ours were not Saints, but Artists; driven to a numb and bleeding madness by the springs of creativity in them for which there was no release. They were Creators, who lived lives of spiritual waste, because they were so rich in spirituality—which is the basis of Art—that the strain of enduring their unused and unwanted talent drove them insane. Throwing away this spirituality was their pathetic attempt to lighten the soul to a weight their work-worn, sexually abused bodies could bear.

What did it mean for a black woman to be an artist in our grandmothers' time? In our great-grandmothers' day? It is a question with an answer cruel enough to stop the blood.

Did you have a genius of a great-great-grandmother who died under some ignorant and depraved white overseer's lash? Or was she required to bake biscuits for a lazy backwater tramp, when she cried out in her soul to paint watercolors of sunsets, or the rain falling on the green and peaceful pasturelands? Or was her body broken and forced to bear children (who were more often than not sold away from her)—eight, ten, fifteen, twenty children—when her one joy was the thought of modeling heroic figures of rebellion, in stone or clay?

How was the creativity of the black woman kept alive, year after year and century after century, when for most of the years black people have been in America, it was a punishable crime for a black person to read or write? And the freedom to paint, to sculpt, to expand the mind with action did not exist. Consider, if you can bear to imagine it, what might have been the result if singing, too, had been forbidden by law. Listen to the voices of Bessie Smith, Billie Holiday, Nina Simone, Roberta Flack, and Aretha Franklin, among others, and imagine those voices muzzled for life. Then you may begin to comprehend the lives of our "crazy," "Sainted" mothers and grandmothers. The agony of the lives of women who might have been Poets, Novelists, Essayists, and Short-Story Writers (over a period of centuries), who died with their real gifts stifled within them.

And, if this were the end of the story, we would have cause to cry out in my paraphrase of Okot p'Bitek's great poem:

> O, my clanswomen
> Let us all cry together!
> Come,
> Let us mourn the death of our mother,
> The death of a Queen
> The ash that was produced
> By a great fire!
> O, this homestead is utterly dead
> Close the gates
> With *lacari* thorns,
> For our mother
> The creator of the Stool is lost!
> And all the young women
> Have perished in the wilderness!

But this is not the end of the story, for all the young women—our mothers and grandmothers, *ourselves*—have not perished in the wilderness. And if we ask ourselves why, and search for and find the answer, we will know beyond all efforts to erase it from our minds, just exactly who, and of what, we black American women are.

One example, perhaps the most pathetic, most misunderstood one, can provide a backdrop for our mothers' work: Phillis Wheatley, a slave in the 1700s.

Virginia Woolf, in her book *A Room of One's Own,* wrote that in order for a woman to write fiction she must have two things, certainly: a room of her own (with key and lock) and enough money to support herself.

What then are we to make of Phillis Wheatley, a slave, who owned not even herself? This sickly, frail black girl who required a servant of her own at times—her health was so precarious—and who, had she been white, would have been easily considered the intellectual superior of all the women and most of the men in the society of her day.

Virginia Woolf wrote further, speaking of course not of our Phillis, that "any woman born with a great gift in the sixteenth century [insert "eighteenth century," insert "black woman," insert "born or made a slave"] would certainly have gone crazed, shot herself, or ended her days in some lonely cottage outside the village, half witch, half wizard [insert "Saint"], feared and mocked at. For it needs little skill and psychology to be sure that a highly gifted girl who had tried to use her gift for poetry would have been so thwarted and hindered by contrary instincts [add "chains, guns, the lash, the ownership of one's body by someone else, submission to an alien religion"], that she must have lost her health and sanity to a certainty."

The key words, as they relate to Phillis, are "contrary instincts." For when we read the poetry of Phillis Wheatley—as when we read the novels of Nella Larsen or the oddly false-sounding autobiography of that freest of all black women writers, Zora Hurston—evidence of "contrary instincts" is everywhere. Her loyalties were completely divided, as was, without question, her mind.

But how could this be otherwise? Captured at seven, a slave of wealthy, doting whites who instilled in her the "savagery" of the Africa they "rescued" her from . . . one wonders if she was even able to remember her homeland as she had known it, or as it really was.

Yet, because she did try to use her gift for poetry in a world that made her a slave, she was "so thwarted and hindered by . . . contrary instincts, that she . . . lost her health. . . ." In the last years of her brief life, burdened not only with the need to express her gift but also with a penniless, friendless "freedom" and several small children for whom she was forced to do strenuous work to feed, she lost her health, certainly. Suffering from malnutrition and neglect and who knows what mental agonies, Phillis Wheatley died.

So torn by "contrary instincts" was black, kidnapped, enslaved Phillis that her description of "the Goddess"—as she poetically called the Liberty she did not have—is ironically, cruelly humorous. And, in fact, has held Phillis up to ridicule for more than a century. It is usually read prior to hanging Phillis's memory as that of a fool. She wrote:

> The Goddess comes, she moves divinely fair,
> Olive and laurel binds her *golden* hair.
> Wherever shines this native of the skies,
> Unnumber'd charms and recent graces rise. [My italics]

It is obvious that Phillis, the slave, combed the "Goddess's" hair every morning; prior, perhaps, to bringing in the milk, or fixing her mistress's lunch. She took her imagery from the one thing she saw elevated above all others.

With the benefit of hindsight we ask, "How could she?"

But at last, Phillis, we understand. No more snickering when your stiff, struggling, ambivalent lines are forced on us. We know now that you were not an idiot or a traitor; only a sickly little black girl, snatched from your home and country and made a slave; a woman who still struggled to sing the song that was your gift, although in a land of barbarians who praised you for your bewildered tongue. It is not so much what you sang, as that you kept alive, in so many of our ancestors, *the notion of song.*

Black women are called, in the folklore that so aptly identifies one's status in society, "the *mule* of the world," because we have been handed the burdens that everyone else—*everyone* else—refused to carry. We have also been called "Matriarchs," "Superwomen," and "Mean and Evil Bitches." Not to mention "Castraters" and "Sapphire's Mama." When we have pleaded for understanding, our character has been distorted; when we have asked for simple caring, we have been handed empty inspirational appellations, then stuck in the farthest corner. When we have asked for love, we have been given children. In short, even our plainer gifts, our labors of fidelity and love, have been knocked down our throats. To be an artist and a black woman, even today, lowers our status in many respects, rather than raises it: and yet, artists we will be.

Therefore we must fearlessly pull out of ourselves and look at and identify with our lives the living creativity some of our great-grandmothers were not allowed to know. I stress *some* of them because it is well known that the majority of our great-grandmothers knew, even without "knowing" it, the reality of their spirituality, even if they didn't recognize it beyond what happened in the singing at church—and they never had any intention of giving it up.

How they did it—those millions of black women who were not Phillis Wheatley, or Lucy Terry or Frances Harper or Zora Hurston or Nella Larsen or Bessie Smith; or Elizabeth Catlett, or Katherine Dunham, either—brings me to the title of this essay, "In Search of Our Mothers' Gardens," which is a personal account that is yet shared, in its theme and its meaning, by all of us. I found, while thinking about the far-reaching world of the creative black woman, that often the truest answer to a question that really matters can be found very close.

In the late 1920s my mother ran away from home to marry my father. Marriage, if not running away, was expected of seventeen-year-old girls. By the time she was twenty, she had two children and was pregnant with a third. Five children later, I was born. And this is how I came to know my mother: she seemed a large, soft, loving-eyed woman who was rarely impatient in our home. Her quick, violent temper was on view only a few times a year, when she battled with the white landlord who had the misfortune to suggest to her that her children did not need to go to school.

She made all the clothes we wore, even my brothers' overalls. She made all the towels and sheets we used. She spent the summers canning vegetables and fruits. She spent the winter evenings making quilts enough to cover all our beds.

During the "working" day, she labored beside—not behind—my father in the fields. Her day began before sunup, and did not end until

late at night. There was never a moment for her to sit down, undisturbed, to unravel her own private thoughts; never a time free from
interruption—by work or the noisy inquiries of her many children.
And yet, it is to my mother—and all our mothers who were not
famous—that I went in search of the secret of what has fed that
muzzled and often mutilated, but vibrant, creative spirit that the
black woman has inherited, and that pops out in wild and unlikely
places to this day.

But when, you will ask, did my overworked mother have time to
know or care about feeding the creative spirit?

The answer is so simple that many of us have spent years discovering it. We have constantly looked high, when we should have looked
high—and low.

For example: in the Smithsonian Institution in Washington, D.C.,
there hangs a quilt unlike any other in the world. In fanciful, inspired,
and yet simple and identifiable figures, it portrays the story of the
Crucifixion. It is considered rare, beyond price. Though it follows no
known pattern of quilt-making, and though it is made of bits and
pieces of worthless rags, it is obviously the work of a person of powerful imagination and deep spiritual feeling. Below this quilt I saw a note
that says it was made by "an anonymous Black woman in Alabama,
a hundred years ago."

If we could locate this "anonymous" black woman from Alabama,
she would turn out to be one of our grandmothers—an artist who left
her mark in the only materials she could afford, and in the only
medium her position in society allowed her to use.

As Virginia Woolf wrote further, in *A Room of One's Own:*

> Yet genius of a sort must have existed among women as it must have
> existed among the working class. [Change this to "slaves" and "the
> wives and daughters of sharecroppers."] Now and again an Emily
> Brontë or a Robert Burns [change this to "a Zora Hurston or a Richard
> Wright"] blazes out and proves its presence. But certainly it never got
> itself on to paper. When, however, one reads of a witch being ducked,
> of a woman possessed by devils [or "Sainthood"], of a wise woman
> selling herbs [our root workers], or even a very remarkable man who
> had a mother, then I think we are on the track of a lost novelist, a
> suppressed poet, of some mute and inglorious Jane Austen. . . . Indeed,

I would venture to guess that Anon, who wrote so many poems without
signing them, was often a woman. . . .

And so our mothers and grandmothers have, more often than not
anonymously, handed on the creative spark, the seed of the flower
they themselves never hoped to see: or like a sealed letter they could
not plainly read.

And so it is, certainly, with my own mother. Unlike "Ma" Rainey's
songs, which retained their creator's name even while blasting forth
from Bessie Smith's mouth, no song or poem will bear my mother's
name. Yet so many of the stories that I write, that we all write, are
my mother's stories. Only recently did I fully realize this: that through
years of listening to my mother's stories of her life, I have absorbed
not only the stories themselves, but something of the manner in which
she spoke, something of the urgency that involves the knowledge that
her stories—like her life—must be recorded. It is probably for this
reason that so much of what I have written is about characters whose
counterparts in real life are so much older than I am.

But the telling of these stories, which came from my mother's lips
as naturally as breathing, was not the only way my mother showed
herself as an artist. For stories, too, were subject to being distracted,
to dying without conclusion. Dinners must be started, and cotton
must be gathered before the big rains. The artist that was and is my
mother showed itself to me only after many years. This is what I
finally noticed:

Like Mem, a character in *The Third Life of Grange Copeland,* my
mother adorned with flowers whatever shabby house we were forced
to live in. And not just your typical straggly country stand of zinnias,
either. She planted ambitious gardens—and still does—with over fifty
different varieties of plants that bloom profusely from early March
until late November. Before she left home for the fields, she watered
her flowers, chopped up the grass, and laid out new beds. When she
returned from the fields she might divide clumps of bulbs, dig a cold
pit, uproot and replant roses, or prune branches from her taller bushes
or trees—until night came and it was too dark to see.

Whatever she planted grew as if by magic, and her fame as a grower
of flowers spread over three counties. Because of her creativity with
her flowers, even my memories of poverty are seen through a screen

of blooms—sunflowers, petunias, roses, dahlias, forsythia, spirea, delphiniums, verbena . . . and on and on.

And I remember people coming to my mother's yard to be given cuttings from her flowers; I hear again the praise showered on her because whatever rocky soil she landed on, she turned into a garden. A garden so brilliant with colors, so original in its design, so magnificent with life and creativity, that to this day people drive by our house in Georgia—perfect strangers and imperfect strangers—and ask to stand or walk among my mother's art.

I notice that it is only when my mother is working in her flowers that she is radiant, almost to the point of being invisible—except as Creator: hand and eye. She is involved in work her soul must have. Ordering the universe in the image of her personal conception of Beauty.

Her face, as she prepares the Art that is her gift, is a legacy of respect she leaves to me, for all that illuminates and cherishes life. She has handed down respect for the possibilities—and the will to grasp them.

For her, so hindered and intruded upon in so many ways, being an artist has still been a daily part of her life. This ability to hold on, even in very simple ways, is work black women have done for a very long time.

This poem is not enough, but it is something, for the woman who literally covered the holes in our walls with sunflowers:

> They were women then
> My mama's generation
> Husky of voice—Stout of
> Step
> With fists as well as
> Hands
> How they battered down
> Doors
> And ironed
> Starched white
> Shirts
> How they led
> Armies

> Headragged Generals
> Across mined
> Fields
> Booby-trapped
> Kitchens
> To discover books
> Desks
> A place for us
> How they knew what we
> *Must* know
> Without knowing a page
> Of it
> Themselves.

Guided by my heritage of a love of beauty and a respect for strength—in search of my mother's garden, I found my own.

And perhaps in Africa over two hundred years ago, there was just such a mother; perhaps she painted vivid and daring decorations in oranges and yellows and greens on the walls of her hut; perhaps she sang—in a voice like Roberta Flack's—*sweetly* over the compounds of her village; perhaps she wove the most stunning mats or told the most ingenious stories of all the village storytellers. Perhaps she was herself a poet—though only her daughter's name is signed to the poems that we know.

Perhaps Phillis Wheatley's mother was also an artist.

Perhaps in more than Phillis Wheatley's biological life is her mother's signature made clear.

[1974]

A SAMPLER OF ESSAYS
FROM PREVIOUS EDITIONS

MAX BEERBOHM

A RELIC

YESTERDAY I found in a cupboard an old, small, battered port-
manteau which, by the initials on it, I recognized as my own property.
The lock appeared to have been forced. I dimly remembered having
forced it myself, with a poker, in my hot youth, after some journey
in which I had lost the key; and this act of violence was probably the
reason why the trunk had so long ago ceased to travel. I unstrapped
it, not without dust; it exhaled the faint scent of its long closure; it
contained a tweed suit of Late Victorian pattern, some bills, some
letters, a collar-stud, and—something which, after I had wondered for
a moment or two what on earth it was, caused me suddenly to murmur, "Down below, the sea rustled to and fro over the shingle."
   Strange that these words had, year after long year, been existing in
some obscure cell at the back of my brain!—forgotten but all the
while existing, like the trunk in that cupboard. What released them,
what threw open the cell door, was nothing but the fragment of a fan;
just the butt-end of an inexpensive fan. The sticks are of white bone,
clipped together with a semicircular ring that is not silver. They are
neatly oval at the base, but variously jagged at the other end. The
longest of them measures perhaps two inches. Ring and all, they have
no market value; for a farthing is the least coin in our currency. And
yet, though I had so long forgotten them, for me they are not worthless. They touch a chord . . . Lest this confession raise false hopes in
the reader, I add that I did not know their owner.
   I did once see her, and in Normandy, and by moonlight, and her
name was Angélique. She was graceful, she was even beautiful. I was
but nineteen years old. Yet even so I cannot say that she impressed
me favorably. I was seated at a table of a café on the terrace of a
casino. I sat facing the sea, with my back to the casino. I sat listening
to the quiet sea, which I had crossed that morning. The hour was late,
there were few people about. I heard the swing-door behind me flap
open, and was aware of a sharp snapping and crackling sound as a lady

in white passed quickly by me. I stared at her erect thin back and her agitated elbows. A short fat man passed in pursuit of her—an elderly man in a black alpaca jacket that billowed. I saw that she had left a trail of little white things on the asphalt. I watched the efforts of the agonized short fat man to overtake her as she swept wraithlike away to the distant end of the terrace. What was the matter? What had made her so spectacularly angry with him? The three or four waiters of the café were exchanging cynical smiles and shrugs, as waiters will. I tried to feel cynical, but was thrilled with excitement, with wonder and curiosity. The woman out yonder had doubled on her tracks. She had not slackened her furious speed, but the man waddlingly contrived to keep pace with her now. With every moment they became more distinct, and the prospect that they would presently pass by me, back into the casino, gave me that physical tension which one feels on a wayside platform at the imminent passing of an express. In the rushingly enlarged vision I had of them, the wrath on the woman's face was even more saliently the main thing than I had supposed it would be. That very hard Parisian face must have been as white as the powder that coated it. "Écoute, Angélique," gasped the perspiring bourgeois, "écoute, je te supplie—" The swing-door received them and was left swinging to and fro. I wanted to follow, but had not paid for my bock. I beckoned my waiter. On his way to me he stooped down and picked up something which, with a smile and a shrug, he laid on my table: "Il semble que Mademoiselle ne s'en servira plus." This is the thing I now write of, and at sight of it I understood why there had been that snapping and crackling, and what the white fragments on the ground were.

I hurried through the rooms, hoping to see a continuation of that drama—a scene of appeasement, perhaps, or of fury still implacable. But the two oddly assorted players were not performing there. My waiter had told me he had not seen either of them before. I suppose they had arrived that day. But I was not destined to see either of them again. They went away, I suppose, next morning; jointly or singly; singly, I imagine.

They made, however, a prolonged stay in my young memory, and would have done so even had I not had that tangible memento of them. Who were they, those two of whom that one strange glimpse had befallen me? What, I wondered, was the previous history of each?

What, in particular, had all that tragic pother been about? Mlle. Angélique I guessed to be thirty years old, her friend perhaps fifty-five. Each of their faces was as clear to me as in the moment of actual vision—the man's fat shiny bewildered face; the taut white face of the woman, the hard red line of her mouth, the eyes that were not flashing, but positively dull, with rage. I presumed that the fan had been a present from him, and a recent present—bought perhaps that very day, after their arrival in the town. But what, *what* had he done that she should break it between her hands, scattering the splinters as who should sow dragon's teeth? I could not believe he had done anything much amiss. I imagined her grievance a trivial one. But this did not make the case less engrossing. Again and again I would take the fan-stump from my pocket, examining it on the palm of my hand, or between finger and thumb, hoping to read the mystery it had been mixed up in, so that I might reveal that mystery to the world. To the world, yes; nothing less than that. I was determined io make a story of what I had seen—a *conte* in the manner of great Guy de Maupassant. Now and again, in the course of the past year or so, it had occurred to me that I might be a writer. But I had not felt the impulse to sit down and write something. I did feel that impulse now. It would indeed have been an irresistible impulse if I had known just what to write.

I felt I might know at any moment, and had but to give my mind to it. Maupassant was an impeccable artist, but I think the secret of the hold he had on the young men of my day was not so much that we discerned his cunning as that we delighted in the simplicity which his cunning achieved. I had read a great number of his short stories, but none that had made me feel as though I, if I were a writer, mightn't have written it myself. Maupassant had an European reputation. It was pleasing, it was soothing and gratifying, to feel that one could at any time win an equal fame if one chose to set pen to paper. And now, suddenly, the spring had been touched in me, the time was come. I was grateful for the fluke by which I had witnessed on the terrace that evocative scene. I looked forward to reading the MS. of "The Fan"—tomorrow, at latest. I was not wildly ambitious. I was not inordinately vain. I knew I couldn't ever, with the best will in the world, write like Mr. George Meredith. Those wondrous works of his, seething with wit, with poetry and philosophy and what not, never had beguiled me with the sense that I might do something similar. I had full consciousness of not being a philosopher, of not being a poet, and of not being a wit. Well, Maupassant was none of these things. He was just an observer like me. Of course he was a good deal older than I, and had observed a good deal more. But it seemed to me that he was not my superior in knowledge of life. I knew all about life through *him*.

Dimly, the initial paragraph of my tale floated in my mind. I—not exactly I myself, but rather that impersonal *je* familiar to me through Maupassant—was to be sitting at that table, with a book before me, just as I *had* sat. Four or five short sentences would give the whole scene. One of these I had quite definitely composed. You have already heard it. "Down below, the sea rustled to and fro over the shingle."

These words, which pleased me much, were to do double duty. They were to recur. They were to be, by a fine stroke, the very last words of my tale, their tranquillity striking a sharp ironic contrast with the stress of what had just been narrated. I had, you see, advanced further in the form of my tale than in the substance. But even the form was as yet vague. What, exactly, was to happen after Mlle. Angélique and M. Joumand (as I provisionally called him) had rushed back past me into the casino? It was clear that I must hear the whole inner history from the lips of one or the other of them. Which? Should M. Joumand stagger out on to the terrace, sit down heavily at the table next to mine, bury his head in his hands, and presently, in broken words, blurt out to me all that might be of interest? . . .

"'And I tell you I gave up everything for her—everything.' He stared at me with his old hopeless eyes. 'She is more than the fiend I have described to you. Yet I swear to you, monsieur, that if I had anything left to give, it should be hers.'

"Down below, the sea rustled to and fro over the shingle."

Or should the lady herself be my informant? For a while, I rather leaned to this alternative. It was more exciting, it seemed to make the writer more signally a man of the world. On the other hand, it was less simple to manage. Wronged persons might be ever so communicative, but I surmised that persons in the wrong were reticent. Mlle. Angélique, therefore, would have to be modified by me in appearance and behavior, toned down, touched up; and poor M. Joumand must look like a man of whom one could believe anything. . . .

"She ceased speaking. She gazed down at the fragments of her fan, and then, as though finding in them an image of her own life, whispered, 'To think what I once was, monsieur!—what, but for him, I might be, even now!' She buried her face in her hands, then stared out into the night. Suddenly she uttered a short, harsh laugh.

"Down below, the sea rustled to and fro over the shingle."

I decided that I must choose the first of these two ways. It was the less chivalrous as well as the less lurid way, but clearly it was the more artistic as well as the easier. The "chose vue," the "tranche de la vie"—this was the thing to aim at. Honesty was the best policy. I must be nothing if not merciless. Maupassant was nothing if not merciless. He would not have spared Mlle. Angélique. Besides, why should I libel M. Joumand? Poor—no, not *poor* M. Joumand! I warned myself against pitying him. One touch of "sentimentality," and I should be lost. M. Joumand was ridiculous. I must keep him so. But—what was his position in life? Was he a lawyer perhaps?—or the proprietor of a shop in the Rue de Rivoli? I toyed with the possibility that he kept a fan shop—that the business had once been a prosperous one, but had gone down, down, because of his infatuation for this woman to whom he was always giving fans—which she *always* smashed. . . . " 'Ah monsieur, cruel and ungrateful to me though she is, I swear to you that if I had anything left to give, it should be hers; but,' he stared at me with his old hopeless eyes, 'the fan she broke tonight was the last—the last, monsieur—of my stock.' Down below,"—but I pulled myself together, and asked pardon of my Muse.

It may be that I had offended her by my fooling. Or it may be that she had a sisterly desire to shield Mlle. Angélique from my mordant art. Or it may be that she was bent on saving M. de Maupassant from a dangerous rivalry. Anyway, she withheld from me the inspiration I had so confidently solicited. I *could not* think what had led up to that scene on the terrace. I tried hard and soberly. I turned the "chose vue" over and over in my mind, day by day, and the fan-stump over and over in my hand. But the "chose à figurer"—what, oh what, was that? Nightly I revisited the café, and sat there with an open mind—a mind wide open to catch the idea that should drop into it like a ripe golden plum. The plum did not ripen. The mind remained wide open for a week or more, but nothing except that phrase about the sea rustled to and fro in it.

A full quarter of a century has gone by. M. Joumand's death, so far too fat was he all those years ago, may be presumed. A temper so violent as Mlle. Angélique's must surely have brought its owner to the grave, long since. But here, all unchanged, the stump of her fan is; and once more I turn it over and over in my hand, not learning its secret—no, nor even trying to, now. The chord this relic strikes in me is not one of curiosity as to that old quarrel, but (if you will forgive me) one of tenderness for my first effort to write, and for my first hopes of excellence.

[1918]

E. M. FORSTER

MY WOOD

A FEW YEARS AGO I wrote a book which dealt in part with the difficulties of the English in India. Feeling that they would have had no difficulties in India themselves, the Americans read the book freely. The more they read it the better it made them feel, and a check to the author was the result. I bought a wood with the check. It is not a large wood—it contains scarcely any trees, and it is intersected, blast it, by a public footpath. Still, it is the first property that I have owned, so it is right that other people should participate in my shame, and should ask themselves, in accents that will vary in horror, this very important question: What is the effect of property upon the character? Don't let's touch economics; the effect of private owner-ship upon the community as a whole is another question—a more important question, perhaps, but another one. Let's keep to psychol-ogy. If you own things, what's their effect on you? What's the effect on me of my wood?

In the first place, it makes me feel heavy. Property does have this effect. Property produces men of weight, and it was a man of weight who failed to get into the Kingdom of Heaven. He was not wicked, that unfortunate millionaire in the parable, he was only stout; he stuck out in front, not to mention behind, and as he wedged himself this way and that in the crystalline entrance and bruised his well-fed flanks, he saw beneath him a comparatively slim camel passing through the eye of a needle and being woven into the robe of God. The Gospels all through couple stoutness and slowness. They point out what is perfectly obvious, yet seldom realized: that if you have a lot of things you cannot move about a lot, that furniture requires dusting, dusters require servants, servants require insurance stamps, and the whole tangle of them makes you think twice before you accept an invitation to dinner or go for a bathe in the Jordan. Some-times the Gospels proceed further and say with Tolstoy that property is sinful; they approach the difficult ground of asceticism here, where I cannot follow them. But as to the immediate effects of property on people, they just show straightforward logic. It produces men of weight. Men of weight cannot, by definition, move like the lightning from the East unto the West, and the ascent of a fourteen-stone bishop into a pulpit is thus the exact antithesis of the coming of the Son of Man. My wood makes me feel heavy.

In the second place, it makes me feel it ought to be larger.

The other day I heard a twig snap in it. I was annoyed at first, for I thought that someone was blackberrying, and depreciating the value of the undergrowth. On coming nearer, I saw it was not a man who had trodden on the twig and snapped it, but a bird, and I felt pleased. My bird. The bird was not equally pleased. Ignoring the relation between us, it took fright as soon as it saw the shape of my face, and flew straight over the boundary hedge into a field, the property of Mrs. Henessy, where it sat down with a loud squawk. It had become Mrs. Henessy's bird. Something seemed grossly amiss here, something that would not have occurred had the wood been larger. I could not afford to buy Mrs. Henessy out, I dared not murder her, and limitations of this sort beset me on every side. Ahab did not want that vineyard—he only needed it to round off his property, preparatory to plotting a new curve—and all the land around my wood has become necessary to me in order to round off the wood. A boundary protects. But—poor little thing—the boundary ought in its turn to be protected. Noises on the edge of it. Children throw stones. A little more, and then a little more, until we reach the sea. Happy Canute! Happier Alexander! And after all, why should even the world be the limit of possession? A rocket containing a Union Jack, will, it is hoped, be shortly fired at the moon. Mars. Sirius. Beyond which . . . But these immensities ended by saddening me. I could not suppose that my wood was the destined nucleus of universal dominion—it is so small and contains no mineral wealth beyond the blackberries. Nor was I comforted when Mrs. Henessy's bird took alarm for the second time and flew clean away from us all, under the belief that it belonged to itself.

In the third place, property makes its owner feel that he ought to do something to it. Yet he isn't sure what. A restlessness comes over him, a vague sense that he has a personality to express—the same sense which, without any vagueness, leads the artist to an act of creation. Sometimes I think I will cut down such trees as remain in the wood, at other times I want to fill up the gaps between them with new trees. Both impulses are pretentious and empty. They are not honest movements towards moneymaking or beauty. They spring from a foolish desire to express myself and from an inability to enjoy what I have got. Creation, property, enjoyment form a sinister trinity in the human mind. Creation and enjoyment are both very very good, yet they are often unattainable without a material basis, and at such moments property pushes itself in as a substitute, saying, "Accept me instead—I'm good enough for all three." It is not enough. It is, as Shakespeare said of lust, "The expense of spirit in a waste of shame": it is "Before, a joy proposed; behind, a dream." Yet we don't know how to shun it. It is forced on us by our economic system as the alternative to starvation. It is also forced on us by an internal defect in the soul, by the feeling that in property may lie the germs of self-development and of exquisite or heroic deeds. Our life on earth is, and ought to be, material and carnal. But we have not yet learned to manage our materialism and carnality properly; they are still entangled with the desire for ownership, where (in the words of Dante) "Possession is one with loss."

And this brings us to our fourth and final point: the blackberries.

Blackberries are not plentiful in this meagre grove, but they are easily seen from the public footpath which traverses it, and all too easily gathered. Foxgloves, too—people will pull up the foxgloves, and ladies of an educational tendency even grub for toadstools to show them on the Monday in class. Other ladies, less educated, roll down the bracken in the arms of their gentlemen friends. There is paper, there are tins. Pray, does my wood belong to me or doesn't it? And, if it does, should I not own it best by allowing no one else to walk there? There is a wood near Lyme Regis, also cursed by a public footpath, where the owner has not hesitated on this point. He has built high stone walls each side of the path, and has spanned it by bridges, so that the public circulate like termites while he gorges on the blackberries unseen. He really does own his wood, this able chap. Dives in Hell did pretty well, but the gulf dividing him from Lazarus could be traversed by vision, and nothing traverses it here.

And perhaps I shall come to this in time. I shall wall in and fence
out until I really taste the sweets of property. Enormously stout,
endlessly avaricious, pseudo-creative, intensely selfish, I shall weave
upon my forehead the quadruple crown of possession until those
nasty Bolshies come and take it off again and thrust me aside into
the outer darkness.

[1926]

4 reasons
for him
not wanting
to own
property

stout (make him feel heavy)
avaricious (should be larger)
pseudo-creative (should do something to it)
selfish (EVERYTHING IS MINE)

D. H. LAWRENCE
ADOLF

WHEN WE WERE CHILDREN our father often worked on the night-shift. Once it was spring-time, and he used to arrive home, black and tired, just as we were downstairs in our nightdresses. Then night met morning face to face, and the contact was not always happy. Perhaps it was painful to my father to see us gaily entering upon the day into which he dragged himself soiled and weary. He didn't like going to bed in the spring morning sunshine.

But sometimes he was happy, because of his long walk through the dewy fields in the first daybreak. He loved the open morning, the crystal and the space, after a night down pit. He watched every bird, every stir in the trembling grass, answered the whinnying of the pewits and tweeted to the wrens. If he could, he also would have whinnied and tweeted and whistled in a native language that was not human. He liked non-human things best.

One sunny morning we were all sitting at table when we heard his heavy slurring walk up the entry. We became uneasy. His was always a disturbing presence, trammelling. He passed the window darkly, and we heard him go into the scullery and put down his tin bottle. But directly he came into the kitchen. We felt at once that he had something to communicate. No one spoke. We watched his black face for a second.

"Give me a drink," he said.

My mother hastily poured out his tea. He went to pour it out into his saucer. But instead of drinking he suddenly put something on the table among the teacups. A tiny brown rabbit! A small rabbit, a mere morsel, sitting against the bread as still as if it were a made thing.

"A rabbit! A young one! Who gave it you, father?"

But he laughed enigmatically, with a sliding motion of his yellow-grey eyes, and went to take off his coat. We pounced on the rabbit.

"Is it alive? Can you feel its heart beat?"

My father came back and sat down heavily in his armchair. He dragged his saucer to him, and blew his tea, pushing out his red lips under his black moustache.

"Where did you get it, father?"

"I picked it up," he said, wiping his naked forearm over his mouth and beard.

"Where?"

"It is a wild one!" came my mother's quick voice.

"Yes, it is."

"Then why did you bring it?" cried my mother.

"Oh, we wanted it," came our cry.

"Yes, I've no doubt you did—" retorted my mother. But she was drowned in our clamour of questions.

On the field path my father had found a dead mother rabbit and three dead little ones—this one alive, but unmoving.

"But what had killed them, daddy?"

"I couldn't say, my child. I s'd think she'd aten something."

"Why did you bring it!" again my mother's voice of condemnation. "You know what it will be."

My father made no answer, but we were loud in protest.

"He must bring it. It's not big enough to live by itself. It would die," we shouted.

"Yes, and it will die now. And then there'll be *another* outcry."

My mother set her face against the tragedy of dead pets. Our hearts sank.

"It won't die, father, will it? Why will it? It won't."

"I s'd think not," said my father.

"You know well enough it will. Haven't we had it all before!" said my mother.

"They dunna always pine," replied my father testily.

But my mother reminded him of other little wild animals he had brought, which had sulked and refused to live, and brought storms of tears and trouble in our house of lunatics.

Trouble fell on us. The little rabbit sat on our lap, unmoving, its eye wide and dark. We brought it milk, warm milk, and held it to its nose. It sat as still as if it was far away, retreated down some deep burrow, hidden, oblivious. We wetted its mouth and whiskers with drops of milk. It gave no sign, did not even shake off the wet white drops. Somebody began to shed a few secret tears.

"What did I say?" cried my mother. "Take it and put it down in the field."

Her command was in vain. We were driven to get dressed for school. There sat the rabbit. It was like a tiny obscure cloud. Watching it, the emotions died out of our breast. Useless to love it, to yearn over it. Its little feelings were all ambushed. They must be circumvented. Love and affection were a trespass upon it. A little wild thing, it became more mute and asphyxiated still in its own arrest, when we approached with love. We must not love it. We must circumvent it, for its own existence.

So I passed the order to my sister and my mother. The rabbit was not to be spoken to, nor even looked at. Wrapping it in a piece of flannel I put it in an obscure corner of the cold parlour, and put a saucer of milk before its nose. My mother was forbidden to enter the parlour whilst we were at school.

"As if I should take any notice of your nonsense," she cried affronted. Yet I doubt if she ventured into the parlour.

At midday, after school, creeping into the front room, there we saw the rabbit still and unmoving in the piece of flannel. Strange grey-brown neutralization of life, still living! It was a sore problem to us.

"Why won't it drink its milk, mother?" we whispered. Our father was asleep.

"It prefers to sulk its life away, silly little thing." A profound problem. Prefers to sulk its life away! We put young dandelion leaves to its nose. The sphinx was not more oblivious. Yet its eye was bright.

At tea-time, however, it had hopped a few inches, out of its flannel, and there it sat again, uncovered, a little solid cloud of muteness, brown, with unmoving whiskers. Only its side palpitated slightly with life.

Darkness came; my father set off to work. The rabbit was still unmoving. Dumb despair was coming over the sisters, a threat of tears before bedtime. Clouds of my mother's anger gathered as she muttered against my father's wantonness.

Once more the rabbit was wrapped in the old pit-singlet. But now it was carried into the scullery and put under the copper fireplace, that it might imagine itself inside a burrow. The saucers were placed about, four or five, here and there on the floor, so that if the little creature *should* chance to hop abroad, it could not fail to come upon some food. After this my mother was allowed to take from the scullery what she wanted and then she was forbidden to open the door.

When morning came and it was light, I went downstairs. Opening the scullery door, I heard a slight scuffle. Then I saw dabbles of milk all over the floor and tiny rabbit-droppings in the saucers. And there the miscreant, the tips of his ears showing behind a pair of boots. I peeped at him. He sat bright-eyed and askance, twitching his nose and looking at me while not looking at me.

He was alive—very much alive. But still we were afraid to trespass much on his confidence.

"Father!" My father was arrested at the door. "Father, the rabbit's alive."

"Back your life it is," said my father.

"Mind how you go in."

By evening, however, the little creature was tame, quite tame. He was christened Adolf. We were enchanted by him. We couldn't really love him, because he was wild and loveless to the end. But he was an unmixed delight.

We decided he was too small to live in a hutch—he must live at large in the house. My mother protested, but in vain. He was so tiny. So we had him upstairs, and he dropped his tiny pills on the bed and we were enchanted.

Adolf made himself instantly at home. He had the run of the house, and was perfectly happy, with his tunnels and his holes behind the furniture.

We loved him to take meals with us. He would sit on the table humping his back, sipping his milk, shaking his whiskers and his tender ears, hopping off and hobbling back to his saucer, with an air of supreme unconcern. Suddenly he was alert. He hobbled a few tiny paces, and reared himself up inquisitively at the sugar basin. He fluttered his tiny fore-paws, and then reached and laid them on the edge of the basin, whilst he craned his thin neck and peeped in. He trembled his whiskers at the sugar, then did his best to lift down a lump.

"*Do* you think I will have it! Animals in the sugar pot!" cried my mother, with a rap of her hand on the table.

Which so delighted the electric Adolf that he flung his hind-quarters and knocked over a cup.

"It's your own fault, mother. If you left him alone—"

He continued to take tea with us. He rather liked warm tea. And he loved sugar. Having nibbled a lump, he would turn to the butter. There he was shooed off by our parent. He soon learned to treat her shooing with indifference. Still, she hated him to put his nose in the food. And he loved to do it. And one day between them they overturned the cream-jug. Adolf deluged his little chest, bounced back in terror, was seized by his little ears by my mother and bounced down on the hearth-rug. There he shivered in momentary discomfort, and suddenly set off in a wild flight to the parlour.

This last was his happy hunting ground. He had cultivated the bad habit of pensively nibbling certain bits of cloth in the hearth-rug. When chased from this pasture he would retreat under the sofa. There he would twinkle in Buddhist meditation until suddenly, no one knew why, he would go off like an alarm clock. With a sudden bumping scuffle he would whirl out of the room, going through the doorway with his little ears flying. Then we would hear his thunderbolt hurtling in the parlour, but before we could follow, the wild streak of Adolf would flash past us, on an electric wind that swept him round the scullery and carried him back, a little mad thing, flying possessed like a ball round the parlour. After which ebullition he would sit in a corner composed and distant, twitching his whiskers in abstract meditation. And it was in vain we questioned him about his outbursts. He just went off like a gun, and was as calm after it as a gun that smokes placidly.

Alas, he grew up rapidly. It was almost impossible to keep him from the outer door.

One day, as we were playing by the stile, I saw his brown shadow loiter across the road and pass into the field that faced the houses. Instantly a cry of "Adolf!"—a cry he knew full well. And instantly a wind swept him away down the sloping meadow, his tail twinkling and zigzagging through the grass. After him we pelted. It was a strange sight to see him, ears back, his little loins so powerful, flinging the world behind him. We ran ourselves out of breath, but could not catch him. Then somebody headed him off, and he sat with sudden unconcern, twitching his nose under a bunch of nettles.

His wanderings cost him a shock. One Sunday morning my father had just been quarrelling with a pedlar, and we were hearing the aftermath indoors, when there came a sudden unearthly scream from the yard. We flew out. There sat Adolf cowering under a bench, whilst a great black and white cat glowered intently at him, a few yards away. Sight not to be forgotten. Adolf rolling back his eyes and parting his strange muzzle in another scream, the cat stretching forward in a slow elongation.

Ha, how we hated that cat! How we pursued him over the chapel wall and across the neighbours' gardens.

Adolf was still only half grown.

"Cats!" said my mother. "Hideous detestable animals, why do people harbour them?"

But Adolf was becoming too much for her. He dropped too many pills. And suddenly to hear him clumping downstairs when she was alone in the house was startling. And to keep him from the door was impossible. Cats prowled outside. It was worse than having a child to look after.

Yet we would not have him shut up. He became more lusty, more callous than ever. He was a strong kicker, and many a scratch on face and arms did we owe to him. But he brought his own doom on himself. The lace curtains in the parlour—my mother was rather proud of them—fell on the floor very full. One of Adolf's joys was to scuffle wildly through them as though through some foamy undergrowth. He had already torn rents in them.

One day he entangled himself altogether. He kicked, he whirled round in a mad nebulous inferno. He screamed—and brought down the curtain-rod with a smash, right on the best beloved pelargonium, just as my mother rushed in. She extricated him, but she never forgave him. And he never forgave either. A heartless wildness had come over him.

Even we understood that he must go. It was decided, after a long deliberation, that my father should carry him back to the wildwoods. Once again he was stowed into the great pocket of the pit-jacket.

"Best pop him i' th' pot," said my father, who enjoyed raising the wind of indignation.

And so, next day, our father said that Adolf, set down on the edge of the coppice, had hopped away with utmost indifference, neither elated nor moved. We heard it and believed. But many, many were the heartsearchings. How would the other rabbits receive him? Would they smell his tameness, his humanized degradation, and rend him? My mother pooh-poohed the extravagant idea.

However, he was gone, and we were rather relieved. My father kept an eye open for him. He declared that several times passing the coppice in the early morning, he had seen Adolf peeping through the nettle-stalks. He had called him, in an odd, high-voiced, cajoling fashion. But Adolf had not responded. Wildness gains so soon upon its creatures. And they become so contemptuous then of our tame presence. So it seemed to me. I myself would go to the edge of the coppice, and call softly. I myself would imagine bright eyes between the nettle-stalks, flash of a white, scornful tail past the bracken. That insolent white tail, as Adolf turned his flank on us! It reminded me always of a certain rude gesture, and a certain unprintable phrase, which may not even be suggested.

But when naturalists discuss the meaning of the rabbit's white tail, that rude gesture and still ruder phrase always come to my mind. Naturalists say that the rabbit shows his white tail in order to guide his young safely after him, as a nursemaid's flying strings are the signal to her toddling charges to follow on. How nice and naïve! I only know that my Adolf wasn't naïve. He used to whisk his flank at me, push his white feather in my eye, and say *"Merde!"* It's a rude word—but one which Adolf was always semaphoring at me, flag-wagging it with all the derision of his narrow haunches.

That's a rabbit all over—insolence, and the white flag of spiteful derision. Yes, and he keeps his flag flying to the bitter end, sporting, insolent little devil that he is. See him running for his life. Oh, how his soul is fanned to an ecstasy of fright, a fugitive whirlwind of panic. Gone mad, he throws the world behind him, with astonishing hind legs. He puts back his head and lays his ears on his sides and rolls the white of his eyes in sheer ecstatic agony of speed. He knows the awful approach behind him; bullet or stoat. He knows! He knows, his eyes are turned back almost into his head. It is agony. But it is also ecstasy. Ecstasy! See the insolent white flag bobbing. He whirls on the magic wind of terror. All his pent-up soul rushes into agonized electric emotion of fear. He flings himself on, like a falling star swooping into extinction. White heat of the agony of fear. And at the same time, bob! bob! bob! goes the white tail, *merde! merde! merde!* it says to the pursuer. The rabbit can't help it. In his utmost extremity he still flings the insult at the pursuer. He is the inconquerable fugitive, the indomitable meek. No wonder the stoat becomes vindictive.

And if he escapes, this precious rabbit! Don't you see him sitting there, in his earthly nook, a little ball of silence and rabbit triumph? Don't you see the glint on his black eye? Don't you see, in his very immobility, how the whole world is *merde* to him? No conceit like the conceit of the meek. And if the avenging angel in the shape of the ghostly ferret steals down on him, there comes a shriek of terror out of that little hump of self-satisfaction sitting motionless in a corner. Falls the fugitive. But even fallen, his white feather floats. Even in death it seems to say: "I am the meek, I am the righteous, I am the rabbit. All you rest, you are evil doers, and you shall be *bien emmerdés!*"

[1920]

JAMES THURBER
THE DOG THAT BIT PEOPLE

PROBABLY NO ONE MAN should have as many dogs in his life as I have had, but there was more pleasure than distress in them for me except in the case of an Airedale named Muggs. He gave me more trouble than all the other fifty-four or -five put together, although my moment of keenest embarrassment was the time a Scotch terrier named Jeannie, who had just had six puppies in the clothes closet of a fourth floor apartment in New York, had the unexpected seventh and last at the corner of Eleventh Street and Fifth Avenue during a walk she had insisted on taking. Then, too, there was the prize winning French poodle, a great big black poodle—none of your little, untrou-blesome white miniatures—who got sick riding in the rumble seat of a car with me on her way to the Greenwich Dog Show. She had a red rubber bib tucked around her throat and, since a rain storm came up when we were halfway through the Bronx, I had to hold over her a small green umbrella, really more of a parasol. The rain beat down fearfully and suddenly the driver of the car drove into a big garage, filled with mechanics. It happened so quickly that I forgot to put the umbrella down and I will always remember, with sickening distress, the look of incredulity mixed with hatred that came over the face of the particular hardened garage man that came over to see what we wanted, when he took a look at me and the poodle. All garage men, and people of that intolerant stripe, hate poodles with their curious haircut, especially the pom-poms that you've got to leave on their hips if you expect the dogs to win a prize.

But the Airedale, as I have said, was the worst of all my dogs. He really wasn't my dog, as a matter of fact: I came home from a vacation one summer to find that my brother Roy had bought him while I was away. A big, burly, choleric dog, he always acted as if he thought I wasn't one of the family. There was a slight advantage in being one of the family, for he didn't bite the family as often as he bit strangers. Still, in the years that we had him he bit everybody but mother, and he made a pass at her once but missed. That was during the month when we suddenly had mice, and Muggs refused to do anything about them. Nobody ever had mice exactly like the mice we had that month. They acted like pet mice, almost like mice somebody had trained. They were so friendly that one night when mother entertained at dinner the Friraliras, a club she and my father had belonged to for twenty years, she put down a lot of little dishes with food in them on the pantry floor so that the mice would be satisfied with that and wouldn't come into the dining room. Muggs stayed out in the pantry with the mice, lying on the floor, growling to himself—not at the mice, but about all the people in the next room that he would have liked to get at. Mother slipped out into the pantry once to see how every-thing was going. Everything was going fine. It made her so mad to see Muggs lying there, oblivious of the mice—they came running up to her—that she slapped him and he slashed at her, but didn't make it. He was sorry immediately, mother said. He was always sorry, she said, after he bit someone, but we could not understand how she figured this out. He didn't act sorry.

Mother used to send a box of candy every Christmas to the people the Airedale bit. The list finally contained forty or more names. No-body could understand why we didn't get rid of the dog. I didn't understand it very well myself, but we didn't get rid of him. I think that one or two people tried to poison Muggs—he acted poisoned once in a while—and old Major Moberly fired at him once with his service revolver near the Seneca Hotel in East Broad Street—but Muggs lived to be almost eleven years old and even when he could hardly get around he bit a Congressman who had called to see my father on business. My mother had never liked the Congressman—she said the signs of his horoscope showed he couldn't be trusted (he was Saturn with the moon in Virgo)—but she sent him a box of candy that Christmas. He sent it right back, probably because he suspected it was trick candy. Mother persuaded herself it was all for the best that the dog had bitten him, even though father lost an important business association because of it. "I wouldn't be associated with such a man," mother said. "Muggs could read him like a book."

We used to take turns feeding Muggs to be on his good side, but that didn't always work. He was never in a very good humor, even after a meal. Nobody knew exactly what was the matter with him, but whatever it was it made him irascible, especially in the mornings. Roy never felt very well in the morning, either, especially before breakfast,

and once when he came downstairs and found that Muggs had moodily chewed up the morning paper he hit him in the face with a
grapefruit and then jumped upon the dining room table, scattering
dishes and silverware and spilling the coffee. Muggs' first free leap
carried him all the way across the table and into a brass fire screen
in front of the gas grate but he was back on his feet in a moment and
in the end he got Roy and gave him a pretty vicious bite in the leg.
Then he was all over it; he never bit anyone more than once at a time.
Mother always mentioned that as an argument in his favor; she said
he had a quick temper but that he didn't hold a grudge. She was
forever defending him. I think she liked him because he wasn't well.
"He's not strong," she would say, pityingly, but that was inaccurate;
he may not have been well but he was terribly strong.

One time my mother went to the Chittenden Hotel to call on a
woman mental healer who was lecturing in Columbus on the subject
of "Harmonious Vibrations." She wanted to find out if it was possible
to get harmonious vibrations into a dog. "He's a large tan-colored
Airedale," mother explained. The woman said that she had never
treated a dog but she advised my mother to hold the thought that he
did not bite and would not bite. Mother was holding the thought the
very next morning when Muggs got the iceman but she blamed that
slip-up on the iceman. "If you didn't think he would bite you, he
wouldn't," mother told him. He stomped out of the house in a terrible
jangle of vibrations.

One morning when Muggs bit me slightly, more or less in passing,
I reached down and grabbed his short stumpy tail and hoisted him
into the air. It was a foolhardy thing to do and the last time I saw
my mother, about six months ago, she said she didn't know what
possessed me. I don't either, except that I was pretty mad. As long
as I held the dog off the floor by his tail he couldn't get at me, but
he twisted and jerked so, snarling all the time, that I realized I
couldn't hold him that way very long. I carried him to the kitchen
and flung him onto the floor and shut the door on him just as he
crashed against it. But I forgot about the backstairs. Muggs went up
the backstairs and down the frontstairs and had me cornered in the
living room. I managed to get up onto the mantelpiece above the
fireplace, but it gave way and came down with a tremendous crash
throwing a large marble clock, several vases, and myself heavily to the
floor. Muggs was so alarmed by the racket that when I picked myself

up he had disappeared. We couldn't find him anywhere, although we whistled and shouted, until old Mrs. Detweiler called after dinner that night. Muggs had bitten her once, in the leg, and she came into the living room only after we assured her that Muggs had run away. She had just seated herself when, with a great growling and scratching of claws, Muggs emerged from under a davenport where he had been quietly hiding all the time, and bit her again. Mother examined the bite and put arnica on it and told Mrs. Detweiler that it was only a bruise. "He just bumped you," she said. But Mrs. Detweiler left the house in a nasty state of mind.

Lots of people reported our Airedale to the police but my father held a municipal office at the time and was on friendly terms with the police. Even so, the cops had been out a couple times—once when Muggs bit Mrs. Rufus Sturtevant and again when he bit Lieutenant-Governor Malloy—but mother told them that it hadn't been Muggs' fault but the fault of the people who were bitten. "When he starts for them, they scream," she explained, "and that excites him." The cops suggested that it might be a good idea to tie the dog up, but mother said that it mortified him to be tied up and that he wouldn't eat when he was tied up.

Muggs at his meals was an unusual sight. Because of the fact that if you reached toward the floor he would bite you, we usually put his food plate on top of an old kitchen table with a bench alongside the table. Muggs would stand on the bench and eat. I remember that my mother's Uncle Horatio, who boasted that he was the third man up Missionary Ridge, was splutteringly indignant when he found out that we fed the dog on a table because we were afraid to put his plate on the floor. He said he wasn't afraid of any dog that ever lived and that he would put the dog's plate on the floor if we would give it to him. Roy said that if Uncle Horatio had fed Muggs on the ground just before the battle he would have been the first man up Missionary Ridge. Uncle Horatio was furious. "Bring him in! Bring him in now!" he shouted. "I'll feed the --- on the floor!" Roy was all for giving him a chance, but my father wouldn't hear of it. He said that Muggs had already been fed. "I'll feed him again!" bawled Uncle Horatio. We had quite a time quieting him.

In his last year Muggs used to spend practically all of his time outdoors. He didn't like to stay in the house for some reason or other—perhaps it held too many unpleasant memories for him. Anyway, it was hard to get him to come in and as a result the garbage man, the iceman, and the laundryman wouldn't come near the house. We had to haul the garbage down to the corner, take the laundry out and bring it back, and meet the iceman a block from home. After this had gone on for some time we hit on an ingenious arrangement for getting the dog in the house so that we could lock him up while the gas meter was read, and so on. Muggs was afraid of only one thing, an electrical storm. Thunder and lightning frightened him out of his senses (I think he thought a storm had broken the day the mantelpiece fell). He would rush into the house and hide under a bed or in a clothes closet. So we fixed up a thunder machine out of a long narrow piece of sheet iron with a wooden handle on one end. Mother would shake this vigorously when she wanted to get Muggs into the house. It made an excellent imitation of thunder, but I suppose it was the most round-about system for running a household that was ever devised. It took a lot out of mother.

A few months before Muggs died, he got to "seeing things." He would rise slowly from the floor, growling low, and stalk stiff-legged and menacing toward nothing at all. Sometimes the Thing would be just a little to the right or left of a visitor. Once a Fuller Brush salesman got hysterics. Muggs came wandering into the room like Hamlet following his father's ghost. His eyes were fixed on a spot just to the left of the Fuller Brush man, who stood it until Muggs was about three slow, creeping paces from him. Then he shouted. Muggs wavered on past him into the hallway grumbling to himself but the Fuller man went on shouting. I think mother had to throw a pan of cold water on him before he stopped. That was the way she used to stop us boys when we got into fights.

Muggs died quite suddenly one night. Mother wanted to bury him in the family lot under a marble stone with some such inscription as "Flights of angels sing thee to thy rest" but we persuaded her it was against the law. In the end we just put up a smooth board above his grave along a lonely road. On the board I wrote with an indelible pencil "Cave Canem." Mother was quite pleased with the simple classic dignity of the old Latin epitaph.

[1933]

EDMUND WILSON

THE OLD STONE HOUSE

As I go north for the first time in years, in the slow, the constantly stopping, milk train—which carries passengers only in the back part of the hind car and has an old stove to heat it in winter—I look out through the dirt-yellowed double pane and remember how once, as a child, I used to feel thwarted in summer till I had got the windows open and there was nothing between me and the widening pastures, the great boulders, the black and white cattle, the rivers, stony and thin, the lone elms like feather-dusters, the high air which sharpens all outlines, makes all colors so breathtakingly vivid, in the clear light of late afternoon.

The little stations again: Barneveld, Stittville, Steuben—a tribute to the Prussian general who helped drill our troops for the Revolution. The woman behind me in the train talks to the conductor with a German accent. They came over here for land and freedom.

Boonville: that pale boxlike building, smooth gray, with three floors of slots that look in on darkness and a roof like a flat overlapping lid—cold dark clear air, fresh water. Like nothing else but upstate New York. Rivers that run quick among stones, or, deeper, stained dark with dead leaves. I used to love to follow them—should still. A fresh breath of water off the Black River, where the blue closed gentians grow. Those forests, those boulder-strewn pastures, those fabulous distant falls!

There was never any train to Talcottville. Our house was the center of the town. It is strange to get back to this now: it seems not quite like anything else that I have ever known. But is this merely the apparent uniqueness of places associated with childhood?

The settlers of this part of New York were a first westward migration from New England. At the end of the eighteenth century, they drove ox-teams from Connecticut and Massachusetts over into the wild northern country below Lake Ontario and the St. Lawrence River, and they established here an extension of New England.

Yet an extension that was already something new. I happened last week to be in Ipswich, Mass., the town from which one branch of my family came; and, for all the New England pride of white houses and green blinds, I was oppressed by the ancient crampedness. Even the House of the Seven Gables, which stimulated the imagination of Hawthorne, though it is grim perhaps, is not romantic. It, too, has the tightness and the self-sufficiency of that little provincial merchant society, which at its best produced an intense little culture, quite English in its concreteness and practicality—as the block letters of the signs along the docks made Boston look like Liverpool. But life must have hit its head on those close and low-ceilinged coops. That narrowness, that meagerness, that stinginess, still grips New England today: the drab summer cottages along the shore seem almost as slit-windowed and pinched as the gray twin-houses of a mill town like Lawrence or Fall River. I can feel the relief myself of coming away from Boston to these first uplands of the Adirondacks, where, discarding the New England religion but still speaking the language of New England, the settlers found limitless space. They were a part of the new America, now forever for a century on the move; and they were to move on themselves before they would be able to build here anything comparable to the New England civilization. The country, magnificent and vast, has never really been humanized as New England has: the landscape still overwhelms the people. But this house, one of the few of its kind among later wooden houses and towns, was an attempt to found a civilization. It blends in a peculiar fashion the amenities of the eastern seaboard with the rudeness and toughness of the new frontier.

It was built at the end of the eighteenth century: the first event recorded in connection with it is a memorial service for General Washington. It took four or five years in the building. The stone had to be quarried and brought out of the river. The walls are a foot and a half thick, and the plaster was applied to the stone without any intervening lattice. The beams were secured by enormous nails, made by hand and some of them eighteen inches long. Solid and simple as a fortress, the place has also the charm of something which has been made to order. There is a front porch with white wooden columns

which support a white wooden balcony that runs along the second
floor. The roof comes down close over the balcony, and the balcony
and the porch are draped with vines. Large ferns grow along the
porch, and there are stone hitching-posts and curious stone orna-
ments, cut out of the quarry like the house: on one side, a round
bottomed bowl in which red geraniums bloom, and on the other, an
unnamable object, crudely sculptured and vaguely pagoda-like. The
front door is especially handsome: the door itself is dark green and
equipped with a brass knocker, and the woodwork which frames it is
white; it is crowned with a wide fanlight and flanked by two narrow
panes of glass, in which a white filigree of ironwork makes a webbing
like ice over winter ponds. On one of the broad sides of the building,
where the mortar has come off the stone, there is a dappling of dark
gray under pale gray like the dappling of light in shallow water, and
the feathers of the elms make dapplings of sun among their shadows
of large lace on the grass.

The lawn is ungraded and uneven like the pastures, and it merges
eventually with the fields. Behind, there are great clotted masses of
myrtle-beds, lilac-bushes, clumps of pink phlox and other things I
cannot identify; pink and white hollyhocks, some of them leaning, fine
blue and purple dye of larkspur; a considerable vegetable garden, with
long rows of ripe gooseberries and currants, a patch of yellow pump-
kin flowers, and bushes of raspberries, both white and red—among
which are sprinkled like confetti the little flimsy California poppies,
pink, orange, white and red. In an old dark red barn behind, where
the hayloft is almost collapsing, I find spinning-wheels, a carder,
candle-molds, a patent bootjack, obsolete implements of carpentry,
little clusters of baskets for berry-picking and a gigantic pair of scales
such as is nowadays only seen in the hands of allegorical figures.

The house was built by the Talcotts, after whom the town was
named. They owned the large farm in front of the house, which
stretches down to the river and beyond. They also had a profitable
grist mill, but—I learn from the county history—were thought to
have "adopted a policy adverse to the building up of the village at the
point where natural advantages greatly favored," since they "refused
to sell village lots to mechanics, and retained the water power on
Sugar River, although parties offered to invest liberally in manufac-

tures." In time, there were only two Talcotts left, an old maid and her widowed sister. My great-grandfather, Thomas Baker, who lived across the street and had been left by the death of his wife with a son and eight daughters, paid court to Miss Talcott and married her. She was kind to the children, and they remembered her with affection. My great-grandfather acquired in this way the house, the farm and the quarry.

All but two of my great-grandfather's daughters, of whom my grandmother was one—"six of them beauties," I understand—got married and went away. Only one of them was left in the house at the time when I first remember Talcottville: my great-aunt Rosalind, a more or less professional invalid and a figure of romantic melancholy, whose fiancé had been lost at sea. When I knew her, she was very old. It was impressive and rather frightening to call on her—you did it only by special arrangement, since she had to prepare herself to be seen. She would be beautifully dressed in a lace cap, a lavender dress and a white crocheted shawl, but she had become so bloodless and shrunken as dreadfully to resemble a mummy and reminded one uncomfortably of Miss Haversham in Dickens' *Great Expectations.* She had a certain high and formal coquetry and was the only person I ever knew who really talked like the characters in old novels. When she had been able to get about, she had habitually treated the townspeople with a condescension almost baronial. According to the family legend, the great-grandmother of great-grandmother Baker had been a daughter of one of the Earls of Essex, who had eloped with a gardener to America.

Another of my Baker great-aunts, who was one of my favorite relatives, had married and lived in the town and had suffered tragic disappointments. Only her strong intellectual interests and a mind capable of philosophic pessimism had maintained her through the wreck of her domestic life. She used to tell me how, a young married woman, she had taught herself French by the dictionary and grammar, sitting up at night alone by the stove through one of their cold and dark winters. She had read a great deal of French, subscribed to French magazines, without ever having learned to pronounce it. She had rejected revealed religion and did not believe in immortality; and when she felt that she had been relieved of the last of her family obligations—though her hair was now turning gray—she came on to

New York City and lived there alone for years, occupying herself with the theater, reading, visits to her nephews and nieces—with whom she was extremely popular—and all the spectacle and news of the larger world which she had always loved so much but from which she had spent most of her life removed.

When she died, only the youngest of the family was left, the sole brother, my great-uncle Tom. His mother must have been worn out with childbearing—she died after the birth of this ninth child—and he had not turned out so well as the others. He had been born with no roof to his mouth and was obliged to wear a false gold palate, and it was difficult to understand him. He was not really simple-minded— he had held a small political job under Cleveland, and he usually beat me at checkers—but he was childlike and ill-equipped to deal with life in any very effective way. He sold the farm to a German and the quarry to the town. Then he died, and the house was empty, except when my mother and father would come here to open it up for two or three months in the summer.

his aunts

I have not been back here in years, and I have never before examined the place carefully. It has become for me something like a remembered dream—unearthly with the powerful impressions of childhood. Even now that I am here again, I find I have to shake off the dream. I keep walking from room to room, inside and outside, upstairs and down, with uneasy sensations of complacency that are always falling through to depression.

These rooms are very well proportioned; the white mantelpieces are elegant and chaste, and the carving on each one is different. The larger of the two living rooms now seems a little bare because the various members of the family have claimed and taken away so many things; and there are some disagreeable curtains and carpets, for which the wife of my great-uncle Tom is to blame. But here are all the things, I take note, that are nowadays sold in antique stores: red Bohemian-glass decanters; a rusty silver snuff-box; a mirror with the American eagle painted at the top of the glass. Little mahogany tables with slim legs; a set of curly-maple furniture, deep seasoned yellow like satin; a yellow comb-backed rocker, with a design of green conch-shells that look like snails. A small bust of Dante with the nose chipped, left behind as defective by one of my cousins when its companion piece,

Desc. of Whats in the house

Beethoven, was taken away; a little mahogany melodeon on which my
Aunt "Lin" once played. Large engravings of the family of Washington and of the "Reformers Presenting Their Famous Protest before
the Diet of Spires"; a later engraving of Dickens. Old tongs and poker,
impossibly heavy. A brown mahogany desk inlaid with yellow bird-
wood, which contains a pair of steel-rimmed spectacles and a thing for
shaking sand on wet ink. Daguerrotypes in fancy cases: they seem to
last much better than photographs—my grandmother looks fresh and
cunning—I remember that I used to hear that the first time my
grandfather saw her, she was riding on a load of hay—he came back
up here to marry her as soon as he had got out of medical school. An
old wooden flute—originally brought over from New England, I remember my great-uncle's telling me, at the time when they traveled
by ox-team—he used to get a lonely piping out of it—I try it but
cannot make a sound. Two big oval paintings, in tarnished gilt frames,
of landscapes romantic and mountainous: they came from the Utica
house of my great-grandfather Baker's brother—he married a rich
wife and invented excelsior—made out of the northern lumber—and
was presented with a solid-silver table service by the grateful city of
Utica.

Wallpaper molded by the damp from the stone; uninviting old black
haircloth furniture. A bowl of those enormous up-country sweet peas,
incredibly fragrant and bright—they used to awe and trouble me—
why?

In the dining room, a mahogany china closet, which originally—in
the days when letters were few and great-grandfather Baker was
postmaster—was the whole of the village post office. My grandmother's pewter tea-service, with its design of oak-leaves and acorns,
which I remember from her house in New Jersey. Black iron cranes,
pipkins and kettles for cooking in the fireplace; a kind of flat iron
pitchfork for lifting the bread in and out, when they baked at the back
of the hearth. On the sideboard, a glass decanter with a gilt black-
letter label: "J. Rum." If there were only some rum in the decanter!—
if the life of the house were not now all past!—the kitchens that trail
out behind are almost too old-smelling, too long deserted, to make
them agreeable to visit—in spite of the delightful brown crocks with
long-tailed blue birds painted on them, a different kind of bird on each
crock.

In the ample hall with its staircase, two large colored pictures of trout, one rising to bait, one leaping. Upstairs, a wooden pestle and mortar; a perforated tin box for hot coals to keep the feet warm in church or on sleigh-rides; a stuffed heron; a horrible bust of my cousin Dorothy Read in her girlhood, which her mother had done of her in Germany. The hair-ribbon and the ruffles are faithfully reproduced in marble, and the eyes have engraved pupils. It stands on a high pedestal, and it used to be possible, by pressing a button, to make it turn around. My Cousin Grace, Dorothy's mother, used to show it off and invite comparison with the original, especially calling attention to the nose; but what her mother had never known was that Dorothy had injured her nose in some rather disgraceful row with her sister. One day when the family were making an excursion, Dorothy pleaded indisposition and bribed a man with a truck to take the bust away and drop it into a pond. But Uncle Tom got this out of the man, dredged the statue up and replaced it on its pedestal. An ugly chair with a round rag back; an ugly bed with the head of Columbus sticking out above the pillows like a figurehead. Charming old bedquilts, with patterns of rhomboids in softened browns, greens and pinks, or of blue polka-dotted hearts that ray out on stiff phallic stalks. A footstool covered in white, which, however, when you step on a tab at the side, opens up into a cuspidor—some relic, no doubt, of the times when the house was used for local meetings. (There used to be a musical chair, also brought back from Germany, but it seems to have disappeared.) A jar of hardly odorous dried rose-leaves, and a jar of little pebbles and shells that keep their bright colors in alcohol.

The original old panes up here have wavy lines in the glass. There are cobweb-filthy books, which I try to examine: many religious works, the annals of the state legislature, a book called *The Young Wife, or Duties of Women in the Marriage Relation,* published in Boston in 1838 and containing a warning against tea and coffee, which "loosen the tongue, fire the eye, produce mirth and wit, excite the animal passions, and lead to remarks about ourselves and others, that we should not have made in other circumstances, and which it were better for us and the world, never to have made." But there is also, I noticed downstairs, Grant Allan's *The Woman Who Did* from 1893.

I come upon the *History of Lewis County* and read it with a certain pride. I am glad to say to myself that it is a creditable piece of work—admirably full in its information on geology, flora and fauna, on history and local politics; diversified with anecdotes and biographies never overflattering and often pungent; and written in a sound English style. Could anyone in the country today, I wonder, command such a sound English style? I note with gratification that the bone of a prehistoric cuttlefish, discovered in one of the limestone caves, is the largest of its kind on record, and that a flock of wild swans was seen here in 1821. In the eighties, there were still wolves and panthers. There are still bears and deer today.

I also look into the proceedings of the New York State Assembly. My great-grandfather Thomas Baker was primarily a politician and at that time a member of the Assembly. I have heard that he was a Jacksonian Democrat, and that he made a furious scene when my grandmother came back from New Jersey and announced that she had become a Republican: it "spoiled her whole visit." There is a photograph of great-grandfather Baker in an oval gilt frame, with his hair sticking out in three spikes and a wide and declamatory mouth. I look through the Assembly record to see what sort of role he played. It is the forties; the Democrats are still angry over the Bank of United States. But when I look up Thomas Baker in the index, it turns out that he figures solely as either not being present or as requesting leave of absence. They tell me he used to go West to buy cattle.

That sealed-up space on the second floor which my father had knocked out—who did they tell me was hidden in it? I have just learned from one of the new road-signs which explain historical associations that there are caves somewhere here in which slaves were hidden. Could this have been a part of the underground route for smuggling Negroes over the border into Canada? Is the attic, the "kitchen chamber," which is always so suffocating in summer, still full of those carpetbags and crinolines and bonnets and beaver-hats that we used to get out of the old cowhide trunks and use to dress up for charades?

It was the custom for the married Baker daughters to bring their children back in the summer; and their children in time brought their children. In those days, how I loved coming up here! It was a reunion with cousins from Boston and New York, Ohio and Wisconsin, as well as with the Talcottville and Utica ones: we fished and swam in the rivers, had all sorts of excursions and games. Later on, I got to dislike

it: the older generation died, the younger did not much come. I
wanted to be elsewhere, too. The very fullness with life of the past,
the memory of those many families of cousins and uncles and aunts,
made the emptiness of the present more oppressive. Isn't it still?—
didn't my gloom come from that, the night of my first arrival? Wasn't
it the dread of that that kept me away? I am aware, as I walk through
the rooms, of the amplitude and completeness of the place—the home
of a big old-fashioned family that had to be a city in itself. And not
merely did it house a clan: the whole life of the community passed
through it. And now for five sixths of the year it is nothing but an
unheated shell, a storehouse of unused antiques, with no intimate
relation to the county.

The community itself today is somewhat smaller than the community of those days, and its condition has very much changed. It must
seem to the summer traveler merely one of the clusters of houses that
he shoots through along the state highway; and there may presently
be little left save our house confronting, across the road, the hot-dog
stand and the gasoline station.*

For years I have had a recurrent dream. I take a road that runs
toward the west. It is summer; I pass by a strange summer forest, in
which there are mysterious beings, though I know that, on the whole,
they are shy and benign. If I am fortunate and find the way, I arrive
at a wonderful river, which runs among boulders, with rapids, between
alders and high weedy trees, through a countryside fresh, green and
wide. We go in swimming; it is miles away from anywhere. We plunge
in the smooth flowing pools. We make our way to the middle of the
stream and climb up on the pale round gray stones and sit naked in
the sun and the air, while the river glides away below us. And I know
that it is the place for which I have always longed, the place of
wildness and freedom, to find which is the height of what one may
hope for—the place of unalloyed delight.

As I walk about Talcottville now, I discover that the being-haunted
forest is a big grove which even in daytime used to be lonely and dark

---

*This description may seem inconsistent with my account of our Talcottville location
in another book, *A Piece of My Mind,* but the main highway was later shifted, put
through along another road, and my mother had succeeded, in the meantime, in getting
rid of the hot-dog stand by buying back the lot across the street.

and where great white Canadian violets used to grow out of the deep black leaf-mold. Today it is no longer dark, because half the trees have been cut down. The river of my dream, I see, is simply an idealized version of the farther and less frequented and more adventurous bank of Sugar River, which had to be reached by wading. Both river and forest are west of the road that runs through the village, which accounts for my always taking that direction in my dream. I remember how Sugar River—out of the stone of which our house is built—used, in my boyhood, so to fascinate me that I had an enlargement made of one of the photographs I had taken of it—a view of "the Big Falls"—and kept it in my room all winter. Today the nearer bank has been largely blasted away to get stone for the new state highway, and what we used to call "the Little Falls" is gone.

I visit the house of my favorite great-aunt, and my gloom returns and overwhelms me. The huge root of an elm has split the thick slabs of the pavement so that you have to walk over a hump; and one of the big square stone fence-posts is toppling. Her flowers, with no one to tend them, go on raggedly blooming in their seasons. There has been nobody in her house since she died. It is all too appropriate to her pessimism—that dead end she always foresaw. As I walk around the house, I remember how, once on the back porch there, she sang me old English ballads, including that gruesome one, "Oh, where have you been, Randall, my son?"—about the man who had gone to Pretty Peggy's house and been given snakes to eat:

"What had you for supper, Randall, my son?"
"Fresh fish fried in butter. Oh, make my bed soon!
For I'm sick at my heart and I fain would lie down!"

She was old then—round-shouldered and dumpy—after the years when she had looked so handsome, straight-backed and with the fashionable aigrette in her hair. And the song she sang seemed to have been drawn out of such barbarous reaches of the past, out of something so surprisingly different from the college-women's hotels in New York in which I had always known her as living: that England to which, far though she had come from it, she was yet so much nearer than I—that queer troubling world of legend which I knew from Percy's *Reliques* but with which she had maintained a real contact through centuries of women's voices—for she sang it without a smile, completely possessed by its spirit—that it made my flesh creep, disconcerted me.

My great-aunt is dead, and all her generation are dead—and the new generations of the family have long ago left Talcottville behind and have turned into something quite different. They were already headed for the cities by the middle of the last century, as can be seen by the rapid dispersal of great grandfather Baker's daughters. Yet there were still, in my childhood, a few who stayed on in this country as farmers. They were very impressive people, the survivors of a sovereign race who had owned their own pastures and fields and governed their own community. Today the descendants of these are performing mainly minor functions in a machine which they do not control. They have most of them become thoroughly urbanized, and they are farther from great-grandfather Baker than my grandmother, his daughter, was when she came back from New Jersey a Republican. One of her children, a retired importer in New York, was complaining to me the other day that the outrageous demands of the farmers were making business recovery impossible, and protesting that if the advocates of the income tax had their way, the best people would no longer be able to live up to their social positions. A cousin, who bears the name of one of his Ipswich ancestors, a mining engineer on the Coast and a classmate and admirer of Hoover, invested and has lost heavily in Mexican real estate and the industrial speculations of the boom. Another, with another of the old local names, is now at the head of an organization whose frankly avowed purpose is to rescue the New York manufacturers from taxation and social legislation. He has seen his native city of Utica decline as a textile center through the removal of its mills to the South, where taxes are lighter and labor is cheaper; and he is honestly convinced that his efforts are directed toward civic betterment.

Thus the family has come imperceptibly to identify its interests with those of what my great-grandfather Baker would have called the "money power." They work for it and acquiesce in it—they are no longer the sovereign race of the first settlers of Lewis County, and in the cities they have achieved no sovereignty. They are much too scrupulous and decent, and their tastes are too comparatively simple for them ever to have rolled up great fortunes during the years of

expansion and plunder. They have still the frank accent and the
friendly eye of the older American world, and they seem rather taken
aback by the turn that things have been taking.

And what about me? As I come back in the train, I find that—other
causes contributing—my depression of Talcottville deepens. I did not
find the river and the forest of my dream—I did not find the magic
of the past. I have been too close to the past: there in that house, in
that remote little town which has never known industrial progress
since the Talcotts first obstructed the development of the water power
of Sugar River, you can see exactly how rural Americans were living
a century and a half ago. And who would go back to it? Not I. Let
people who have never known country life complain that the farmer
has been spoiled by his radio and his Ford. Along with the memory
of exaltation at the immensity and freedom of that countryside, I have
memories of horror at its loneliness: houses burning down at night,
sometimes with people in them, where there was no fire department
to save them, and husbands or wives left alone by death—the dark
nights and the prisoning winters. I do not grudge the sacrifice of the
Sugar River falls for the building of the new state highway, and I do
not resent the hot-dog stand. I am at first a little shocked at the sight
of a transformer on the road between Talcottville and Boonville, but
when I get to the Talcottville house, I am obliged to be thankful for
it—no more oil-lamps in the evenings! And I would not go back to
that old life if I could: that civilization of northern New York—why
should I idealize it?—was too lonely, too poor, too provincial.

I look out across the Hudson and see Newburgh: with the neat-
windowed cubes of its dwellings and docks, distinct as if cut by a
burin, built so densely up the slope of the bank and pierced by an
occasional steeple, undwarfed by tall modern buildings and with only
the little old-fashioned ferry to connect it with the opposite bank, it
might still be an eighteenth-century city. My father's mother came
from there. She was the granddaughter of a carpet-importer from
Rotterdam. From him came the thick Spanish coins which the children of my father's family were supposed to cut their teeth on. The
business, which had been a considerable one, declined as the sea trade
of the Hudson became concentrated in New York. My father and
mother went once—a good many years ago—to visit the old store by

the docks, and were amazed to find a solitary old clerk still scratching up orders and sales on a slate that hung behind the counter.

And the slate and the Spanish coins, though they symbolize a kind of life somewhat different from that evoked by Talcottville, associate themselves in my mind with such things as the old post office turned china closet. And as I happen to be reading Herndon's *Life of Lincoln,* that, too, goes to flood out the vision with its extension still further west, still further from the civilized seaboard, of the life of the early frontier. Through Herndon's extraordinary memoir, one of the few really great American books of its kind, which America has never accepted, preferring to it the sentimentalities of Sandburg and the ladies who write Christmas stories—the past confronts me even more plainly than through the bootjacks and daguerreotypes of Talcottville, and makes me even more uneasy. Here you are back again amid the crudeness and the poverty of the American frontier, and here is a man of genius coming out of it and perfecting himself. The story is not merely moving, it becomes almost agonizing. The ungainly boorish boy from the settler's clearing, with nobody and nothing behind him, hoping that his grandfather had been a planter as my great-aunt Rosalind hoped that she was a descendant of the Earls of Essex, the morbid young man looking passionately toward the refinement and the training of the East but unable to bring himself to marry the women who represented it for him—rejoining across days in country stores, nights in godforsaken hotels, rejoining by heroic self-discipline the creative intelligence of the race, to find himself the conscious focus of its terrible unconscious parturition—his miseries burden his grandeur. At least they do for me at this moment.

> Old Abe Lincoln came out of the wilderness,
> Out of the wilderness, out of the wilderness—

The echo of the song in my mind inspires me with a kind of awe—I can hardly bear the thought of Lincoln.

Great-grandfather Baker's politics and the Talcottville general store, in which people sat around and talked before the new chain store took its place—Lincoln's school was not so very much different. And I would not go back to that.

Yet as I walk up the steps of my house in New York, I am forced to recognize, with a sinking, that I have never been able to leave it.

This old wooden booth I have taken between First and Second Avenues—what is it but the same old provincial America? And as I open the door with its loose knob and breathe in the musty smell of the stair-carpet, it seems to me that I have not merely stuck in the world where my fathers lived but have actually, in some ways, lost ground in it. This gray paintless clapboarded front, these lumpy and rubbed yellow walls—they were probably once respectable, but they must always have been commonplace. They have never had even the dignity of the house in Lewis County. But I have rented them because, in my youth, I had been used to living in houses and have grown to loathe city apartments.

So here, it seems, is where I must live: in an old cramped and sour frame-house—having failed even worse than my relatives at getting out of the American big-business era the luxuries and the prestige that I unquestionably should very much have enjoyed. Here is where I end by living—among the worst instead of the best of this city that took the trade away from Newburgh—the sordid and unhealthy children of my sordid and unhealthy neighbors, who howl outside my windows night and day. It is this, in the last analysis—there is no doubt about it now!—which has been rankling and causing my gloom: to have left that early world behind yet never to have really succeeded in what was till yesterday the new.

[1933]

JAMES BALDWIN

NOTES OF A NATIVE SON

ON THE 29th of July, in 1943, my father died. On the same day, a few hours later, his last child was born. Over a month before this, while all our energies were concentrated in waiting for these events, there had been, in Detroit, one of the bloodiest race riots of the century. A few hours after my father's funeral, while he lay in state in the undertaker's chapel, a race riot broke out in Harlem. On the morning of the 3rd of August, we drove my father to the graveyard through a wilderness of smashed plate glass.

The day of my father's funeral had also been my nineteenth birthday. As we drove him to the graveyard, the spoils of injustice, anarchy, discontent, and hatred were all around us. It seemed to me that God himself had devised, to mark my father's end, the most sustained and brutally dissonant of codas. And it seemed to me, too, that the violence which rose all about us as my father left the world had been devised as a corrective for the pride of his eldest son. I had declined to believe in that apocalypse which had been central to my father's vision; very well, life seemed to be saying, here is something that will certainly pass for an apocalypse until the real thing comes along. I had inclined to be contemptuous of my father for the conditions of his life, for the conditions of our lives. When his life had ended I began to wonder about that life and also, in a new way, to be apprehensive about my own.

I had not known my father very well. We had got on badly, partly because we shared, in our different fashions, the vice of stubborn pride. When he was dead I realized that I had hardly ever spoken to him. When he had been dead a long time I began to wish I had. It seems to be typical of life in America, where opportunities, real and fancied, are thicker than anywhere else on the globe, that the second generation has no time to talk to the first. No one, including my father, seems to have known exactly how old he was, but his mother had been born during slavery. He was of the first generation of free men. He, along with thousands of other Negroes, came North after 1919 and I was part of that generation which had never seen the landscape of what Negroes sometimes call the Old Country.

He had been born in New Orleans and had been a quite young man there during the time that Louis Armstrong, a boy, was running errands for the dives and honky-tonks of what was always presented to me as one of the most wicked of cities—to this day, whenever I think of New Orleans, I also helplessly think of Sodom and Gomorrah. My father never mentioned Louis Armstrong, except to forbid us to play his records; but there was a picture of him on our wall for a long time. One of my father's strong-willed female relatives had placed it there and forbade my father to take it down. He never did, but he eventually maneuvered her out of the house and when, some years later, she was in trouble and near death, he refused to do anything to help her.

He was, I think, very handsome. I gather this from photographs and from my own memories of him, dressed in his Sunday best and on his way to preach a sermon somewhere, when I was little. Handsome, proud, and ingrown, "like a toe-nail," somebody said. But he looked to me, as I grew older, like pictures I had seen of African tribal chieftains: he really should have been naked, with war-paint on and barbaric mementos, standing among spears. He could be chilling in the pulpit and indescribably cruel in his personal life and he was certainly the most bitter man I have ever met; yet it must be said that there was something else in him, buried in him, which lent him his tremendous power and, even, a rather crushing charm. It had something to do with his blackness, I think—he was very black—with his blackness and his beauty, and with the fact that he knew that he was black but did not know that he was beautiful. He claimed to be proud of his blackness but it had also been the cause of much humiliation and it had fixed bleak boundaries to his life. He was not a young man when we were growing up and he had already suffered many kinds of ruin; in his outrageously demanding and protective way he loved his children, who were black like him and menaced, like him; and all these things sometimes showed in his face when he tried, never to my knowledge with any success, to establish contact with any of us. When he took one of his children on his knee to play, the child always became fretful and began to cry; when he tried to help one of us with our homework the absolutely unabating tension which emanated from him caused our minds and our tongues to become paralyzed, so that he, scarcely knowing why, flew into a rage and the child, not knowing why, was punished. If it ever entered his head to bring a surprise home for his children, it was, almost unfailingly, the wrong surprise and even the big watermelons he often brought home on his back in the summertime led to the most appalling scenes. I do not remember, in all those years, that one of his children was ever glad to see him come home. From what I was able to gather of his early life, it seemed that this inability to establish contact with other people had always marked him and had been one of the things which had driven him out of New Orleans. There was something in him, therefore, groping and tentative, which was never expressed and which was buried with him. One saw it most clearly when he was facing new people and hoping to impress them. But he never did, not for long. We went from church to smaller and more improbable church, he found himself in less and less demand as a minister, and by the time he died none of his friends had come to see him for a long time. He had lived and died in an intolerable bitterness of spirit and it frightened me, as we drove him to the graveyard through those unquiet, ruined streets, to see how powerful and overflowing this bitterness could be and to realize that this bitterness now was mine.

When he died I had been away from home for a little over a year. In that year I had had time to become aware of the meaning of all my father's bitter warnings, had discovered the secret of his proudly pursed lips and rigid carriage: I had discovered the weight of white people in the world. I saw that this had been for my ancestors and now would be for me an awful thing to live with and that the bitterness which had helped to kill my father could also kill me.

He had been ill a long time—in the mind, as we now realized, reliving instances of his fantastic intransigence in the new light of his affliction and endeavoring to feel a sorrow for him which never, quite, came true. We had not known that he was being eaten up by paranoia, and the discovery that his cruelty, to our bodies and our minds, had been one of the symptoms of his illness was not, then, enough to enable us to forgive him. The younger children felt, quite simply, relief that he would not be coming home anymore. My mother's observation that it was he, after all, who had kept them alive all these years meant nothing because the problems of keeping children alive are not real for children. The older children felt, with my father gone, that they could invite their friends to the house without fear that their friends would be insulted or, as had sometimes happened with me, being told that their friends were in league with the devil and intended to rob our family of everything we owned. (I didn't fail to wonder, and it made me hate him, what on earth we owned that anybody else would want.)

His illness was beyond all hope of healing before anyone realized that he was ill. He had always been so strange and had lived, like a prophet, in such unimaginably close communion with the Lord that his long silences which were punctuated by moans and hallelujahs and snatches of old songs while he sat at the living room window never seemed odd to us. It was not until he refused to eat because, he said, his family was trying to poison him that my mother was forced to accept as a fact what had, until then, been only an unwilling suspicion. When he was committed, it was discovered that he had tuberculosis and, as it turned out, the disease of his mind allowed the disease of his body to destroy him. For the doctors could not force him to eat, either, and, though he was fed intravenously, it was clear from the beginning that there was no hope for him.

In my mind's eye I could see him, sitting at the window, locked up in his terrors; hating and fearing every living soul including his children who had betrayed him, too, by reaching towards the world which had despised him. There were nine of us. I began to wonder what it could have felt like for such a man to have had nine children whom he could barely feed. He used to make little jokes about our poverty, which never, of course, seemed very funny to us; they could not have seemed very funny to him, either, or else our all too feeble response to them would never have caused such rages. He spent great energy and achieved, to our chagrin, no small amount of success in keeping us away from the people who surrounded us, people who had all-night rent parties to which we listened when we should have been sleeping, people who cursed and drank and flashed razor blades on Lenox Avenue. He could not understand why, if they had so much energy to spare, they could not use it to make their lives better. He treated almost everybody on our block with a most uncharitable asperity and neither they, nor, of course, their children were slow to reciprocate.

The only white people who came to our house were welfare workers and bill collectors. It was almost always my mother who dealt with them, for my father's temper, which was at the mercy of his pride, was never to be trusted. It was clear that he felt their very presence in his home to be a violation: this was conveyed by his carriage, almost ludicrously stiff, and by his voice, harsh and vindictively polite. When I was around nine or ten I wrote a play which was directed by a young, white schoolteacher, a woman, who then took an interest in me, and gave me books to read and, in order to corroborate my theatrical bent, decided to take me to see what she somewhat tactlessly referred to as "real" plays. Theater-going was forbidden in our house, but, with the really cruel intuitiveness of a child, I suspected that the color of this woman's skin would carry the day for me. When, at school, she suggested taking me to the theater, I did not, as I might have done if she had been a Negro, find a way of discouraging her, but agreed that she should pick me up at my house one evening. I then, very cleverly, left all the rest to my mother, who suggested to my father, as I knew she would, that it would not be very nice to let such a kind woman make the trip for nothing. Also, since it was a schoolteacher, I imagine that my mother countered the idea of sin with the idea of "education," which word, even with my father, carried a kind of bitter weight.

Before the teacher came my father took me aside to ask *why* she was coming, what *interest* she could possibly have in our house, in a boy like me. I said I didn't know but I, too, suggested that it had something to do with education. And I understood that my father was waiting for me to say something—I didn't quite know what; perhaps that I wanted his protection against this teacher and her "education." I said none of these things and the teacher came and we went out. It was clear, during the brief interview in our living room, that my father was agreeing very much against his will and that he would have refused permission if he had dared. The fact that he did not dare caused me to despise him: I had no way of knowing that he was facing in that living room a wholly unprecedented and frightening situation.

Later, when my father had been laid off from his job, this woman became very important to us. She was really a very sweet and generous woman and went to a great deal of trouble to be of help to us, particularly during one awful winter. My mother called her by the highest name she knew: she said she was a "christian." My father could scarcely disagree but during the four or five years of our relatively close association he never trusted her and was always trying to surprise in her open, Midwestern face the genuine, cunningly hidden, and hideous motivation. In later years, particularly when it began to be clear that this "education" of mine was going to lead me to perdition, he became more explicit and warned me that my white friends in high school were not really my friends and that I would see, when I was older, how white people would do anything to keep a Negro down. Some of them could be nice, he admitted, but none of them were to be trusted and most of them were not even nice. The best thing was to have as little to do with them as possible. I did not feel this way and I was certain, in my innocence, that I never would.

But the year which preceded my father's death had made a great change in my life. I had been living in New Jersey, working in defense plants, working and living among southerners, white and black. I knew about the south, of course, and about how southerners treated Negroes and how they expected them to behave, but it had never entered my mind that anyone would look at me and expect *me* to behave that way. I learned in New Jersey that to be a Negro meant, precisely, that one was never looked at but was simply at the mercy of the reflexes the color of one's skin caused in other people. I acted in New Jersey as I had always acted, that is as though I thought a great deal of myself—I had to *act* that way—with results that were, simply, unbelievable. I had scarcely arrived before I had earned the enmity, which was extraordinarily ingenious, of all my superiors and nearly all my co-workers. In the beginning, to make matters worse, I simply did not know what was happening. I did not know what I had done, and I shortly began to wonder what *anyone* could possibly do, to bring about such unanimous, active, and unbearably vocal hostility. I knew about jim-crow but I had never experienced it. I went to the same self-service restaurant three times and stood with all the Princeton boys before the counter, waiting for a hamburger and coffee; it was always an extraordinarily long time before anything was set before me; but it was not until the fourth visit that I learned that, in fact, nothing had ever been set before me: I had simply picked something up. Negroes were not served there, I was told, and they had been waiting for me to realize that I was always the only Negro present. Once I was told this, I determined to go there all the time. But now they were ready for me and, though some dreadful scenes were subsequently enacted in that restaurant, I never ate there again.

It was the same story all over New Jersey, in bars, bowling alleys, diners, places to live. I was always being forced to leave, silently, or with mutual imprecations. I very shortly became notorious and children giggled behind me when I passed and their elders whispered or shouted—they really believed that I was mad. And it did begin to work on my mind, of course; I began to be afraid to go anywhere and to compensate for this I went places to which I really should not have gone and where, God knows, I had no desire to be. My reputation in town naturally enhanced my reputation at work and my working day became one long series of acrobatics designed to keep me out of trouble. I cannot say that these acrobatics succeeded. It began to seem that the machinery of the organization I worked for was turning over, day and night, with but one aim: to eject me. I was fired once, and contrived, with the aid of a friend from New York, to get back on the payroll; was fired again, and bounced back again. It took a while to fire me for the third time, but the third time took. There were no loopholes anywhere. There was not even any way of getting back inside the gates.

That year in New Jersey lives in my mind as though it were the year during which, having an unsuspected predilection for it, I first contracted some dread, chronic disease, the unfailing symptom of which is a kind of blind fever, a pounding in the skull and fire in the bowels. Once this disease is contracted, one can never be really carefree again, for the fever, without an instant's warning, can recur at any moment. It can wreck more important things than race relations. There is not a Negro alive who does not have this rage in his blood—one has the choice, merely, of living with it consciously or surrendering to it. As for me, this fever has recurred in me, and does, and will until the day I die.

My last night in New Jersey, a white friend from New York took me to the nearest big town, Trenton, to go to the movies and have a few drinks. As it turned out, he also saved me from, at the very least, a violent whipping. Almost every detail of that night stands out very clearly in my memory. I even remember the name of the movie we saw because its title impressed me as being so patly ironical. It was a movie about the German occupation of France, starring Maureen O'Hara and Charles Laughton and called *This Land Is Mine.* I remember the name of the diner we walked into when the movie ended: it was the "American Diner." When we walked in the counterman asked what we wanted and I remember answering with the casual sharpness which had become my habit: "We want a hamburger and a cup of coffee, what do you think we want?" I do not know why, after a year of such rebuffs, I so completely failed to anticipate his answer, which was, of course, "We don't serve Negroes here." This reply failed to discompose me, at least for the moment. I made some sardonic comment about the name of the diner and we walked out into the streets.

This was the time of what was called the "brown-out," when the lights in all American cities were very dim. When we reentered the streets something happened to me which had the force of an optical illusion, or a nightmare. The streets were very crowded and I was facing north. People were moving in every direction but it seemed to me, in that instant, that all of the people I could see, and many more than that, were moving toward me, against me, and that everyone was white. I remember how their faces gleamed. And I felt, like a physical sensation, a *click* at the nape of my neck as though some interior string connecting my head to my body had been cut. I began to walk. I heard my friend call after me, but I ignored him. Heaven only knows what was going on in his mind, but he had the good sense not to touch me—I don't know what would have happened if he had—and to keep me in sight. I don't know what was going on in my mind, either; I certainly had no conscious plan. I wanted to do something to crush these white faces, which were crushing me. I walked for perhaps a block or two until I came to an enormous, glittering, and fashionable restaurant in which I knew not even the intercession of the Virgin would cause me to be served. I pushed through the doors and took the first vacant seat I saw, at a table for two, and waited.

I do not know how long I waited and I rather wonder, until today, what I could possibly have looked like. Whatever I looked like, I frightened the waitress who shortly appeared, and the moment she appeared all my fury flowed towards her. I hated her for her white face, and for her great, astounded, frightened eyes. I felt that if she found a black man so frightening I would make her fright worth-while.

She did not ask me what I wanted, but repeated, as though she had learned it somewhere, "We don't serve Negroes here." She did not say it with the blunt, derisive hostility to which I had grown so accustomed, but, rather, with a note of apology in her voice, and fear. This made me colder and more murderous than ever. I felt I had to do something with my hands. I wanted her to come close enough for me to get her neck between my hands.

So I pretended not to have understood her, hoping to draw her closer. And she did step a very short step closer, with her pencil poised incongruously over her pad, and repeated the formula: ". . . don't serve Negroes here."

Somehow, with the repetition of that phrase, which was already ringing in my head like a thousand bells of a nightmare, I realized that she would never come any closer and that I would have to strike from a distance. There was nothing on the table but an ordinary water-mug half full of water, and I picked this up and hurled it with all my strength at her. She ducked and it missed her and shattered against the mirror behind the bar. And, with that sound, my frozen blood abruptly thawed, I returned from wherever I had been, I *saw*, for the first time, the restaurant, the people with their mouths open, already, as it seemed to me, rising as one man, and I realized what I had done, and where I was, and I was frightened. I rose and began running for the door. A round, pot-bellied man grabbed me by the nape of the neck just as I reached the doors and began to beat me about the face. I kicked him and got loose and ran into the streets. My friend whispered, *"Run!"* and I ran.

My friend stayed outside the restaurant long enough to misdirect my pursuers and the police, who arrived, he told me, at once. I do not know what I said to him when he came to my room that night. I could not have said much. I felt, in the oddest, most awful way, that I had somehow betrayed him. I lived it over and over and over again, the way one relives an automobile accident after it has happened and one finds oneself alone and safe. I could not get over two facts, both equally difficult for the imagination to grasp, and one was that I could have been murdered. But the other was that I had been ready to commit murder. I saw nothing very clearly but I did see this: that my life, my *real* life, was in danger, and not from anything other people might do but from the hatred I carried in my own heart.

[2]

I had returned home around the second week in June—in great
haste because it seemed that my father's death and my mother's
confinement were both but a matter of hours. In the case of my
mother, it soon became clear that she had simply made a miscalcula-
tion. This had always been her tendency and I don't believe that a
single one of us arrived in the world, or has since arrived anywhere
else, on time. But none of us dawdled so intolerably about the business
of being born as did my baby sister. We sometimes amused ourselves,
during those endless, stifling weeks, by picturing the baby sitting
within in the safe, warm dark, bitterly regretting the necessity of
becoming a part of our chaos and stubbornly putting it off as long as
possible. I understood her perfectly and congratulated her on showing
such good sense so soon. Death, however, sat as purposefully at my
father's bedside as life stirred within my mother's womb and it was
harder to understand why he so lingered in that long shadow. It
seemed that he had bent, and for a long time, too, all of his energies
towards dying. Now death was ready for him but my father held back.

All of Harlem, indeed, seemed to be infected by waiting. I had never
before known it to be so violently still. Racial tensions throughout this
country were exacerbated during the early years of the war, partly
because the labor market brought together hundreds of thousands of
ill-prepared people and partly because Negro soldiers, regardless of
where they were born, received their military training in the south.
What happened in defense plants and army camps had repercussions,
naturally, in every Negro ghetto. The situation in Harlem had grown
bad enough for clergymen, policemen, educators, politicians, and social workers to assert in one breath that there was no "crime wave"
and to offer, in the very next breath, suggestions as to how to combat
it. These suggestions always seemed to involve playgrounds, despite
the fact that racial skirmishes were occurring in the playgrounds, too.
Playground or not, crime wave or not, the Harlem police force had
been augmented in March, and the unrest grew—perhaps, in fact,
partly as a result of the ghetto's instinctive hatred of policemen.
Perhaps the most revealing news item, out of the steady parade of
reports of muggings, stabbings, shootings, assaults, gang wars, and
accusations of police brutality, is the item concerning six Negro girls

who set upon a white girl in the subway because, as they all too
accurately put it, she was stepping on their toes. Indeed she was, all
over the nation.

I had never before been so aware of policemen, on foot, on
horseback, on corners, everywhere, always two by two. Nor had I ever
been so aware of small knots of people. They were on stoops and on
corners and in doorways, and what was striking about them, I think,
was that they did not seem to be talking. Never, when I passed these
groups, did the usual sound of a curse or a laugh ring out and neither
did there seem to be any hum of gossip. There was certainly, on the
other hand, occurring between them communication extraordinarily
intense. Another thing that was striking was the unexpected diversity
of the people who made up these groups. Usually, for example, one
would see a group of sharpies standing on the street corner, jiving the
passing chicks; or a group of older men, usually, for some reason, in
the vicinity of a barber shop, discussing baseball scores, or the numbers, or making rather chilling observations about women they had
known. Women, in a general way, tended to be seen less often together—unless they were church women, or very young girls, or prostitutes met together for an unprofessional instant. But that summer
I saw the strangest combinations: large, respectable, churchly ma-
trons standing on the stoops or the corners with their hair tied up,
together with a girl in sleazy satin whose face bore the marks of gin
and the razor, or heavy-set, abrupt, no-nonsense older men, in company with the most disreputable and fanatical "race" men, or these
same "race" men with the sharpies, or these sharpies with the
churchly women. Seventh Day Adventists and Methodists and
Spiritualists seemed to be hobnobbing with Holyrollers and they were
all, alike, entangled with the most flagrant disbelievers; something
heavy in their stance seemed to indicate that they had all, incredibly,
seen a common vision, and on each face there seemed to be the same
strange, bitter shadow.

The churchly women and the matter-of-fact, no-nonsense men had
children in the Army. The sleazy girls they talked to had lovers there,
the sharpies and the "race" men had friends and brothers there. It
would have demanded an unquestioning patriotism, happily as un-
common in this country as it is undesirable, for these people not to
have been disturbed by the bitter letters they received, by the newspa-

per stories they read, not to have been enraged by the posters, then to be found all over New York, which described the Japanese as "yellow-bellied Japs." It was only the "race" men, to be sure, who spoke ceaselessly of being revenged—how this vengeance was to be exacted was not clear—for the indignities and dangers suffered by Negro boys in uniform; but everybody felt a directionless, hopeless bitterness, as well as that panic which can scarcely be suppressed when one knows that a human being one loves is beyond one's reach, and in danger. This helplessness and this gnawing uneasiness does something, at length, to even the toughest mind. Perhaps the best way to sum all this up is to say that the people I knew felt, mainly, a peculiar kind of relief when they knew that their boys were being shipped out of the south, to do battle overseas. It was, perhaps, like feeling that the most dangerous part of a dangerous journey had been passed and that now, even if death should come, it would come with honor and without the complicity of their countrymen. Such a death would be, in short, a fact with which one could hope to live.

It was on the 28th of July, which I believe was a Wednesday, that I visited my father for the first time during his illness and for the last time in his life. The moment I saw him I knew why I had put off this visit so long. I had told my mother that I did not want to see him because I hated him. But this was not true. It was only that I *had* hated him and I wanted to hold on to this hatred. I did not want to look on him as a ruin: it was not a ruin I had hated. I imagine that one of the reasons people cling to their hates so stubbornly is because they sense, once hate is gone, that they will be forced to deal with pain.

We traveled out to him, his older sister and myself, to what seemed to be the very end of a very Long Island. It was hot and dusty and we wrangled, my aunt and I, all the way out, over the fact that I had recently begun to smoke and, as she said, to give myself airs. But I knew that she wrangled with me because she could not bear to face the fact of her brother's dying. Neither could I endure the reality of her despair, her unstated bafflement as to what had happened to her brother's life, and her own. So we wrangled and I smoked and from time to time she fell into a heavy reverie. Covertly, I watched her face, which was the face of an old woman; it had fallen in, the eyes were sunken and lightless; soon she would be dying, too.

In my childhood—it had not been so long ago—I had thought her beautiful. She had been quick-witted and quick-moving and very generous with all the children and each of her visits had been an event. At one time one of my brothers and myself had thought of running away to live with her. Now she could no longer produce out of her handbag some unexpected and yet familiar delight. She made me feel pity and revulsion and fear. It was awful to realize that she no longer caused me to feel affection. The closer we came to the hospital the more querulous she became and at the same time, naturally, grew more dependent on me. Between pity and guilt and fear I began to feel that there was another me trapped in my skull like a jack-in-the-box who might escape my control at any moment and fill the air with screaming.

She began to cry the moment we entered the room and she saw him lying there, all shriveled and still, like a little black monkey. The great, gleaming apparatus which fed him and would have compelled him to be still even if he had been able to move brought to mind, not beneficence, but torture; the tubes entering his arm made me think of pictures I had seen, when a child, of Gulliver, tied down by the pygmies on that island. My aunt wept and wept, there was a whistling sound in my father's throat; nothing was said; he could not speak. I wanted to take his hand, to say something. But I do not know what I could have said, even if he could have heard me. He was not really in that room with us, he had at last really embarked on his journey; and though my aunt told me that he said he was going to meet Jesus, I did not hear anything except that whistling in his throat. The doctor came back and we left, into that unbearable train again, and home. In the morning came the telegram saying that he was dead. Then the house was suddenly full of relatives, friends, hysteria, and confusion and I quickly left my mother and the children to the care of those impressive women, who, in Negro communities at least, automatically appear at times of bereavement armed with lotions, proverbs, and patience, and an ability to cook. I went downtown. By the time I returned, later the same day, my mother had been carried to the hospital and the baby had been born.

[3]

For my father's funeral I had nothing black to wear and this posed a nagging problem all day long. It was one of those problems, simple, or impossible of solution, to which the mind insanely clings in order to avoid the mind's real trouble. I spent most of that day at the downtown apartment of a girl I knew, celebrating my birthday with whiskey and wondering what to wear that night. When planning a birthday celebration one naturally does not expect that it will be up against competition from a funeral and this girl had anticipated taking me out that night, for a big dinner and a night club afterwards. Sometime during the course of that long day we decided that we would go out anyway, when my father's funeral service was over. I imagine *I* decided it, since, as the funeral hour approached, it became clearer and clearer to me that I would not know what to do with myself when it was over. The girl, stifling her very lively concern as to the possible effects of the whiskey on one of my father's chief mourners, concentrated on being conciliatory and practically helpful. She found a black shirt for me somewhere and ironed it and, dressed in the darkest pants and jacket I owned, and slightly drunk, I made my way to my father's funeral.

The chapel was full, but not packed, and very quiet. There were, mainly, my father's relatives, and his children, and here and there I saw faces I had not seen since childhood, the faces of my father's one-time friends. They were very dark and solemn now, seeming somehow to suggest that they had known all along that something like this would happen. Chief among the mourners was my aunt, who had quarreled with my father all his life; by which I do not mean to suggest that her mourning was insincere or that she had not loved him. I suppose that she was one of the few people in the world who had, and their incessant quarreling proved precisely the strength of the tie that bound them. The only other person in the world, as far as I knew, whose relationship to my father rivaled my aunt's in depth was my mother, who was not there.

It seemed to me, of course, that it was a very long funeral. But it was, if anything, a rather shorter funeral than most, nor, since there were no overwhelming uncontrollable expressions of grief, could it be called—if I dare to use the word—successful. The minister who preached my father's funeral sermon was one of the few my father had still been seeing as he neared his end. He presented to us in his sermon a man whom none of us had ever seen—a man thoughtful, patient, and forbearing, a Christian inspiration to all who knew him, and a model for his children. And no doubt the children, in their disturbed and guilty state, were almost ready to believe this; he had been remote enough to be anything and, anyway, the shock of the incontrovertible, that it was really our father lying up there in that casket, prepared the mind for anything. His sister moaned and this grief-stricken moaning was taken as corroboration. The other faces held a dark, non-committal thoughtfulness. This was not the man they had known, but they had scarcely expected to be confronted with *him;* this was, in a sense deeper than questions of fact, the man they had not known, and the man they had not known may have been the real one. The real man, whoever he had been, had suffered and now he was dead: this was all that was sure and all that mattered now. Every man in the chapel hoped that when his hour came he, too, would be eulogized, which is to say forgiven, and that all of his lapses, greeds, errors, and strayings from the truth would be invested with coherence and looked upon with charity. This was perhaps the last thing human beings could give each other and it was what they demanded, after all, of the Lord. Only the Lord saw the midnight tears, only He was present when one of His children, moaning and wringing hands, paced up and down the room. When one slapped one's child in anger the recoil in the heart reverberated through heaven and became part of the pain of the universe. And when the children were hungry and sullen and distrustful and one watched them, daily, growing wilder, and further away, and running headlong into danger, it was the Lord who knew what the charged heart endured as the strap was laid to the backside; the Lord alone who knew what one *would* have said if one had had, like the Lord, the gift of the living word. It was the Lord who knew of the impossibility every parent in that room faced: how to prepare the child for the day when the child would be despised and how to *create* in the child—by what means?—a stronger antidote to this poison than one had found for oneself. The avenues, side streets, bars, billiard halls, hospitals, police stations, and even the playgrounds of Harlem—not to mention the houses of correction, the jails, and the morgue—testified to the potency of the poison while remaining silent as to the efficacy of whatever antidote, irresistibly raising the question of whether or not such an antidote existed; raising, which was worse, the question of whether or not an antidote was desirable; perhaps poison should be fought with poison. With these several schisms in the

mind and with more terrors in the heart than could be named, it was
better not to judge the man who had gone down under an impossible
burden. It was better to remember: *Thou knowest this man's fall; but
thou knowest not his wrassling.*

While the preacher talked and I watched the children—years of
changing their diapers, scrubbing them, slapping them, taking them
to school, and scolding them had had the perhaps inevitable result of
making me love them, though I am not sure I knew this then—my
mind was busily breaking out with a rash of disconnected impressions.
Snatches of popular songs, indecent jokes, bits of books I had read,
movie sequences, faces, voices, political issues—I thought I was going
mad; all these impressions suspended, as it were, in the solution of the
faint nausea produced in me by the heat and liquor. For a moment
I had the impression that my alcoholic breath, inefficiently disguised
with chewing gum, filled the entire chapel. Then someone began
singing one of my father's favorite songs and, abruptly, I was with
him, sitting on his knee, in the hot, enormous, crowded church which
was the first church we attended. It was the Abyssinia Baptist Church
on 138th Street. We had not gone there long. With this image, a host
of others came. I had forgotten, in the rage of my growing up, how
proud my father had been of me when I was little. Apparently, I had
had a voice and my father had liked to show me off before the
members of the church. I had forgotten what he had looked like when
he was pleased but now I remembered that he had always been grinning with pleasure when my solos ended. I even remembered certain
expressions on his face when he teased my mother—had he loved her?
I would never know. And when had it all begun to change? For now
it seemed that he had not always been cruel. I remembered being
taken for a haircut and scraping my knee on the footrest of the
barber's chair and I remembered my father's face as he soothed my
crying and applied the stinging iodine. Then I remembered our fights,
fights which had been of the worst possible kind because my technique
had been silence.

I remembered the one time in all our life together when we had
really spoken to each other.

It was on a Sunday and it must have been shortly before I left home.
We were walking, just the two of us, in our usual silence, to or from
church. I was in high school and had been doing a lot of writing and

I was, at about this time, the editor of the high school magazine. But I had also been a Young Minister and had been preaching from the pulpit. Lately, I had been taking fewer engagements and preached as rarely as possible. It was said in the church, quite truthfully, that I was "cooling off."

My father asked me abruptly, "You'd rather write than preach, wouldn't you?"

I was astonished at his question—because it was a real question. I answered, "Yes."

That was all we said. It was awful to remember that that was all we had *ever* said.

The casket now was opened and the mourners were being led up the aisle to look for the last time on the deceased. The assumption was that the family was too overcome with grief to be allowed to make this journey alone and I watched while my aunt was led to the casket and, muffled in black, and shaking, led back to her seat. I disapproved of forcing the children to look on their dead father, considering that the shock of his death, or, more truthfully, the shock of death as a reality, was already a little more than a child could bear, but my judgment in this matter had been overruled and there they were, bewildered and frightened and very small, being led, one by one, to the casket. But there is also something very gallant about children at such moments. It has something to do with their silence and gravity and with the fact that one cannot help them. Their legs, somehow, seem *exposed*, so that it is at once incredible and terribly clear that their legs are all they have to hold them up.

I had not wanted to go to the casket myself and I certainly had not wished to be led there, but there was no way of avoiding either of these forms. One of the deacons led me up and I looked on my father's face. I cannot say that it looked like him at all. His blackness had been equivocated by powder and there was no suggestion in that casket of what his power had or could have been. He was simply an old man dead, and it was hard to believe that he had ever given anyone either joy or pain. Yet, his life filled that room. Further up the avenue his wife was holding his newborn child. Life and death so close together, and love and hatred, and right and wrong, said something to me which I did not want to hear concerning man, concerning the life of man.

After the funeral, while I was downtown desperately celebrating my birthday, a Negro soldier, in the lobby of the Hotel Braddock, got into a fight with a white policeman over a Negro girl. Negro girls, white policemen, in or out of uniform, and Negro males—in or out of uniform—were part of the furniture of the lobby of the Hotel Braddock and this was certainly not the first time such an incident had occurred. It was destined, however, to receive an unprecedented publicity, for the fight between the policeman and the soldier ended with the shooting of the soldier. Rumor, flowing immediately to the streets outside, stated that the soldier had been shot in the back, an instantaneous and revealing invention, and that the soldier had died protecting a Negro woman. The facts were somewhat different—for example, the soldier had not been shot in the back, and was not dead, and the girl seems to have been as dubious a symbol of womanhood as her white counterpart in Georgia usually is, but no one was interested in the facts. They preferred the invention because this invention expressed and corroborated their hates and fears so perfectly. It is just as well to remember that people are always doing this. Perhaps many of those legends, including Christianity, to which the world clings began their conquest of the world with just some such concerted surrender to distortion. The effect, in Harlem, of this particular legend was like the effect of a lit match in a tin of gasoline. The mob gathered before the doors of the Hotel Braddock simply began to swell and to spread in every direction, and Harlem exploded.

The mob did not cross the ghetto lines. It would have been easy, for example, to have gone over to Morningside Park on the west side or to have crossed the Grand Central railroad tracks at 125th Street on the east side, to wreak havoc in white neighborhoods. The mob seems to have been mainly interested in something more potent and real than the white face, that is, in white power, and the principal damage done during the riot of the summer of 1943 was to white business establishments in Harlem. It might have been a far bloodier story, of course, if, at the hour the riot began, these establishments had still been open. From the Hotel Braddock the mob fanned out, east and west along 125th Street, and for the entire length of Lenox, Seventh, and Eighth avenues. Along each of these avenues, and along each major side street—116th, 125th, 135th, and so on—bars, stores, pawnshops, restaurants, even little luncheonettes had been smashed open and entered and looted—looted, it might be added, with more

haste than efficiency. The shelves really looked as though a bomb had
struck them. Cans of beans and soup and dog food, along with toilet
paper, corn flakes, sardines, and milk tumbled every which way, and
abandoned cash registers and cases of beer leaned crazily out of the
splintered windows and were strewn along the avenues. Sheets, blankets, and clothing of every description formed a kind of path, as
though people had dropped them while running. I truly had not
realized that Harlem *had* so many stores until I saw them all smashed
open; the first time the word *wealth* ever entered my mind in relation
to Harlem was when I saw it scattered in the streets. But one's first,
incongruous impression of plenty was countered immediately by an
impression of waste. None of this was doing anybody any good. It
would have been better to have left the plate glass as it had been and
the goods lying in the stores.

It would have been better, but it would also have been intolerable,
for Harlem had needed something to smash. To smash something is
the ghetto's chronic need. Most of the time it is the members of the
ghetto who smash each other, and themselves. But as long as the
ghetto walls are standing there will always come a moment when these
outlets do not work. That summer, for example, it was not enough to
get into a fight on Lenox Avenue, or curse out one's cronies in the
barber shops. If ever, indeed, the violence which fills Harlem's
churches, pool halls, and bars erupts outward in a more direct fashion,
Harlem and its citizens are likely to vanish in an apocalyptic flood.
That this is not likely to happen is due to a great many reasons, most
hidden and powerful among them the Negro's real relation to the
white American. This relation prohibits, simply, anything as uncomplicated and satisfactory as pure hatred. In order really to hate white
people, one has to blot so much out of the mind—and the heart—that
this hatred itself becomes an exhausting and self-destructive pose. But
this does not mean, on the other hand, that love comes easily: the
white world is too powerful, too complacent, too ready with gratuitous humiliation, and, above all, too ignorant and too innocent for
that. One is absolutely forced to make perpetual qualifications and
one's own reactions are always canceling each other out. It is this,
really, which has driven so many people mad, both white and black.
One is always in the position of having to decide between amputation
and gangrene. Amputation is swift but time may prove that the ampu-

tation was not necessary—or one may delay the amputation too long.
Gangrene is slow, but it is impossible to be sure that one is reading
one's symptoms right. The idea of going through life as a cripple is
more than one can bear, and equally unbearable is the risk of swelling
up slowly, in agony, with poison. And the trouble, finally, is that the
risks are real even if the choices do not exist.

"But as for me and my house," my father had said, "we will serve
the Lord." I wondered, as we drove him to his resting place, what this
line had meant for him. I had heard him preach it many times. I had
preached it once myself, proudly giving it an interpretation different
from my father's. Now the whole thing came back to me, as though
my father and I were on our way to Sunday school and I were
memorizing the golden text: *And if it seem evil unto you to serve the
Lord, choose you this day whom you will serve; whether the gods
which your fathers served that were on the other side of the flood, or
the gods of the Amorites, in whose land ye dwell: but as for me and
my house, we will serve the Lord.* I suspected in these familiar lines
a meaning which had never been there for me before. All of my
father's texts and songs, which I had decided were meaningless, were
arranged before me at his death like empty bottles, waiting to hold
the meaning which life would give them for me. This was his legacy:
nothing is ever escaped. That bleakly memorable morning I hated the
unbelievable streets and the Negroes and whites who had, equally,
made them that way. But I knew that it was folly, as my father would
have said, this bitterness was folly. It was necessary to hold on to the
things that mattered. The dead man mattered, the new life mattered;
blackness and whiteness did not matter; to believe that they did was
to acquiesce in one's own destruction. Hatred, which could destroy
so much, never failed to destroy the man who hated and this was an
immutable law.

It began to seem that one would have to hold in the mind forever
two ideas which seemed to be in opposition. The first idea was acceptance, the acceptance, totally without rancor, of life as it is, and men
as they are: in the light of this idea, it goes without saying that
injustice is a commonplace. But this did not mean that one could be
complacent, for the second idea was of equal power: that one must
never, in one's own life, accept these injustices as commonplace but

must fight them with all one's strength. This fight begins, however, in the heart and it now had been laid to my charge to keep my own heart free of hatred and despair. This intimation made my heart heavy and, now that my father was irrecoverable, I wished that he had been beside me so that I could have searched his face for the answers which only the future would give me now.

[1955]

NORMAN MAILER
MIAMI BEACH

THEY SNIPPED the ribbon in 1915, they popped the cork, Miami Beach was born. A modest burg they called a city, nine-tenths jungle. An island. It ran along a coastal barrier the other side of Biscayne Bay from young Miami—in 1868 when Henry Lum, a California 'forty-niner, first glimpsed the island from a schooner, you may be certain it was jungle, coconut palms on the sand, mangrove swamp and palmetto thicket ten feet off the beach. But by 1915, they were working the vein. John S. Collins, a New Jersey nurseryman (after whom Collins Avenue is kindly named) brought in bean fields and avocado groves; a gent named Fisher, Carl G., a Hoosier—he invented Prestolite, a millionaire—bought up acres from Collins, brought in a work-load of machinery, men, even two elephants, and jungle was cleared, swamps were filled, small residential islands were made out of baybottom mud, dredged, then relocated, somewhat larger natural islands adjacent to the barrier island found themselves improved, streets were paved, sidewalks put in with other amenities—by 1968, one hundred years after Lum first glommed the beach, large areas of the original coastal strip were covered over altogether with macadam, white condominium, white luxury hotel and white stucco flea-bag. Over hundreds, then thousands of acres, white sidewalks, streets and white buildings covered the earth where the jungle had been. Is it so dissimilar from covering your poor pubic hair with adhesive tape for fifty years? The vegetal memories of that excised jungle haunted Miami Beach in a steam-pot of miasmas. Ghosts of expunged flora, the never-born groaning in vegetative chancery beneath the asphalt came up with a tropical curse, an equatorial leaden wet sweat of air which rose from the earth itself, rose right up through the baked asphalt and into the heated air which entered the lungs like a hand slipping into a rubber glove.

The temperature was not that insane. It hung around 87° day after day, at night it went down to 82°, back to the same 87° in the

A.M.—the claims of the News Bureau for Miami Beach promised that in 1967 temperature exceeded 90° only four times. (Which the Island of Manhattan could never begin to say.) But of course Miami Beach did not have to go that high, for its humidity was up to 87° as well—it was, on any and every day of the Republican Convention of 1968, one of the hottest cities in the world. The reporter was no expert on tropical heats—he had had, he would admit, the island of Luzon for a summer in World War II; and basic training in the pine woods of Fort Bragg, North Carolina, in August; he had put in a week at Las Vegas during July—temperatures to 110°; he had crossed the Mojave Desert once by day; he was familiar with the New York subway in the rush hour on the hottest day of the year. These were awesome immersions—one did not have to hit the Congo to know what it was like in a hothouse in hell—but that 87° in Miami Beach day after day held up in competition against other sulphuric encounters. Traveling for five miles up the broken-down, forever in-a-state-of-alteration and repair of Collins Avenue, crawling through 5 P.M. Miami Beach traffic in the pure miserable fortune of catching an old taxi without air conditioning, dressed in shirt and tie and jacket—formal and implicitly demanded uniform of political journalists—the sensation of breathing, then living, was not unlike being obliged to make love to a 300-pound woman who has decided to get on top. Got it? You could not dominate a thing. That uprooted jungle had to be screaming beneath.

Of course it could have been the air conditioning: natural climate transmogrified by technological climate. They say that in Miami Beach the air conditioning is pushed to that icy point where women may wear fur coats over their diamonds in the tropics. For ten miles, from the Diplomat to the Di Lido, above Hallandale Beach Boulevard down to Lincoln Mall, all the white refrigerators stood, piles of white refrigerators six and eight and twelve stories high, twenty stories high, shaped like sugar cubes and ice-cube trays on edge, like mosques and palaces, shaped like matched white luggage and portable radios, stereos, plastic compacts and plastic rings, Moorish castles shaped like waffle irons, shaped like the baffle plates on white plastic electric heaters, and cylinders like Waring blenders, buildings looking like giant op art and pop art paintings, and sweet wedding cakes, cottons of kitsch and piles of dirty cotton stucco, yes, for ten miles the hotels

for the delegates stood on the beach side of Collins Avenue: the Eden
Roc and the Fontainebleau (Press Headquarters), the Di Lido and the
De Lano, the Ivanhoe, Deauville, Sherry Frontenac and the Monte
Carlo, the Cadillac, Caribbean and the Balmoral, the Lucerne, Hilton
Plaza, Doral Beach, the Sorrento, Marco Polo, Casablanca, and At-
lantis, the Hilyard Manor, Sans Souci, Algiers, Carillon, Seville, the
Gaylord, the Shore Club, the Nautilus, Montmartre, and the Prome-
nade, the Bal Harbour on North Bay Causeway, and the Twelve
Caesars, the Regency and the Americana, the Diplomat, Versailles,
Coronado, Sovereign, the Waldman (dig!), the Beau Rivage, the
Crown Hotel, even Holiday Inn, all oases for technological man. Deep
air conditioning down to 68°, ice-palaces to chill the fevered brain—
when the air conditioning worked. And their furnishings were monu-
mentally materialistic. Not all of them: the cheaper downtown hotels
like the Di Lido and the Nautilus were bare and mean with vinyl
coverings on the sofas and the glare of plastic off the rugs and tables
and tiles, inexpensive hotel colors of pale brown and buff and dingy
cream, sodden gray, but the diadems like the Fontainebleau and the
Eden Roc, the Doral Beach, the Hilton Plaza (Headquarters for
Nixon), the Deauville (Hq for Reagan) or the Americana—Rockefeller and the New York State delegation's own ground—were lavish
with interlockings, curves, vaults and runs of furnishings as inter-
twined as serpents in the roots of a mangrove tree. All the rivers of
the very worst taste twisted down to the delta of each lobby in each
grand Miami Beach hotel—rare was the central room which did not
look like the lobby of a movie palace, imitation of late-Renaissance
imitations of Greek and Roman statues, imitations of baroque and
rococo and brothel Victorian and Art Nouveau and Bauhaus with gold
grapes and cornucopias welded to the modern bronze tubing of the
chair, golden moldings which ran like ivy from room to room, chande-
liers complex as the armature of dynamos, and curvilinear steps in the
shape of amoebas and palettes, cocktail lounge bars in deep rose or
maroon with spun-sugar white tubes of plaster decor to twist around
the ceiling. There was every color of iridescence, rainbows of vulgarity, aureoles of gorgeous taste, opium den of a middle-class dollar,
materialistic as meat, sweat, and the cigar. It is said that people born
under Taurus and Capricorn are the most materialistic of us all. Take
a sample of the residents in the census of Miami B.—does Taurus

predominate more than one-twelfth of its share? It must, or astrology is done, for the Republicans, Grand Old Party with a philosophy rather than a program, had chosen what must certainly be the materialistic capital of the world for their convention. Las Vegas might offer competition, but Las Vegas was materialism in the service of electricity—fortunes could be lost in the spark of the dice. Miami was materialism baking in the sun, then stepping back to air-conditioned caverns where ice could nestle in the fur. It was the first of a hundred curiosities—that in a year when the Republic hovered on the edge of revolution, nihilism, and lines of police on file to the horizon, visions of future Vietnams in our own cities upon us, the party of conservatism and principle, of corporate wealth and personal frugality, the party of cleanliness, hygiene, and balanced budget, should have set itself down on a sultan's strip.

That was the first of a hundred curiosities, but there were mysteries as well. The reporter had moved through the convention quietly, as anonymously as possible, wan, depressed, troubled. Something profoundly unclassifiable was going on among the Republicans and he did not know if it was conceivably good or a concealment of something bad—which was the first time a major social phenomenon like a convention had confused him so. He had covered others. The Democratic Convention in 1960 in Los Angeles which nominated John F. Kennedy, and the Republican in San Francisco in 1964 which installed Barry Goldwater, had encouraged some of his very best writing. He had felt a gift for comprehending those conventions. But the Republican assembly in Miami Beach in 1968 was a different affair— one could not tell if nothing much was going on, or to the contrary, nothing much was going on near the surface but everything was shifting down below. So dialogue with other journalists merely depressed him—the complaints were unanimous that this was the dullest convention anyone could remember. Complaints took his mind away from the slow brooding infusion he desired in the enigmas of conservatism and/or Republicanism, and any hope of perspective on the problem beyond. The country was in a throe, a species of eschatological heave. The novelist John Updike was not necessarily one of his favorite authors, but after the assassination of Robert F. Kennedy, it was Updike who had made the remark that God might have withdrawn His blessing from America. It was a thought which could not be

forgotten for it gave insight to the perspectives of the Devil and his
political pincers: Left-wing demons, white and Black, working to
inflame the conservative heart of America, while Right-wing devils
exacerbated Blacks and drove the mind of the New Left and liberal
middle class into prides of hopeless position. And the country roaring
like a bull in its wounds, coughing like a sick lung in the smog, turning
over in sleep at the sound of motorcycles, shivering at its need for new
phalanxes of order. Where were the new phalanxes one could trust?
The reporter had seen the faces of too many police to balm his dreams
with the sleep they promised. Even the drinks tasted bad in Miami
in the fever and the chill.

[1968]

EDWARD HOAGLAND
THE COURAGE OF TURTLES

TURTLES ARE a kind of bird with the governor turned low. With the same attitude of removal, they cock a glance at what is going on, as if they need only to fly away. Until recently they were also a case of virtue rewarded, at least in the town where I grew up, because, being humble creatures, there were plenty of them. Even when we still had a few bobcats in the woods the local snapping turtles, growing up to forty pounds, were the largest carnivores. You would see them through the amber water, as big as greeny wash basins at the bottom of the pond, until they faded into the inscrutable mud as if they hadn't existed at all.

When I was ten I went to Dr. Green's Pond, a two-acre pond across the road. When I was twelve I walked a mile or so to Taggart's Pond, which was lusher, had big water snakes and a waterfall; and shortly after that I was bicycling way up to the adventuresome vastness of Mud Pond, a lake-sized body of water in the reservoir system of a Connecticut city, possessed of cat-backed little islands and empty shacks and a forest of pines and hardwoods along the shore. Otters, foxes and mink left their prints on the bank; there were pike and perch. As I got older, the estates and forgotten back lots in town were parceled out and sold for nice prices, yet, though the woods had shrunk, it seemed that fewer people walked in the woods. The new residents didn't know how to find them. Eventually, exploring, they did find them, and it required some ingenuity and doubling around on my part to go for eight miles without meeting someone. I was grown by now, I lived in New York, and that's what I wanted on the occasional weekends when I came out.

Since Mud Pond contained drinking water I had felt confident nothing untoward would happen there. For a long while the developers stayed away, until the drought of the mid-1960s. This event, squeezing the edges in, convinced the local water company that the pond really wasn't a necessity as a catch basin, however; so they bulldozed a hole in the earthen dam, bulldozed the banks to fill in the bottom, and landscaped the flow of water that remained to wind like an English brook and provide a domestic view for the houses which were planned. Most of the painted turtles of Mud Pond, who had been inaccessible as they sunned on their rocks, wound up in boxes in boys' closets within a matter of days. Their footsteps in the dry leaves gave them away as they wandered forlornly. The snappers and the little musk turtles, neither of whom leave the water except once a year to lay their eggs, dug into the drying mud for another siege of hot weather, which they were accustomed to doing whenever the pond got low. But this time it was low for good; the mud baked over them and slowly entombed them. As for the ducks, I couldn't stroll in the woods and not feel guilty, because they were crouched beside every stagnant pothole, or were slinking between the bushes with their heads tucked into their shoulders so that I wouldn't see them. If they decided I had, they beat their way up through the screen of trees, striking their wings dangerously, and wheeled about with that headlong, magnificent velocity to locate another poor puddle.

I used to catch possums and black snakes as well as turtles, and I kept dogs and goats. Some summers I worked in a menagerie with the big personalities of the animal kingdom, like elephants and rhinoceroses. I was twenty before these enthusiasms began to wane, and it was then that I picked turtles as the particular animal I wanted to keep in touch with. I was allergic to fur, for one thing, and turtles need minimal care and not much in the way of quarters. They're personable beasts. They see the same colors we do and they seem to see just as well, as one discovers in trying to sneak up on them. In the laboratory they unravel the twists of a maze with the hot-blooded rapidity of a mammal. Though they can't run as fast as a rat, they improve on their errors just as quickly, pausing at each crossroads to look left and right. And they rock rhythmically in place, as we often do, although they are hatched from eggs, not the womb. (A common explanation psychologists give for our pleasure in rocking quietly is that it recapitulates our mother's heartbeat *in utero*.)

Snakes, by contrast, are dryly silent and priapic. They are smooth movers, legalistic, unblinking, and they afford the humor which the humorless do. But they make challenging captives; sometimes they don't eat for months on a point of order—if the light isn't right, for instance. Alligators are sticklers too. They're like war-horses, or German shepherds, and with their bar-shaped, vertical pupils adding emphasis, they have the *idée fixe* of eating, eating, even when they choose to refuse all food and stubbornly die. They delight in tossing a salamander up towards the sky and grabbing him in their long mouths as he comes down. They're so eager that they get the jitters, and they're too much of a proposition for a casual aquarium like mine. Frogs are depressingly defenseless: that moist, extensive back, with the bones almost sticking through. Hold a frog and you're holding its skeleton. Frogs' tasty legs are the staff of life to many animals—herons, raccoons, ribbon snakes—though they themselves are hard to feed. It's not an enviable role to be the staff of life, and after frogs you descend down the evolutionary ladder a big step to fish.

Turtles cough, burp, whistle, grunt and hiss, and produce social judgments. They put their heads together amicably enough, but then one drives the other back with the suddenness of two dogs who have been conversing in tones too low for an onlooker to hear. They pee in fear when they're first caught, but exercise both pluck and optimism in trying to escape, walking for hundreds of yards within the confines of their pen, carrying the weight of that cumbersome box on legs which are cruelly positioned for walking. They don't feel that the contest is unfair; they keep plugging, rolling like sailorly souls—a bobbing, infirm gait, a brave, sea-legged momentum—stopping occasionally to study the lay of the land. For me, anyway, they manage to contain the rest of the animal world. They can stretch out their necks like a giraffe, or loom underwater like an apocryphal hippo. They browse on lettuce thrown on the water like a cow moose which is partly submerged. They have a penguin's alertness, combined with a build like a Brontosaurus when they rise up on tiptoe. Then they hunch and ponderously lunge like a grizzly going forward.

Baby turtles in a turtle bowl are a puzzle in geometrics. They're as decorative as pansy petals, but they are also self-directed building blocks, propping themselves on one another in different arrangements, before upending the tower. The timid individuals turn fearless, or vice versa. If one gets a bit arrogant he will push the others off the rock and afterwards climb down into the water and cling to the back of one of those he has bullied, tickling him with his hind feet until he bucks like a bronco. On the other hand, when this same milder-mannered fellow isn't exerting himself, he will stare right into the face of the sun for hours. What could be more lionlike? And he's at home in or out of the water and does lots of metaphysical tilting. He sinks and rises, with an infinity of levels to choose from; or, elongating himself, he climbs out on the land again to perambulate, sits boxed in his box, and finally slides back in the water, submerging into dreams.

I have five of these babies in a kidney-shaped bowl. The hatchling, who is a painted turtle, is not as large as the top joint of my thumb. He eats chicken gladly. Other foods he will attempt to eat but not with sufficient perseverance to succeed because he's so little. The yellow-bellied terrapin is probably a yearling, and he eats salad vora-ciously, but no meat, fish or fowl. The Cumberland terrapin won't touch salad or chicken but eats fish and all of the meats except for bacon. The little snapper, with a black crenelated shell, feasts on any kind of meat, but rejects greens and fish. The fifth of the turtles is African. I acquired him only recently and don't know him well. A mottled brown, he unnerves the green turtles, dragging their food off to his lairs. He doesn't seem to want to be green—he bites the algae off his shell, hanging meanwhile at daring, steep, head-first angles.

The snapper was a Ferdinand until I provided him with deeper water. Now he snaps at my pencil with his downturned and fearsome mouth, his swollen face like a napalm victim's. The Cumberland has an elliptical red mark on the side of his green-and-yellow head. He is benign by nature and ought to be as elegant as his scientific name *(Pseudemys scripta elegans)*, except he has contracted a disease of the air bladder which has permanently inflated it; he floats high in the water at an undignified slant and can't go under. There may have been internal bleeding, too, because his carapace is stained along its ridge. Unfortunately, like flowers, baby turtles often die. Their mouths fill up with a white fungus and their lungs with pneumonia. Their organs clog up from the rust in the water, or diet troubles, and, like a dying man's, their eyes and heads become too prominent. Toward the end, the edge of the shell becomes flabby as felt and folds around them like a shroud.

While they live they're like puppies. Although they're vivacious, they would be a bore to be with all the time, so I also have an adult wood turtle about six inches long. Her shell is the equal of any seashell for sculpturing, even a Cellini shell; it's like an old, dusty, richly engraved medallion dug out of a hillside. Her legs are salmon-orange bordered with black and protected by canted, heroic scales. Her plastron—the bottom shell—is splotched like a margay cat's coat, with black ocelli on a yellow background. It is convex to make room for the female organs inside, whereas a male's would be concave to help him fit tightly on top of her. Altogether, she exhibits every camouflage color on her limbs and shells. She has a turtleneck neck, a tail like an elephant's, wise old pachydermous hind legs and the face of a turkey—except that when I carry her she gazes at the passing ground with a hawk's eyes and mouth. Her feet fit to the fingers of my hand, one to each one, and she rides looking down. She can walk on the floor in perfect silence, but usually she lets her shell knock portentously, like a footstep, so that she resembles some grand, concise, slow-moving id. But if an earthworm is presented, she jerks swiftly ahead, poises above it and strikes like a mongoose, consuming it with wild vigor. Yet she will climb on my lap to eat bread or boiled eggs.

If put into a creek, she swims like a cutter, nosing forward to intercept a strange turtle and smell him. She drifts with the current to go downstream, maneuvering behind a rock when she wants to take stock, or sinking to the nether levels, while bubbles float up. Getting out, choosing her path, she will proceed a distance and dig into a pile of humus, thrusting herself to the coolest layer at the bottom. The hole closes over her until it's as small as a mouse's hole. She's not as aquatic as a musk turtle, not quite as terrestrial as the box turtles in the same woods, but because of her versatility she's marvelous, she's everywhere. And though she breathes the way we breathe, with scarcely perceptible movements of her chest, sometimes instead she pumps her throat ruminatively, like a pipe smoker sucking and puffing. She waits and blinks, pumping her throat, turning her head, then sets off like a loping tiger in slow motion, hurdling the jungly lumber, the pea vine and twigs. She estimates angles so well that when she rides over the rocks, sliding down a drop-off with her rugged front legs extended, she has the grace of a rodeo mare.

But she's well off to be with me rather than at Mud Pond. The other turtles have fled—those that aren't baked into the bottom. Creeping up the brooks to sad, constricted marshes, burdened as they are with that box on their backs, they're walking into a setup where all their enemies move thirty times faster than they. It's like the nightmare most of us have whimpered through, where we are weighted down disastrously while trying to flee; fleeing our home ground, we try to run.

I've seen turtles in still worse straits. On Broadway, in New York, there is a penny arcade which used to sell baby terrapins that were scrawled with bon mots in enamel paint, such as KISS ME BABY. The manager turned out to be a wholesaler as well, and once I asked him whether he had any larger turtles to sell. He took me upstairs to a loft room devoted to the turtle business. There were desks for the paper work and a series of racks that held shallow tin bins atop one another, each with several hundred babies crawling around in it. He was a smudgy-complexioned, serious fellow and he did have a few adult terrapins, but I was going to school and wasn't actually planning to buy; I'd only wanted to see them. They were aquatic turtles, but here they went without water, presumably for weeks, lurching about in those dry bins like handicapped citizens, living on gumption. An easel where the artist worked stood in the middle of the floor. She had a palette and a clip attachment for fastening the babies in place. She wore a smock and a beret, and was homely, short and eccentric-looking, with funny black hair, like some of the ladies who show their paintings in Washington Square in May. She had a cold, she was smoking, and her hand wasn't very steady, although she worked quickly enough. The smile that she produced for me would have looked giddy if she had been happier, or drunk. Of course the turtles' doom was sealed when she painted them, because their bodies inside would continue to grow but their shells would not. Gradually, invisibly, they would be crushed. Around us their bellies—two thousand belly shells—rubbed on the bins with a mournful, momentous hiss.

Somehow there were so many of them I didn't rescue one. Years later, however, I was walking on First Avenue when I noticed a basket of living turtles in front of a fish store. They were as dry as a heap of old bones in the sun; nevertheless, they were creeping over one another gimpily, doing their best to escape. I looked and was touched to discover that they appeared to be wood turtles, my favorites, so I bought one. In my apartment I looked closer and realized that in fact this was a diamond-back terrapin, which was bad news. Diamond-backs are tidewater turtles from brackish estuaries, and I had no sea water to keep him in. He spent his days thumping interminably against the baseboards, pushing for an opening through the wall. He drank thirstily but would not eat and had none of the hearty, accepting qualities of wood turtles. He was morose, paler in color, sleeker and more Oriental in the carved ridges and rings that formed his shell. Though I felt sorry for him, finally I found his unrelenting presence exasperating. I carried him, struggling in a paper bag, across town to the Morton Street Pier on the Hudson. It was August but gray and windy. He was very surprised when I tossed him in; for the first time in our association, I think, he was afraid. He looked afraid as he bobbed about on top of the water, looking up at me from ten feet below. Though we were both accustomed to his resistance and rigidity, seeing him still pitiful, I recognized that I must have done the wrong thing. At least the river was salty, but it was also bottomless; the waves were too rough for him, and the tide was coming in, bumping him against the pilings underneath the pier. Too late, I realized that he wouldn't be able to swim to a peaceful inlet in New Jersey, even if he could figure out which way to swim. But since, short of diving in after him, there was nothing I could do, I walked away.

[1968]

Acknowledgments (cont'd)

"Ellen Terry" from *The Moment and Other Essays* by Virginia Woolf, copyright 1948 by Harcourt Brace Jovanovich, Inc., and renewed 1976 by Marjorie T. Parsons. Reprinted by permission of Harcourt Brace Jovanovich, Inc., the Executors of the Virginia Woolf Estate, and The Hogarth Press.

Excerpt from "A Sketch of the Past" from *Moments of Being* by Virginia Woolf, copyright © 1976 by Quentin Bell and Angelica Garnett. Reprinted by permission of Harcourt Brace Jovanovich, Inc., the Executors of the Virginia Woolf Estate, and The Hogarth Press.

"A Hanging" and "Shooting an Elephant" from *Shooting an Elephant and Other Essays* by George Orwell, copyright 1950 by Sonia Brownell Orwell and renewed 1978 by Sonia Pitt-Rivers, reprinted by permission of Harcourt Brace Jovanovich, Inc., and the estate of the late Sonia Brownell Orwell and Martin Secker & Warburg.

"Politics and the English Language" by George Orwell, copyright 1946 by Sonia Brownell Orwell and renewed 1974 by Sonia Orwell, reprinted from *Shooting an Elephant and Other Essays* by permission of Harcourt Brace Jovanovich, Inc., and the estate of the late Sonia Brownell Orwell and Martin Secker & Warburg.

"Marrakech" and "Why I Write" from *Such, Such Were the Joys* by George Orwell, copyright 1953 by Sonia Brownell Orwell, renewed 1981 by Mrs. George K. Perutz, Mrs. Miriam Gross, Dr. Michael Dickson, Executors of the Estate of Sonia Brownell Orwell, reprinted by permission of Harcourt Brace Jovanovich, Inc., and the estate of the late Sonia Brownell Orwell and Martin Secker & Warburg.

"Once More to the Lake," copyright 1941 by E. B. White; "Death of a Pig," copyright 1947 by E. B. White; "The Ring of Time," copyright 1956 by E. B. White; "On a Florida Key," copyright 1941 by E. B. White; specified excerpt from "Foreword" (titled "The Essayist"), copyright 1977 by E. B. White; all from *The Essays of E. B. White.* Reprinted by permission of Harper & Row, Publishers, Inc.

"Death in the Open" and "The Iks" from *The Lives of a Cell* by Lewis Thomas. Copyright © 1947 by Lewis Thomas. All rights reserved. Reprinted by permission of Viking Penguin, a division of Penguin Books USA, Inc.